W0016657

9781442233843

Concise Dictionary of
American Grammar
and Usage

Concise Dictionary of American Grammar and Usage

Edited by

ROBERT C. WHITFORD

Professor of English, Pratt Institute

and JAMES R. FOSTER

Professor of English, Long Island University

PHILOSOPHICAL LIBRARY

NEW YORK

Foreword

This *Concise Dictionary* is primarily a manual for people who aspire to write a clear and forceful American in accord with current good use. It has grown out of our *Little Dictionary of English Usage* (1946) but differs from that earlier handbook in emphasis and content because this new book includes a considerable number of words and phrases which lately have become current in the United States or have acquired new meanings in recent years. The aim here is to be positive, not negative. Conservative schoolmasters who have written about grammar and diction in the past have devoted much space to condemnation of turns of phrase which seemed to violate accepted principles or old rules of grammar or rhetoric. In this wordbook, on the contrary, we endeavor to recommend effective new modes of expression which have the approving stamp of use by good writers of our own day. Many words formerly regarded as slang or vulgarisms are now accepted as good colloquial American; others formerly colloquial, familiar, or informal have become standard literary diction. Such changes in the standing of words we have indicated in several instances derived from our authorities or our own observation of the present practice of good writers and speakers. Many of our statements concerning grammatical usages are made after consulting Otto Jespersen's *Essentials of English Grammar* (1933), George O. Curme's *Syntax* (1931), H. W. Fowler's *Dictionary of Modern English Usage* (1926), *Webster's New International Dictionary*, second edition (1934), and the *American College Dictionary* (1947).

In order that our guidebook may be as dependable as possible we have freely made use of the works of recognized authorities. We are especially indebted to George Philip Krapp's *The English Language in America* (1925), *The Knowledge of English* (1927), and *A Comprehensive Guide to Good English* (1927), Arthur G. Kennedy's *Current English* (1935), and H. T. Horwill's *A Dictionary of Modern American Usage* (1935), as well as the revised edition of H. L. Mencken's *The American Language* (1936) and *The American Language, Supplements One and Two* (1945, 1948). We have also turned to *A Glossary of Literary Terms* (1941) by Dan S. Norton and Peters Rushton for help in defining critical terms and to *Current English Usage* (1935) by Sterling Andrus Leonard, the *American English Grammar* (1940) of Charles C. Fries, and *British and American English Since 1900* by Eric Partridge and John W. Clark for stimulating suggestions on many debatable points. The *Dictionary of Americanisms* of the Chicago University Press is the standard background word-book.

Because of limitations of space we have avoided including in our list the most common words and, at the other extreme, many highly technical terms which are new, to be sure, but are not in general use. On the other hand, we have tried to explain American terms which might puzzle visitors from Australia, Canada, or other parts of the British Commonwealth, and we have warned our American readers against some of the expressions which are polite enough in America but are vulgar or improper in the United Kingdom. Our basis for selection has been eclectic, and usefulness has been our prime objective.

For college freshmen or other students of the art of composition, our *Dictionary* constitutes a combined handbook of diction, grammar, and rhetoric. It enables the theme-writer to turn to a general discussion of the type or genre of writing in which he is interested, a solution of the problem of punctuation that troubles him, or a definition of the word that he may have misused. To the instructor or theme-reader it affords the greatest possible freedom in the use of signs and abbreviations for textual emendation. He need not commit to memory or assign to his students for rote memorization a set of symbols or a chart. All he has to do is to write in the margin of a theme the first letters of the name of the fault or the rhetorical principle on which his student must seek enlightenment. The abecedarian arrangement of the *Dictionary* does the rest. Thus he might write *Syl* in the margin when the word at the end of a line is wrongly divided, and so refer the student to the entry regarding Syllabication. Or he might simply underline a word or phrase the use of which is discussed in the *Dictionary*, adding such a marginal notation as *sl.* for *slang* or *colloq.* for *colloquial*.

But the theme-reader may conveniently use conventional proofreader's marks if he prefers to do so. Many of these are included in the alphabetical series under the heading of "Signs and Symbols"; such, for example, are || meaning *not parallel* and # asking for more space. Others like the dele sign (ꝃ) and l.c., *lower case,* are listed separately.

In discussing such matters of mechanical procedure as capitalization, spelling, and compounding, we have endeavored to follow the recommendations of the *United States Government Printing Office Style Manual* (1945) unless we have seen strong reason for contrary suggestions.

In general we have devoted little of our limited space to historical or critical discussion of the changes in meanings of words. But if the origin or development of a word seemed very remarkable or oddly related to present American use, we have indicated the etymology briefly within square brackets [ ] after the definition. In choosing between contradictory etymologies we have leaned conservatively toward Skeat's *Etymological Dic-*

tionary of the English Language, the *Oxford English Dictionary,* and the smaller dictionaries published in America by the John C. Winston Company, rather than toward the interpretations of the popular experts in semasiology.

The alphabetical sequence in the text includes concise articles on grammatical and stylistic topics ("Letters," for example), as well as a large number of brief vocabulary items. The short entries concerned with the current usage of individual terms are typically arranged as follows: First is the word itself in boldface type with its principal parts if it is an irregular verb, comparison if it is an unusual adjective or adverb, variant spellings if any variants are in general use. Italicized abbreviation indicates the part or parts of speech in which the word may be used. Next come the definitions. If in the first of the senses given the word under discussion is not standard American English, an italicized abbreviation preceding the definition indicates a practical classification as slang, colloquial, archaic, or British. Acceptable meanings of the term are presented with commas separating synonyms but semicolons separating distinct definitions. For a few words commonly mispronounced, however, we have indicated acceptable pronunciations in parentheses before the definitions. In these instances the diacritical marks used are:

ā ē ī ō ū o͞o (skāte, ēve, īce, nōte, mūte, mo͞ot)
ă ĕ ĭ ŏ ŭ o͝o (săck, nĕck, sĭt, nŏt, cŭt, co͝ok)
ä as in pärt; á as in ásk (in New England); oi ou aw (boil, bout, bawl)
The unmarked vowels are mute *e*'s; e.g., the *a* in Chīna.

Abbreviations used in the text include:

abbr. abbreviation, abbreviated
adj. adjective
adv. adverb
Am. American, Americanism, of the United States
arch. archaic, antiquated
Br. British, Briticism
colloq. colloquial, colloquially
conj. conjunction
dial. dialect, dialectal
Du. Dutch, Netherlandish
fig. figurative
Fr. French
Ger. German, Germanic
Gr. Greek
gram. grammar, grammatical
interj. interjection
L. Latin
LL. late Latin

n. noun
OE. Old English, Anglo-Saxon
OF. Old French
p. past, preterit
part. participle, participial
pl. plural
prep. preposition, prepositional
pron. pronoun
q.v. which see
sing. singular
sl. slang
sp. spelled, spelling
stand. lit. standard literary language or usage
tech. trade or technical term
v. verb
v.i. intransitive verb
v.t. transitive verb

In the course of years, we have gratefully received helpful suggestions from many associates. Two whose assistance has been especially valuable are Dr. George A. Finch of Pratt Institute and Lt. Col. Victor H. Streit, U.S.M.C. Ret.

R.C.W.

Brooklyn, N.Y.
April, 1954

Concise Dictionary of
American Grammar and Usage

A

abandon, desert, forsake, *v*. When one gives something up completely, especially when he leaves it to the mercy of someone or something, he *abandons* it. When he quits something (except a place) in violation of legal or moral claims upon him, he *deserts* it. When he leaves something familiar or someone dear to him, he *forsakes* it or him. "*Abandon* a ship; *desert* one's regiment; *forsake* one's children."

Abbreviation. Shortened or contracted form of word or phrase; e.g., *C.O.D.* Mainly used in reference citations, tabulated matter, and technical writing.

abecedarian, *adj*. Alphabetical; childishly simple. An *abecedarian* poem is one consisting of twenty-six lines, beginning with the letters of the alphabet in order.

abhorrence, *n*. Loathing; hatred.

ability, capacity, *n*. *Ability* means the power of putting physical or mental energy to use; *capacity*, the power of receiving and holding ideas. "He is a man of great *capacity* but of little *ability*."

A-bomb, *n*. Atom bomb; missile causing devastation by setting off a chain of molecular fission.

a-borning, *adv. Colloq.*, in the process of being born.

about, *adv. Colloq.*, in the sense of *almost*, as in "She was *about* ready to cry"; *near*, as in "They looked to see whether there was anyone *about*"; and *in active pursuit of duties*, as in "He is not yet up and *about*."

above, *prep*. Can be used as an *adj.*, as in "the *above* statement," but this is not recommended for any except the most humdrum and mechanical of contexts. On a level with *inst., ult., prox.*, in letters. Substitute *the preceding, the foregoing, the matter already referred to.*

abri (à brē'), *n*. Shelter; dugout; hut. [*Fr.* shelter.]

absenteeism, *n*. Frequent absence from work. "*Absenteeism* cuts down production."

Absolute Construction. Participial phrase or equivalent not formally connected with the main clause. "She stood there, *arms akimbo and head back*" for "She stood there *with* her arms akimbo and head back." Sometimes called the nominative absolute because the noun in the phrase is felt to be in the nominative case. "*He being tired and I fresh*, everybody insisted on my going." "*These difficulties being evident*, the diplomats proceeded cautiously." A literary rather than a *colloq.* construction, and one to be handled with discretion.

absquatulate, *v. Arch. colloq.*, depart, get up and go.

abstention, *n*. Refraining; refraining from voting.

Abstract. Abstract terms such as *goodness, equality, nature,* and so on are symbols of general ideas and qualities. Their function is to fix a concept until a more definite content can be given to it by concrete particulars. If not given this content, the abstract term is likely to be vague or evasive and can be manipulated dishonestly. As a rule, it is more effective to present material in concrete or specific than in abstract or general terms.

accede, *v*. Attain; give adherence, used with *to*.

accent, *v*. Stress, give prominence to.

Accent. Stress laid upon a syllable of a

word or part of a phrase or sentence. Variation in accent often distinguishes nouns from verbs, *con'duct, n., conduct', v.;* and nouns from adjectives, *min'ute, n., minute', adj.*

accent, accentuate, *v.* Choose the latter when the sense is figurative. "Poverty *accentuates* the other forms of human misfortune." "He *accented* the wrong syllable."

accept, except, *v. Accept* means take; *except,* as transitive, exclude, bar, omit, and as intransitive, take exception to. "I *accept* your terms but wish to *except* item four from the list."

accidentally, *adv.* Casually, by chance.

accommodate, *v.* Bring into agreement; provide with something needed, help out; furnish living quarters for.

accompanied by, with. *By* is nearly always used unless the idea is that of combining or supplementing. "She was *accompanied by* a crowd of admirers," but "She *accompanied* the words *with* a knowing smile."

accord, *n.* Agreement, concurrence; unofficial agreement between representatives of states or nations.

accord, *v.* Grant, award; agree [*L.,* to the heart].

account, *v.* With *to, for,* and (in the passive) *of,* but does not admit of *as* before the complement of *account.* Write "I *account* it (not *it as*) a stroke of luck."

ace, *n.* Playing card Number One of a suit, card of highest value in many games; expert; combat pilot who has shot down a certain number of enemy planes. The *pl. aces* is slang as an *adj.* meaning highly esteemed.

acquaint, *v.* Make known, make to know, used with *with.*

acquaintance, *n.* Personal knowledge; a person one has met but does not know intimately.

acquaintanceship, *n.* Personal knowledge; *Br.* substitute for *acquaintance.*

acquainted as an *adj.,* familiar, on friendly terms, is *Am. colloq.*

acquiesce, *v.* Rest satisfied with, idiomatically used with *in.*

acquire, attain, obtain, procure, *v.* To *acquire* is to take on or to gain possession of, usually by one's own exertions. To *attain* is to arrive at, touch upon. To *obtain* is to get a desired thing. To *procure* is to get by search or request. "*Acquire* knowledge, *attain* a goal, *obtain* a position, *procure* a specimen."

acre, *n.* Land measure of 4,840 square yards. The *abbr.* a. should be used but rarely.

acronym, *n.* Name coined as an acrostic, combining initials or initial syllables of the words in a long name or title. See *radar, Unesco,* for example.

across, *adv.* and *prep.* To the opposite side. To put an idea *across* is *colloq.* metaphor from the theatrical performer's obligation to send his effects across to the audience on the other side of the footlights.

acrost, *adv.* and *prep. Vulgar,* across.

acrostic, *n.* Set of lines in which initial letters spell out a message; similar poem or series of prose lines in which final letters make a word or message.

act, *n.* Deed; *tech.* in literary criticism, major division of a play. A Roman tragedy regularly consisted of five *acts.*

Action or Plot. In the narrative the incidents should be arranged in the order of increasing interest. All the details requisite to an understanding of the story must be given before the climax is reached, but there must be no anticlimax. The action should progress steadily and fairly rapidly, and lead directly to the point of culmination. Having made the most of the climax, the author should end the story while the reader's interest is still alive.

activate, *v.* Charge with chemical energy; make ready for work; organize a military unit for active duty.

actual, *adj.* Real; being done.

ad, *n.* The handy *colloq.* stump of *advertisement. Ad-writer, want-ad, ad-man,* etc., are *trade* or *tech.* (journalism).

addicted, devoted, *part., adj. Addicted* means inclined or given to a practice or habit or pursuit (often bad); *devoted,* habitually attached to something or someone (always taken in a good sense). *"Devoted* to music, *addicted* to smoking."

adherent, *adj.* Closely connected; sticking to; so placed as to indicate close connection. An adjective preceding a noun is in the *adherent* position.

adherent, *n.* Partisan, loyal follower.

Adjective. The name of something presented as a quality or attribute.

Adjective and **Adverb.** Do not mistake an *adj.* for an *adv.* It is sometimes difficult to tell them apart because many words can be used as either without change of form. The tendency is to use the shorter form, which is frequently, although not always, the *adj.*

Do not write:

considerable *for* considerably
powerful *for* powerfully
real *for* really
sure *for* surely

After verbs like *look, sound, feel, taste, smell,* use the *adj.* except in the rare cases when an *adv.* of manner is needed to describe the action of the *v.* "The persimmon tastes *sour* (not *sourly*)."

For adjectives that may stand for adverbs, see **Quasi Adverbs.**

adjust, *v.* Make exact, bring to agreement; psychological *tech.,* arrive at improved relationship with environment.

ad·lib, *v. Theatrical tech.,* talk freely, improvise instead of reciting memorized lines. [*L.,* at pleasure.]

administer, *v.* Manage; give as medicine.

administrate, *v. Bureaucratic jargon,* administer.

admissible, *adj.* Worthy to be allowed, acceptable as evidence.

admit, *v.t.* Let in, concede, own, confess. As *v.i.* it is used with *to* in the sense of give entrance or access, and with *of* in the sense of permit, allow, grant. The construction with *of* is limited to use with impersonal subjects. Write "His absolute sincerity *admits of* no question," not "He *admits of* no question concerning his sincerity."

advantage, *n.* With *over* or *of* when the meaning is superiority, stronger position, mastery; with *of* when the meaning is gain, profit, opportunity, or circumstance especially favorable to a desired end. "The man who can think has the *advantage over* the man who can only remember." "He took *advantage of* my ignorance." "You have the *advantage of* me" often means "You know me but I do not know you," i.e., you are no acquaintance of mine. The *adj.* is *advantageous.*

adventurer, *n.* Soldier of fortune; man willing to undertake hazardous enterprises.

adventuress, *n.* Wily woman seeking to attain wealth or power by dubious devices.

Adverbs. In conversation, the tone of the voice helps to indicate the idea to be limited by an adverb; in writing, position is everything. Yet even in the best literary style such adverbs as *only* need not always precede what they modify. Thus in "We *only* had two sandwiches left," where the *adv.* is in the preverbal position, there is no ambiguity. But in "I *only* shot a dozen ducks" or "I *only* hired the healthy," where *only* is in the same position, the idea is not expressed clearly. Whether a certain position is correct or not depends largely upon the phrase in which the *adv.* occurs, but, of course, an *adv.* should in general stand as near as possible to the word it modifies.

Some adjectives can be made into adverbs by adding *-ly.* But do not forget that some adverbs do not end in *-ly: slow, fast, much, first.* There is an *adv. slowly,* but *fastly* and *muchly* are *vulgar.* Note the difference between *sharp* and *sharply* in "The play begins at 8:40 *sharp*" and "He turned *sharply* to the left." Usually some such distinction in meaning as this is necessary to keep the short and the *-ly* form of the same *adv.* in active use.

adverse, averse, *adj. Adverse,* hostile, not conducive to success, unfavorably disposed. "These *adverse* circumstances did not deter him." *Averse,* having a dislike of or an aversion to. "They were *averse to* a peaceful settlement of the question." Do not write *averse from.*

advise, *v. Trade* or *tech.* (business) in the sense of say, tell, inform.

adviser, *n.* Consultant; counselor. Ad-

visor is a variant spelling preferred in some types of educational counseling.

advisory, *adj.* Concerned with or containing advice or counsel. *n.* Bulletin of advice.

aegis (ē′jĭs), *n.* Ancient Greek accouterment or shield; a shield or protection. A poeticism as used with *under* in newspapers in the sense of *auspices, patronage, care,* or in place of *for.* "The girls are selling cookies *under the aegis of* (better *for*) the Dog Club."

aerodrome, *n.* Airfield; large hangar for storage of planes or dirigibles.

aesthetic, *adj.* (also *sp. esthetic*). Pertaining to beauty, sensitive to or possessing a sense of beauty. A man or a movement may be *aesthetic,* but the term is not a substitute for *beautiful.* Write "a *beautiful* picture or town" not "an *aesthetic* picture or town."

affect, effect, *v. Affect* means to act on, feign, cultivate, make an ostentatious display of liking; *effect,* to bring about, accomplish. "The bad news *affected* him deeply." "He *effected* an opening somehow." The *n. affect* is obsolete except *trade* or *tech.* (psychological term for feeling, emotion, or desire). The *n. effect,* meaning result, purport, impression is, of course, in good use.

affix, *v.* Fasten (to); attach; append.

affix (ă′fĭx), *n.* Prefix or suffix; something attached.

after. Not needed with a *p. part.,* as in "Having come (not *after* having come) as far as St. Charles, we had just as well go on to St. Louis."

agendum, *pl.* **agenda,** *n.* Something that must be done; *pl.,* items of work for a meeting of a committee or a deliberative or legislative body.

aggravate, *v.* Increase in weight or seriousness. "His mental condition *aggravates* the disease." In the sense of *exasperate, annoy, provoke,* it is chiefly *dial.* "That merchant's method of dealing with customers *aggravates* (better *irritates*) me."

aggregate, *n.* Mass or sum of many particulars; *tech.,* hard material in lumps of graduated sizes used in mixture with ce-

ment to form concrete. The sum of several amounts of money is a total rather than an *aggregate.*

aggregate, *v. Colloq.* meaning to reach in the aggregate to. "That makes it *aggregate (stand. lit. amount to)* a hundred."

ago. Do not use with *since,* as in "It is nearly twenty years *(ago)* since he was here."

agree, *v.* Used with *to, on, in,* and *with.* "We *agree* to your proposition." "We *agree* on this price." "We *agree* in theory." "We *agree with* you."

Agreement. Conformity or concord between *pron.* and antecedent in number, between subject and *v.* in points they have in common, i.e., number and person; or between *pron.* and antecedent in number, person, and gender if indicated [or between *this, that,* and a *sing. n.* and *these, those,* and a *pl. n.*]. For example, a collective *n.* or compound subject considered as a whole takes a *sing. v.* "The grand jury *is* sitting." "Soul and mind *is* all." But if such a subject is considered as combined units it takes a *pl.* verb. "The jury *are* disagreed." "Soul and mind *are* in conflict."

None may take either *sing.* or *pl. v.,* but the other indefinite pronouns, *each, neither, everyone,* etc., as a rule take a *sing. v.,* and if they are antecedents, are followed by *sing.* pronouns. "*Neither* of these women has kept *her* appointment."

For concord of *v.* forms in subordinate clauses, see **Conformity of Tenses.**

aim to, *v. Am. stand. lit.,* intend to. *Br.* usage prefers *aim at* in the figurative sense.

ain't, *v. Abbr.* of *am not* or *are not,* wrongly used for *is not, has not,* and *have not;* often *sp. a′n′t* or *hain′t.* In the first person *sing. ain't* is *low colloq.* "I suppose I'm the last one, *ain't* I?" In other persons it is careless or *vulgar.* "*Ain′t* that terrible!" "*Ain′t* you goin'?" Do not use *aren't I?* as a substitute for *ain't I?*

airlift, *n.* Systematic air transport, especially that which supplied Berlin during the blockade in 1948; air ferry over hostile territory.

aisle, *n.* Passage between seats of a theater or assembly room; side division of a church, set off by a row of pillars.

alcoholic, *n*. Person whose excessive drinking has become a disease.

alert, *adj*. On watch, awake. *v*. Rouse as by alarm of military attack, put on the alert.

Alexandrine, *n*. Verse consisting of six iambic feet; ninth line of a Spenserian stanza.

alfalfa, *n*. Lucern, sturdy forage plant of the pea family.

alfresco, *adj*. Open-air.

Algonquian, *adj*. Belonging to any of a group of Indian languages which includes the tongues of the Blackfeet, Chippewas, Crees, and Ottawas as well as the Algonquins.

alibi, *n*. *Tech*. (law), the plea of having been, at the alleged time of the commission of an offense, elsewhere than at the alleged place of commission. *Colloq*., an excuse, a plausible excuse.

allegory, parable, fable, fabliau. The *allegory* is a story in which persons and things are symbols and the action itself is symbolic, as in *Pilgrim's Progress*. The *allegory*, the *parable*, and the *fable* teach moral lessons by presenting abstract ideas in the guise of concrete images. In the *fable*, talking animals, or even plants, are substituted for persons. The term *parable* is confined to religious subjects. In general, more attention is given to the manner of presentation in the *allegory*, which is also usually much longer than the *parable* or *fable*. All three are related to the metaphor. A *fabliau* (*pl. fabliaux*) is a witty realistic narrative told for its own sake, e.g., Chaucer's *Miller's Tale*.

alley, *n*. Narrow passage; narrow street; *fig*., "down his *alley*," suited to his natural ability.

alligator pear, *n*. Avocado. This is apparently an instance of the change of a foreign name by folk etymology, illiterate Americans having mumbled "avocado" until they thought they were saying *alligator*.

all in all. This favorite way of introducing a conclusion or a generalization is be-

coming trite. "*All in all*, it was a good show."

Alliteration, Assonance. *Alliteration*, the recurrence of the same sound, whether consonant or vowel, initially. Used principally in poetry. Oliver Herford's "Tugged till the toadstool toppled in two." *Assonance*, the similarity of the accented vowels (and those that follow if there be any) in words at the ends of verses or elsewhere, the consonants being unlike, as in *fāte* and *tāke*, *lādy* and *bāby*.

all of a thing. Logically, since *of* as a partitive denotes part of something that has been divided, e.g., "She is the prettiest *of* the blondes," *all of* before something that has not been divided would be incorrect. Yet this is not so. The construction with nouns is extremely common. The following expressions are correct: "*All of* the nations of the world"; "*all of* them"; "*all of* these tribes"; "*all of* the books."

allot, allotted, allotting, *v*. Distribute by lot; distribute.

allow, *v*. When used for *think, be of opinion, declare, assert*, it is *low colloq*. or *dial*. "She's a big one, I'll *allow*." The *stand. lit. allow* is less formal and positive than *permit*. "Sometimes they *allow* smoking in this room." As a *v.i.* it is used with *for*. "Are you *allowing* for the baggage?"

all right. To be written so, not *alright, allright*, or *all-right*. *Colloq*. in the sense of *gratifying, satisfactory, correct, satisfactorily*, and as an expression of assent. "This plan is *all right*." "*All right*, I'll go." Much better than its slang equivalent, *O.K. Low colloq*. or *slang* when used as an *adv*. to mean certainly, undoubtedly. "She's gone, *all right*." "The car knocked him down, *all right*."

all the farther, faster, quicker. *Low colloq*. for *as far as, as fast as, as quickly as*. "This is *all the farther* I can go."

allude, refer, *v*. *Allude* means to indicate by indirection or suggestion; *refer*, to introduce or mention a particular definite person or thing. "He *alluded* to a recent business transaction; he *referred* to his commission of 12 per cent."

allusion, illusion, *n*. An *allusion* is an

indirect reference or a hint; an *illusion*, a perception that does not correspond to reality. "She made an *allusion* to a silly habit of mine." "This is an optical *illusion*."

Allusion, Irrelevant. In using a saying or quoting a phrase, make sure that you do not distort its real meaning and that this meaning is appropriate, with no part of it pointless or ambiguous in the context in which you place it. The devil-and-the-sea allusion does not belong in the following passage, for here the alternatives are pleasant ones and not the horns of a dilemma. Besides, one is usually *caught*, not *torn*, between the devil and the sea. "The book dealer who is also a collector is often *torn between the devil and the deep blue sea*—the thrill of making a profit on a rare book, and the inner satisfaction of keeping the volume for himself."

Make sure also that your phrase has not been used too often, like *dim religious light, poor as Job's turkey* (he had to lean on a fence to gobble), *feast of reason and flow of soul*. An unadorned plain statement is much better than such clichés.

ally (ă lī'), *v.* Unite with or to; connect. *n.* Confederate, associate; one of the nations in alliance against the Central Powers in World War I. The *pl.* is often pronounced ăl'līs.

almost, *adv.* Condensed to *most* (*q.v.*) in careless speech.

aloud, *adv.* In full speaking voice, out loud.

already, all ready. *Already* is an *adv.* meaning *previously* or *before a specified time.* "*Already* the geese are flying south."

also, *adv.* In addition, moreover. When used as a co-ordinating *conj.* it is *colloq.* unless accompanied with *and* or *as.* "She asks you to accept this present, *also* (*stand. lit. and also*) begs you not to forget your promise to return." Sometimes *but* appears alone as the second member of the correlative pair *not only . . . but* (*also*), but never *also.*

altar, *n.* Table or other raised structure on which sacrifices are offered to a god.

alter (awl'tr), *v.* Change; remodel. *Altar*

and *alter* are pronounced the same.

alternate (awl'ter năt, ăl'ter năt), **alternative** (awl tur'nå tĭv, ăl tur'nå tĭv), *adj.* *Alternate* means occurring by turns, every other (one); *alternative*, mutually exclusive (usually said of two things). "He came on *alternate* days." "French and English I are not *alternative* courses; both may be taken the same year." The *n. alternative* means a choice between two (or more) of the things so offered. "The *alternatives* are delay or war."

Alternate, n., means a substitute. "The *alternate* took the appointment because the original appointee refused it."

altogether, *adv.* Utterly, in all respects. Do not confuse with *all together,* which means all at once, simultaneously.

altruistic, *adj.* Devoted to or devised or conceived for the good of others.

aluminum, *n.* Metallic element no. 13, symbol Al. The *Br. sp.* is *aluminium* (ăl ū mĭn'ē um).

alumnus, *n. Am.,* college graduate, man with a degree from a certain college. The *pl.* is *alumni;* the female graduate of an American college is an *alumna;* two or more female graduates are *alumnae.* In *colloq.* use, all former students who will pay dues to the association are *alumni.*

alveolar (ăl vē'ō lä), *adj. Tech.,* pertaining to vocal tones produced while the tongue is pressed against a ridge behind the upper front teeth.

amateur (ăm'å tŭr, ăm'å tūr), *n.* An athlete, sportsman, artist, collector; not a professional. *Amateur* is often confused with *novice,* a beginner.

amateurish, *adj.* Unprofessional, with connotations of futility and immaturity. Contrast "the old college try" which connotes the do-or-die type of Am. sportsmanship without the snobbery of the *Br.* "old school tie."

ambiguous, *adj.* Of uncertain meaning. An expression that seems to mean two things, when the author of it meant only one, is *ambiguous.* E.g.: "And a young man who wears a flower in his hair gives away quarters and whistles in Carnegie Hall."

amenity, *n.* Appropriate or agreeable

behavior, often used in the *pl.*, "the amenities of social intercourse."

Americanism. An *Americanism* is a word or phrase that differs in form or meaning from the expression that would commonly be used in England to mean the same thing. It may or may not have originated in the United States, but it is the American way of expressing a certain idea. The *hood* of an automobile, an *Americanism,* is called the *bonnet* in England. Thus *bonnet* is a **Briticism,** *q.v.*

Americanize, *v.* Transform to conform to customs or manners in the United States.

americium, *n.* Recently discovered element, radioactive and unstable, No. 95, symbol Am.

ammo, *n. Sl.,* ammunition.

among, between, *prep. Among* is used in referring to several persons or things. "She went *among* the Gypsies." *Between* may be used in referring to two, or more than two, persons or things. "She swept *between* the pews." *Between* always implies separation, its primary meaning being *in the time or space that keeps things apart,* whereas, on the contrary, *among* carries an implication of sharing.

Amongst is the poetic form of *among.*

amorphous, *adj.* Shapeless, vague, disorganized.

amount, number. Use the first in referring to the total bulk or mass, the latter in referring to individuals or units. "A small *amount* of gasoline; a large *number* of cars."

ample, *adj.* "They have an *ample supply* of water" is better than "They have *ample* water" because in the sense of *plenty of, ample* is preferably used only with nouns denoting abstractions or immaterial things.

an, a. *An* is used before words beginning with a vowel sound. Everyone writes *a* before any *h* that is pronounced, but a few follow the old custom of writing *an* before *h* beginning an unaccented syllable, as *an her ba'rium, an ho tel', an his to'rian, an hy poth'esis.* Still fewer use *an* before a word beginning with a *ū* sound: *a(n) European.*

Anachronism. The misplacing of something historically, especially the introduction of a modern invention before its time, as a radio announcement of the fall of Troy.

Analogy. Similarity; a comparison. Reasoning by *analogy* is reasoning from parallel cases. Such reasoning appeals to the imagination but by itself is inconclusive and even misleading because it is nearly always based on an oversimplification or a false or superficial parallelism. Can you say that because a man can make a long journey more quickly if he does not take too fast a pace, an automobile on a long trip should be driven only at a moderate speed? If you cannot, the *analogy* is false.

analysis, *n.* Taking to pieces; classification; partition; reduction of a complex object to its components. This critical catchword is often misused by pseudoscientific writers.

anapest, *n.* Dactyl reversed; metrical foot consisting of two short or unaccented syllables followed by one long or stressed syllable. In scansion, the anapest is represented by ⏑ ⏑ — or x x x'.

anaphora, *n.* Repetition of a word at the beginnings of successive clauses.

and etc. If you must write the *and* before *etc.,* write *and so forth.*

and/or, *conj.* Used in business and legal documents. Of questionable value. The jocular use: "Today the President will have occasion to make another historical *and/or* political speech at Vincennes, Indiana."

and, to. With a *v.* after *go, come, send, try,* etc., *and* can be used, although the more fastidious insist upon the infinitive with *to.* Generally, *come and see* is stronger than *come to see; go and get it* than *go to get it.* But if you wish to express nothing but purpose, use *to.*

anecdote, *n.* Condensed narrative; account of a short incident usually to illustrate a point or describe an odd trait of character or a whimsical turn of events. Do not confuse with *antidote,* a remedy to counteract poison.

anent. A poeticism meaning *about, con-*

cerning, in respect to. Write "Concerning (not *anent*) butter prices quoted, we can say . . ."

anesthetic, *n.* Drug producing insensitiveness to pain. [*Gr.,* adapted from an earlier *tech.* medical term, *anesthesia,* by Dr. Oliver Wendell Holmes.]

angel, *n.* Messenger of God; heavenly being.

angle, *n.* Place where two lines meet, space between two lines that are about to meet; point of view; side. *Angle* is now *stand. lit.* in the sense of *point of view, standpoint, aspect,* or *phase,* although not entirely free from the taint of having been journalese. One may say, "He is approaching the problem *from* another *angle,*" but it would be more logical to say, "He is approaching the problem *at* another *angle.*" The *colloq. slant* is similar, meaning point of view, attitude, or opinion that is personal or particular, as "Considered from his *slant,* it does seem different." In the slang of racketeers, *angles* are unfair advantages arising from sharp practices.

Anglicized Word. A word that came from a foreign language and is now modified in some way, as in pronunciation, to conform to native English word habits. The foreign word that becomes so useful as to be a familiar part of the common vocabulary usually is made to conform more quickly than the word used by a few persons only. The Anglicized pronunciation of *esplanade* is *ĕsplanād',* and is preferred *to ĕsplanäd',* which is nearer the Spanish.

announcer, *n. Radio tech.,* maker of introductions, explanations, or advertising announcements in connection with radio programs.

antagonist, *n.* Adversary; opponent of the protagonist in a tragedy.

antagonize, *v.* Alienate, incur the enmity of.

ante, *n.* Stake in the pool in a poker game [*L.,* before].

Antecedent. In grammar, the *n.* which precedes a *pron.,* and to which the *pron.* is said to refer. In "This was the man who had flown around the world," *man* is the antecedent of *who.* See REFERENCE.

antenna, *n.* Wire used in sending or receiving electromagnetic waves. In this sense the *pl.* is *antennas.*

anti, *adj.* and *n.* Against; in opposition; chronic opponent.

anticipate, expect, *v. Anticipate* means to foresee, get a foretaste of, forestall, introduce too soon. The general meaning of *expect* is to look forward to something likely or confidently counted on to happen. "A full list of prizes has been secured and Mr. Lister *expects* (not *anticipates*) a big crowd."

anticlimax, *n.* See CLIMAX.

antidote, *n.* See ANECDOTE.

Antithesis. Balanced contrast. Pope's heroic couplets are built upon antitheses. "In words as fashions the same rule will hold,

Alike fantastic if too new or old:
Be not the first by whom the new is tried,
Nor yet the last to lay the old aside."

Antonym. Word of opposite meaning; *heavy* is the *antonym* of *light.* Cf. *synonym,* which means a word of approximately the same meaning.

anxious, *adj.* Although often objected to when used in the sense of *eager,* or *calculated to cause worry,* it may be so used. "Gertrude is *anxious* to meet the new boy." "You will find out that it is a very *anxious* business."

any, *adv.* To any extent, in any degree, at all. "Did he work *any* this week?" "That didn't help them *any.*" "I can't stay *any* longer." The *adj.* means *an indefinite single one* (indifferently) *of an indefinite number, quantity, or degree; some.* After a negative it means *appreciable.* "We hadn't been gone for *any* length of time." As a *pron.* it generally takes the place of *some* in questions and negative or conditional statements. Cf. "Give him *some,*" and "Don't give him *any.*" "*Some* of my uncle's money, if he had *any,* should come to me." "Did *any* of the passengers survive?"

anybody else's. Present-day usage prefers to give the possessive ending to the *else* rather than to *anybody.* Write *anybody else's, anyone else's,* etc.

anyplace, every place, someplace, *adv.*
Colloq. for *anywhere, everywhere,* and
somewhere. "I will go *anyplace* (*stand. lit.*
anywhere) you say." "Is there *any place*
where I can write?" is *stand. lit.*
anyway, anyhow, *adv.* Practically synonymous. *Anyway* means anywise, at all, in
any case, anyhow. *Anyways* means *anywise,*
but for *anyhow* or *in any case* or *at any*
rate it is *dial.* or *vulgar,* as in "*Anyways,*
Fanny told me you hid it."
anywheres, *adv.* The final *s* of *any-*
wheres, everywheres, and *somewheres* is
dial.
Anzac, *n.* Australian and New Zealand
Army Corps; member of that military
force. [acronym]
Anzus, *n.* Australia, New Zealand,
United States, associated in a system of
collective security. See *acronym.*
Apache (á pä′chä or ă pă′chĭ), *n.* American Indian tribesman of a roving Southwestern group; as occasionally applied to
Parisian gangsters the name is printed
without capitalization and is commonly
pronounced ä päsh′.
aphorism, *n.* Pithy sentence; maxim;
concise wise saying.
aplenty. *Stand. lit.* as an *adj.,* as in "He
had cloth *aplenty,*" but slang as an *adv.,* as
in "He was worried *aplenty.*"
apocope (a pŏk′o pĕ), *n.* Omission of the
last syllable of a word; clipping. [*Gr.*]
Apostrophe. Punctuation mark (′) used
for the following purposes:
1. To indicate the omission of one or
   more letters from a word, or one or
   more figures from a date. *I'll, 'tis,*
   ne'er, Ass'n, Class of '40. It is not
   needed before *twenties, thirties,* etc.,
   denoting the decades of a century, although the *nineteen,* etc., has been
   omitted. "That style was popular in
   the *twenties.*"
2. To form the plurals of letters, figures,
   signs, and words used as words only.
   "She chose the *8's,* the *9's,* and the
   13's." "Watch your *n's,* your final *g's,*
   and your *don't's.*"
3. Followed by an *s,* to form the possessive of *sing.* and *pl. n.* not ending in

an *s* or *z* sound. The *apostrophe* with
s is used with one-syllable *sing.* nouns
ending in an *s* or *z* sound, and with
polysyllabic *sing.* nouns having this
ending and a primary or secondary
accent on the final syllable. The *apos-*
trophe with *s* is often less ambiguous
than the *apostrophe* alone (*Alberts'*
and *Albert's* sound alike) and is preferred in most modern proper names
of more than one syllable, even when
the accent falls on the next-to-last syllable. "The hunter's horse"; "the children's games"; "Louise's program";
"Lewis's novels"; "Dickens's influence"; "Wells's ideas."
4. Without an *s,* to form the possessive
   of *pl.* nouns ending in an *s* or *z* sound,
   except a few forming their *pl.* by internal vowel change. "The hunters'
   horses"; "the commuters' tickets";
   "the Browns' Cafeteria"; "the mice's
   nests"; "the geese's feathers."
5. Without an *s,* to form the possessive
   of some (especially the two-syllable)
   classical or foreign proper names and
   certain common nouns ending in an
   s or *z* sound. Nouns coming before
   sake, and others like *actress, inno-*
   cence, heiress, etc., usually drop the *s*
   (and sometimes may drop the *apos-*
   trophe) especially in poetry or when
   the next word begins with a hissing
   sound. *Zeus's, Brutus', Atlas', Cer-*
   vantes', "For goodness' (or goodness)
   sake . . ."
6. With an *s,* to form the *group posses-*
   sive. The *apostrophe* and *s* are added
   to the final member of a group of two
   or more when the reference is to joint
   ownership. Similarly, they are added
   to the last *n.* to form the possessive of
   two or more nouns in apposition or
   in the same construction. "Joan and
   Jennie's· table finished first." But
   "Both Joan's and Jennie's letters were
   sent." "The member from Ohio's motion was adopted."

Follow local usage in the matter of place
names and titles. The apostrophe is often

omitted. "The Teachers Club"; "Clarices Inn."

No apostrophe is used with the pronouns *his, hers, its, ours, yours, theirs.*

Apostrophe. A turning away. The rhetorical device (mainly poetical and oratorical) of breaking off the discourse to address some deity, person(s), or personified thing, present or (more usually) absent.

Arethusa. Do what, sir? Would sleep?
Philaster. For ever, Arethusa. Oh, you Gods,
Give me a worthy patience!
Have I stood
Naked, alone, the shock of many fortunes?
    —BEAUMONT AND FLETCHER,
        Philaster, III, 2

appearance, *n.* Semblance, external show; apparition. Careless spellers should note the spelling.

appendix, *pl.* **appendixes, appendices,** *n.* Something added or appended; outgrowth; supplement.

appointee, *n.* Officer designated by another officer or by a small group; official not elected.

apposite, opposite, *adj. Apposite* means relevant, fitting (often used with *to); opposite,* contrary, set over against. "The man who sat *opposite* made the *apposite* remark that it was nobody's business."

Appositive. A *n.* or *n.* equivalent set beside another (usually without connective) as an explanatory or restricting adjunct or as an attributive. In "I see that Rex Pipes, the *plumber,* has honored us with another visitation—the *fifth* this month," *plumber* and *fifth* are in apposition to *Pipes* and *visitation.*

The *adj.* in the *appositive* position— "The morning, *dull* and *listless* . . ."—is less connected with its *n.* than if it were *adherent,* i.e., "The *dull* and *listless* morning . . ."

appraise, *v. t.* Set a value on; estimate the worth of.

appreciate, *v.* Set a just value upon; approve; be thankful for; increase in value (opposite of *depreciate);* cause to rise in value.

apprehend, comprehend, *v. Apprehend* means to seize; *comprehend,* to understand fully.

apprise or **apprize,** *v.* Notify, inform, with *of.* Cf. **advise.**

appropriate, *v. Am.,* set apart or assign for a certain use; *Br.,* steal, take for oneself, except when the purpose is specified.

apropos (ăp'rō pō), *adv.* Opportunely, suitably, with respect to, by the way. May be used with *to,* but *of* is generally preferred. "*Apropos,* it is worth your while to notice his casual remarks" illustrates the absolute use. *Adj.* "A remark very *apropos;* that is, to the point."

apt, *adj. Stand lit.,* fit, suitable; *Am.,* likely.

apt, likely, liable. *Apt* emphasizes the idea of predisposition. "A sentimental person is *apt* to cry." *Likely* emphasizes that of probability. "It is *likely* to rain." But these words are often interchanged, especially *colloq.* One may say *colloq.* "It is *apt* (or *liable*) to rain," but the *stand. lit. liable* implies lack of defense against something, as in "Children are *liable* to get measles."

aquiline, *adj.* Hooked like an eagle beak.

Archaism. Antiquated word or expression: *whilom, I trow yon, perchance.* Most archaisms are poeticisms *(q.v.),* and some are used only in special phrases; e.g., *yore* in *of yore.* An obsolete word is one no longer in use; *archaisms* are obsolescent.

archiepiscopal (är'kǐ ē pǐs'kō păl), *adj.* Like an archbishop.

area, *n.* Part, division; journalistic *adj.,* local; regional.

aren't I? A bad substitute for the *colloq. ain't I? Aren't* is a contraction of *are not* as in "*Aren't* they there yet?"

argot (är'gō, är'gŏt), *n.* Secret language of thieves and vagabonds. Sometimes used to mean the special language of a trade, or of a professional or social group; i.e., *trade* or *tech.* language.

Argument. The presentation of one side of a controversial subject. See **Fallacy, Analogy** and **Blurred Thinking; Persuasion.**

arise, rise, *v.* The first is more poetical and dignified.

around, *adv.* and *prep.* On all sides; *colloq.*, about, approximately; *Am. st. lit.*, at the other side of.

around, round. *Around, adv.*, is correctly used in the senses of *all about, here and there, somewhere near, in every direction, to the rearward.* "Fred looked *around.*" "They were standing *around.*" *Round* is sometimes incorrectly used for *around*, as in "There was not enough chicken to go *round*" (better *around*). As a *prep. around* is *colloq.* in the sense of *about*, as in "*Around* 900 men will be needed," and "He arrived *around* nine o'clock."

The *Am. colloq. adj. all-around*, possessing general ability, excellence, usefulness, is the *Br. all-round.* "The best *all-around* American athletes will compete."

In general, *around* directs attention inward toward a center, and *round* outward to the circumference or to motion along it. "The trees danced *round* and *round.*"

Arrangement. Have you arranged your ideas in the most effective order? The perfectly arranged composition meets the requirements of the four essentials: time, interest, facility, and expediency. See CLIMAX.

arsis, *pl.* **arses,** *n.* Accented syllable of a metrical foot. [*Gr.*, rising.]

artery, *n.* Tubular vessel carrying blood from the heart; important or central road or thoroughfare.

articulate, *v.* Connect, link; connect sounds in clear and fluent speech.

articulation, *n.* Connection in smooth sequence; expression of orderly thought in appropriate phrasing.

as, *relative pron.* After *the same, such, so,* and *as,* it may introduce a relative clause. "She will never be *the same as* she was before." "He is just *such* a man *as* they have been looking for." But *as* for *who* or *that,* as in "Though I say it *as* shouldn't," or "I don't know *as* he is here," is *dial.* or *low. colloq.*

as, *conj. As if* is better than *as though* in sentences like "It looks as *if* it were going to snow." *As is* is *trade* or *tech.* (business) for without guarantee. "I will sell it *as is* for twenty dollars."

as, *adv.* **as . . . as, so . . . as,** *correlatives.* The *as . . . as* used always in affirmative constructions—"He ran *as* well *as* could be expected"—is correct also in negative ones, "He doesn't write *as* well now *as* formerly." However, many writers prefer *so . . . as* in negative constructions: "Your task is not *so* difficult *as* his."

as how. *Provincial* or *dial.*, whether; *old colloq.*, that.

ascent (ăs sĕnt′), *n.* Rise, upward climb. Cf. *assent.*

ashcan, *n.* Equivalent to *Br.* dustbin.

aside, *adv.* Apart; *n.* actor's speech which, by convention, is not overheard by other players on the stage.

aside from, *prep. phrase. Colloq.* for *apart from, in addition to,* and *except for.* "*Aside from* (*stand. lit.* except *for*) a black eye, he showed no sign of having been in a fight."

ask (New England, àsk; General American ăsk), *v.* Do not pronounce *àst* or *ăst. Past, dance, half, can't* and similar words are pronounced with the *à* in New England and *ă* in the rest of the country, except the South where the *ă* is likely to be somewhat broader.

as long as, *conj.* A causal as well as a temporal *conj.* Temporal: "*As long as* the sailing was easy, she was willing to help with the cooking." Causal: "*As long as* (since, inasmuch as) he is already there, he may remain in the hospital for treatment over the week end."

aspect, *n.* Countenance; appearance, view; *grammatical tech.*, variation in form of a verb to represent (1) a general truth or (2) action in progress. The present indicative form is commonly used to show the first or "terminal" aspect, as in the wise saying, "Cows ruminate." A present participle combined with a form of the verb *to be* shows the progressive aspect. "The cow is, was, has been chewing."

aspirant (ăs pī′rănt), *n.* One who desires eagerly. "The presidential aspirant was pleased when *Pravda* called him a warmonger."

aspirin, *n.* Acetylsalicylic acid, an efficient pain-killer; *colloq.*, five-grain tablet of this drug. [*a* from acetyl, *spir* from spiraeic, the alternate name for salicylic acid, + suffix *-in*.]

assent, *n.* Agreement; affirmative response; *v.* agree; express concurrence.

Assonance. Repetition of the same vowel sound in several stressed syllables in a line or successive lines of verse. See AL-LITERATION.

assurance, *n.* State of being assured; confidence; insurance.

as . . . than. Do not try to make a double comparison, such as "Jenkins is *as* tall if not taller *than* Perkins." If *as* introduces an *adj.* in a comparison, use another *as* to complete the construction, "Jenkins is *as* tall *as* Perkins, if not taller" or "Jenkins is *as* tall *as,* if not taller *than,* Perkins."

as to. The lazy man's *prep.* of all work. Nearly always another *prep.* would be more accurate and expressive. *As to* before *whether, how, when, where,* and so on makes a very awkward construction. Write "I do not know *whether* (not *as to whether*) she is here yet." "He didn't say a thing *as to* (better *about*) money." However, *as to* is useful at the beginning of a sentence when something is to be specified: "*As to* the truth of this report, we know nothing."

astronomical, *adj.* In accord with principles or customs of astronomy; *colloq.,* mathematically vast, like the numerical symbols used by astronomers.

astrophysics, *n.* Physical science of the heavenly bodies.

as well as, *conj.* Does not take the objective case unless an objective precedes it.

at, *prep.* Redundant in the *low colloq.* use with *where,* as in "Where'll she be *at* at ten o'clock tomorrow?" "Where's she *at* now?" "Business wants to know where it is *at.*"

atabrine, *n.* Synthetic drug useful in treatment of malaria.

athlete, *n.* Participant in physical exercise or contests. Note that this word is a dissyllable.

Atmosphere. In painting or description, the mood of the scene expressed in terms of human emotion.

atom, *n.* Small particle; smallest possible particle. [*Gr.,* indivisible.]

at that. *Colloq.* for *even so, without further ado, anyway, moreover, nevertheless.* "Perhaps Mr. Robinson's intelligent discussion of their shortcomings is having its effect, *at that.*" "Finally she made a scene, and in a public place *at that.*"

attributive, *adj.* Having the quality of an adjective standing with its noun to denote assumed qualification; not predicative.

audience, *n.* Group of hearers; formal interview granted by an important personage.

audio, *adj.* Concerned with direct hearing. The audio wave conveys direct transmission of a radio program from a studio. It contrasts with the carrier wave of a broadcasting station.

audition, *n.* Hearing; *v.* give a hearing to, consider for a job as a vocal entertainer.

auditorium, *n.* Large hall in which meetings are held.

aureomycin, *n.* Antibiotic differing from penicillin in that it has a specific effect on viruses.

author, *v. Colloq.* write, compose. "President Truman authored a new declaration of foreign policy."

autochthonous, *adj.* Native, aboriginal, sprung from the ground. This is one of Walt Whitman's pet words.

auxiliary, *adj.* Assisting, assistant, conferring help.

averse. See ADVERSE.

avocado, *n.* Pulpy fruit of *Persea persea,* usually sliced for salad.

avocation, *n.* Secondary pursuit, field of minor activity; major hol by.

avocation, vocation. "His *vocation* is advertising, his *avocation* gardening."

away, *adv.* In the meaning of *far distant in time or space* it is written *colloq. 'way.* " '*Way* down south in Dixie, *'way* down on the third floor, *'way* back in 1889." *Colloq.* in the sense of *unhesitatingly, without delay.* "Haul *away,* fiddle *away.*"

a ways, *adv. Colloq.* and *dial.* for *a way.* "She walked *a* long *ways* before we caught up with her."

awful, *adj.* Like *dreadful, ghastly, horrible,* and *terrible,* it has become a counterword. Used *colloq.* in such sentences as "The soup was *awful,*" "The weather was *awful.*" See **Counterwords.** The *adv.* is *awfully,* not *awful. Colloq.* in "I'm *awfully* tired."

Awkwardness. The opposite of **Effectiveness and Economy,** *q.v.* Specifically, some of the common causes of awkwardness are the use of the double passive, lack of parallelism, stringy off-balance sentences, illogical or missing transition, lack of directness, intruders, mixed construction, faulty comparison, and inadequate vocabulary.

AWOL, *adj. Military tech.,* absent without leave, absconding.

axiom, *n.* Self-evident truth; principle received without question.

axis, *n.* Straight line around which a figure revolves or upon which measurements are based. The *pl.* is pronounced ăx′ēz, whereas the *pl.* of ax or axe, also spelled *axes,* is pronounced ăx′ĭz.

aye (ā), *adv.* Ever. *Aye* (ī, *pl.* īz), *adv.* Yes. Both these words are sometimes *sp.* ay. The second *aye* as a *n.* means an affirmative vote. "The *ayes* have it."

B

bach, *v. Colloq.,* live as a bachelor, commonly with vague object *it;* live alone and like it.

back, *adj. Colloq.* for *in arrears.* "I am *back* in my payments to Scott"; *Dial.* for *ago.*

back and forth, *adv. phrase.* To and fro.

backbite, *v.* Speak evil (of an absent person); slander.

back down, *v.* Like *back out, colloq.* in the sense of *withdraw from an engagement, fail to keep a promise,* etc.

backlash, *n.* Wind and rain following hurricane.

back of. *Colloq.* contraction of *in back of. In back of,* which is *Am.* and less formal than *behind,* has won acceptance because of its resemblance to such phrases as *in front of* and *on top of.* "He stood *back of* (*stand. lit. behind*) the fence." *At the back of* is on a par with *behind.*

Back water, *v.,* to retract one's words, to "crawfish," and **back talk,** *n.,* impertinent reply, are also *colloq.*

bacteriophage, *n.* Destroyer of disease germs; antibiotic which destroys bacteria.

bacterium, *pl.* **bacteria,** *n.* Germ; microbe; unicellular microorganism of the type causing disease or fermentation.

bade, *v.* Old past tense of *bid.*

badger, *v.* Worry, bait; tease.

badger game, *n.* Blackmail based on threatened disclosure of compromising situation. See *frame.*

badly, *adv.* Low *colloq.* in the sense of *very much.* "She wanted to buy that dress *badly.*" Use *badly* only when it describes the manner of action. "He feels bad because he dances *badly.*"

baggage, *n.* Luggage, is *Br.* equivalent.

bags, *n. Br.,* slacks.

bail, *n.* Security for return of a prisoner released until trial or hearing; half-hoop or ring used as handle for kettle or support for canopy.

bait, *n.* Lure; food placed in a trap as lure for animals; anything used to attract or entice; food; pause for rest and a meal.

balance, *n. Colloq.,* remainder, the rest. In business *tech.* a *balance* is either an amount in excess on one side of an account or a state of equipoise between credit and debit. Do not refer to "the *balance* of the day"; say rather, "the rest of the day."

bale, *n.* Large package compressed and bound tightly.

Ballad, *n.* A popular poem or song that tells a story objectively in a series of simple stanzas, generally with a refrain; a "mammy," "pal," or "torch" song, or similar sentimental romantic effusion.

ball up, *v.* Slang for *confuse.* "She got everything all *balled up.*"

baloney, *n.* and *adj. Slang,* nonsense. [*It.,* Bologna]

banality, *n.* Triteness; *pl.,* dull everyday phrases.

bandanna, *n.* Cotton kerchief printed in bright colors. [Hindu, *dyc.*]

bandit, *n.* Robber, outlaw. The *pl.* banditti is used in the special sense of Italian freebooters or the romantic robbers appearing in musical dramas and Gothic novels.

banjo, *n.* Long-necked, round-bodied stringed instrument played by plucking or strumming. [*Sp.,* West Indian name]

bank (up)on, *v. Colloq.* for *rely on, count on.* "Are you *banking on* the credulity of the customers?"

banquet, *n.* Public dinner, not always sumptuous.

Barbarism. An uncouth expression concocted or used by a person who does not know, or disregards, standard usage and the legitimate ways of word formation. An unnecessary coinage not in accepted use, e.g., *to enthuse, disremember, concertize, citify.*

A word may be in good use although composed of parts coming from different languages, e.g., *amoral* (Greek, Latin), *automobile* (Greek, Latin), *beautiful* (French, English). Such words are called *hybrids.* Some people pretend to dislike *bureaucrat, pacifist, television, electrocute,* terms which survive, like others of their kind, because they are useful and because good substitutes for them have not been found.

An *impropriety* is the misuse of a good expression, as a *n.* for a *v.,* when there is no authority for such use, e.g., *to concession, to error.*

A *solecism* is an unidiomatic construction, e.g., *to go in bed, to be different than,* or one which violates the rules of syntax.

barbecue, *n.* Feast for which animals are roasted whole; *v.t.* to cook meat before open fire.

barbiturate, *n.* Sedative drug; derivative of barbituric acid.

barge, *n.* Large freight boat, usually without its own motive power; large and clumsy passenger boat or wagon.

barker, *n. Slang,* guide, lecturer; crier outside a cheap show.

barn, *n.* Farm building for storage of hay or grain; *Am.,* enclosed shelter for horses or cattle.

barnstormer, *n.* Itinerant actor; aviator who performs at, or above, fairs and carnivals.

barnstorming, *n.* Touring the countryside with a show, originally for one-night stands in improvised playhouses.

barter, *n.* Direct exchange; trade without use of money or credit.

barytron, *n.* Unstable particle derived from cosmic rays; mesotron.

basic, *adj.* Fundamental. "Basic English is a system of simplified English based upon a vocabulary of 850 words and a minimum number of grammatical rules."

Basic English, *proper n.* Copyrighted list of words making up a linguistic bridge between any foreign language and full English.

basis, *pl.* **bases,** *n.* Foundation; groundwork. The *pl.* is pronounced bās'ēz, whereas the *pl.* of *base* is pronounced bā'sīz.

bathetic, *adj.* Commonplace; dull.

bathos, *n.* Commonplace material in vulgarly pretentious style; false pathos; descent from an elevated to commonplace style.

battery, *n.* Baseball tech., pitcher and catcher.

battle, *v. tr. Am.,* combat, fight against.

bawl out, *v. Sl.* for *reprimand, scold.* "Don't *bawl* him *out.*"

bazooka, *n.* Burlesque musical instrument made of gaspipe and a funnel; portable rocket gun.

be. Principal parts: *am, was, been.* The infinitive is *to be.*

beam, *n.* Large timber; wooden cylinder on which a weaver's warp is wound; ray; collection of parallel rays of light, heat, or electricity.

beam, *v.* Smile warmly; direct in accord with a radio beam; direct.

beat, *n. Low colloq.* in the sense of anyone or anything that would surpass or better. "I never saw his *beat* at bragging." *Beat the band* is *colloq.* "It rained to *beat the band.*" A *beat* or *dead beat* is slang for one who never pays debts. The *v.* in the meanings of baffle, defraud, worst, win from or over, get ahead of, is *colloq. Beat out* in "He *beat out* (arrived ahead of) the throw to first base" is also *colloq. Beat,*

beat up, *adj. slang.* worn out, weary. *Beat, n.* journalism, publication of a story before other newspapers, an exclusive story.

beautician, *n.* Aide in a beauty parlor; specialist in the field of beautifying.

be-bop, *n.* A development of jazz music characterized by atonality and frequent solo improvisations.

because, *adv.* By reason. "You will be late *because* of the accident." *Conj.* After *the reason is* . . . the clause containing the reason commonly begins with *that,* not *because,* the *conj.* "The *reason* he had always avoided the issue is *that* he knew it would lead to trouble." *Because, conj.,* correctly used: "He was gratified *because* they had promised to join next week."

becoming, *adj.* Appropriate, suitable; *colloq.,* suitable or suited to one's style or physique.

bed, *v.* Prepare a bed for, put to bed. Often with *down* (the preposition rather than the fine feathers).

beef, *v. Slang,* complain, find fault.

been, past participle of **be.** *Dial.* with *to,* gone, traveled, as in "Have you been to town lately?"

beetle, *v. Colloq.,* shamble, walk like a beetle; overhang, jut over.

beg, *v.* Business politeness in *beg to advise, beg to say,* etc. Out of place anywhere but in a business letter, and even here its presence is rarely a help.

begin, *v.* Principal parts, *begin, began, begun. Colloq.* in negative comparisons. "She can't begin to make pies like her Grandmother's." Idiomatically the words *begin to* have here the effect of an adverbial phrase, *at all, in the least.*

behind, *prep.* At the back of. The *colloq. in back of* is an elegant substitute. *Colloq.* in arrears. "He is *behind* in his payments."

beholden, *participle* as *adj. Arch.* obliged, indebted.

behoove, *v.* Now slightly archaic and bookish. Chiefly impersonal. "It *behooves* (is proper or necessary for, incumbent upon) you to answer their appeal."

being as, *conj.* Vulgar substitute for *since, seeing that, because,* or *inasmuch as.*

"The mother is happy *because* (not *being as*) her children are all provided for."

belay, *v.* Wind around a cleat or pin to make fast; *fig.,* slow down; *slang,* stop, put a stop to.

believe, *v.* Put faith in, have confidence in. Note the spelling.

belittle, *v.* Strictly, to depreciate, disparage, speak slightingly of, but often carelessly used for *deride* or *ridicule.* "He *belittled* their efforts to influence the press and ridiculed their publicity." The verb was reputedly coined by Thomas Jefferson.

bellhop, *n.* Hotel messenger, bellboy.

belly-ache, *v. Colloq.* complain, find fault.

belong, *v.* Be the property of, with *to;* with *among, in,* or *with,* to be attached to, to be classified among; *colloq.* with *to,* to be a member of; to be socially acceptable, "He doesn't *belong.*"

benefit, benefited, benefiting, *v.t.* Be beneficial to, do good to or for; *v.* profit.

beset, *v.* Trouble, attack, hamper.

beside, besides. Sometimes interchangeable, but *beside* is usually the more formal and emphatic, and almost always a *prep.* employed in a local sense. It means *near, at the side of,* and, figuratively, *compared with.* "*Beside* modern cars, those of twenty years ago seem quaint antiques." In a few set phrases it means *aside from,* e.g., "That is *beside* the question." *Besides* is usually an *adv.* meaning *moreover, over and above, in addition.* As a *prep.* it means *beside* and *in addition to.* "*Besides* running the business and taking care of his mother, he is taking extension courses in engineering."

besiege, *v.* Beleaguer, lay siege to, surround with hostile military forces. Note the spelling of *besieging, besieged.*

best. See *good.*

best, *v. Stand. lit.* in the sense of *excel, outdo, vanquish.* "Nat *bested* the other runners by saving himself on the hills." Also as an *adj.* in the sense of *most, largest.* "She stayed awake the *best* part of the night."

best-seller, *n.* Book widely circulated; popular success.

bet, *v.* Less genteel but more virile, *bet* has almost completely routed *wager*—at least, in America. Overworked as an expletive: "I *betcha!*" "You *bet!*"

better, *adj.* Can be used for *larger,* as in "She was sick the *better* part of a year," but it cannot stand for *had better,* as in "You *better* (had better) go home." *Better half* for *wife* is trite.

between, *prep.* Used of two or of more than two. Some prefer *after every inning, every round* to *between each inning, each round,* but everyone has to say "There was a screen *between* each bed and the next one." "They do not know the difference *between* wheat, oats, and barley." Never say "between you and I." Cf. **among.**

Bibliography. List of books and articles given to indicate sources consulted in the preparation of a composition, and to help persons interested in the same subject find material on it. A typical bibliographical note:

Garnett, A. Campbell, *The Mind in Action,* New York, 1932.

bid, *n.* Colloq. for *invitation.*

big, *adj.* Chiefly *colloq.* in the senses of *great, fine, leading, important, outstanding,* or as an *adv.* "What is the *big* idea?" "He was the *big* butter-and-egg man from Keokuk." "It went over *big.*"

bilious, *adj.* Suffering from disorder of the liver. See *humor.*

bill, *n.* Piece of paper money, banknote; statement of an account due; statement showing debit or credit; printed sheet of paper, handbill; billboard.

billboard, *n.* Panel, wall, or fence on which advertising sheets are displayed.

billion, *n.* One thousand million, a Fr. *milliard.* In German and British notation, a *billion* is a million million.

billy, *n.* Club or truncheon of the type carried by policemen.

binge, *n.* Slang, period of excessive indulgence; spree.

Biography (bĭ ŏg'rǎ fĭ). Written narrative of a life. *Autobiography,* the story of the author's own life.

biopsy, *n. sing. tech.,* removal and examination of organs for diagnosis.

biotics, *n.* Science of life, especially of the destruction of life. This word is *sing.* in its prime sense but *pl.* as a name for characteristic modes of action of living things. See **mathematics, electronics.**

biscuit, *n.* Small unit of raised bread; *Br.* cracker, unleavened bread.

bistro, *n.* Petty night club; small bar or tavern.

bit, *n.* Stand. *lit.* in the meaning of trivial amount or degree. "That's not a *bit* polite." *Colloq.* when applied to time, as "We worked a little *bit* just before noon." *Every bit* is colloq. for in every way, positively. "She's *every bit* as good as you."

bit, *n.* Theatrical *tech.,* small talking part in a play.

bite, *n.* Mouthful; *slang,* impost, tax, commission, cut, discount.

biweekly, *adv.* Once in two weeks.

black, the, *n.* Profit side of the ledger, where entries are in black ink.

blackguard (blăg'grd, blăg'gärd), *n.* Scullion; scoundrel.

blackleg, *n. Br.,* non-union strike-breaker; scab.

blacklist, *v.* Place on the black list; classify among persons worthy of being barred from social or business relations.

blackmail, *n.* Extortion by intimidation or threat of publication of damaging secrets; *Scottish,* tribute for protection against robbery.

blackout, *v.* Obscure by extinguishing lights; *fig.,* faint.

blame, *v.t.* Accuse, reproach, find fault with. "I *blame* you for this; you *blame* society." The use with *on* or *upon,* as in "He *blames* this *on* you," is *colloq.*

blank, *adj.* Colorless; vacant, plain. Blank verse is unrhymed iambic pentameter. See **meter.**

blank, *n.* Paper form with spaces to be filled in.

bleachers, *n. pl.* Unroofed seating space, especially tiered seats for spectators at baseball games.

blend, *n.* Smooth mixture; combination of parts of two words to express their combined meanings; e.g., tragicomedy. Writers for *Time* affect a style involving many such coinages. "The old GOPartisan was in his anecdotage."

blimp, *n.* Dirigible with motor and cabin within a suspended fuselage.

blitz, *n.* Lightning attack; devastating bombardment from airplanes. [G. = lightning war]

blizzard, *n.* Snowstorm, especially such a storm with high wind that causes drifting.

bloc, *n.* Association of politicians or political groups for a common purpose.

block, *n.* City square, space enclosed by four streets or, rarely, three; *colloq.,* large building in a small town. "Dr. Smith's office is in the Crumb Block at the corner of Smith and South Salina Streets."

blockbuster, *n.* Aerial bomb weighing more than four tons.

bloodbank, *n.* Reserve supply of blood plasma for transfusion.

blow, *v.* The *p.* is *blew,* and the *p. part.* is *blown.*

blow, *v. Slang,* depart hurriedly.

blue angel, *n.* Barbiturate sleeping pill.

blue plate, *n.* Meal served on one plate divided into compartments by low partitions; hence, a simplified meal.

bluff, *n.* Promontory, cliff on a peninsula; attempted deceit through false pretense of strength.

bluff, *adj.* Broad; abrupt, crusty; *v.* deceive by pretense of strength; attempt to deceive as in draw poker.

blurb, *n. Colloq.* word coined by Gelett Burgess. Laudatory remarks, especially if extravagant, on the jacket of a book or in the advertising columns. *Colloq.* as a *v.* meaning to advertise as in a *blurb.*

Blurred Thinking. Vague thinking, or not thinking at all. To cure, try to see clearly what you desire to say. Focus your attention sharply so that logical relations are thrown into clear relief. Separate ideas that should be separated, and link those that belong together. Do not let an important idea get into the blind spot. And remember that your reader will not be a mind reader. See **Fallacy.**

board, *v.* Enter upon any vehicle or conveyance, whether ship, railroad car, or bus.

bobby-soxer, *n.* Girl who wears ankle socks; adolescent devotee of swing music.

body, *n.* Alone and in the sense of *person,* chiefly *dial.* Usually found in combination: *everybody, busybody,* etc.

bogus, *adj.* Sham, counterfeit, spurious.

boiled, *adj. Colloq.,* starched, as a shirt; *slang,* drunk.

bolt, *v.t.* Fasten; *colloq.,* rush away from; *v.i.,* run away.

bombast, *n.* Windy style, claptrap; pretentious verbiage [formerly *stuffing, padding,* from OF, cotton, L, silk].

bonanza, *n.* Fabulously rich goldmine; extraordinarily successful business.

bone or **boner,** *n. Slang.* A stupid or ridiculous mistake. Often with the *v. pull.*

bone-dry, *adj.* Completely dry; banning all alcoholic drinks.

bonehead, *n.* A stupid person. The *adj. bonehead* or *boneheaded* is slang.

boob, *n. Slang.* Stump of *booby.* Simpleton. Ponderous comic compounds derived from *b.* include the fascistically contemptuous *boobocracy.*

booby hatch, *n.* Insane asylum; jail.

bookstore, *n.* Bookshop.

boom, *n.* Rush, rapid increase in profitable activity. [Possibly derived from the boom of chains and timbers which holds an accumulation of floating logs upstream from a sawmill.]

boondoggling, *n.* Useless work done by recipients of disguised doles during hard times. [Boy Scout coinage, boondoggle, braided lanyard.]

boost, *v. Colloq.* in the sense of *help* by lifting or pushing, but *slang* in the figurative senses of *praise, endorse, help along.* The opposite of the *slang knock.* The nouns *boost* and *booster* are also *colloq.* in their literal and *slang* in their figurative senses.

booster, *n. Colloq.* disseminator of favorable propaganda.

boot, *n.* High and heavy footgear; *slang,* beginner, freshman; *tech.,* U.S.M.C., recruit undergoing basic training.

bootleg, *v.* Sell illegally or without paying taxes.

borne (bōrn), *v. P. part.* of *bear.* Carried. Note the difference between this word and **born** (pron. bawrn).

borscht, borsht, *n.* Beet soup.

boss, *n. Colloq.* in the sense of a man in charge of workers; foreman, manager. It is slang meaning a politician who controls votes or brings pressure to bear upon the administrative officers. As a *v.t.* meaning to manage, direct, superintend (especially officiously), and as a *v.i.* meaning to rule, be master, it is *colloq. Bossy, adj.,* domineering, inclined to be a *boss,* is also *colloq.* "He's too *bossy* to suit me."

both, *adj., pron.* The two, the pair. "*Both* sisters." "*Both* are there." As a *conj., both* precedes the first of two or more words or phrases joined by *and.* These must be parallel, e.g., "*Both* he and she are young." "In *both* Europe and America" is to be preferred to "*Both* in Europe and in America." *Both* may be applied to more than two objects, e.g., "*Both* man and woman and child."

The both, as in "I hate *the both* of you," is vulgar. Do not use *each* to refer to *both.* Instead of "*Both* boxers were afraid of *each* other," write "*Each* boxer was afraid of the other." Strictly, *both alike* is redundant since *alike* means *one thing like another. Both of the* before a *n.* is *colloq.* The *stand. lit.* prefers to omit the *of,* "*Both* the cooks left."

botheration, *n. Colloq.* Something that bothers; act of annoying or perplexing; state of being bothered.

bottleneck, *n.* Place or point on an assembly line at which delays occur; step in a process which slows up the entire series; log jam.

bound, *past part.* of *bind.* The general meaning is *certain, tied, destined, obliged.* In U.S. it also has the *colloq.* meanings of *bent on, resolved to, determined to.* "He is *bound* to succeed." "She was *bound* to go out in the storm."

bourgeois (bōōr zhwä′), *adj.* Borrowed from the French to provide an *adj.* for *burgess,* a borough dweller; not a noble or peasant. Then used as a *n.* (bōōr zhwä′, bōōr′ zhwä) with *pl.* the same as the *sing.,*

and meaning a member of the middle class or *bourgeoisie* (bōōr zhwä zē′). **Bourgeoise,** *n.* and *adj.,* the feminine of *bourgeois,* is one of the rare examples of the French distinction between masculine and feminine being kept in English. It is pronounced (bōōr zhwäz′) in the *sing.* and the *pl.*

bowl, *n.* Hemispherical dish; amphitheatre.

bows, *n. pl.* Frames of spectacles, including earpieces.

boxy, *adj.* Square cut; like a box coat.

bra, *n. Colloq.,* brassiere.

brace, *n.* Symbol to mark relation of one line or group of lines to another; similar mark of punctuation. { }

braces, *n. pl. Br.,* suspenders.

bracket, *n.* Support beneath a shelf; level of classification; group of individuals or families with about the same annual income.

Brackets [ ]. Explanatory remarks inserted in the text by the author or editor are enclosed in *brackets.* "Nov. 6: This week a book by the same author [probably Willa Cather] came to my desk." Here the editor is explaining an item appearing in a diary. *Brackets* serve as parentheses within parentheses. "He bragged about knowing this district and pointed out Old Piney (he thought that it was Old Piney [it was really Mt. Million] and said it was five miles away) but we simply laughed at him."

brain, *adj.* Cerebral; intellectual, used with some of the connotations of **highbrow.** "He had a brain tumour." "Moley, Tugwell, and Berle were the original Brain Trust."

brainwashing, *n.* Torture to produce avowal or recantation in accord with Communist doctrine.

brainy, *adj. Colloq.,* clever, intelligent, alert. "He's a brainy fellow."

brand, *n.* Burn, scar from burning; identifying scar on an animal, cattleman's mark of ownership; trade-mark, product identified by a protected trade-mark; *arch.,* partly burned stick; sword.

brand, *adj.* Associated with a trade-mark. "When you buy a product and find it good, you can buy more of the same only because it has a *brand* name."

brand new, *adj.* Strikingly new and fresh, fire-new.

brassard (brăs'rd), *n.* Badge worn on the arm, arm-band. The band of black cloth worn above the left elbow of a light-colored jacket to indicate that the wearer is in mourning is a *b.* A special policeman not in uniform usually wears an identifying *b.*

bratting, *n.* Slang, baby-sitting.

breach, *n.* Break; violation of agreement; rupture of friendship; *colloq.,* hernia.

breadgrains, *n.* Cereals; grains from which bread is baked.

break, *v.* In reference to news, to become public with sensational effect; reach the point when news of some criminal investigation, etc., can be made public. Also as a *n.* meaning the point at which a piece of news can be published; the first news so published. Slang as a *n.* meaning equal or fair chance, advantageous favor or opportunity. "Give him a *break.*" "He got the *breaks,*" i.e., luck was with him. Also slang for *social blunder, unwise remark.*

breech, *n.* Hinder part; stern; rear part of a gun.

breeches (brĭch'ĭz), *n. pl.* short trousers; outer pants.

brief, *v.* *Military tech.,* give detailed direction, instruct in planned procedure; hence, *colloq.,* inform. Used with *on.*

brief, *n.* *Legal tech.,* organized summary of the facts of a case. In rhetoric a brief is a complete outlined plan of the logical sequence to be demonstrated in a formal argument. It consists of introduction, proof, and conclusion, and the heads and subheads belonging to these divisions. These headings must be complete statements, and in the "proof" division, connected by *for.*

bring, *v.* *Principal parts* **bring, brought, brought.** Come carrying or escorting. *Brung* or *brang* as *p.* and *brung* as *part.* are vulgar.

Britannic, *adj.* British, of Great Britain. Misspellers have trouble with the Latin title of the great *Encyclopaedia Britannica.*

Briticism. A word or expression peculiar to England, as opposed to an Americanism.

broadcast, *v.* The *p.* is *broadcast* (the more usual form) or *broadcasted.*

broadloom, *n.* Type of woven fabric; *slang,* carpet.

brogan (brŏg'ăn), *n.* Heavy shoe of rough brown leather. [Gaelic, little shoe]

bromide, *n. sl.,* dull, commonplace person; utterance of such a person. [Coinage attributed to Mr. Gelett Burgess.]

bromidic, *adj.* Like a bromide.

brontosaurus, *n.* American dinosaur of the Jurassic period; thunder lizard.

Brooklynese, *n.* *Colloq.,* a tough way of talking common in metropolitan New York but not peculiar to any one borough.

brunch, *n.* *Colloq.,* repast in late forenoon; breakfast and lunch combined. A blend or portmanteau word.

brushoff, *n.* *Sl.,* brusque dismissal or rejection; denial of acquaintance.

bub, *n.* Boy, used commonly in direct address. [G., boy]

buck, *n.* Buckeye, horse chestnut. *Passing the buck, buck-passing,* avoiding responsibility by passing it on, as in the game of hide-the-thimble.

buck, *n.* *Sl.,* dollar.

buckaroo, *n.* Cowboy. [Spanish *vaquero,* L., cow herd]

bucolic, *adj.* Pastoral, rustic.

buddy-buddy, *adj.* *Sl.,* very friendly, often used derisively.

buffalo, *v.* *Colloq.,* bewilder; intimidate or confuse by a display of power.

buffet (bŭf ā'), *n.* Sideboard; buffet luncheon.

buffet (bŭf'ĭt), *v.* Strike with heel of the hand or with fist.

bug, *n.* Insect; *slang,* defect.

bughouse, *adj.* Slang, deranged; *n.* hospital for nervous diseases.

bugs, *adj.* Slang, insane, mad.

bulldoze, *v.* *Colloq.,* bully.

bulldozer, *n.* Large metal blade, usually of steel, used for clearing land of heavy and bulky obstacles; tractor with such a blade mounted frontally.

bull pen, *n.* *Baseball tech.,* side enclosure

where pitchers warm up during a game.

bum. Slang as *v.*, *n.*, or *adj.* "That *bum* tried to *bum* a nickel and I gave him a *bum* one."

bumper, *n.* Buffer, fender.

bunch, *n.* As a general term to designate objects in groups, aggregates of things of the same kind, *bunch* is correctly used unless the situation calls for a more specific term, such as *class, squad, bevy, herd, covey,* or *flock.* It is *colloq.* meaning an intimate group of people. "Won't you join our *bunch?*"

bungalow, *n.* One-story house of East Indian type.

bunk, *n.* Speech, doctrine, sentiment, etc., that is hypocritical, pretentious, false. As a *v.* it means to humbug. The *v.* **debunk,** to rid of *bunk,* the *n.* **debunker,** are slang.

bureau, *pl.* bureaus, bureaux *n.* Chest of drawers; government department directed by officers who are appointed rather than elected.

bureaucracy (bū rō′crắ sĭ, *colloq.*, bū rŏk′rắ sĭ), *n.* Government by bureaucrats, civil servants not elected by popular vote; a perversion of democracy.

burglarize, *v. Colloq.*, rob after forcible entry.

burgle, *v. Colloq.*, break into and enter in order to steal.

burlesque (br lĕsk′), *n.* Mocking imitation. The common literary types of *b.* are *mock-heroic* in which trivialities are presented in dignified style and *travesty* in which important characters and action (of the Trojan War, for example) are vulgarized by low style and setting.

burlesque, *adj.* Consisting of mocking imitation; *U.S.*, relating to or characteristic of the type of musical show which includes dancing, short comic numbers, broad jests, and sensuous display. See *ecdysiast.*

burp, *v.i. Colloq.*, belch; *v.t.*, cause to belch. "After feeding, always burp the baby before you lay him down."

burying ground, *n. Colloq.*, graveyard, churchyard, cemetery.

busboy, *n.* Subordinate restaurant worker who removes dishes, brings glasses of water, and carries trays for full-fledged waiters. [omnibus]

bushel, *n.* Dry measure approximately 2,150 cubic inches, slightly less than *Br.* bushel.

Business Correspondence. See **Letters.**

business suit, *n.* Ordinary daytime dress of businessman or professional man; British equivalent is lounge suit.

bust, *v. Low colloq.* for *burst.* Slang in the senses of *failure, spree, to bankrupt, to go bankrupt,* and *to break a horse.*

But, The "But" Habit. Almost any clause that is slightly contrasting or contradictory may be introduced by *but,* and as a result *but* is frequently used when *although, though, however, nevertheless, notwithstanding, while, on the contrary,* etc., would be more exact. Because *but* is a sharp adversative, a sequence of *but* clauses is bewildering. "It is more difficult to train a horse than a dog, *but* the results are perhaps more pleasing; *but* who would not think it worth his time and trouble had he *but* sufficient leisure?"

Avoid redundant negatives after *but,* e.g., "How can you tell *but* that two months hence he may *not* be tired of his job?"; illogical *but's,* "In vain he struggled and kicked, *but* he could not get free," and *however* after *but,* as in "The men left the theater, *but* they returned, *however,* with more overripe fruit."

but, *prep.* or *conj.* Most grammarians prefer to regard *but* as a *conj.* in sentences like "There was no one going there *but* I." Yet when an objective construction occurs just before *but,* an objective must follow, as in "They had no guardian but *me.*"

In negative expressions, *but,* alone or with *that,* can be used as a relative connective. "There is no mother *but* wishes to please her children." "There are *but* three cigars in the box."

but what. *Stand. lit.* in "I will do nothing *but what* I am told to do." Here *but* means *except* and governs the *what* clause. The *but what* occurring after negatives and used instead of *but that* is low colloq.

or vulgar. "I wouldn't be a bit surprised *but what* you're right."

butt, *n.* Stub or stump; thick end or lower end.

butt, *v.* Push with head or horns.

butt in or **into,** *v.* Slang for interrupt, break in, intrude, interfere. Cf. the slang *horn in* and *muscle in.*

butyraceous, *adj.* Butter, buttery, like butter.

buzz, *v.* Hum continuously, *colloq.,* telephone; annoy with gossip; fly an airplane dangerously low.

by hook or by crook, *adv. phrase.* Somehow; by any available means. There is said to have been a custom or rule in medieval forests that peasants might not cut down any tree but might take limbs or branches they could tear away with a pruning hook or a shepherd's crook.

by-line, *n. Journalistic tech.,* newspaper man's signature; attribution or acknowledgement of authorship.

by-pass, *n.* Secondary passage; other road.

by-pass, *v.* Evade, get around.

C

cabby, *n. Colloq.,* driver of a taxicab, cabdriver, hacky.

cablese, *n. Journalistic tech.,* condensed style used in cablegrams.

caboose, *n.* Galley on deck of a ship; car for workmen or traincrew at end of a freight train.

Cacophony. Harsh or unpleasant sound combination. The repetition of a sound until it becomes noticeable or unpleasant. See **Jingle.** "These writers give away the plots of their stories in the descriptions of circumstances in these short chapters."

cactus, *pl.* **cactuses, cacti,** *n.* Prickly plant native to the American desert.

caddy, *n.* Container for tea. [Malay kati, weight of about a pound]

caddy, *n.* Unskilled servant; boy who carries clubs for a golfer. [*Fr.,* cadet]

cadence, *n.* Rhythmic flow, regular rhythm whether strictly metrical or not.

caesura (sĭ zhū'ra), *n.* Pause in verse;

pause due to the ending of a word inside a metrical foot.

cafeteria, *n.* Self-service restaurant. [Spanish]

cagey, *adj. Colloq.,* shrewd, cautious, not gullible.

cajun (kā'jǎn), *n.* Rustic of French descent in Louisiana. [Acadian]

calaboose, *n. Slang,* jail. [Spanish, prison cell]

calculate, *v.* Compute, reckon, shape for a purpose, rely on, count on, estimate. *Colloq.* in the senses of *plan, expect, think, suppose, intend.* "I *calculate* to interest my neighbors in the scheme."

calendar, *n.* Tabulation of the days, weeks, months of a year. [*L.,* account book]

calender, *n.* Machine for pressing cloth or paper; dervish.

call, *v.* Shout; pay a social visit; communicate by telephone or radiotelephone; *v.t.,* summon.

call off, *v.* Cancel.

call down, *v.* Slang in the sense of *reprove, scold, correct.* "She *called* him *down* right."

Calliope (kăl ī'ŏ pē), *Proper n.* Muse of epic poetry. See **Muse.**

calliope (kăl'ē ōp), *n.* Circus steam-piano; series of whistles played from a keyboard.

"I am the calliope
    Tootin' hope, tootin' hope."
                        —Vachel Lindsay.

[Gr., beautiful voice]

calorie, *n.* Unit of heat; amount which will raise one kilogram of water one degree centigrade.

campus, *n.* College yard; grounds of a college or school. [*L.,* field, parade ground]

can, *n.* Metal container; equivalent of *Br.* tin; *colloq.* jail; latrine.

can, *v.* have power; be able. [OE, know how]

can, *v.t.* pack in containers whether of metal or glass; *slang,* discard, discharge.

can, may, *v.* Usually *can* (*p.* form *could*) means to be able to, have the right to do, but sometimes it expresses permission, of-

ten tinged with a mild imperative, as in "You *can* go now, Freddie." Permission, however, is usually expressed by *may* (*p.* form *might*). *May* also expresses possibility, a wish, or a request. "It *may* be so; you *might* call at the bank and find out."
Cannot (often written *can not,* especially in America) and *can only* are often carelessly used for *may not* and *may only.*

candidacy, *n.* Standing for office, running for office. Chiefly *Br.* equivalent is *candidature.*

candidate, *n.* Person who has been nominated for an elective or appointive office. [*L.,* dressed in white]

cane, *n.* Walking stick, whether large of small, heavy or light.

canine, *n.* Sometimes the names of families or orders can be used as nouns; *canine, bovine, simian, feline.* Often, however, this use lacks precision or is affected. For example, *canine, n.,* may mean a tooth, any member of the dog family, or simply a dog. To use it merely to avoid repeating the word *dog* is "elegant" variation, and affected. To vary *beaver* with *castor* would be taking chances, for *castor* is now chiefly *arch.* Cf. **human, humane.**

canoe, *n.* Small, light boat propelled by paddling. To paddle your own canoe is to be independent. [Haitian]

cant, *n.* Now chiefly used in the sense of hypocritical mouthing of moral or pious sentiments. Sometimes used to mean *argot* or a *trade or technical dial. term. Argot* or *trade or tech.* is better when the meaning is *secret language of thieves and vagabonds* or *expression belonging to a special group, technical jargon.* Strictly, *jargon* is a mixture of two or more languages. *Lingo* is a contemptuous term for any manner of speech not understood.

can't hardly. Like *haven't hardly,* a low *colloq.* double negative. Write *can hardly* or *..ave hardly.*

cantankerous, *adj. Colloq.,* cross, cranky.

cantilever, *n.* Projecting beam supported only at one end; *v.* construct like a cantilever bridge.

canvas, *n.* Heavy hempen cloth; tents of a circus.

canvass, *v.* Examine, scrutinize; solicit votes or orders for purchases.

capable, susceptible, *adj.* These words touch at one point only, in the meaning of *admitting, able to receive;* but even here the active nature of the first and the passive nature of the second assert themselves. One would say "This passage is *susceptible of* another interpretation" rather than ". . . *capable of* another interpretation." *Capable* commonly means *able, competent, having the power or fitness to. Susceptible* commonly means *impressionable, readily acted upon,* and is used with *to* when the acting force is an influence or an agency, and with *of* before an action or condition. "*Susceptible of* change; *susceptible* to abuse."

capacity, *n.* Utmost that may be contained, content (pron. cŏn'tĕnt); *adj.* to the utmost, to the limit. See **Ability.**

capital, capitol, *n.* The chief meanings of *capital* are wealth, money, goods, a capital city. *Capitol* denotes the building in which Congress or a state legislature holds its sessions.

Capitals, *Abbr., caps.* Capitalize the first word of a sentence, proper names, names of languages or races, titles, and abbreviations of proper names. A title in the second person is capitalized; "Your Honor," "Mr. Secretary."

caption, *n.* Heading of a newspaper article; title of an illustration.

car, *n.* Railway carriage or van; automobile, motor car.

caramel (kă'rà mĕl), *n.* Piece of sticky candy composed of or flavored with burnt sugar; burnt sugar.

card, *n. Colloq.* in the sense of witty, eccentric, or droll person. "Elmer is a *card!*"

care, *n.* Supervision, control. *Take care of* may have a sinister meaning, get rid of, put out of the way.

career, *n.* Act of running; course of life, progressive achievement in a chosen calling; vocation of professional grade; *adj.,* professionally trained and experienced. "He was a career man in the consular service." *In full career* means at full speed.

caret, *n.* Proofreader's mark to indicate

that something is to be inserted. ∧

caribou, *n.* North American reindeer. [Algonquian, scratcher]

carnival, *n.* Period of revelry before Lent; combination of shows, rides, and games under one management.

carom, *n.* Shot in billiards for which the *Br.* term is *cannon.* The cueball strikes two other balls in succession.

carpet-bagger, *n.* Politician not long resident in his district; especially a Northerner (Yankee) resident in the South for political advantage.

carport, *n.* Roof projecting over a driveway in lieu of a garage; *porte-cochere.*

carry, *v.* Convey; *colloq.,* have in stock; *tech.,* include in a program of study or in the contents of a periodical.

Case. Form in *n.* (common and possessive case) and *pron.* (nominative, possessive, and objective) indicating grammatical status in the sentence. The object of a *v.,* or the *n.* or *pron.* in a *prep.* phrase, is in the objective case. Since the subject of an infinitive is in the objective case, a linking *v.* used in the infinitive is logically followed by the objective. "He said he wished me to be *me,* to be *myself.*" The *pron.* immediately preceding a gerund is in the possessive. "*My doings.*" For formation of the possessive, see **Apostrophe.**

case, *v. Sl.,* investigate with a view to robbery; check on conditions.

case, instance, *n.* In the sense of *illustration* or *example, instance* is the general term, *case* meaning *a particular situation* or *special illustrative instance.* "This *case* of malnutrition is an *instance* of what poverty and indolence will do." Use *case* in sentences like "If I were in your *case,* I would be despondent," "This is a *case* in point," or "Such being the *case,* I think we had better go." Use *instance* when the meaning is *instigation, suggestion, request,* or *step in an action.* "He wrote the poem at the *instance* of his friend."

In case of is likely to be redundant, as in "Older customers will, at least *in the case of* those who knew what Elmer meant to the store, regret that he is leaving."

cash-and-carry, *adj.* Self-service, applied

to a type of grocery or general store.

casket, *n. Elegant Am.,* coffin.

casual, *adj.* Chance; accidental, haphazard; informal.

catastrophe, *n.* Sudden calamity; final event in a tragedy.

catch, *v.* Principal parts, **catch, caught, caught.** *Catched* as *p.* and *p. part.* is vulgar. *Catch on* is *colloq.,* understand. Pron. *kĕtch* is vulgar.

catchword, *n. Theatrical tech.,* cue word; word printed over a column of a dictionary, being a reprint of the first word of the first or last entry on the page; hence, word or phrase repeatedly associated with a subject or cause.

catharsis, *n. Med. tech.,* purge; *critical tech.,* effect of a work of art in exhausting capacity for emotion. Aristotle in the *Poetics* describes the effect of tragedy as "purgation of pity and fear." [*Gr.*]

catholic, *adj.* All inclusive; all-embracing; with capital C, *adj.* or *n.,* adherent of one of the authoritarian Christian churches, Greek Catholic, Anglo-Catholic, or, and this is the common *Am.* use, Roman Catholic.

cation, kation (kăt′ī ŏn), *n.* Positively electrified ion.

caucus, *n.* Political meeting to select candidates and agree on procedure.

caused by. See **due to.**

cause is due to. *Due to* is redundant in sentences like "The chief cause of his retirement is *due to* his domestic troubles." But one can say "His retirement is *due* chiefly *to* his domestic troubles."

cede, *v.* Yield, grant; assign.

cedilla, *n.* Mark under the letter c to show that it sounds like s. [Spanish, little zeta, *Gr.* letter z]

cell, *n.* Small room; prison unit; nucleus, office, or group for disseminating propaganda.

cemetery (sĕm′ĕ tĕ′rĭ), *n.* Burying ground; graveyard; place set apart for burial of the dead. The *Br.* pronunciation is sĕm′ĕ trĭ, almost identical with *symmetry.* [*Gr.,* sleeping place]

censer, censor, censure, *n. Censer* is an incense burner; *censor,* a person who passes judgment on books, pictures, plays, etc.; *censure* is the act of finding fault with or condemning as wrong.

cereal, *n.* Grain used as food; porridge, pre-cooked or hot from the stove.

ceremonial, ceremonious, *adj.* *Ceremonial* is applied to occasions, costumes, etc., fit for, pertaining to, or performed with rituals or formalities; *ceremonious* means *formal, punctilious, precise,* and is commonly applied to persons. But either *ceremonial* or *ceremonious* can be applied to some words, although the meaning is always changed; e.g., A *ceremonious entry* (that of a pompous person); *ceremonial* entry (that of a religious procession, regiment, etc.).

cermet, *n.* *Tech.,* ceramic and metal alloy.

certificate, *n.* Authenticated statement, document attesting to educational or other achievement.

Cf. *abbr.* confer; compare.

chain-store, *n.* One of a group of shops belonging to one owner or affiliated proprietors.

chair, *v.t.* *Colloq.,* act as chairman of.

challenge, *v.* Invite to fight, dare; stimulate to active participation or opposition. *Challenging* is a cant word of writers of blurbs.

chance, *n.* Probability; luck; fortuitous event; *colloq.,* opportunity.

chapbook, *n.* *Arch.,* booklet of folk literature for street sale; *stand. Am.,* modern small book, in tone aesthetic and scholarly rather than businesslike.

chaperon, chaperone (shăp′ ė rōn), *n.* Married woman who accompanies or watches over unmarried women for propriety's sake; man or woman officially representing a school or college at a student party. Note that the spelling with -e is appropriate only for a woman.

chaps, *n.* Overalls or leggings of leather and sheepskin [Spanish, chaparajos]. The word is often pronounced shăps.

character, *n.* Symbol; letter; style of handwriting; moral nature, aggregate of qualities of an individual or group. Often used loosely to stand for the abstract suf-

fixes *-ness, -ty,* etc. "Because of its oily *character,* this shampoo . . ." Better: "Because of its *oiliness,* this shampoo . . ." "Owing to the antique *character* of this highboy, the price . . ." Better: "Owing to its *antiquity,* this highboy should fetch a high price."

chare, char, *n.* Task, chore; odd job.

charge, *n.* Quantity of static electricity existing on an insulated electric conductor; *sl.,* thrill, pleasant experience.

charwoman, *n.* *Br.,* cleaning woman. See *chore.*

chauvinism (shō′vĭn ĭzm), *n.* Exaggerated patriotism; devotion to a lost cause. [*Fr.,* Chauvin, name of a Napoleonic veteran]

check, *n.* Written order authorizing payment of money by a bank or banker, which in Britain is called *cheque;* flaw in metal; ticket, record slip, token for a garment or package left in temporary storage.

checkers, *n.* Game of draughts.

checkoff, *n.* Deduction of union-member's dues from his pay.

checkroom, *n.* Place for temporary storage of garments or packages on payment of a small fee or tip.

check up, *v.* Investigate.

cheeseburger, *n.* Hamburger with cheese.

chichi, chi-chi, *adj.* *Slang,* chic, efficient and graceful; excellent.

chicken, *n.* Young fowl; euphemism of menus, fowl, be it never so old and tough; *adj.,* cowardly.

chicken, *adj.* *Slang,* cowardly, chicken-hearted.

chicle, *n.* Sap from which chewing gum is made. [Central American Indian]

childish, childlike. The suffix *-ish* usually adds a depreciatory sense to a *n.,* e.g., *mannish, womanish, selfish, sheepish.* Applied to adults *childish* implies blame, but applied to children it does not. A child's expression should be *childish,* not *childlike.* In an adult, *childlike* simplicity or enthusiasm may or may not be a merit.

chili, chilli, *n.* Red pepper. [Mexican Indian]

chinchilla, *n.* Soft grey fur of a South

American rodent; woolen imitation of this fur; the rodent from which the fur is derived. [Spanish, bedbug]

chipmunk, *n.* Small, striped rodent of the squirrel family. [Algonquian]

chisel(l)er, *n.* An unscrupulous "nickel gatherer" who harvests beyond the line of strict honesty. Jamieson's *Dictionary of the Scottish Language*, 1808, records the *v. chizzel*, meaning to cheat. The *n.* and the *v. chisel* are now listed as slang but seem destined to become standard.

chivvy, *v.t. Colloq.*, maneuver, deceive; *Br.*, hunt, chase.

chocolate (chŏc'ō lĭt), *n.* Cacao seeds roasted and ground to powder. [Central American Indian] Pronunciation chawk'-uh lŭt or chawk'lĭt is inelegant but widespread.

choice, *n.* Selection; hence the *colloq. adj.*, select, good, exclusive.

Choppy Sentences. Choppy sentences are monotonous, wasteful, and tiring. Avoid monotony, excessive predication, faulty emphasis, and the primer style. Yet do not make all of your sentences long. Short ones consciously employed for emphasis or to give the effect of rapid action are not choppy sentences. If several short sentences are used to express an idea and the notions closely related to that same idea, it looks as if a good sentence with a main clause and some subordinate clauses had been deliberately chopped up into bits. "Father is in Chicago. He is away from home. The twins have been bad. They minded father. They do not mind mother." This should be in one sentence.

chop suey, *n.* Flavorful hash of beansprouts, sliced meat, etc., prepared by Chinese cooks for Occidental customers. The "American national dish" in that it is popular in all parts of the U.S. and nowhere else. [Chinese, *mixture, hash*]

chore, *n.* Small task: unit of farm work, usually in *pl.* This thoroughly *Am.* word is related to the *Br. char* or *chare*, do minor task such as cleaning, sweeping, disposing of refuse. [OE., *turn over, turn*]

chorister, *n.* Member of a choir; precentor, choir-master.

chorus, *n.* Group of singers; body of dancers in a modern musical entertainment; character in Elizabethan drama who speaks prologue or epilogue.

chow, *n.* Perky little dog of Chinese origin; *colloq.*, food, diet. [Military slang, possibly from Chinese]

chowchow, *n.* Mixture; kind of mixed pickles. [Pidgin English]

chowderhead, *n. Slang*, simpleton.

chow mein, *n.* Meat stew with noodles. [Cantonese Chinese, *fried dough*]

chum, *n.* Close friend. For synonyms, see **pal.**

cinch, *n.* Slang in the sense of *a certainty; something easy or sure,* as in "It's a cinch I'm not going to beg for it." The *v.* in the sense of *make certain of,* as in "I'm going to cinch that deal now," is also slang.

cinch, *n.* Saddle girth; tight pack strap; *sl.*, easy undertaking.

Cincinnati (sĭn sĭn nắt'uh or sĭn sĭn nắt'ĭ), *proper n.* City on the Ohio River. This name is often misspelled by people who do not note that it is the plural form of the name of the patriotic Roman Cincinnatus. The city was named in honor of the Society of the Cincinnati, an association of American and French officers who served in the American Revolution.

cinerama, *n.* System of motion picture projection which adds to the illusion of depth.

C.I.O., *abbr.* Congress of Industrial Organizations, an affiliation of industry-wide labor unions.

circuitous, *adj.* Indirect, roundabout.

circumlocution, *n.* Roundabout expression; periphrasis.

cist, *n. Architectural tech.*, box for sacrificial utensils.

cyst, *n. Medical tech.*, abnormally closed pouch or sac.

claim, *v.* Ask for as due one by right. *Dial.* or *low colloq.* for *say, think, represent,* or for *assert,* or *maintain* when there is no question of the assertion or maintenance of one's rights. "He *claims* (better *asserts*) that the retailers are to blame." "She *claims* to be (better *she says that she is*) a cook."

clambake, *n.* Social gathering outdoors at which clams are baked; *sl.,* a raucous party.

clarity, *n.* Clearness; lucidity of style.

class, *n.* In sentences like "That player has *class*," class is slang for quality. *Classy, adj.* is also slang.

classic, *adj.* Of the highest quality; conservatively excellent in accord with principles of harmony, restraint, and moderation.

classical, *adj.* Conforming to the rules of ancient Greek or Roman literature or art; excellent in conformity with established principles or traditional cultural criteria.

Classification. Grouping items on a basis of some similarity, as logical relation, physical resemblance, etc.

Clause. A word group containing a subject and a predicate. Main or independent clauses can stand alone; subordinate or dependent clauses cannot, and are functionally equivalent to *n., adj.,* or *adv.*

clean up, *v. Colloq.* in the sense of *make oneself clean,* or *gather everything up.* Slang in the meaning of *defeat badly,* or *make a "cleanup,"* i.e., get all the money.

clear, *adv. Colloq.,* all the way, utterly. "She drove *clear* to Chicago."

clearance, *n.* Removal of obstacles or obstructions; open space beside or above a vehicle or other mobile object.

Clearness. A cardinal virtue in writing. On the negative side, it means freedom from anything that dims, blurs, or obscures the meaning. On the positive side it means that the exact word has been put in the right place; that the idea has found perfect representation. Faults that hinder clearness are: (1) faulty reference, (2) badly placed modifiers, (3) misplaced words, (4) poor diction, (5) bad arrangement, (6) misleading parallelism, (7) faulty connective, (8) useless shifts, (9) mixed constructions, (10) faulty emphasis. Have you omitted something necessary to the comprehension of the idea? Do you need a definition? Revise.

clench, clinch, *v.* One *clenches* the teeth

or hands but *clinches* nails or an argument, or in a boxing match.

clergyman, *n.* Ordained minister, religious leader of a congregation. This loose use is *Am.;* in *Br.* usage a clergyman is a priest or deacon of the Church of England.

clerk (clurk, *Br.,* clårk), *n.* Salesperson; secretary, keeper of records or accounts.

clerk, *v.* Serve as a salesman. To *clerk it* is dialectal.

Cliché (klē shā'). In writing, a stereotyped or trite phrase: "The psychological moment"; "stood like a sentinel silhouetted against the western sky." Avoid social clichés like "those with whom we come in contact," business clichés like "your esteemed favor received and contents noted" and "by return mail," and critical clichés like "extremely well written"; "to coin a phrase." Don't use such a phrase. In the cant of the mystery program, "you can't get away with it!" "Nothing could be farther from the truth."

click, *v.* Meaning to function in an efficient manner, like a well-oiled and nicely adjusted machine, *click* is slang. "The football team is *clicking.*" "My mind isn't *clicking.*"

client, *n.* Grateful follower of a patron; person to whom a lawyer gives advice or service; beneficiary of public money and pseudo-scientific advice from social worker or welfare agency. [Latin]

climatic, *adj.* Pertaining to climate or the weather.

climax, *n.* Popularly, the culminating member of a series of ideas, words, sentences, or situations presented in the order of increasing importance; the highest point. The opposite is *anticlimax,* a comedown brought about by having something relatively trivial as the keystone of an ascending series. The *anticlimax* may be used intentionally, for humor, as when Sterne writes that Dr. Slop stood at the parlor door for a full minute and a half "with all the majesty of mud." Any inadvertent sudden drop from the serious to the trivial is *bathos.*

clink, *n. Colloq.,* prison, jail, always with the definite article.

clip, *n. Dialect,* rate of speed. "The mare trotted right along at a two-twenty clip."

clip, *v.* Cut as with scissors; *slang,* cheat.

Clipped Sentence. Elliptical sentence. Such a sentence is legitimate since what it lacks to be grammatically complete could be supplied (if it were necessary) by the reader or listener, who understands what is meant because he knows the context. The clipped sentence is typical of the *colloq.* style. "Well, if it isn't Napoleon (then who is it?)." Not to be confused with the *fragmentary sentence,* an incorrect construction.

close, *adj.* Narrow, confined, fast shut. See **shut.**

close call, *n.* Narrow escape.

close shave, *n.* Narrow escape.

closed shop, *n.* Business place where workers must be members of a certain union.

closet, *n.* Wardrobe; *Br.,* lavatory, latrine, watercloset.

close-up (klōs' ŭp), *n.* Moving-picture term for a view taken at closer quarters than in the main part of the picture. Hence, a photograph taken at close range; a close view or examination of something.

coach, *n. Tech.,* instructor or guide for competitors in sports; coacher.

coal, *pl.* **coal.** *Br. pl.,* **coals** is not used in U.S. in ordinary sense; **coals,** in *Am.* use, are types of coal.

coalesce (kō ăl ĕs'), *v.* Combine into one body.

coalition, *n.* Combination or alliance among persons or political groups or parties. A coalition government is formed by an agreement among a number of political parties.

coarse, *adj.* Unrefined, rough.

co-author, *n.* One of the authors. Often there is an implication that the other author did more work; associate writer.

coaxial, *adj.* Having axes that coincide.

cocaine, *n.* Alkaloid derived from coca leaves and used as an anesthetic.

cockeyed, *adj.* Having a squinting eye. Slang in the senses of *silly, awry, drunk, twisted.* A *cockeyed* guess would be a very wild one.

cocksure, *adj.* Confident, overconfident; confident as a fighting cock.

coed or **co-ed,** *n. Am.,* a female student in a coeducational college or university.

cogent, *adj.* Convincing; strongly rational.

Coherence. A close and natural sequence of parts. The parts of a sentence or the sentences in a paragraph or the sections of the whole composition must have a clear and logically consistent connection with what goes before and what comes after. Related parts should be placed together; unrelated parts kept asunder. Use connectives that express the exact relation between the ideas expressed, and repeat connectives, pronouns, and auxiliary verbs when clearness requires repetition. Transition from one thought to the next should be easy, clear, adroit, and logical. See **Arrangement** and **Transitions.**

cohort, *n.* Company, Roman military unit; *Sl.,* henchman.

coincidence, *n.* In the narrative, events that coincide unexpectedly, accidentally, or almost miraculously. Do not use to mean any happening or event. Correct in "It was a remarkable *coincidence* that John should turn up in Shanghai just when we needed him."

Coined Word. Usually a useless neologism; a newly made word or expression not yet established. The good coined word meets a real need, straightforwardly and unpretentiously giving a needed name for a new invention, discovery, or idea, e.g., *gas.* The useless coinage does not meet the reasonable requirements that a word should be intelligible, pleasing, needed, and made by adding genuine prefix or suffix to a real root, with some regard to precedent. *To uglify, groceteria, eatery, to suicide, endorsation, redecontamination, deratization,* fail to meet one or more of these requirements.

Often coined words are made because the plain term is not sufficiently pompous or pretentious, or is to be avoided for some reason, such as low connotation. A *repossessed* motor car sounds better than a *secondhand* one. Commercial trade names are usually coined: *Socony, Kodak, Listerine.* Although such words commonly disregard all the rules of word formation, they can be accepted as a special class. Yet license such as this should not be carried into the language proper. See **Neologism.**

cola, *n.* Extract of the cola nut, used in manufacture of soft drinks.

cold deck, *v. Sl.,* cheat; deceive as with marked cards.

collaboration, collusion, *n. Collaboration* means working together on the same thing, as a painting, book, or invention; *collusion,* a secret agreement to co-operate for the purpose of obtaining something fraudulently. "This discovery was the result of *collaboration.*" "The surprising verdict was the result of *collusion.*"

collaborationist, *n.* Traitor who cooperates with enemies of his country.

collage, *n. Art tech.* abstract or surrealist composition of string, newspaper clippings, bits of cloth, and other odds and ends. [*Fr.,* pasting]

collect, *v. Colloq.,* secure payment due.

Collective Noun. See **Agreement.**

Colloquial. Conversational: having the qualities of the speech that is neither technical, professorial, formal, nor vulgar and illiterate. *Colloquial* speech is not limited to a certain region as is *provincial or dialectal* speech (localisms), or to a special class as is *trade or technical* language. It is standard; but *low colloq.,* which is less accurate and correct, without being illiterate, is not. *Colloquial* grammar and usage are freer and less precise than those of the *standard literary* language. Although not capable of doing the work usually allotted to the more formal style, colloquial English has richness, color, and the strength of straightforward utterance, and often exerts a healthful restraining influence on a formal manner that tends to become stilted or artificial. "If you were I" is *stand. lit.;* "If you were me" is *colloq.;* and "If you was me" is vulgar.

collusion, *n.* Complicity; participation or involvement as an accomplice in an evil or illegal deed or plan.

Colon. Punctuation mark (:) used for the following purposes:

1. To introduce a formal list of particulars. A list of words following a colon begins with a small letter, but a phrase or sentence may begin with a capital. "The subjects of his satire may be put into three classes: the die-hard conservative, the obscurantist, and the rabble rouser."

2. To introduce a long or formal or unusually important direct quotation, or a direct question. "He quoted this line from 'Adonais': 'He has outsoared the shadow of our night.' "

3. To set off an appositive clause, or a phrase restating the idea expressed in a preceding clause. In this construction *to wit, that is,* etc., may or may not be written. "His prescription for the happy life contains three ingredients: he prescribes simplicity of living, health of body, and courage to meet life as it comes."

4. To separate certain items in references or in groups of numbers. "8:10 A.M." "New York: Henry Holt and Company."

5. To follow the salutation in a business letter or in an address. "Gentlemen:" "Mr. President, students of the university, and friends:" The first word of a formally introduced series of items or phrases after a colon may be capitalized.

colossal, *adj.* Vast and tremendous; absurdly overworked catchword of Hollywood advertising.

colossus, *n.* Gigantic structure; figuratively, huge and intricate industrial or economic organization. [The Colossus of Rhodes, ancient statue of vast proportions astride the entrance to the harbor, was one of the Seven Wonders of the World.]

columnist (kŏl′ŭm nĭst, *colloq.,* kŏl′-yŭm nĭst), *n.* Editor or writer of a daily or periodical department in a newspaper.

combine (kăm′bīn), *n. Colloq.,* combination of two or more companies or corporations; *tech.,* automobile agricultural machine uniting the various functions involved in harvesting wheat or other grain; *Canadian*, monopoly.

come, *v.* Principal parts, *come, came, come. Come* for *came* is vulgar. The following expressions are *colloq.*: *come out,* end, declare (oneself) publicly, as in "It *came out* all right," "He *came out* against the unions"; *come down on,* as in "The doctor *came down on* (rebuked) him hard," *come up to scratch,* meet expectations, *come back,* regain former position, and the *n.* **comeback.**

The *adj.* **come-at-able,** accessible, attainable, and the *n.* **come-down,** disappointment, anticlimax, are *stand. lit.*

The following are slang: *come across,* pay, hand over; *come across with,* deliver; *come it over,* bully; *come off of,* quit; *come through,* win, do what is expected of one.

come-back, *n.* Rehabilitation after illness, victory after defeat.

comeback, *n.* and *v.* Retort; and **come-on,** *n.,* an easy mark, challenge, lure.

comedy, *n.* Play having a happy ending; situation or patter producing amusement or hilarity.

comforter, *n. Colloq.* or *dial.,* quilt, comfortable.

comic, comical, *adj.* The first means designed to amuse; like a comedy. A humorous literary sketch, if successful, is *comic.* If unsuccessful, it might be *comical,* since anything laughable or mirth-provoking, whether this reaction was intended or not, is *comical.* "*Comic* pictures"; "a *comical* face."

Comma. The most difficult of the punctuation marks to use because of the nice discrimination that must be made between pauses that do not require a comma or any other mark, those that do require a comma, and those that require the heavier marks. Moreover, in ordinary descriptive or narrative writing the modern tendency is to use commas only when they are plainly needed to avoid ambiguity (the *open* system). But in the more formal, compact, and involved types of composition, all of the rhetorical pauses are punctuated (the *close* system). Open: This book is a mixture of parody, burlesque and glorious nonsense. Close:

This book is a mixture of parody, burlesque, and glorious nonsense.

The chief uses of the *comma* are the following:

1. To separate independent clauses joined by the co-ordinating conjunctions *and, but, or, for.* If one or more of the clauses is broken up by commas, use a semicolon to mark the chief turn in the sentence. If the clauses are short, the comma may be omitted. "Several seasons ago I read and commented upon an excellent book called *The Mere Living,* but today I cannot call to mind a single feature of it." "She will be angry but she will get over it."

2. To set off words, phrases, and clauses that are independent, parenthetical, or used as appositives. When a *n.* and its appositive form one idea, as in "My friend George is here," the comma is omitted.

   Interjection: "Oh, don't go if you don't want to."

   Nouns of Direct Address: "Mr. President, may I proceed?"

   Unattached Participial Phrase: "Generally speaking, the market is firm."

   Appositive: "Alexander, the famous pitcher, is there."

   Parenthetical: "His temper, an even one it must be admitted, was now sorely tried."

3. To set off words, phrases, or clauses in a series. "She was clever, industrious, and attractive." "He rang the doorbell, put down his bag, and waited for someone to come to the door." "Add 19, 23, and 57." When the second of two adjectives preceding a *n.* relates more closely to the *n.* than the first, or when the first *adj.* modifies both the second *adj.* and the *n.,* the comma is not used; e.g., "a lively comic sketch"; "a brilliant literary critic."

4. To separate contrasted words, words out of their natural position, and consecutive words that otherwise

would be ambiguous or absurd. "We need cash, not promises." "That the opposition has won, I concede." "In his correspondence with Gertrude, Jones had always been prompt."

5. To separate a main clause from subordinate elements, such as a long adverbial clause at the beginning of the sentence, or a nonrestrictive relative clause. The adverbial clause following a main clause is not set off by comma except when it is clearly nonrestrictive and is introduced by *because, since, as, though.* "If you had only been willing to hurry through breakfast, you would have caught the train." "This famous elm, which stood at the corner of Sixth and William Streets, has been cut down and made into firewood."

6. To set off transitional or directive words, adverbs of response, and adverbs and adverbial phrases that modify an entire clause or sentence. When the conjunctive adverbs *therefore, moreover, however, nevertheless,* are used transitionally, they are set off by commas; otherwise a semicolon precedes them; e.g., "The opportunity, therefore, has not passed." "They thought, for instance, that he never smoked." "Afterwards, we shall go to the Ritz." "Yes, they will play us." "On the contrary, he is absolutely honest."

7. To separate a short informal quotation, an interrogative clause, or an adverbial phrase containing a participle, gerund, or infinitive, from the rest of the sentence. "He suddenly asked, 'Why did you do it?' " "What do you think, Nick?" "Immediately upon receiving the letter, he telephoned Mary."

8. To indicate the omission of a word common to two parts of a sentence but not repeated, and to separate two adjacent words that are identical, or two sets of figures. The comma is also used after *namely, that is, e.g.,* and *i.e.,* introducing an illustration

or example. "The word *honest* implies fairness; the word *sincere,* desire to conform to the truth." "In 1936, 238 new families arrived." "If you say it does, does that make it so?" "The chief end in view, namely, to eliminate the unfit, is not aided by this attitude."

Omit the comma when it would coincide with a dash, question mark, or exclamation point.

A comma at the end of a quoted statement comes before the closing quotation marks.

Comma Splice. The "comma fault" or "comma hitch." Using nothing but a comma to join two independent clauses where there should be a semicolon, or a comma and a co-ordinating conjunction. "Their lack of distinction possibly accounts for the low rating he gave them, [and] their poor performance accounts for the indifference of the audience."

commandos, *n. pl. Br.,* amphibian or airborne shock troops corresponding to *Am.* rangers.

commence, *v.* Much more pompous than *start* or *begin.*

commencement, *n.* Ceremony of graduation and awarding of degrees in college or university. This event now commonly takes place at the close of each academic year.

commentate, *v.* Comment in the manner of a newscaster. [Superfluous and ugly back formation from *commentator.*]

commentator *n.* Person who comments; broadcaster of news and his opinions.

commercial, *n.* Radio *tech.,* brief broadcast of advertising within a sponsored program.

commission, *n.* Authority in writing, authorization; body of persons authorized for a specified undertaking; assignment of responsibility as an officer.

common, *adj.* Vulgar; commonplace; shared by two or more individuals. Cf. **mutual.**

commonplace, *n.* Passage marked for ready reference; stock expression voicing what is obvious or well known. One may resort to the stock expression because he cannot think of anything else, or because the customary remark is expected or is the conventional thing to say; e.g., "How time flies." A commonplace may be a *truism*, i.e., a self-evident truth so obvious that no one but a bore or a parrot would repeat it. Or it may be a *platitude*, a flat or trite utterance. As an *adj.*, *commonplace* means trite, ordinary, usual, common.

commute, *v.* Change, transfer; travel regularly between home and place of business using a weekly or monthly season ticket.

commuter, *n.* Traveler who changes and reduces the cost of his transportation by paying fares in advance.

comparative, *adj.* Pertaining to degrees of similarity; relative; concerned with similarity or extent of possession of a quality by two persons or things.

compare to, compare with. The first is used when the idea is that of suggesting or stating a similarity, the second when the idea is that of competition or of estimating the degree of a supposed or real similarity. "He *compared* a tiger *to* a cat." "His horses cannot be *compared with* mine in breeding or speed."

comparison, *n.* Gram. tech., change of form of adjective or adverb (or modification by *more* and *most*) to denote degrees of intensity of quality corresponding to singular, dual, and plural numbers of nouns. Positive: tall, comparative: taller, superlative: tallest.

Comparisons. In "His obstinacy was worse than a mule" an abstraction is compared to an object, but the rule is that like must be compared to like. If *'s* were added to *mule*, the comparison would be logical and complete. In sentences like "Men of today are much more tolerant" the thought necessary to make the comparison complete ("than the men of yesterday") must be explicitly expressed in written discourse unless it is perfectly obvious from the context, but in *colloq.* usage the situation usually makes what is meant clear and the comparison therefore complete.

In "His mental level is higher than the average person" *that of* should be inserted after *than*, or *person* made *person's*. *Other* must follow *any* in *greater . . . than any*, etc. Write "This year's team has a *better* record than *any other* team that has represented the college."

Adjectives like *full, complete, perfect, straight*, etc., although logically not susceptible of comparison, are in actual practice compared. "Your collection is *more complete* than mine."

For figurative comparisons that clash see **Mixed Metaphor.**

compensation, *n.* Salary, pay; amends for loss or injury.

complacent, complaisant, *adj. Complacent* means self-satisfied; *complaisant* means affable or obliging. "She could forgive everything but his *complacent* ignorance." "Our host was genteel and *complaisant.*"

complected, *adj.* Dial. for *complexioned.* "She was light *complexioned*," or better, "She had a light complexion."

complement, compliment, *n. Complement* means *that which completes,* the *act of completing.* In grammar it is used to denote a word or word group that completes a predication, e.g., *fine* in "The weather is *fine.*" *Compliment* means *praise* or *congratulation.* "She paid him a splendid *compliment.*"

Completeness. Not all the thought of a sentence has to be stated explicitly; some of it can be suggested, and some left to be inferred from the context. But the thought or idea must be complete; there must be no loose ends, no fragments. A fragment that masquerades as a sentence, or a sentence from which indispensable words or phrases have been omitted, is a sign of incompetence or carelessness. In "Nee added, 'But of course something may come up later that he can't compete at Ohio State or any other school,'" *that he can't* should be expanded to *that will make it impossible for him to.* In "Shot guns are being oiled to drive the wolves away," the clause *so that they can be used* should be inserted after *oiled.*

Common forms of incompleteness are:

(1) fragmentary sentence, (2) incomplete comparison (see **Comparisons**), (3) necessary word or words omitted, (4) telegraphic style, (5) uncompleted idea, (6) transition omitted, (7) failure to repeat a connective that should have been repeated.

Do not confuse the *fragmentary* with the *clipped sentence.* The omissions that are made in the latter are legitimate.

Complex Sentence. A complex sentence includes at least one subordinate or dependent clause. Subordinate clauses may be classified in the parts of speech as: substantive or noun clauses, relative or adjective clauses, adverbial clauses.

complex, *n.* The general meaning of *complex* is a whole made up of parts that are interrelated. As a *trade* or *tech.* (psychological) term it means the subconscious desires or memories influencing the personality. *Complex* is loosely used to mean an exaggerated emotional attitude toward something, as "the woman *complex.*" In the last two senses *complex* is overworked; perhaps *egotism* will do for *inferiority complex,* and other plain terms for some of the other *complexes.*

complimentary, *adj.* Flattering; expressive of praise and respect.

compose, comprise, *v. Compose* means to put together, constitute, be made of, make calm; *comprise,* to include, make up, be made up of. "This substance was *composed* of three ingredients." "These are the sections that *comprise* Chapter One."

composition, *n.* Art of writing; written exercise, theme; planned and organized work of art.

Compound Word. A term made by combining two or more simpler words, and used as a single word. The older true compounds are usually written solid and stressed on the first syllable, e.g., *black' board.* The newer ones are likely to be written separately (*foun'tain pen'*—here both elements have stress) either with or without the hyphen, e.g., *like'mind'ed.* In the plural of a compound term the significant word takes the plural form. Examples are: attorneys general, daughters-in-law, lieutenant colonels, maid servants,

justices of the peace. The plural of a compound term in which neither original word is a noun is made by adding *-s* to the last word.

comprehend. See APPREHEND.

comprehensible, *adj.* Susceptible of being understood, more than "readable."

con, *v.t.* Study carefully. *Am. sl.* to swindle, from confidence game or man.

concede, *v.* Admit, surrender, yield; grant.

conceit, *n.* Clever idea; far-fetched and extended metaphor of the kind ingeniously developed by Jacobean poets; also self-conceit, vanity, excessively high opinion of one's own powers or virtues.

conceptualize, *v. Psych. tech.,* form mental images that correspond to general ideas; think in general ideas.

concert master, *n.* First violinist; concertmeister; assistant to leader of an orchestra.

concessionaire, *n.* Holder of concession granted by government or other authority; operator of a sideshow.

conclude, *v.* End, close; *Am. stand. lit.,* decide finally, arrive at an opinion. (Horwill cites Acts xxi: 25.)

Conclusion. A good conclusion is not long-winded, flowery, abrupt, stereotyped, or irrelevant, nor does it broach a new subject.

concourse, *n.* Assemblage; place of assembly; open space where several streets meet.

Concrete, Abstract. Material presented in concrete or specific terms is commonly more effective than if presented in abstract or general terms. *Concrete* means perceptible to the senses, e.g., *the spotted dog, the greasy spoon; abstract* means perceptible to the intellect, e.g., *truth, freedom, avarice. General* denotes relation to the whole genus, hence not *particular* or *specific. Flowers* is general, *calla lily,* specific. Words in summarizing and topic sentences must perforce be abstract and general very often, but the sentences that describe, define, and illustrate should as a rule be concrete and specific.

condition, *v.* Stipulate, put in proper or

fit form for competition, use, etc. The *trade or tech.* (psychological) meaning, to build up a new attachment of stimulus and response, should not be extended to serve as a synonym for *habituate, persuade,* or *affect the mind and feelings.* "Our customers are *conditioned* to use (better *in the habit of using*) Bellax Tea."

condition, *n.* State; *sport tech.,* fitness for athletic competition; limiting provision; understanding that a deficiency will be made up; in collegiate parlance, a deficiency; euphemism for disease.

conduct (kŏn dŭkt'), *v.* Lead, guide; direct as a leader.

conduct (kŏn'dŭkt), *n.* Guidance; behavior.

Conformity of Tenses. The relation in tense between verbs in main and dependent clauses, especially in sentences containing purpose clauses or indirect quotation. In general, if the *v.* of the main clause is in the present or future tense, a *v.* in an indirect quotation remains as it was in the direct quotation. If the *v.* in the main clause is in any other tense, the tense as it was in the direct quotation is changed from present to past, from future to past future, or from present perfect to past perfect. In purpose clauses use the present with present or future, and past with past or past perfect. "We *are* going in order that we *may* see the Joneses." "We *were* going so that we *might* see the Joneses."

conjugation, *n.* Inflectional forms of a verb arranged in a systematic series.

Conjunction. A word or several joining words or phrases of the same class, as *n.* with *n., adj.* with *adj.,* independent clause with independent clause (the co-ordinating conjunctions *and, but,* etc.), and subordinate clause to the word that governs it (*when, where, because, although, if, that,* etc.).

Conjunctive Adverbs. When *accordingly, also, still, nevertheless, so, therefore,* etc., join independent clauses, they normally follow a semicolon.

connection, *n.* Do not let the wordy *in connection with* take the place of more concise and precise prepositions such as *for, about,* etc. "Regulations *in connection with* (better *for*) admitting aliens . . ."

Connective. Usually a *conj., prep.,* or relative *pron.,* but the term may be used for phrases, clauses, and sentences that point out relations between ideas. "*However that may be,* let me go on." Take care to select the connective that will express the exact relation you wish to indicate. Do not use *like* or *without* as a conjunction. "When I couldn't catch up with the bus, it honked *like* (better *as if*) an insult was intended." "They will be left in the lurch *without* (better *unless*) they do this."

When clearness demands it, a connective in a parallel series should be repeated. "She was considered a saint *by* people who knew her, and especially members of her church" (especially *by* members of her church).

connoisseur (kŏn'i sŭr', kŏn i sūr'), *n.* A judge of art, beauty, wine, etc.

Connotation. The emotional and imaginative effect of a word; the quality of all of the ideas commonly associated with a word. *Denotation* is the bare meaning of a word; *a faulty implication* is an unintended *denotation.* A political party might be called Sons of Liberty or the Young Republicans by friends, but enemies might call it the Red Radical Party when they wish to profit by the bad *connotation* given by the lying label or the question-begging appellation that assumes or imputes that the things so named have been definitely proved bad, false, or dangerous. Then, too, there are question-begging names that connote excellence, truth, safety, when the presence of these qualities is dubitable.

conscious, aware, *adj.* Not exactly synonymous, although nearly so. *Conscious* may mean *aware* of either an inward state or outward fact, but it is most often used with reference to the former. "He was *conscious* of a desire to go home." "He became *aware* of a ticking noise." *Conscious* also means deliberate or intentional: "a *conscious* lie." Hyphenated use of *-conscious* is tritely prevalent in psychological jargon.

consequence, consequential. *Consequence* is a *n.* meaning result, importance; *consequential* is an *adj.* meaning self-important, consequent. "The *consequence* was that he caught a bad cold." "Even the *consequential* gentleman in the frock coat had to apologize for being there."

considerable, *adj. Low colloq.* for the *adv. considerably,* as in "He was *considerable* flustered." *Stand. lit.* for *rather large in extent,* but *colloq.* for *rather large in amount,* and as a *n.* meaning a *rather large amount, considerable degree,* or *extent. Stand. lit.:* "The drought affected a *considerable* territory." *Colloq.:* "He gave a *considerable* sum to charity."

consider as, *v.* "I do not *consider* it absolutely necessary" is better than "I do not *consider* it *as* absolutely necessary." Here *consider* is roughly synonymous with *regard as,* the *as* attaching itself to *consider,* where it is not needed.

consist of, consist in. In designating the parts or material of which anything is composed, use *consist of;* in defining the nature of an abstract idea or term, use *consist in.* "The committee *consists of* ten men." "Optimism *consists in* right living and right thinking."

contact, *n.* One can be in *contact* with someone socially or on business, but the *v.,* meaning to make such contacts, is *colloq.;* e.g., "A reporter *contacted* Mr. Roe." "*Contacting* you has been such a pleasure."

containment, *n.* Military *tech.,* keeping an enemy in a position from which he can advance in a given direction only; preventing or offsetting propaganda or economic pressure by a potential enemy.

contemptuous, contemptible, *adj.* Contemptuous expresses an attitude toward the vile and worthless, such as scorn or disdain; *contemptible* means *worthy of contempt.* "A *contemptuous* smile; a *contemptible* sneak."

content, *n.* Correctly used in "The vitamin *content* of this milk," but do not broaden the term to make it stand for quality, property, or value of any kind. Write "This is an instructive book," not "This book has a high educational *content.*"

Context. The enveloping idea; the warp and woof of expression that surrounds a certain unit, such as a word or a sentence; what goes before and after.

continual, continuous, *adj. Continual* means *occurring on every occasion, recurring at short intervals, seemingly incessant; continuous* means *uninterrupted.* "The puppy's *continual* howling kept him awake nights." "The bombardment was *continuous* from Monday until Friday."

Contractions. Contracted words are typical of the *colloq.* style. *I've* for *I have, we've* for *we have, don't* for *do not, let's* for *let us, you'd* for *you would* or (less frequently) *you had,* and so on. The contraction *'ll* is for *will,* not *shall.* Do not confuse *your* or *its* with *you're* or *it's.* Contracted words are contractions in pronunciation; abbreviations are contractions in spelling. Stump words, *phone, ad, gym,* serve the same purpose as contracted words. Both make for economy, ease, and rapidity, qualities much desired in conversation.

Contracted and (less frequently) clipped sentences are used even in formal English. In contracted sentences or clauses (they are always co-ordinate) a certain portion which is common to two members is expressed only once and is to be supplied in the other. For a common fault in this type of sentence see **Counterfeit Repetition.**

In the clipped sentence the part to be supplied is not necessarily the same in form as the portion expressed. "Will you go?" "*Certainly*" (I will go). The following sentence is both contracted and clipped. "There would be danger of ill-advised legislation affecting the enterprise, but [there would be] no more [danger] so than [there is] now."

contraption, *n. Dial.* or *colloq.* with humorous connotation, a queer machine or newfangled contrivance.

contrast, *v.* (kŏn trăst′), *n.* (kŏn′trăst). The *v.* is usually followed by *with* and the *n.* by *to.* Write "The brilliant sunset *contrasted with* (or *was a contrast to*) the gloomy woods," not "The brilliant sunset *contrasted* the gloomy woods." But "*Contrast* (arrange so as to set off or bring out differences) the poor and the rich lands" is correct.

contumely (kŏn'tū mē'lĭ), *n.* Abusive rudeness, insulting language, insolent treatment.

Co-ordination, Excessive. There are several methods of cutting down excessive numbers of long unemphatic sentences held loosely together by *and's, but's,* and *or's.*

1. Use a compound predicate and suppress the second subject.
2. Substitute a subordinate clause for one or more of the main clauses.
3. Condense one of the main clauses into an appositive *n.* or modifier.
4. Convert an independent clause into a phrase or a gerund or participial construction.

corny, *adj. Slang,* banal, passé, sentimental; a snob term popular among the young.

Correlatives. Paired conjunctions: *both . . . and, either . . . or, neither . . . nor, not . . . or, whether . . . or, not only . . . but (also). Nor* commonly follows *neither,* but it is not limited to that construction, for *nor* may follow negatives such as *not, no, never,* etc., when the expression demands strong opposition of elements. Cf. "Will he *not* affirm *or* deny it?" (one or the other) with "Will he *not* affirm *nor* deny it?" (not either). "This is *not* to be forgotten, *nor* even to be forgiven." Place correlatives before corresponding parts of speech.

costumer, *n. Local,* hatrack, clothes rack.

could not help but. Mixed construction. Write "He *could not help* scolding him."

couldn't scarcely. Like *hadn't only, never . . . nothing,* a double negative. Vulgar.

council, counsel, *n.* A *council* is a board or assembly. One who sits on such a board is a councilor. *Counsel* means consultation, advice, or a lawyer or group of lawyers. A *counselor* gives advice.

Counterfeit Repetition. A word not actually repeated which is thought of as being adequately represented by a single appearance in another member of a compound construction, but which does not fit in the sentence grammatically or idiomatically. "I always have [*drive*] and shall continue to *drive* my own car." The first *drive* is not grammatical and therefore *driven* must be written instead. Often the counterfeit repetition takes the form of a word (often the *prep. of*) which is repeated wrongly or unnecessarily. "This is eloquent testimony *to* the limits of this kind of legislation, and *of* (wrongly for *to,* which does not have to be repeated here) the efficiency of the right methods of curbing reckless lawmaking."

"I shut and locked him in" is correct, but "I scolded and sent him to bed" is not. In "The conservatives will howl when they find out that in the four-year period ending [   ] and including *last year,* the government has increased the public debt ten billion dollars," *last year* is wrongly made to do the work of both *adv.* and *n.*

Colloq. and in informal writing, when the reader can supply the (omitted) correct form, it does not have to be spoken or written down, "He *hates* all criticism, but I [hate] nothing but unfair criticism." It should be remembered that in the clipped sentence the omitted part to be supplied by the reader or listener does not have to be identical with the corresponding portion that is expressed. "*Will you* write him?" "Of course" (*I will*). See **Contractions.**

Counterwords. One of the chief differences between the *colloq.* and the formal languages is in attitudes toward *counterwords.* The written language could hardly do without general utility words of broad meaning and of such general application that they can be used in a great many ways and in differing contexts with no special change of meaning; e.g., *affair, business, fact, person, situation, stuff, thing, feature.* But the counterword, which represents a more advanced stage of "fading" or loss of individuality through generalization, is not usually admitted in formal writing.

Yet *colloq.* speech, with its rapid tempo and its dependence upon the situation itself to fill out the meaning, admits coun-

terwords, especially when there is no special call for expressing minutely specified
ideas. The talker will say that the show was
good rather than *entertaining, instructive,
artistically presented,* etc. He will say *somebody* rather than *plumber, agent, salesman,* or *gardener.* However, the talker who
uses overworked expressions all the time is
indolent, vague, unoriginal, and trite. *Awful, fierce, nice, keen, highbrow, fine, horrid, funny, grand, pretty, marvelous, cute,*
are typical counterwords.

coup (c̄oo), *n.* Blow, sudden and successful revolutionary uprising; among Plains
Indians, achievement by which a brave
earned the right to wear another feather
in his warbonnet.

course, *n.* Planned path of progress; behavior, way of doing; prescribed series of
studies; planned series of lectures, discus-
sions, experiments, or tests; racetrack; in
nautical parlance, the direction in which
a ship is or should be moving.

crack, *n. Colloq.* in the senses of *shot* or
*blow, person or thing of superior excel-
lence;* cf. the slang *crackajack* or *cracker-
jack. Crack* or *wisecrack* is slang for *retort,
quip, joke.* As an *adj.* it is *stand. lit.* "It
was a *crack* team." **Crack,** *v.* is slang in the
sense of *fail* or *break down.* **Crack up,** *v.,*
is *trade* or *tech.* for *wreck a plane,* and *colloq.* in the sense of *laud* or *cry up.* **Crackpot,** *n.* and *adj.,* a harmless lunatic, crazy,
as in "a *crackpot* scheme," is slang.

crawfish, *v. Colloq.,* to back out, retract.

creditable, credible, credulous, *adj.
Creditable* means estimable, *credible*
means believable, and *credulous* means inclined to believe, especially on insufficient
evidence. "He made a *creditable* record."
"It is scarcely *credible* that she did that by
herself." "*Credulous* people are victimized
by quacks."

creek, *n.* Bay or inlet; *Am.,* stream
smaller than a river, bigger than a brook.

crocodile, *n.* Long-nosed, thick-skinned,
carnivorous, aquatic reptile of Asia or
Africa, resembling the American alligator;
unit of a million electron-volts used in
measuring neutrons.

Crocodile tears, *n. pl.* Insincere evidence of sympathy or regret.

crook, *n. Colloq.* for *sharper, swindler,
thief.* The *adj.* crooked, meaning dishonest, is *stand. lit.*

crow, *n.* To have a *crow to pick* is to
have some fault to find or some awkward
matter to settle with someone. To *eat crow*
is to recant, withdraw formally what one
has said, or have to accept what one has
tried to defeat or make impossible. *To eat
humble pie* is to be submissive, especially
under the humiliating circumstances of
being forced to *eat crow* or retreat from a
position. The *v.,* as in "That's nothing to
crow over," means to express exultation,
brag.

crowd, *n.* A throng, a great number of
persons. Also a group, clique, set. "My
crowd is rather lively." The *v.* when used
to mean *put pressure on, urge payment,* is
colloq.

cunning, *adj.* Counterword in the sense
of *pretty, sweet, piquant, interesting,* etc.
"What a *cunning* dress."

cups full, cupfuls. The first means *full
cups,* the second, *cup measures.* In general,
when the parts of compound words or
phrases are separate or hyphenated, the
chief element takes the *-s* marking the *pl.*
If the compound is so fused that there is
no element dominant, the *-s* is added finally.

man-eaters
brothers-in-law
editors-in-chief
poets laureate
the Misses Burney, or the Miss Burneys.

Cups may stand for *cupfuls, colloq.* "Put in
two *cups* of flour."

curious, *adj.* Eager to learn; inquisitive;
colloq., odd, strange; *arch.,* intricate.

cuss. *Colloq.* as a *v.* or *n.* meaning *curse.*
Also as an *adj.* in *cuss-word,* and as the
stump of *customer,* as in "He's a queer *cuss*
and a tough *cuss.*" The reference may be
to an animal, person, or thing, and the
word is usually thought of as humorous
but rather indefinite in meaning. *Cuss one
out* is slang. *Cussed* (kŭs'ĕd, kus'ĭd), *adj.,*

is *colloq.* for *cursed. Cussedness* is *stand. lit.*

custodian-engineer, *n. Tech.,* building superintendent employed by N.Y. City Board of Education.

custom, *adj.* Made to order in contrast to *ready-made.*

cut, *n. Business tech.,* reduction.

cut, *v. Colloq.* in *cut* and *run, cut glass, cut a figure (caper, dido),* and *cut in,* take another's dancing partner. Also when meaning *exclude* or *snub. Cut* or *cut out* in the sense of *stop doing, using,* etc., is slang. *Trade or tech.* (motion pictures), to stop the photographing of, to edit by cutting out or rearranging parts of a film.

cutback, *n. Motion picture tech.,* return to earlier point in narrative sequence; *bus.,* reduction in rate of production.

cute, *adj.* Feminine counterword of approbation. "Isn't it a *cute* little apartment?" *Colloq.* for *clever* or *shrewd.*

cybernetics, *n. sing.* Comparative study of unrelated systems; specifically, study of the human nervous system in comparison with a mechanical or electrical communication system.

cycle, *n.* Circle, complete revolution; *radio tech.,* complete swing of an electric vibration.

cyclotron, *n.* Radio oscillator devised for study of the internal structure of atoms.

D

◌, delete letters or words indicated.

dactyl, *n.* Metrical foot consisting of one accented syllable and two unaccented syllables (– ◡ ◡). Think of your forefinger with its one long joint and two short ones. [*Gr.,* finger]

Dadaism, *n.* Parisian cult of irrationality in art and literature, a movement which flourished about 1920.

daemon (dē'mŏn), *n.* Guardian spirit, tutelary deity as discussed by Socrates of Plato's dialogues.

daffy, *adj.* Silly, imbecile; daft.

daimon (dī'mon), *n.* Daemon.

dairy, *n.* Place where milk is kept, processed, or sold.

dais (dā'ĭs), *n.* Elegant term for a platform, especially the platform supporting the head table at a banquet.

damning (dăm'ing), *present part.* In the *adj.* uses where it means *fatally conclusive,* the *n* is often sounded, i.e., dăm'ning, as it always is in *damnable.* "That admission is *damning.*"

dandy, *n.* A dude. *Colloq.* or slang for anything especially good, a "daisy." As an *adj.,* a *colloq.* counterword. "Isn't she just *dandy?*"

Dangling Participle. A "loose" or "hanging" *participle;* that is, without a *n.* to modify, or not near enough to the *n.* it is supposed to modify; e.g., "His face is gaunt, *making* his cheek bones protrude." Cf. "He filled his mouth with peanuts, *making* his cheeks protrude." In general, a participle is likely to modify the subject of the nearest finite *v.*

Certain participles represent a development approximating adverbial or prepositional use. These need not modify a *n.* and therefore cannot be said to dangle. Some of the participles that can be used in this way are *allowing, coming, counting, failing, granting, talking, speaking, using, assuming, leaving, looking, making, returning, taking,* and *turning.* However, in using these special participles, one must avoid ambiguity. Ambiguous: "Generally *speaking,* little men are fiercer than big men." Possible: "*Making* due allowances, the picture is a success."

dare, *v.* Has two forms of the third person present indicative, *dare* and *dares.* "He *dare* not; he *dares* not . . ." Also two forms of the *p.* tense, *dared* and *durst. Dares* and *dared* are usually preferred. *Dasn't* is a *dial.* form.

darn, *adj.* Euphemistic intensive, unpleasant, damned, disapproved [possibly from tarnal < eternal].

Dash. A punctuation mark like a hyphen but twice as long (–). It is used:

1. To indicate the point where a sentence breaks off or changes abruptly in some way. "Would you like me to give particulars—but I see that you are not interested."

2. To mark off a parenthetical inset too detached to be indicated by commas and not detached enough to need parentheses. "This combination—the weirdest the world ever saw—proved remarkably effective."

3. To take the place of commas setting off parenthetical matter which contains commas. "The net effect of the play—which, by the way, ran only two weeks, and should have closed earlier—was as discordant as a backyard quarrel and a hymn to morning."

4. To indicate an emphatic conclusion. "It came to me all at once—Charlotte had married him!"

5. To serve as a light colon before a summarizing expression. "Electricity, gas, and gasoline—these eat up our profits."

6. To join capitalized two-word names used as a compound *adj.*, and, meaning *to and including*, to join the first and last items of dates and numbers (preferably an *en* dash). "The Chicago—Denver express." "Pages 80–95." ". . . the years 1929–1937."

7. To indicate the omission of a word or of letters in a word (usually a two *em* dash). "He called you a —— hypocrite." "The d——l you say!"

Do not use the *dash* for or with a comma or period. It is hardly ever needed with a colon; e.g., it could be omitted in *as follows:—*.

data (dä′tà, dă′tà, dä′tà), *n.* The *pl.* of the rarely used *datum.* There is a growing tendency to use *data* as if it were a collective taking the *sing.*, e.g., "This *data is* just what we need to prove our point."

date, *n. Colloq.* in the sense of social engagement, business appointment. Hence the newly coined slang *dateless,* as in "They promised to observe the rule of three *dateless* nights each week." In "That book has already begun to *date,*" the *v. date* means to show signs of belonging to a past period and belongs to the *trade or tech.* language of the critic. *To date up,* make an appointment, and *date,* person

with whom appointment is made, are slang.

davenport, *n.* Couch, divan; *Br.,* type of desk. (Horwill)

daylight-saving time, *n.* Setting back of clocks to make summer days seem longer. Britons call it summer-time.

de, *French prep.,* of. In foreign names, *de,* like *d′, della, van,* and *von,* is capitalized unless preceded by a title or forename. In *Am.* names of foreign origin such prepositions are commonly capitalized as if they were unit names. *L.* prefix *de-,* from, has value or force of a negative in such coined words as *de*frost, *de*contaminate, *de*nazify.

deaconess, *n.* Fem. officer whose functions include administration of charitable activities of a church or congregation.

dead, *adv. Colloq.,* utterly, absolutely; *adj.,* very weary.

deadpan, *adj. Sl.,* expressionless, like a dead face; betraying no emotion.

deal, *n. Colloq.,* transaction, agreement, often with an implication of underhandedness or dishonesty.

deal, *n.* Portion, indefinite amount. *Colloq.* for *a large amount, a good deal.* "This is a *deal* too much for me." Usually qualified by *great* or *good* in *stand. lit.,* and often used adverbially, *by* being understood. "She is *a good deal* worse." *Colloq.* in *square deal, new deal,* etc., and for *bargain* or *secret business* or *political agreement.* **Deal with,** *v.* means to treat of, discuss. **Deal in** means to sell.

debenture, *n.* Certificate of debt issued by a corporation.

debonair, debonaire, *adj.* Genial, gay.

debouch (dĕ boosh′), *v.* Emerge; open out, fan out. [*F.* < *L., cheek*]

debunk, *v.* Slang for *rid of bunk, i.e.,* false idealism, affectation, and misrepresentation.

debut (dā bü′, the French *u;* dĕ bū′, *Br.,* dā′b͞oo).

deceit, *n.* Fraud attempted, whether successful or not; intentional deception. A tough word for bad spellers.

decent, *adj.* Respectable, fitting; seemly,

not immodest or obscene; *colloq.*, moderately skillful; kind, good-hearted; *theatrical tech.*, not nude, presentable.

decibel, *n.* Unit of measure of sound.

decided, decisive, *adj. Decided* means unquestionable, definite, obvious, positive; *decisive* means conclusive, certain, final. There is some overlapping, but one would always write "That makes a *decided* difference" and "That difference is *decisive.*"

decor, *n.* Decorative scheme or system; combined effect of the embellishment of a room or series of rooms.

decorum, *n.* Propriety; fitness of language or behavior.

deep-freeze, *adj.* Adapted to refrigeration at a much lower temperature than that of an icebox; *n.* deep-freeze locker, refrigerator for storage of food and other organic substances at temperatures below 32° F.

defenestration, *n.* Casting out (of a person or thing) through a window.

Define. You have used a term that needs defining.

definite, definitive, *adj. Definite* means defined, exact, unmistakable; *definitive* means fixed, positive, final. *Definite* terms are those that are clear; *definitive* terms are those that are final.

dehorn, *v.* Amputate the horns of; make helpless; deprive of vitality.

dehumidify, *v.t.* Take moisture from, reduce the humidity in.

dehydrate, *v.t.* Render free of water; figurative, make dry, vapid, or dull.

Delete. Take out, strike out words indicated.

deleterious (dĕ lĕ tē'rĭ ŭs), *adj.* Harmful, hurtful.

deliberate, *adj.* Considered; intentional; careful and slow. [*LL.*, weighed well]

delinquent, *n.* Person who neglects duty or offends against authority; juvenile offender.

delouse, *v.* Remove lice from. The *Br.* equivalent is disinfect.

demean, *v.t.* Two words. One means to behave, comport oneself; the other *colloq.*, to lower or debase oneself. "Will you *demean* yourself with the proper dignity?"

"I wouldn't *demean* myself by answering his libelous insults."

demography, *n.* Statistical science of peoples or of mankind.

demon, *n.* Evil spirit, devil; minor god; daemon; *Sl.* one having a liking for or facility in. "A speed demon," "A demon for study."

demonstrate, *v.* Explain by example; prove logically.

demoralize, *v.* Deprive of morale, poise, or strength of character.

demote, *v.* Reduce in rank. [Coined by analogy from promote]

denatured alcohol, *n.* Methylated spirit or spirits.

denazification, *n.* Elimination of Nazi traits or ideas; modern exorcism.

dengue (dĕng'gā), *n.* Breakbone fever, a tropical disease. [Spanish]

denigrate, *v.t.* Blacken, soil; defame.

Denotation. The bare meaning of a word as distinguished from *connotation,* the emotional and imaginative overtones.

denouement (dā nōō'män), *n.* The final untying of the complications in a narrative. The issue or solution of a tangled situation in real life.

depend, *v.* With *on* or *upon* when the meaning is *be dependent,* but alone or with *on* in the other meanings. "His promotion *depends on* whether he continues to improve." "He has learned to *depend upon* himself." "That all *depends.*"

dependability, *n.* Reliability.

dependent, *adj.* Subordinate; relying (on); hanging (from); *n.* person who relies on another for support.

depot (dĕ'pō, *colloq.* dē'pō), *n.* storehouse; *colloq.*, railroad station. The pronunciation dā pō is provincial.

deprecate, depreciate, *v. Deprecate* means disapprove, plead against; *depreciate* means disparage, belittle, undervalue, and as *v.i.*, fall in value. "His action was *deprecated* by all his friends." "After they are placed on sale, fresh fruits *depreciate* rapidly."

derby, *n.* Hard felt hat, bowler; with *cap.* D, classic horserace run annually at

Churchill Downs. The *Br.* horserace is pronounced dȧr'bĭ.

dereliction, *n.* Wilful failure; shortcoming.

derelict, *adj.* Abandoned; *stand. lit. Am.,* with *in,* delinquent, failing; *n.* waterlogged hulk; *colloq.,* social outcast, bum.

dermatoplasty, *n.* Skin grafting; plastic surgery involving transplanting skin.

descendant, *n.* Offspring; grandchild or person more remotely descended; *adj.* descendent, coming down from an ancestor.

descent, *n.* Going down; act of changing from higher to lower; pedigree.

Description. The form of discourse that gives an account of human experience chiefly by portraying sensory details; "representation" of a unified composite of sense impressions.

desert, *v.* See *abandon.*

déshabillé, *adj.* Undressed.

desirous, *adj.* Eager, full of desire. With *of* or an infinitive with *to.* Pompous in "Introducing Mr. Potts, who is *desirous of* opening an account." Say "who *wishes* or *wants* to."

dessert, *n.* Sweet course near the end of dinner. [*Fr.,* clear the table]

detail, *n.* Group of men assigned for a particular task.

Details. Do you have enough details to support your general statements or to make your description vivid and circumstantial? A paucity of detail is much more common than a superfluity. But omit the trivia! and the petty unless a certain context makes these important. Do not bury your leading ideas under a mountain of details or lose them among disorganized details. But have enough details. See **Concrete.**

determinist, *n.* Philosopher who believes that outside causes limit or control economic and social progress and acts of the individual will; economic determinist.

develop, *v.* To unfold by degrees or in detail; bring or come from what is latent, rudimentary, or immature into a more advanced state. Not exactly equivalent to *be close,* or *transpire.* "It *developed* (better

was disclosed) today that the Bruins have bought five new players."

development, *n.* Growth, unfolding; *real estate tech.,* planned use of a parcel or tract of land for housing or industry.

deviltry, *n.* Mischief; less commonly, devilry, Satanic machinations.

devitalize, *v.* Weaken; kill.

devoted. See **addicted.**

diacritical, *adj.* Serving to distinguish. A mark over or on a letter to distinguish its sound from others represented by the same letter is a diacritical mark. Such marks include acute accent (´), grave accent (`), tilde (˜), circumflex accent (^), dieresis, and cedilla. They are used in foreign words which have not been thoroughly Americanized.

Diaeresis or **Dieresis.** A mark (¨) placed over a vowel to indicate that it is to be pronounced as a separate syllable; e.g., *aërate, Brontë.*

Dialect. *Local dialect* is the language of a given community or region where the pronunciation, vocabulary, or grammar differs from that of the standard or literary language. It is not a degenerate form of the standard language, but simply a language that did not become standard over large areas. *Class or social dialect* is the special language of a trade, profession, or sport, or of a special group of people having some interest or activity in common.

dialectic, *n.* Logical procedure, logical system for testing the validity of assertions. *Dialectics* is a *sing. n.* of similar meaning. "Marx adapted the Hegelian *dialectic.*"

dialog, dialogue, *n.* Conversation between two or more persons. A *monologue* is a *soliloquy.* A *colloquy* is a conversation, especially a rather formal conference or discussion.

diaphragm, *n.* Thin partition; wall of muscle between abdomen and thorax; vibrating disc of telephone.

diary, *n.* Journal; daily record of personal experiences and views.

dichotomy, *n.* Cutting in two, division, forking; *biological tech.,* bifurcation.

dickey, *n.* Collar and shirtfront worn instead of a shirt; *Br.*, rumble seat or small back seat of motor car.

Diction, *n.* Words; style; mode of utterance; choice and use of words. Good diction is the use of the words that fit the ideas, suggest the associated emotions, and are perfectly adjusted to the tone of the context.

die, *v.* With *of, by, from,* or *through* but not *with.* "To die *of love by* Cupid's dart *from* pure delight *through* wantonness."

dieresis, diaeresis, *n. Prosody,* pause or break in a verse at the coincident end of a word and a metrical foot. Contrast the *caesura.*

different, *adj.* The standard idiom is *different from,* although *different to* is sometimes used, especially in England. *Different than* may occasionally be found in writings of good standing, but it is nevertheless *colloq.* or *low colloq.* "It is said that fat people have *different* temperaments *than* (better *have temperaments different from those of*) skinny ones." But here the idiom demands *other than,* or *which differ from.*

Different is often misused for *differently,* e.g., "We know *different.*" It is often redundant after *many* or plurals, *e.g.,* "The delegates had *many (different)* opinions upon the tariff."

differ from, differ with, *v.* For expressing unlikeness *from* is the most common *prep.*, if a *prep.* is used. Both *differ from* and *differ with* may mean *be of conflicting opinion or sentiment.* Use *with* when the meaning is to dispute, contend, *have a difference.* "I must *differ with* you on that point." "They *differ from* each other in nearly every particular."

dig, *v.* Principal parts, *dig, dug* or *digged, dug* or *digged. Digged* is somewhat archaic. *Colloq.* in the sense of *study laboriously, drudge,* and as a *n.* meaning *a plodding student; a poke,* as in "I gave him a *dig* in the ribs"; and *a verbal* thrust, *an intimation.* "There was many a sly *dig* in her description of his manners." *Sl.,* rejoin, as in "Plant you now; dig you later."

Digest. A compact summary that does not (as the précis does) follow the proportions of the original but gives most attention to the salient point or section and minimizes other units.

dilapidated, *adj.* Ready to fall to pieces; on the verge of ruin or decay. This adj. is used chiefly of buildings.

dilemma, *n.* Properly a difficult or awkward situation in which one must choose between bad alternatives. Do not use it to mean other kinds of difficulties.

dilettante (dĭl'e tăn'tĭ), *n.* Has two plurals, *dilettanti* (-tē) and *dilettantes* (-tĭz). An amateur; a person with more fondness for, than accurate or professional knowledge of, the arts.

diligent, *adj.* Industrious. Note the spelling.

dime novel, *n.* Paper back of fifty years ago, superseded and outclassed by the "quarter books" of today.

diner, *n.* Dining car; restaurant car.

dinner, *n.* The principal meal of the day, whether eaten at noon or in the evening.

dinner-pail, *n.* Container for a workman's lunch, lunchbox including a container for liquid. "The full d." was long a symbol of the dignity and prosperity of labor.

diphtheria (dĭf thē'rē yȧ), *n.* Throat ailment characterized by the formation of a membrane in the air passages. Careful pronunciation leads to correct spelling. Note that the *th* is not voiced.

dipper, *n.* Long-handled drinking cup; *Br.* equivalent is pannikin.

directive, *n. Tech.,* general set of instructions or statement regarding administrative policy.

directly, *adv.* Chiefly *low colloq.* when used as a *conj.* meaning *as soon as* or *immediately after.* "I will sign your paper directly *(stand. lit. as soon as)* I get home." *Stand. lit.* in "He went *directly* to the doctor."

dirigible (dĭr'ĭ jĭbl), *n.* Balloon that can be steered; blimp.

dirndl, *n.* Tyrolean peasant dress, with full skirt, gathered waist, and tight bodice.

disadvise, *n. Pedagogical jargon,* advise against.

disappoint, *v.* Accomplish less than was expected; frustrate, fail to achieve as much as was expected by. This word is often misspelled.

disassemble, *v.* Take apart.

disc jockey, *n.* Conductor of radio program of recorded music.

discophile, *n.* Connoisseur of phonograph records.

discover, *v.* Find; uncover.

discreet, *adj.* Judicious; cautiously reticent.

discrete, *adj.* Separate and distinct. Pron. *dĭs'krēt* is Brit.

discriminate, *v.* Observe clearly; perceive differences, make nice distinctions; show favoritism or prejudice.

discrimination, *n.* Faculty of perceiving differences; *colloq.,* displaying prejudice, unfairly deciding against minority groups.

disinterested, uninterested, *adj. Disinterested* means showing a lack of interest, apathetic, impartial; *uninterested* means indifferent to, without property or interest in. "I am sure that her decision is a *disinterested* one." "Her *disinterested* manner irked me." "Never did you see anyone as *uninterested* in a play as he."

disk, disc, *n.* Flat, circular object; phonograph record.

disparity, *n.* Dissimilarity; difference in condition.

disqualify, *v.* Bar from eligibility for competition.

disremember, *v. Dial.* and *low colloq.* To forget; fail to remember.

dissenter, *n.* Person who disagrees; *Br.,* nonconformist, hence adherent of any Protestant church or sect other than the Church of England in England or the Presbyterian establishment in Scotland.

dissimilarity, *n.* Unlikeness, point or detail of difference.

dissipate, *v.t.* Scatter; use up; *v.i. colloq.* waste energy in pleasurable excesses.

district attorney, *n.* Public prosecutor in town or county. For prosecutions by the State, the official is the States Attorney.

dither, *v. Arch.,* shiver; cause to shiver.

n. Colloq., state of nervous excitement, mild jitters.

diurnal, *adj. Arch.* and poetic, daily.

divide, *n.* Watershed. The ridge at the top of the Rocky Mountains is the Great Divide, with water flowing toward the Mississippi on one side and toward the Pacific or the Rio Grande on the other.

do, *v.* Principal parts, *do, did, done. Done* for *did,* or *did* for *done* is vulgar. "*Do* you have . . . ?" is *colloq.* for "Have you . . . ?" There is a tendency to overwork the *p:* emphatic, using *did go* for *went.*

Do is regularly used to stand for another *v.* so that it will not have to be repeated. In this construction *do* is used in conjunction with *as, so, neither, nor,* or a *pron.* "The Caribs *ate* human flesh, as *did* certain tribes in the Sandwich Islands." "Margery didn't *wait,* but *who did?*" With *neither* this construction is *colloq.* "You do not like mackerel, and *neither do* I."

Do is *colloq.* in the senses of trick, cheat, as in "I was *done* out of my share"; visit as a tourist, as in "We want to *do* France in three weeks"; serve a term in prison.

do in, *v. Sl.,* kill.

do up, *v. Colloq.,* wash and iron, launder.

dock, *n.* Landing platform; wharf.

doctor, *n.* Person qualified to teach; possessor of a doctoral degree; physician; dentist; veterinarian. [*L.,* teacher]

doctor, *v.t. Colloq.* in the sense of *treat as a doctor does, fix to suit one's own purposes, tamper with.* As a *v.i. colloq.* for *take* or *practice medicine.* "He's *doctoring* himself."

documentary, *n.* Motion picture that presents historical facts or news without fictional modification.

doggerel, *n.* Slipshod, uninspired, irregular, trivial, or comic verse.

doghouse, *n.* Kennel; shelter for a watchdog. *In the doghouse* means in disgrace or disfavor.

dogie, *n.* Motherless calf in a range herd.

dogma, *pl.* dogmas, dogmata; *n.* Tenet; doctrine; unit of doctrine, esp. religious teaching.

doll, *n. Sl.,* attractive woman, frequently used in personal address.

doll up, *v.* Dress up.

domestic, *adj.* Homelike, not foreign, home.

Dominant Impression. In description, harmonious unity of effect obtained by careful selection of the objects, the aspects of the objects to be presented, and the words used to describe these. Mood, tone, or point of view that the writer makes predominant.

donate, *v.* Coined from *donation* and called a pretentious and grandiloquent vulgarism by its many enemies. But it seems to be useful and to have a shade of meaning, or, at least, a connotation different from *give.* The pompous writer will say "Mrs. Ophelia Vandeventer *donated* a trousseau of slumber-wear." Why not write "She *gave* a half-dozen nightgowns"?

done, *p. part.* of *do.* Vulgar for *did,* as in "He *done* it." *Done with* for *completed* or *disposed of* is *colloq.* in "I'm glad I'm *done with* that job."

don't. *Colloq.* contraction of *do not. Low colloq.* or vulgar for *does not. I don't doubt but* is a double negative.

dope, *n. Colloq.,* anything dipped, sauce into which one dips; any thick, viscous liquid; drug; harmful drug; *slang,* drugged person; fool; information; inside information; *v.*—often with *out*—predict by the aid of special information, guess, make out or understand the inner workings of something. "I couldn't *dope out* her part in the affair." [Dutch, sauce]

dormitory, *pl.* **dormitories,** *n.* Bedroom containing several beds; building providing bedrooms and other rooms for students, patients, or prisoners.

dossier (dŏs'yā), *n.* File or set of papers on any subject; records concerning a member of an organization or candidate for employment. [*F.,* bundle]

double-breasted, *adj.* Overlapping and having two vertical rows of buttons; having the appearance of being susceptible of being buttoned on either right or left. Actually the buttonholes on the left side fit buttons on the right side of a man's d.-b. coat.

Double Capacity, Word in. The same as **Counterfeit Repetition,** q.v. *About* in "Smith is interested and curious *about* magic" is said to be a word in a double capacity as it is the *prep.* for *magic* and the understood *prep.* after interested. But since one does not say *interested about,* the construction is faulty. The sentence should be "Smith is interested in and curious *about* magic."

Double Genitive or Double Possessive. "A friend *of* my brother*'s.*" Correct grammatically.

Double Negative. A construction typical of popular or vulgar speech. It consists of negative expressions like *can't, won't, ain't,* followed by *none, nothing, no, not, never, hardly, barely,* or *scarcely.* "I *ain't never* goin' to do that *no* more" is a triple negative.

Not is redundant in sentences like "I shouldn't wonder if it did*n't* turn to rain this afternoon." Write ". . . if it *turned* to rain . . ."

Double Passive. An awkward and incorrect construction used because it seems to be like a correct construction in which the subject of two passives would be the object of both verbs if they were made active; e.g., "This boy *was chosen to be sent.*" In the active this would be "They chose the boy to send him." These sentences are correct. But in "Considerable time *was managed to be wasted,*" a double passive, *time* was *wasted* but was not *managed.* Write "We cannot hope that a higher bid will be made," not "No higher bid can be *hoped* to be made." Write "No man can say *what should be done* (not *what is wanted to be done*) in regard to the gold plank."

doublet, *n.* Closefitting uppergarment worn in Elizabethan England; unit of a pair; *philological tech.,* one of two words derived from the same word in another language, as *glamor* and *grammar.*

double talk, *n.* Comedian's jargon of meaningless or distorted phrases; a speech (especially political) filled with contradictions.

doubt, *v.* Except when the main assertion is interrogative, as "Do they *doubt that* he is here?" or negative, as "There is *no doubt that* he is ambitious," or "It is *no* longer *doubtful* that she will recover," *doubt* and *doubtful* are regularly followed by *whether*. "I *doubt whether* he will come." "I've *no doubt but what* . . ." is standard.

In modern speech and writing the *-ly* is omitted from the *adv. doubtless* (*ly*). "*Doubtless* you are right."

dough, *n. Colloq.,* money.

doughboy, *n.* Soldier; enlisted infantryman of the AUS [traditionally taken from buttons as big as dumplings, the buttons on formal U.S. Army uniforms about 1846].

doughty, *adj.* Strong; swaggeringly courageous.

dour (door), *adj.* Sourly severe; grimly sullen.

dove (dōv), *v. Colloq.* for *dived.*

doxy, *n. Slang,* woman, mistress, common-law wife. [Gypsy]

d.p., *n.* Displaced person; civilian made homeless by war; released prisoner or slave laborer who has been unable to go home.

Drama (drä'ma, drăm'a). A play; art, literature, or affairs of the theater. Figuratively, it means events in real life having dramatic qualities. There are three main types of drama. In the *tragedy* the protagonist suffers because of some flaw in his nature or because of the circumstances in which he is placed. In the *comedy* the characters are involved in humorous or amusing situations but finally solve or escape from their difficulties. In the *melodrama* the situations are sensational, for they are selected to move the audience rather than to make it think.

dramatic, theatrical, *adj.* In figurative use *dramatic* means striking, vivid, effective, as in a good play; *theatrical* means exaggerated, sentimental, tawdry, as in a melodramatic play. "A violent and insincere *theatrical* display of emotions"; "a *dramatic* exit."

drawing room, *n.* Parlor, reception hall;

railroad tech., sleeping car room having three berths.

dream, *v.* Principal parts, *dream, dreamed* (drēmd) or *dreamt* (drĕmt), *dreamed* or *dreamt.*

dredge, *n.* Machine for drawing or dragging solid matter up from the bottom of a body of water.

dresser, *n.* Dressing table; low chest-of-drawers with a mirror; *Br.,* sideboard with platerails.

drink, *v.* Principal parts, *drink, drank, drunk.* The *p. part. drunken* is rare except as a verbal *adj.* meaning *intoxicated. Drunk* as a *n.* is slang.

drive, *n.* Campaign; planned rapid progress toward a goal; *journalistic cant,* any vigorous, concerted effort for any purpose; psychological urge to action.

drone, *n.* Aircraft remotely controlled.

drown, *v.* Principal parts, *drown, drowned* (pronounced drownd), *drowned.* The *p.* form *drownded* is vulgar.

druggist, *n.* Pharmacist, apothecary, equivalent to *Br.,* chemist.

dry, *pl.* **dries,** *n.* Prohibitionist.

dry, *adj.* Prohibitionist; characterized by or advocating prohibition of the sale of intoxicating liquors.

D.T., D.T.'s, *n.* Delirium tremens; disease caused by prolonged use of intoxicants and characterized by frightful hallucinations and violent trembling. Also **d.t.** and **d.t.'s.**

dubious, *adj.* Doubtful; ethically questionable.

dud, *n.* Slang for a bomb or shell that fails to explode; hence, a person or thing that disappoints. In the *pl., colloq.* for *clothes.*

dude, *n.* Well dressed man, dandy; Easterner in the West, city man in the country.

due to, *adj. Due to, caused by,* and *owing to* are by origin adjectival expressions, but now *owing to* can be used as either *adj.* or *prep.* As an *adj.* "This slip was *owing to* his nervousness." As a *prep.,* "*Owing to* his nervousness, he made a slip." *Due to* may be used as an *adj.* but its use as a *prep.* is not yet thoroughly established. *Stand. lit.,* "His failure was *due to* carelessness."

As a *prep.*, *"Due to* carelessness, he failed." *Caused by* is never used as a *prep.*

dues, *n. pl.* Membership fees, subscription to a club.

duke, *n.* Ruler of a duchy in continental Europe; *Br.*, nobleman of highest hereditary rank below royalty; *slang*, fist.

dumb, *adj. Colloq.* in the sense of *dull-witted, stupid.* **Dumbbell,** *n.,* is slang for a stupid person.

dumbwaiter, *n.* Service lift, hand-power elevator for dishes, linen, etc.

dunk, *v. Colloq.*, immerse, dip hard food in liquid, as doughnut in coffee. [Pennsylvania German, dip]

dustbin, *n. Br.*, garbage can, ashcan.

dust-bowl, *n.* Desolate region from which surface soil has been blown away; a section of Oklahoma.

Dutch, *adj. Colloq.*, German as well as Netherlandish.

dynamic personality. As trite as *downy couch* or *tired but happy.*

dyne, *n.* Unit of force causing a mass of one gram to accelerate one centimeter per second; technical term involved in such radio advertising cant words as *heterodyne* and *superheterodyne.*

E

each, *pron., sing. "Each* of the women brought *her* (not *their*) dog(s)." *Each other* applies to *two; one another* applies to more than two. "The twins laughed at *each other's* antics." "The jurymen were whispering to *one another."*

earth, *n.* Planet between Venus and Mars; loam, dirt. The name of the globe on which we live is capitalized only if used in association with capitalized names of other astronomical bodies. The same is true of *sun* and *moon.*

easy mark, *n. Sl.*, sucker, gull.

eat, ate, eaten, *v.i.* Take meals, take nourishment; *v.t.* consume food. See **crow.**

eats, *n. Sl.*, food.

ecdysiast (ĕk dĭz'ĭ ăst), *n.* Dancer who undresses; burlesque performer who does a "strip tease."

Echoic Word. A word imitating the sound it stands for: *clank, boom, moo.* A term easier to handle than *onomatopoetic,* which means the same.

eclectic, *adj.* Unsystematic; selected or selecting from various sources.

Economy. As applied to the sentence, *economy* denotes efficiency and directness. Ideas should be presented in such a fashion that the reader will consume the least possible amount of time and attention in receiving them. But *economy* does not entail the omission of the concrete and the specific. It demands that unnecessary wordiness, fumbling, and awkwardness be avoided. See **Effectiveness and Economy.**

ecstasy, *n.* Emotional obsession; state of being overwhelmed by pleasant passion. A hard word to spell.

edit, edited, editing, *v.t.* Prepare for publication; revise; supervise (a periodical publication).

Editorial We. Except in editorials it is an affectation to refer to yourself as if you were an editor, but the *editorial we* is better than substitutes like "the author of these fragments." Avoid false modesty.

e'en, e'er, *adv.* Poetic for *even* and *ever.*

effect, *n.* Consequence, issue, outcome, effectiveness; *pl.* possessions. See **affect.**

effective, *adj.* Operative, working; in force (of a law or regulation).

Effectiveness and Economy. The effective sentence transmits its idea clearly and with a minimum of loss. It is economical because it is direct, precise, and graceful. Some of the ways of attaining *effectiveness and economy* follow:

1. By use of the parallel construction; i.e., the same arrangement of word, phrase, or clause repeated to economize attention. "Experience keeps a dear school, but fools will learn in no other."

2. By placing modifiers and antecedents correctly.

3. By the use of the right kind of variety and the avoidance of the wrong kind.

4. By Stability and Directness, *q.v.*

5. By avoiding stringy or choppy sentences.

6. By avoiding mixed constructions and faulty comparisons.

7. By good diction.

efficiency, *n.* Degree or quality of accomplishment in proportion to expenditure of time, wealth, or energy. **Proficiency** means skill, expertness, being competent.

efficient, *adj.* Causative; accurate, energetic, and active; satisfactorily productive in proportion to energy and capital expended.

e.g. *Abbr.* of *exempli gratia,* for example, and means *for instance.* It does not have to be italicized or followed by a comma, but may be. Do not use *i.e. (that is)* when you mean *e.g.*

egghead, *n.* Derisive and abusive term for an *intellectual.*

egoist, egotist, *n.* An egoïst is a person given to excessive love and thought of self; an *egotist* is a person addicted to the practice of speaking of, or writing about, or praising himself too much.

egregious (ē grē'jŭs), *adj.* Select, eminent, conspicuous, as "an *egregious* ass." Now applied only to nouns expressing contempt.

either (initial sound of *either* preferably ē), *adj.* and *pron.* Strictly, *one of two,* but sometimes *one of two or more.* Do not use for *each* or *both.* The correlatives *either . . . or, neither . . . nor,* belong immediately before the words or word groups (which must be similar) that are contrasted. "*Either I* am a wizard *or you* are one," not "I am *either* a wizard *or you* are one." "You must fear *neither* God *nor* devil," not "You must *neither* fear God *nor* devil." Used as an *adv.* to emphasize the word that precedes it, usually in negative expressions. "She is not young or pretty *either.*"

eke out, *v.* To piece out or supplement by the addition of something scanty, inferior, or obtained with difficulty; to live or make a living in scanty fashion.

elective, *adj.* Optional, subject to whim or selection.

electronarcosis, *n.* Treatment of mental disorder by feeding into the brain a relatively weak electrical current, an improvement on shock therapy.

electronics, *n.* Science of electrons, branch of physics related to radio, radar, and television.

elegant, *adj.* Refined, over-refined; stylish; *colloq.,* excellent.

Elegant Variation. See **Variations, Fancy.**

elegy, eulogy, *n. Elegy* is a poem of lamentation; *eulogy,* a laudatory discourse.

element, factor, phase, *n.* An *element* is a part which goes into the making of a whole. A *factor* is something that produces a result. A *phase* is a state or stage of change or development, or an aspect of something which varies. "Words are the *elements* of the sentence." "The price is a *factor* that must be considered." "This is a new *phase* of the movement."

elevator, *n.* Compartment or open platform for raising or lowering passengers or freight; the *Br.* equivalent is lift.

elicit, illicit. *Elicit* is a *v.* meaning to bring out or draw forth; *illicit,* an *adj.* meaning unlawful. "He *elicited* the information that led us to believe that the transaction was *illicit.*"

ell, *n.* Wing of a building shaped like an L; *arch.,* cloth measure of about a yard.

ellipsis, *n.* Omission; mark of omission, commonly three asterisks or three periods spaced by em quadrats.

Elliptical Sentence. A clipped sentence, grammatically incomplete but not fragmentary.

else, *pron.* Do not use *but* as the correlative of *else.* Write "A ferret is nothing *else than* (not *but*) a trained weasel." Better than either construction is "A ferret is *merely* (or *only,* or *simply*) a trained weasel." Do not use *else* as a *conj.* in place of *or* or *otherwise,* as in "Give me succor, *else* I perish." Write "Help me *or* I die."

Somebody else's, anybody else's, someone else's, everyone else's, anyone else's, nobody else's, and *who else's,* as in "*Who else's* hat?" are in good use.

elude, *v.* Avoid, escape, escape from.

elusive, elusory, illusory, *adj. Elusive* means evasive, impossible or difficult to grasp physically or mentally; *elusory* is synonymous with *elusive; illusory* means illusive, unsatisfying or disappointing. "Our halfbacks 'are *elusive*." "Our seeming success was *elusory*."

em, *n.* Letter M; type measure, em pica, 0.166 inch.

'em, *pron.* Used *colloq.* as a contraction of *them.* "Up and at *'em.*"

emanate, *v.* Issue, come out; emit.

embarrass, *v.* Disconcert; confuse; impede (in business matters).

emigrate, immigrate, *v. Emigrate* means to go from a country; *immigrate,* to come into a country.

eminent, imminent, *adj. Eminent* means distinguished; *imminent* means impending. "The visit of the *eminent* statesman is *imminent.*"

emotive, *adj.* Causing emotion; referring to emotion, as *e.* critical terminology; synonymous with secondary meaning of *emotional,* appealing to or stirring the feelings.

empennage, *n.* Stabilizing combination of planes at the tail of a dirigible.

Emphasis. Making the most of your important ideas by presenting them in a forceful and distinctive way and by keeping the less important in the background. Common faults under this head are: (1) placing the important material in a poor position, (2) failing to throw out or subordinate unimportant ideas, (3) failing to arrange material in the order of climax, (4) neglecting to repeat when repetition would give needed stress, (5) failing to separate ideas that should be set off, (6) using the weak passive voice instead of the active, (7) gross exaggeration, or overemphasis.

empiric, *n.* Charlatan.

empirical, *adj.* Experimental; learning from experience.

enervate, innervate, *v. Enervate* (ĕn'er vāt) means to weaken, enfeeble, unnerve; *innervate* (ĭ nĕr' vāt) means to give nerves to, stimulate an organ or nerves. "The climate is *enervating.*" "This change will *innervate* the frog's heart."

engage in, indulge in. One *engages in* an occupation or employment; one *indulges in* something that gratifies one's tastes or desires.

engineer, *n.* Member of one of the sci-

entific professions related to machines and construction; driver of a locomotive, one who manages a stationary engine or motor; officer or soldier concerned with military construction work.

English (ĭng'glĭsh), **England** (ĭng'glănd).

English, Levels of. From the highest level down, *standard literary American English, colloquial, low colloquial,* and *vulgar.* In course of time words may pass from one level to another; a *sl.* or *colloq.* word may in time become *stand. lit.* For example, see **mob.**

enhance, *v.* Augment, increase in value, etc. Use preferably with other than a personal object or subject. "Anger *enhanced* her beauty" is better than "She *enhanced* her beauty by being angry."

enjambement, *n. Critical tech.,* carrying over a sentence in poetry in such a way that closely connected words are in different lines. [*Fr.,* straddling]

enjoin, *v.* Ban or prohibit by injunction; *Br.* and *arch.,* command.

enlisted men, *n.* Soldiers who are not commissioned officers; rank and file.

entail, *v.* Limit (a line of inheritance); involve; necessitate.

enthuse, *v.* An old but bad coinage. *Low colloq.* Say *inspire, create enthusiasm, become enthusiastic,* or *speak effusively.*

entity, *n.* Whole, unit.

entomology, *n.* Science of insects.

entourage, *n.* Surrounding group; official family.

entropy, *n.* Source or measure of energy produced by a thermodynamic system but not available for use.

entry, *n. Colloq.,* lobby, entrance, hallway, foyer.

envelop (ĕn vĕl'ŭp), *v.* The *n.* is sometimes *sp. envelop* and pronounced like the *v.,* but the preferred *sp.* for the *n.* is *envelope* and the preferred pronunciation (ĕn'vĕ lōp).

environment, *n.* Surroundings, *milieu* [said to have been coined by Thomas Carlyle].

enzyme, *n.* Organic substance which acts as a catalyst to facilitate digestion; ferment. Pepsin is an enzyme.

epic, *n.* Long narrative poem recounting the deeds of one hero and representing the ideas and ideals of a race, a nation, or a culture group.

Epigram. Saying remarkable for brevity and point. Many of the proverbs are *epigrams;* e.g., "Three may keep a secret if two are dead."

Epithet. Bookish term for an *adj.* or title that hits off a trait or idea with such striking fitness that it sticks and is used regularly in a certain connection, like a nickname. "Fidus Achates," "rosy-fingered dawn," "honest Iago," "conspicuous waste." Without a qualifying *adj.,* such as *offensive,* it does not mean an abusive expression or bad name.

epos, *n.* Monumental epic.

equally as. Not in good use for *just as, equally,* or *as.* Write "Skating is *as* difficult as dancing" not "Skating is *equally as* difficult as dancing." *Equally as good* is due to confusion between *equally good* and *just as good as.* Use either of the last-mentioned phrases.

equip, equipping, equipped, *v.* Fit out; supply with whatever is needed.

equity, *n.* Right, common justice; property right.

eradicate, *v.* Tear out by the roots; eliminate completely.

ergophobia, *n.* Horror of work.

ersatz, *adj.* Artificial, substitute. [German]

erstwhile, *adj.* Fancy for *former.* "We tried to restore him to his *erstwhile* (former) good humor."

escapist, *n.* Person inclined toward substitution of imaginary activity instead of confronting unpleasant reality.

especial, *adj.* See *special.*

Esq., *abbrev.* Esquire. This somewhat formal courtesy title is written after the name of a landowner or a lawyer. If *Mr.* precedes the name, *Esq.* must not follow it.

essay (ĕs sā′), *v.* Try, undertake. **Essay** (ĕs′sā), *n.,* an attempt, especially a piece of writing which is less pretentious and less thorough than a *treatise* or a *monograph.*

essence, *n.* Fundamental being; alcoholic solution of oil extracted from a plant; necessary and distinguishing part. Avoid the trite, "Time is of the essence."

essential, necessary, requisite, *adj.* Essential means absolutely necessary; *necessary* means indispensable, obligatory, or inevitable; *requisite* means required by circumstances or for a certain purpose. In an automobile, wheels are *essential,* tires are *necessary,* and *balloon tires* are *requisite* from the point of view of easy riding.

esthetic, *adj.* See **aesthetic.**

etc. (ĕt sĕt′e rà). In reading it may be pronounced *and so forth.* Write: "Hay, corn, oats, *etc.*" Try to keep *etc.* out of writing that is not commercial or technical. Certainly do not often permit it to take the final emphatic position in the sentence. Sometimes you can avoid the final *etc.* by introducing an enumeration with *such as* or *for example.* "We saw a variety of terriers there, *such as* Wirehairs, Sealyhams, and Scotties."

-ette, Suffix indicating diminutive size or feminine gender, in such modern terms as *kitchenette, luncheonette* and *usherette.*

Etymological Fallacy. The erroneous belief that the meaning of a word at some earlier period (especially in its earliest known form) or in some cognate language is decisive in determining the current meaning of a word. If the original meaning of *mail,* i.e., *bag,* is retained, the compound *mailbag* is tautological, and the use of *mail* should be confined to the meaning of a *bag of letters.* But it is an etymological fallacy to believe that this must be done. The word *mail,* at least in America, by common custom is used for *letters* or anything else transmitted through the postal service. Also *to mail* (letters, etc.) is correct and much more usual than the *v. post. Usage,* not *origin,* determines present meaning.

etymon, *n.* Linguistic root; original word from which another word is derived. [Gr., authentic, real]

Euphemism. The same as *genteelism. Transient boys* is *a euphemism* for *vagrants.* Do not confuse with *Euphuism,* the style employed by the novelist Lyly, who wrote *Euphues, or the Anatomy of Wit.*

Euphony. Does this combination of letters or words produce a pleasant sound? Is it easy to pronounce? Cf. **Cacophony.**

evaluate, *v.* Estimate the worth of. For collegiate registrars *e.* has the special meaning, translate in terms of degree credit.

eventuate, *v.* Chiefly journalese for the plainer *happen, turn out,* or *have as a consequence.*

ever, *adv.* Do not put for *every* as in "She comes here *ever* (*every*) now and then." Compounds made with *ever* and *how, what,* or *where* (usually but not always written solid) when used as interrogative adverbs (expressing wonderment or perplexity) are *colloq.* "However (*stand. lit. how*) did you find out?" "Whatever made him do that?" "Wherever have you been?"

every, *adj. Stand. lit.* in *every now and then* but *colloq.* in *every once in a while, every so often,* and *every which way.* Sometimes *ever* is wrongly put for *every* in these phrases and in others like *ever* (*every*) *bit as good. Everywheres* is *dial.* and *colloq.* for *everywhere.*

every which way, *Colloq.,* unsystematically, in all directions at once.

everyone . . . they. In such sentences as "Because *everyone* wanted to enter at once, *they* had to form a line," the *pl. they* is not *stand. lit.* In *colloq.* usage *everyone, everybody,* may take a *pl.* reference word (especially when several words intervene) if the idea of individual units rather than solid unity is uppermost in the speaker's mind. "*Everybody* seemed to feel better and to recover *their* (*stand. lit. his*) energy after dinner."

every place. *Colloq.* for *everywhere.*

evidentiary, *adj. Legal tech.,* belonging to or having to do with evidence.

evidently, *adv.* Plainly, clearly.

evocative, *adj.* Calling forth; *pedagogical cant,* stirring emotion rather than reasoning.

evolute, *v.* A useless coinage. The more complex forms of life have *evolved,* not *evoluted,* from the simpler. As a *n.,* a geometrical term.

ex- *prefix.* Former; *slang n.,* former wife or husband.

Exact Word. Does the word you have used fit the thought exactly? Do not be content with approximations. Do not say *evade* when *elude* is the word that expresses the idea better. Yet do not think that long words are superior to short ones, for if you do, you may be guilty of writing a *malapropism* or be accused of *fine writing.*

Exaggeration. Do not lay it on with a trowel. Restraint or even understatement is often more effective than overstatement. The Greek name for the figure of speech is *hyperbole;* e.g., "The world's smoothest ride."

excelsior, *n.* Curly shavings or shreds of wood. The *Br.* term is wood-wool. [*L.,* loftier]

except, accept, *v. Except* means to exclude, omit; *accept,* to receive. As a *conj.* meaning *unless, except* is archaic, but *except that* may be used to mean *save for the fact that.* "I would like to go myself *except that* I must stay here with mother." "All passed *except she*" is questionable. Most writers prefer "All passed *except her,*" taking *except* as a *prep.* See **but** and **accept.**

exceptionable, *adj.* Objectionable; liable to objection.

exceptional, *adj.* Extraordinary; not according to rule.

Excessive Predication. The fault of not integrating short sentences that are not economical as they stand.

exchange, *n.* Telephone central office.

excision, *n.* Cutting out.

Exclamation Point. Its uses are the following:

1. To close an exclamatory sentence, as in "What a beating we got!" Sometimes a long, mildly exclamatory sentence may be closed with a period.

2. Sometimes to make a simple declarative sentence exclamatory. "He had just sat down to supper!" Use sparingly.

3. An interjectory word that is an independent sentence element is followed by an exclamation point. "Oh! I forgot to give you the letter." Otherwise

the exclamation point is not used: "O for a spin in the car."

When belonging to a quoted sentence or within parentheses, the exclamation point is placed inside the closing quotation mark or parenthesis.

exclusive, adj. Excluding, shutting out; colloq., high-class, excellent.

excoriate, v. Flay; scold, condemn publicly and harshly.

excuse, v. Forgive, overlook. The formal request for permission to leave a room or the presence of a superior is "Excuse me!" But in this sense, both "Pardon me!" and "Beg pardon!" are Am. stand. lit.

exegesis, n. Critical explanation of Scripture; exposition. [Gr., interpretation] **Epexegesis** is explanation of explanation, supplementary interpretation.

exemplar, n. Representative; one who exemplifies.

exemplum, n. Example; brief narrative used to illustrate a moral truth, especially such a story used by a preacher in a sermon.

exert, v. Exercise; put to use. The less common verb exsert means protrude, push out.

exhilarate, v. Enliven, cheer up. Do not confuse e. with accelerate.

existence, n. State of being; vital reality.

existentialism, n. A philosophical and literary movement which postulates a universe indifferent to man and emphasizes the importance for man of self discovery and personal decision.

exorbitant, adj. Excessive, beyond legal limits, out of line. [L., off the track]

expansionist, n. Advocate of aggressive extension of national influence; advocate of inflation of currency.

expect, suspect, v. Expect means to regard as likely to come or happen, regard as due. It is colloq. in the sense of be inclined to think, suppose, and when it is used for conjecture with reference to the present or past, as in "I expect he was pretty tired by that time." In formal use it applies only to the future and is never substituted for suspect. Suspect means to distrust, be suspicious of, imagine someone to be guilty or something to be true or false or likely. "I suspect collusion; they suspect Alexis."

expedite, v.t. Remove obstacles to prompt action concerning, hasten. Cant term of people in government jobs.

expediter, n. Specialist in putting plans into effect without delay; one who facilitates action or sees to it that things are done quickly.

experience, n. Living; enduring a series of events or sensations; accumulated effect of living through an extensive series of direct, personal impressions.

Expletive (ĕks'plē tĭv). Word or phrase not necessary to the thought of the sentence but thrown in for emphasis or to express feeling. Often the expletive is a more or less disguised oath. O my! Good gracious! O dear! Gee! Golly! Jimminy Crickets!

It and there, when anticipatory subjects, are grammatical expletives. The expletive it is followed by a sing. v. "It is the rumblings of the old volcano that they hear." There is followed by sing. or pl., depending on the number of the deferred subject. "There is a boy here." "There are a great many boys here."

explore, v. Search, search thoroughly, make a journey through for purposes of scientific investigation. "Explore every avenue" is as trite as "in touch with the situation" or "not in the picture."

Exposition. Explanatory writing. The adj. is expository or expositive. See **Forms of Discourse.**

express, adj. Special, direct, quick; clear, precise; transporting directly.

express, n. Messenger sent on a specific errand; company organized for speedy delivery of goods and messages.

extemporaneous, adj. Not unprepared but not memorized.

extempore, adv. Offhand, without memorization.

extend, v. Reach out; offer, present, tender.

extension course, n. Series of lessons offered for adults by a college or university without degree credit.

extent, n. Duration, size.

extra, *adj.* Can be used as an *adv.* meaning beyond the usual in size, extent, or degree. "These actors are *extra* good." Some writers prefer *unusually* in this construction.

extragalactic, *adj.* Existing outside the galaxies. This *tech.* term of astronomy is typical of modern coinages made by combining classical roots and affixes.

extrapolate, *v.* Continue (a line) in both directions.

extrasensory, *adj.* Outside the senses, telepathic.

extravert. See *extrovert.*

extrovert, *n.* Personality or person interested in tangible objects, physical relationships, and other personalities.

extrude, *v.* Push out; cause to protrude.

exuberant, *adj.* Abundant, lavish, effusive [*L.,* being fruitful].

F

F., *abbr.* Fahrenheit, on the Fahrenheit thermometric scale.

fable, *n.* See **allegory.**

fabliau, *pl.* **fabliaux,** *n.* Merry tale, salty anecdote; smutty story; e.g., Chaucer's *Miller's Tale.*

fact, *n.* Thing done or existing. It is established in the phrases *in fact, as a matter of fact, the fact is, the fact of the matter is.* These are preferable to *as a fact,* as in "The prosecuting attorney has been warned about this more than once; *as a fact* (better *as a matter of fact*) he knows very well that he is being very obstinate." *Fact* is an overworked word.

Fact or Opinion? Have you, as you should, let your reader know whether you are giving facts or personal opinion? It is a good rule to give the facts first and the comments and interpretations afterward, making the transition from the one to the other clear and sharp. Likewise mark the limits of indirect quotation, and keep separate from your own material.

factitious, *adj.* Sham. Not equivalent to *fictitious,* contrived, fabulous.

factor, *n.* Agent; element tending to bring about a certain result; quantity or symbol which, multiplied together with other quantities or symbols, will produce a certain product. "The factors of 10 are 5 and 2." "In juvenile delinquency environment is a stronger factor than heredity."

factual, *adj.* Involving or presenting details of doing.

faculty, *n.* One of the senses; one of the departments of knowledge represented in a university; professors and doctors concerned with such a department; entire teaching staff of a college or university.

fail, *v. Colloq.* as used in "The instructor *failed* James because he *failed* the exam" but *stand. lit.* in "James *failed* to pass because he *failed* in a course."

faint, *v.* Become unconscious; swoon.

fair, *adv. Dialect,* utterly. "I declare I'm *fair* tuckered out."

fairly, *adv.* Positively; moderately.

fairy, *n. Slang,* sissy, effeminate youth, female impersonator. *Fag* has the same meanings.

fake, *n. Colloq.* for *fraud* or *fraudulent person.* As a *v.,* meaning to imitate for the purpose of deceiving, "doctor up," etc., it is *colloq.* The *colloq. n. faker,* street peddler, should not be confused with the *stand. lit. fakir,* a religious mendicant.

fall, *v.* Principal parts, *fall, fell, fallen. Colloq.* in *fall down* (*fail*), as in "He *falls down* in math." Slang in *fall for,* succumb to. "Don't *fall for* that line." **Falls,** *n.* takes a *pl. v.* "The falls *are* nearly dry."

Fall, *n.* Autumn. *Fall* is more frequently used in U.S.

fall for, *v. Colloq.,* be charmed by, be beguiled by; believe.

Fallacy. A fault or flaw in a chain of reasoning. Illogical proof. It may follow from poorly defined terms, from an error in matters of fact, or from a false step in the process of reasoning. Some common fallacies:

1. Hasty generalization, reasoning to a general rule from too few specific cases.
2. False analogy. To argue that because tomato juice is good for you it is good for your dog, would be to base your reasoning on a *false analogy.*

3. Faulty causal reasoning: It is bad luck to break a mirror.
4. Begging the question, taking for granted a contention upon which the argument depends, and then using the inference as evidence.
5. Ignoring the question. Abusing one's opponent, appealing to popular prejudice, substituting another proposition, etc., instead of reasoning on the question.

fallout, *n.* Radioactive dust dispersed in the air by explosion of an atomic or hydrogen bomb.

False Lead. Do not bring up a topic as if you were going on with it when you cannot without making a new paragraph within the one you are writing. Do not feign an attack upon one subject when another is your real object.

False or Weak Reasoning. If your conclusions are not warranted by the evidence, or if you do not produce every part of the evidence bearing upon the argument, your reasoning is false or weak. See **garble** and **Fallacy.**

False Proportion. In description *false proportion* is often the consequence of disregarding perspective or physical point of view. In any kind of writing, it means that you have given too much attention to unimportant ideas and too little to the important ones.

False Series. Misleading parallelism; lack of parallelism. See **Parallelism.**

family, *pl.* **families** *n.* Associated group of people physically related; related group; husband, wife, and children.

famous, *adj.* Renowned; favorably known. Cf. **notorious.**

fan, *n.* An enthusiast, generally of some sport or form of entertainment. Stump of *fanatic* or *the fancy* (Regency term for *sportsmen*). A useful word, but now recorded as slang.

fantail, *n.* Tail shaped like a fan; arch with struts that radiate like feathers of a peacock's tail; semicircular deck at stern of a Naval vessel.

fare, *n.* Sum paid for transportation.

farm-hand, *n.* Agricultural laborer; hired man.

fascinate, *v.* Charm; enchant.

fascinator, *n.* Crocheted hat.

fascist, *n.* Advocate of totalitarian government other than Communism; advocate of strong central power in a benevolent oligarchy; *sl.,* rascal, selfish person.

fatal, fateful, *adj. Fatal* means fixed by fate, mortal, causing death; *fateful,* full of fate, either good or bad. "The accident was *fatal;* the day was *fateful.*"

fatuous, *adj.* Complacently stupid, silly; unreal.

fault, *n. At fault* means wrong, puzzled; *in fault,* which is *colloq.,* means culpable, to blame.

Faulty Implication. See **Implication, Unintentional.**

favor, *n. Trade or tech.* (business) for *letter;* **favor,** *v.* Be kind or partial to. The *v.* **favor** in the sense of *resemble in features* is now *stand. lit.* "She *favors* her mother."

faze, *v.* Variant of *feeze. Colloq.* for *disturb, worry, disconcert.* "It takes more than that to *faze* me."

F.B.I., *abbr.* Federal Bureau of Investigation.

feasible, possible, *adj. Feasible* means readily carried out, capable of being done or dealt with; *possible,* much the broader term, means that which may exist or occur if given the proper conditions. "Your campaign plan is *feasible,* your election *possible.*"

feature, *v. Colloq.* in the sense of give special prominence to, make a feature of. "The paper will *feature* sports this week." As a *n.* it is *stand. lit.* in the senses of marked peculiarity, anything conspicuous, any particularly attractive thing offered by theater, store, etc., and part of the face; full length motion picture.

fed-up, *adj.* Also *fed up.* Slang for tired of, surfeited, bored. "I am *fed up* with movies."

feed, *v.t.* Provide with food; provide as food (to).

feel like, *v. Colloq.* in the sense of have the inclination for, want to. "I *feel like* going home." "You must *feel like* resting." "I *feel like* doing something for those people."

feel of. *Feel* is a *n.* in the correct sentence, "It has the *feel* of sandpaper." The *of* in **feel of,** *v.,* is usually superfluous. "Let me *feel* (of) that cloth." But the *of* in "They began to *feel of* their pockets to find out whether the coin was there," is perhaps justified.

feint, *v.* Pretend a blow; feign an attack at one point or in one direction to divert defense from the object or objective of real attack.

fellow, *n. Colloq.,* man; person; male sweetheart; beau.

female, *n.* In reference to persons, prefer *girl* or *woman* unless you wish to give special emphasis to the idea of sex.

feminine, *adj.* Like a woman. In prosody, a *f.* ending is an unaccented syllable at the end of a verse, and a *f.* is a double rhyme, the second syllables being identical.

fender, *n.* Mudguard of an automobile. The *Br.* equivalent is *wing.*

fest, *n.* Party, fiesta, feast. Common in slang compounds such as *slugfest, gabfest.* [Ger.]

few, *adj.* Of small number. In the idioms *a very few* and *a few, f.* becomes a *n.*

fewer, less. *Fewer* is the correct word to use in referring to quantity measurable in numbers, *less,* in referring to quantity not measurable in numbers, to degree, and to value. "*Fewer* accidents and *less* expense."

fiancé, *n. masc.,* **fiancée,** *n. fem.* (fē änsä'). Betrothed person; future spouse.

fiend, *n. Colloq.* for a person addicted to some harmful practice, or one who works hard at, or is very clever in, some pursuit, such as a study. "He's a math *fiend.*"

fifth column, *n.* Secretly active traitors within lines of a nation at war; body of traitors behind a line of defense. In 1936 General Emilio Mola said that he commanded four columns attacking Madrid and a fifth within the city.

fifth wheel, *n.* Useless superfluity.

fifty-fifty, *adv.* and *adj.* Equally.

figurative, *adj.* Not literal, supplying a comparison based on one resemblance between two objects otherwise unlike.

figure, *v.* Estimate, calculate; *figure on,* expect, allow for; *figure up,* estimate arithmetically; *figure out,* work out, calculate, devise.

figure (fĭg'ūr), *n. Colloq.* in the sense of *price* or *amount.* "They are asking a high *figure.*" As a *v.i.* it is *colloq.* in the meanings of reckon in figures, calculate, plan, scheme, contrive, as in "He is *figuring* for a job on the paper." *Figure in,* to include in a computation or list, is also *colloq.* "Did you *figure* that *in*?" But *figure on,* take thought of in planning or reckoning, count on; *figure out,* solve, make out, understand; and *figure up,* to total figures, are *stand. lit.* "I couldn't *figure out* what she was doing there."

figurehead, *n.* Wooden image at the prow of a ship beneath the bowsprit; officer with executive title but little or no authority.

Figure of Speech. A simile, metaphor, etc. Avoid mixed metaphors (q.v.), and trite figures such as *almighty dollar, acid test, bathed in tears, busy as a bee, fly in the ointment.* See **Reading, The Art of.**

file, *v.t.* Put away for reference; loosely, present, offer, put into the record. "I want to *file* my protest right now."

filibuster, *v.* Smuggle munitions; delay legislative action by talking at great length. [Dutch, freebooter]

fill, *v.* Stuff, make full; *colloq.,* fulfil. *Fill out, v.* make entries in blank spaces of a printed form. The corresponding *Br.* locution is *fill up.*

filling station, *n.* Place where gasoline is sold.

finagle, *v.* Renege, revoke; accomplish by trickery; cheat. [*Ger.,* name of a tricky whist-player]

finale, *n.* Closing number of a concert or musical entertainment; last of a series of games.

finalize, *v.* End. This is bureaucratic jargon for finish. See **gobbledygook.**

find, *n.* Something found. It is *colloq.* in

the meaning of an excellent performer who is found by chance or is suddenly found to possess unsuspected ability.

fine, *adj.* Of high quality, delicate, nice, subtle, thin, bright. *"Fine distinction; fine tobacco; fine lines."* Much overworked as a counterword for anything excellent, smart or pleasant. The *adv.* is *finely. Fine* as an *adv.* is *dial.* and *colloq.* "This time our scheme worked just *fine."*

Fine Writing. Used ironically to designate a style that is windy, highflown, elaborate, and ornamental rather than clear, thoughtful, and controlled.

finish, *v.t. Colloq.* in the sense of *settle matters completely, overcome* or *exhaust utterly.* "That just about *finished* me."

fink, *n. Slang,* strike-breaker, scab; informer.

fire, *v. Colloq.* in the senses of *eject by force* (often with *out*) and *discharge from employment.* In the latter meaning it is being replaced by the slang *can, get the gate, get the air, give him the gate.*

fire-new, *adj.* Fresh from the forge, brand-new.

fire-water, *n.* Whiskey, rum; presumably a name given by the Indians.

firstly, *adv.* Most writers prefer *first.*

first-rate, *adj.* and *adv. Colloq.* in the sense of *extremely good* and *very well.* "She is *first-rate;* she did *first-rate."*

fissionable, *adj.* Susceptible of cleavage, especially of nuclear fission.

fit, *v.t.* Suit exactly, meet physical requirements; prepare (for college) in the New England prep. school manner. "He entered a fitting school when his twin sister entered a finishing school."

fiver, *n. Sl.,* five dollar bill.

fives, *n.* Old game of handball.

fivespot, *n. Slang,* five dollar bill.

fix, *v.* To make fast, settle, secure, arrange, adjust. *Colloq.* in the senses of bribe, tamper with, satisfy, repair, get even with, hurt. *Well-fixed,* provided with money, supplies, is *colloq.* **Fix,** *n.* is *colloq.* for *predicament.*

fixation, *n.* State of being fixed or established, concentration on an object; *psych. tech.,* centering upon an object of love.

fizzile, *adj. Neologism,* effervescent; unstable, likely to set off chain reactions.

fizzle, *v. Colloq.,* fail; disappoint like a firecracker with a broken fuse.

flabbergast, *v. Colloq.* for frighten, astonish, or disconcert.

flaccid (flăk'sĭd), *adj.* Flabby [L.].

flagrant, *adj.* Conspicuous, obvious. "Flagrant disregard" is a trite combination.

flair, *n.* By origin a French word meaning literally *dog's sense of smell,* and figuratively, *perspicacity.* Hence *liking, bent, taste combined with talent.* Overworked and often misused, as in "In the career period it became the *flair* (better *fashion*) for young women to specialize in business." Note *sp.*

flak, *n.* Antiaircraft fire.

flash, *n.* Short newspaper item received by telegraph; similar news item announced by a gossipy radio commentator.

flashback, *n.* Explanatory presentation of facts that occurred before the formal beginning of action in a motion picture, story, or play.

flatfoot, *n. Colloq.,* policeman.

flat-footed, *adj.* Blunt, absolute. "He came out flat-footed for Stassen."

flaunt, flout, *v.* To *flaunt* means to display ostentatiously; to *flout,* to mock, treat with contempt.

flay, *v.* Chiefly journalese in the sense of censure, rebuke harshly. "Smith *flays* Mayor."

fleep, *n.* Jeep with wings; flying jeep.

fleet, *n.* Large orderly series or associated group of ships, trucks, or airplanes. All the ships of the Navy available in one Ocean.

float, *n.* Heavy car or wagon, pageant wagon.

Floating Subject. In *low colloq.* English the subject is sometimes repeated unnecessarily, e.g., "Ned and Nat, *they* make me mad." "Natalie, *she's* a good girl."

flop, *v.i. Colloq.* for move like a fish out of water, throw oneself heavily or flabbily, change sides suddenly, fail completely. The *n.* in the sense of *sleep* or *utter failure* is slang. "Take a *flop;* the show's a *flop."*

flopperoo, *n. Slang,* complete failure;

utterly bad performance, play, or concert.

fluff, *v. Radio tech.,* confuse, read badly; *n.,* error in speech.

flunk, *v.* Often with *out;* in the sense of *fail in a course* it is *colloq.* **Flunker,** *n.,* is also *colloq.,* but **flunk,** *n.,* is slang.

fogy, *n.* Conservative; old-fashioned person ready to fight for his convictions. *Old fogy* or *old fogey* has the same meanings. A young woman may be an *o.f.*

folkways, *n. pl.* Customs of the common people of a region.

folks, *n.* The *pl. folk,* as in *townsfolk,* is somewhat archaic; e.g., *country folk* for *country people. Folk* is often found in compounds: folklore, folk music, folk dance. *Folks* meaning *family and kin* is *colloq.,* as are *folksy,* sociable, and *folksiness.*

follow. In introducing a list of items write *as follows.* The *v.* is *sing.* "The order is *as follows:* first . . ." **Follow-up,** *adj.,* is *stand. lit.* in "This was a *follow-up* visit," but *colloq.* and *trade or tech.* (business) in "These *follow-up* letters were the first part of a *follow-up* program of advertising."

font, *n.* Baptismal bowl; style of type, full set of type of one style.

fool, *v.* To trifle, deceive, trick. *Colloq.* for *meddle* (usually with *with*) or *waste time,* and as an *adj.* stump of *foolish.* "To *fool* with that was a *fool* mistake."

footling, *adj.* Feet first, awkward.

Footnote. A note at the foot of a page and explaining a word or passage in the text, or referring to an article or book that has been consulted or quoted from or is to be consulted. A typical footnote:*

* Arthur G. Kennedy, *Current English,* 1935, p. 43.

forbear, *v.* Refrain. Also variant spelling of *n. forebear.*

forceful, forcible, *adj. Forceful* means effective; *forcible,* got by compulsion. "He made a *forceful* speech." "The thief made a *forcible* entry."

Forceful versus Languid Sentences. Ideas in languid sentences are presented in a weak, straggling, or complicated way. Avoid excessive co-ordination, the stringy and the choppy sentence, the tandem construction, faulty repetition, and the weak passive.

Fordizatzia, *n.* Mass production and prosperity based on turnover. [Russian, Ford-like behavior]

forebear, *n.* Forefather, ancestor, commonly used in *pl. forebears.*

forecast, *v.* The *p.* and *p. part. forecast* is regularly used but *forecasted* is not incorrect. "Mr. Kimball *forecast* this rainy weather."

Foreign Words. Whether one knows a foreign language or not, it is a temptation to garnish plain English with an exotic word or two. We pay this tribute to the prestige of foreign languages, especially French. There is no absolute rule concerning the use of foreign words. What one is writing, the public addressed, and sense of style determine whether such expressions can be used advantageously, and how many of them can be used without offending good taste. Sometimes it is more natural to employ the foreign term than the native one; sometimes it is necessary since there is no native word for the idea you wish to express. Consequently, do not trouble yourself to find native substitutes for *entrepreneur, laissez-faire, debris, esprit de corps, chaperon, sabotage.* Indeed, some of these cannot be called foreign as they have become Anglicized. Italicize foreign terms not yet Anglicized.

Make sure that the form of your foreign word is grammatically correct for the position in which you put it. The authors of the following sentences have exposed their ignorance by not using their foreign embellishments correctly. "This man must be *personae gratia (persona grata?)* with the staff." "Have him write us and give a complete *curriculus vita (curriculum vitae?).*" But this never would be used. "Our hero is another Titan *in petto (di piccola statura?).*"

forename, *n.* Name, other than the final surname; given name. All the italicized words in the following example are forenames: *Emeline Eloisa Johnson Forbes Dorislaus.*

foreword, *n.* Introductory note by a person other than the author. Cf. *preface, introduction.*

for keeps, *adv. phrase. Slang,* permanently, for permanent possession.

Formal or Literary English. *Abbr. stand. lit.* The English of the formal speech or the serious book. See **English, Levels of.**

former, *adj.* "The *former* secretary of the club is here." Used as a *pron.* meaning the *first of two.* See **latter.**

formerly, *adv.* In the past.

Forms of Discourse. When the various kinds of written composition are classified according to purpose, form, and characteristic subject matter, one finds that there are four main types: (1) *description,* the portrayal of the sound and look and feel of things, (2) *exposition,* logical or systematic explanation, (3) *argument,* the presentation of one side of a controversial subject, and (4) *narration,* the account of a sequence of related events.

In any composition there is likely to be more than one of these types, but each composition, when viewed as a whole with the form and dominant purpose taken into account, will fall more or less neatly into the classification just given. For instance, *description* turns up in *exposition* as illustration and example, and in *narration* to paint action, character, and background. Expository passages are often controversial in nature. Yet viewed as a whole, the composition is an *exposition* or a *narration.*

formula, *pl.* **formulas** or **formulae,** *n.* Recipe; prescribed form, form of combination. The *pl. formulae,* taken directly from the Latin, is somewhat stilted.

forsake, *v.* See *abandon.*

forsythia (fŏr sĭth'ē á, fŏr sĭth'ĭ á), *n.* Ornamental shrub of the olive family, bearing golden yellow bell-shaped blooms in early spring. It is the official floral symbol of Brooklyn.

fort, forte, *n.* Both are pronounced (fōrt). *Fort* means fortification; *forte,* the thing in which one excels. "Spelling is her *forte.*"

forth, *adv.* Outward, onward.

fortnight, *n.* Two weeks, fourteen days.

for to, to. *To* after verbs like *say* and *like,* and before an infinitive, when purpose is not implied, and *for to,* meaning in order to, are *low colloq.* or vulgar. "Father said *to* stay." "Mr. Snow would *like for* you *to* see the colt." "She went *for to* see if the chickens were hatched."

fortuitous, fortunate, *adj. Fortuitous* means accidental, occurring by chance. *Fortunate* means lucky, occurring by good chance. "Our meeting was entirely *fortuitous.*" "You are always *fortunate* in your friends."

four-flusher, *n.* Empty boaster, dishonest bluff.

fox-hole, *n.* Shallow trench to shelter one or two men.

Fragmentary Sentence. A dependent clause or other construction that cannot stand alone as a sentence, even in a context. See **Clipped Sentence.**

frame, *v.* Often with *up.* It is slang when it means to manufacture false evidence or arrange circumstances so that a person will appear to be guilty of a criminal action. **Frame-up,** *n.,* is also slang.

frankfurter, *n.* Small sausage, reddish and highly seasoned. [*G.,* Frankfort)

frantic, *adj.* Frenzied; mentally deranged.

frantically, *adv.* Like mad.

free-and-easy, *adj.* Informal.

free verse, *n. Vers libre;* poetry that is rhythmical but not regularly metrical.

freight, *n.* Goods transported by land, water, or air. A *freightcar* is the *Am.* equivalent of *Br.* goods van. In *Br., freight* is principally heavy goods transported by water.

freighter, *n.* Cargo ship; vessel devoted chiefly to carrying freight.

frequency, *n.* Brevity of interval between recurrences; *radio tech.,* number of sound waves that can be transmitted in a standard length of time, usually one second.

fresh, *adj. Sl.,* intoxicated, presumptuous, impudent, too familiar, impertinent.

friend, *n.* Intimate; trusted associate, affectionate and esteemed.

Friend, *n.* Member of the religious Society of Friends; Quaker.

frightened, *adj.* Thrown into a state of alarm. *Colloq.* for *afraid. Stand. lit.:* "He ran like a *frightened deer." Colloq.:* "Are you *frightened at* (stand. lit. afraid of or frightened by) bulls?" See **scare.**

frill, *n.* Fluted edging of cloth or paper; affectation or unnecessary adornment, usually in *pl.;* showy addition to a school program or curriculum.

frit, *n.* Fused basic material for glass or enamel.

from whence, *adv. phrase.* Strictly, *from* with *whence* is redundant, for *whence* means *from where.* Yet *from whence* is sometimes used when *whence* is an interrogative or relative *pron.,* e.g., "*From whence* (what place) is he?" *Whence* and *thence* are old-fashioned.

front, *n. Colloq.* in the sense of external show or pretentious appearance of wealth, prosperity, social eminence, or success. A recent development is the figurative use of *front* in the sense of *vanguard;* e.g., peace front, united front, popular front.

front, *n. Colloq.,* nominal head or public representative of an organization; figurehead; false pretense, assumption of prestige.

frustrate, *v.* Balk, baffle.

frustration, *n.* Condition of being balked; failure to achieve objects of desire.

fry, *v. Slang,* die by electrocution.

fuchsia (fū'sha), *n.* Evening primrose of a pinkish red; *adj.* having the color of a fuchsia.

fuddy-duddy, *n. Slang,* old-fashioned person concerned about tradition and conventionality.

fudge, *n.* Sugar candy of several types; nonsense.

fuller. "His glass is *fuller* than mine" is illogical if *full* means *absolutely full,* as, strictly, it does. However, the logic of speech is not so rigid or nice as to object to this sentence, or to *more complete, more perfect, rounder, straighter,* and other adjectives insusceptible of comparison when considered in strict logic.

function, *v.i.* To operate, perform official or professional duties. Pompous in trivial contexts, e.g., "My alarm clock has stopped *functioning* (running)."

functional, *adj.* Designed for use; practical; concerned with operation rather than origin, history, or structure. "Functional grammar" was a pedagogical cant phrase of a decade ago.

functionalist, *n.* Architect or other artist whose avowed aim is to adapt form to use, regardless of tradition or convention.

function word, *n. Grammatical tech.,* word having little or no meaning apart from the grammatical idea it expresses. C. C. Fries in his *American English Grammar* [1940], p. 109, explains that "prepositions, conjunctions, participles are the names used by conservative grammarians" for the classes of words which he calls *function words.*

fundamental, *adj.* Basic, at the foundation.

fundamentalist, *n.* Believer in "the letter of the Bible"; one who holds that belief in Scriptural miracles is fundamental to Christianity. Often capitalized.

funeral, *n.* Burial, ceremonies at graveside; ritual preceding interment; memorial services; obsequies.

funnies, *n. pl.* Comic picture stories published serially; dramatic series of drawings thus published, no matter how completely they lack comic quality.

funny. Counterword meaning comic, comical, ludicrous, ridiculous, droll, amusing, humorous, witty, merry, facetious, waggish, sportive. *Colloq.* in the sense of strange, queer, and odd. *Low colloq.* for strangely, *adv.* "He's been acting *funny* for weeks."

furnishings, *n.* Household equipment, including furniture.

further, farther, *adv.* In actual usage interchanged freely. *Further* is the more common and is preferred when the meaning is *in addition, besides, to a greater extent.* "*On further* investigation we found that this was true." *Farther* is preferred for reference to distance.

All the *further* (*farther*), as in "This is all the *further* I can go," is *low colloq.* or *dial.*

fusion, *n.* Political coalition including members of various parties or groups.

fuss, *n.* A stir, a pother, a to-do; a person who makes an unnecessary ado. As a *v.i.,* meaning to be unduly agitated about trifles, it is *stand. lit.,* but as a *v.t.,* meaning to bother, annoy with trifles, it is *colloq.*

futile (fū′tĭl), *adj.* Vain, useless. The *pron.* fū′tīl is dialect.

G

G., *Slang,* $1,000.

gab, *v. Colloq.,* chatter idly or without letup in flow or speed. The *n.* is scarcely used except in the phrase *gift of gab* (*colloq.*).

gadget, *n.* Slang counterword for any contrivance or device. A "jigger," "dingus," "doodad," "rigamajig," "thingabob," "gismo," or contraption (*colloq.*). [Possibly from Fr. *gachette,* machine]

gaffe (găf), *n.* Blunder. [*Fr.*]

gag, *n.* Joke, jest. [Presumably from gag, choker]

gait, *n.* Manner of walking, rate of speed.

gal, *n.* Phonetic spelling of *girl* as vulgarly pronounced.

Galaxy, *n.* The Milky Way; with lower case initial, island universe; group of theatrical stars or other famous people.

gall, *n.* Pancreas; indignation; insolence, impudence.

Gallicism. A French expression translated word for word rather than made to conform to English idiom: e.g., *a deaf noise* (a muffled noise), *but that makes nothing* (but that makes no difference), *to do one's possible* (to do one's best), *to jump* (or *leap*) *to the eyes* (to be strikingly obvious). "How the town has degenerated *jumps to the eyes* (better is *strikingly obvious*) as we walk down Main Street." The use of Gallicisms is ill-advised unless there is a special purpose.

gallon, *n.* A gallon is 46 cubic inches bigger in Canada or Great Britain than in the United States.

galore. *Colloq.* as an *adv.* meaning in abundance, and as a *n.* meaning an abundance. "Wine and food *galore.*" [*Irish,* plenty, enough]

gamble, *v.i.* Play for wagers; *v.t.,* stake.

gambol, *v.* Cavort; bound about in playful dance.

game, *n.* Slang when applied figuratively to a business or vocation, as the *real-estate game,* the *advertising game.* The *adj.* **game** in the sense of *lame,* as in "Look out! that's my *game* leg," is *colloq.*

garbage, *n.* Kitchen waste; orts.

garble, *v.* To misrepresent facts, evidence, a report, speech, etc., by selecting what will support the impression the writer or speaker wishes to give, and omitting all else. Although *garbling* stops short of falsifying and misquoting, the intention is the same, to favor one side or party.

gas, *n. Colloq.* as stump of *gasoline. Step on the gas* is slang for *hurry up.* **Gas,** *v.,* in the sense of *talk in a vapid or deceitful or boasting fashion, regale with empty talk,* is slang.

gat, *n. Sl.,* gun, revolver. [Stump of *Gatling gun*]

gate-crasher, *n. Sl.,* person who attends a show or a party without ticket or invitation.

gauche, *adj.* Clumsy, graceless, tactless. [*Fr.*]

gaucho (gou′chō), *n.* Argentine cowpuncher.

gauntlet, *n.* Glove. To *run the gauntlet* is a trite *fig.* allusion to an old style of military punishment. See the article, "Gauntlet" in the *Encyclopaedia Britannica.*

geisha (gā′shà), *pl.* **geisha** or **geishas,** *n.* Professional dancer, singer, entertainer; geisha girl. [Japanese]

Gender. The genders are masculine, feminine, and neuter. A *pron.* agrees with its antecedent in gender. "The played a trick on *Mary* by pretending that *she* was invited to the party." Yet gender cannot be shown by some pronouns; e.g., *this, some, one,* and the generic *he, him, his,* can stand for either man or woman. "Make the swimmer, whether boy or girl, try the crawl as soon as *he* has mastered the deadman's float." See **Agreement.**

gene, *n.* Factor of the chromosome influencing hereditary traits.

General. If your statements are too general they need to be limited to a precise meaning or application. Be specific and concrete.

genetics, *n.* Science of origin of individuals through heredity; study of the likenesses and differences between organisms of similar descent.

genius, genus, genie, *n.* The most common meaning of *genius* (*pl. geniuses*) is *a person possessing extraordinary ability* and *extraordinary power of conception and execution in art or science.* *Genus* (*pl. genera,* and rarely *genuses*) in biology means the group between family and species. A *genie* (*pl. genii* or *genies*) is an Oriental demon.

genocide, *n.* Deliberate destruction of racial or culture groups by homicide or sterilization or destruction of cultural vortexes.

genre (zhȧnr), *n.* Kind; type of literary work. [*Fr.,* kind]

Genteelism. The same as *euphemism.* The substitution of a dignified or elevated term for one that is plain, common, or too frank. The motives of such a substitution are false delicacy or refinement, an erroneous idea of what constitutes a good style, or the desire to avoid what might be considered an unpleasantly strong term. Anyone is permitted to avoid a word with a low connotation when this does not harmonize with the context, but the user of genteelisms habitually chooses the elevated (and often periphrastic) expression regardless of circumstances. He will say *mortician* for *undertaker, the late unpleasantness* for the *War between the States, indisposed* for *sick,* and *artificial dentures* for *false teeth.*

genuine (jĕn'ū ĭn), *adj.* Real, authentic; not counterfeit. The pronunciation jĕn'ū-ĭn is dialect or whimsical *Am.*

geochemist, *n.* Scientist whose field is the chemistry of the crust of the earth.

Geographic Names. The spelling of geographic proper names should conform to the decisions of the United States Board on Geographic Names.

geopolitics, *n.* Science of the bearing of geography on politics.

Gerund. A verbal *n.* ending in *-ing.* If there is danger of ambiguity, the agent in the gerund phrase should be the same as the agent in the sentence proper. Compare "On *returning,* the mother's condition had improved," which is faulty, with the correct "On *returning,* I found that the mother's condition had improved." The *pron.* or the *n.* (if it has a possessive case) is put in the possessive case before a gerund. "Excuse *my* stuttering."

The good writer displays his knowledge of idiom by recognizing when a gerund with a *prep.* is required rather than an infinitive. He will write *able to see* but *equal to* performing. Employ the infinitive after *agree, ask, care, desire, expect, hope,* and the gerund after *avoid, endure, help* (keep from), *postpone, stop, tolerate.* Both constructions are correct after *begin, continue, omit,* and *prefer.*

gesso (jĕs'sō), *n.* Plaster of Paris used as a basis for painting.

gesture, *n.* Expressive motion of the body and limbs. The word has developed the meaning of *something done or said for effect without expectation of its being taken seriously.* "Their signing the treaty was only a *gesture.*" Do not use as a mere counterword for any sort of action, movement, offer, threat, or deed.

gesundheit, *n.* Health! Good health to you! An expression used commonly to ward off the devil after a sneeze.

get, *v.* Principal parts, *get, got, got,* and *gotten,* which is chiefly *Am. colloq. Colloq.* the *got* in "I have *got* a cold" is not regarded as superfluous, for in such sentences the *have* is taken as the auxiliary *have,* as in "I *have* caught a cold." "*Have* you a cold?" is not as natural as "I *have* a cold," or as natural or strong as "Have you got a *cold?*" Moreover, the word order of "*Have* you *got* a cold?" corresponds to that of the ordinary question: "*Did* you *get* a cold?" *Have* (or *has*) got is especially frequent when the idea of *recent acquisition* is to be stressed: "He *has got* himself a radio at last." The use before the infinitive to express *necessity* is good *colloq.* "They have got to (*stand. lit.* must) stop that."

The *Am. colloq. gotten* for *become* or *acquire,* as in "In the meantime she'd *gotten* much worse," or "They've *gotten* in a whole lot of supplies," is less frequently seen. Elsewhere *gotten* occurs only in combination, e.g., *ill-gotten gains.*

Get (along with *grow, fall, turn, become,* etc.) is often used to call attention to the initial or the final (result) stage of an action or state; e.g., "He often *gets* tired," "He's *getting* rich." "They *got* the kidnaper," and the *colloq.* "She didn't want to go by the time we *got* started." In the present tense, *getting* is often substituted for *becoming.* "I am *getting* (*becoming*) bald." Although *get* and *become* overlap somewhat, the context usually indicates which to use. "He is *getting* (not *becoming*) excused." "To *get* (not *become*) gossiping together."

As a passive auxiliary *get* is used *colloq.* as a more expressive actional form than *be.* "He *gets* (*stand. lit.* is) scolded every time he brings a dog home." "She *gets* (*stand. lit.* is) invited so often that she *gets* (*is*) fed up with it." "For once you *got* (*were*) caught."

Get, meaning find a way to, be able to, as in "I didn't *get* to meet her," is provincial. *Get* is used in many *colloq.* expressions: *get* six months (receive a sentence of six months); *get ahead of; get around; get away with* (in the sense of *carry off, get the better of*). But *get away with* in the sense of *do something without being penalized for it* is slang, as are: *get behind,* support, *get by, get next to,* bribe, get power over, *get the facts of, get over,* get across, *get off,* as in "She told him where to *get off,*" *get it? get me?* understand, and *get back at.*

Do not use *get* for *make,* as in "This business *gets* me disgusted," or for *lay hold of, fascinate,* as in "That song *gets* me."

Pronounce *got to* as written, not *gotta.*
getaway, *n.* and *adj. Sl.,* escape.
g.i., *abbr. Med. tech.,* gastro-intestinal.
G.I., *n.* Soldier in the Army of the United States. An **ex-G.I.** is an American veteran of World War II or Korea. [abbr. for "government issue," stamped on garments and utensils]

gig, *n. Obsolete,* spinning top; one-wheeled carriage drawn by one horse; spear for fish; painfully exaggerated posture of military attention.

gig, *v.* Spear, tease, haze; *Army slang,* require to stand stiffly at attention.

gigantic, *adj.* Huge; giant. [*L.*]

gimbals, *n. pl.* Pivoted rings used as a frame for a gyroscope or compass.

gimmick, *n. Slang,* trick; ingenious device; specialized tool.

git-fiddle, *n. Southern provincial,* guitar.

give, *v.* Principal parts, *give, gave, given. Give* for *gave* or *given* is vulgar. *Give out* is *stand. lit.* in the senses of *be unable to exert oneself longer, unable to operate or supply further, be exhausted. Give away* is *colloq.* for *tell a secret,* and *give it to* for *scold.*

giveaway, *n.* and *adj.* Type of radio or TV program in which prizes are awarded at random.

glad-hand, *v.* Express false cordiality by smile and handshake. *Gladhanding* is typical of Middle Western middlemen.

gladiolus, gladioli *or* **gladioluses** (glăd-ĭ′ō lŭs *or* glăd ē ō′lŭs), *n.* Flowering plant with sword-shaped leaves; iris. The *pl.* glăd ĭ′ō lī is as hard to say as gladioluses. Most fanciers call these interesting blooms "glads." [*L.,* Roman sword]

glamor, glamour, *n.* Magic; supernatural charm; glorifying effect of association with motion picture stars or other great folk [Scottish, ultimately from *Gr.,* letter] *Glamour* is a doublet of *grammar.*

glide, *v.* Move smoothly and quietly; fly without motor; volplane.

glider, *n.* Person or thing that glides; motorless airplane.

glimpse, glance, *n.* A *glimpse* is a fleeting sight or view of something; a *glance* is a hasty look at something. "It was only a hurried *glance,* but I caught a *glimpse* of Fred and the whole crowd at the table."

global, *adj.* Worldwide.

G-man, *n.* Federal agent; F.B.I. operative or agent.

go, *p.* went, *p. part.,* gone. *n. Stand. lit.* in "It's a go," i.e., a success, but *colloq.* in "She certainly has lots of *go,*" "She is always on the *go,*" "She is all the *go,*" "I'll have a *go* at painting," and "It's no *go.*" The *v.* is *colloq.* in "Do not *go back on* me," "I'll *go* you one better," "What he says *goes,*" "Do that again and I'll *go for* you with an ax," "That ought to *go over* big," "I can't *go* spats," "They *go in for* bridge," and "If we don't help France she's likely to *go* Communist." *To go places* is slang for *visit places of amusement* or *get ahead in the world. Go-getter* and (give someone the) *go-by* are also slang.

gob, *n. Slang,* sailor, rating in the U.S.N.; *colloq.,* lump.

go-back, *adj. Colloq.,* abandoned, uncultivated. "*Go-back* farm land has been permitted to go back to grass."

gobbledygook, *n.* Swollen lingo of bureaucrats. [Reputedly coined by the Hon. Maury Maverick in imitation of the cries of a turkey cock]

go-getter, *n.* Aggressive salesman; dogged fighter for selfish advantage. [A dog retrieving a stick is urged, "Go-get, boy, go-get it!"]

going on, *adj. Colloq.* and *dial.* in the sense of approaching in time. "She's five and *going on* (almost) six." "It was eleven o'clock and *going on* twelve."

goings on, *n. pl.* Activity; happenings.

gold-brick, *v.* Loaf by pretending to be busy. [This Army slang obviously originated from the swindle of selling .as a stolen ingot a brick coated with gold.]

gondola (gŏn'dō là), *n.* Boat used on canals of Venice; barge; (gŏn dō'là) roofless freightcar.

goo, *n. Sl.,* viscous liquid; sentimentality; *adj.* gooey.

goober, *n. Dial.,* peanut [African, *nguba,* perhaps].

good, better, best, *adj. Get the best of* is *Am. stand. lit.* comparable to *Br. get the better of.* As a predicate adj., use *good;* "I feel good," "She looks good." The adverb is *well:* "He did well." But *well* is also an *adj.* meaning *healthy:* "I feel well." See also *make good.*

good and, *adv. Colloq.,* very as in *good and sweet, good and cold; good and plenty* means thoroughly.

goods, *n.* Property, wares, chattels; *Br.,* freight; *slang, truth,* evidence, incriminating information.

goof off, *v. Sl.,* go to sleep; be foolish.

G.O.P., *n.* Republican Party [Grand Old Party].

gossip, *n.* Pointless or malicious talk about neighbors and associates; person who does such talking, gossip monger.

got, *past participle of* **get** (*q.v.*). Purists condemn the idiomatic, "I have got to go." Obviously it involves a redundancy. The fact remains that it is in common use among fairly careful speakers.

gotten, *p. part.* Got.

gouge, *v.* Tear out; extract money by unfair or violent means.

grade, *n.* Level, class, classification; slope, gradient.

grade, *v.* Classify, assort, sort.

gradient, *n.* Slope; ramp.

graduate, *v.t.* Admit to degree or rank. *v.i. Colloq.,* attain such rank, finish a course of study. One may graduate a cup by marking a scale upon it, but one graduates *from,* or is graduated *from,* a school. In the passive *graduated* is commonly followed by *from,* rarely by *by* or *at.*

graduate, *n.* Person who has completed a course of study; alumnus.

graft, *n.* Scion; transplanted bud or shoot of a plant.

graft, *n.* The getting of money or power by dishonest or questionable means; the money so obtained. The *v.* is *colloq.* Also *grafter.*

Grammar. The science treating of the use and application of language rules. Common mistakes in grammar are: (1) faulty agreement, (2) wrong case of *pron.,* (3) wrong tense, (4) *adj.* for *adv.,* (5) wrong form of the *v.*

gramophone, *n.* British phonograph.

grand, *adj.* Magnificent, imposing, noble. Used as a counterword to express approval. *Colloq.* in *had a grand time,* *look grand, in grand condition.* Slang for *one thousand dollars.*

grandstand, *n.* Principal seating space for spectators at outdoor games or shows. *Playing to the grandstand* is individual display of skill or prowess at the expense of teamwork.

grange, *n.* Agricultural society.

grapevine, *n.* Grapevine telegraph; scuttlebutt; secret means of informal communication; also the substance of such communication, rumor, gossip.

graphology, *n. Colloq.,* false science of interpreting character from handwriting.

graveyard, *n.* Churchyard; cemetery; marble orchard.

greaser, *n.* One who greases wagons; *sl.* Mexican, Latin-American. This vulgar term is as opprobrious as *gringo.*

great deal. See **deal.**

gridcaster, *n.* Broadcaster of play-by-play accounts of football games.

gridiron, *n.* Football field, the lines of which resemble the grated iron used for broiling food.

grifter, *n. Sl.,* con man; petty grafter; gambling concessionaire at a carnival.

grill, *v.* Broil on a gridiron; test or question cruelly, torture.

gringo, *n.* North American or Briton as contemptuously viewed by Latin Americans. [*Sp.,* gibberish]

groom, *n.* Bridegroom; less commonly, hostler, stableboy.

groove, *n.* Slot, sunken line. *In the groove, slang,* means reliable, perfect.

Groovey, groovy, *adj. Sl.,* excellent.

grotesque, *n.* Sculpture or painting in which incongruous details of flowers, foliage, and animal or human forms are represented; such art as a whole; such incongruities considered as phase of reality.

grotesque, *adj.* Involving heterogeneous and inconsistent details.

grouch, *v. Colloq.* for *grumble, feel sullen, morose, feel resentment.* Also as a *n.* meaning a sullen person, a fit of sulkiness; and as an *adj., grouchy,* and *adv. grouchily.*

ground floor, *n.* First floor, street floor. The "first storey" in a *Br.* building would be called either second floor or mezzanine in the U.S.

group, *n.* In danger of being overworked, as it is used to mean anything from five plumbers to fifty thousand Democrats. Use the specific term: *society, squad, class, party,* etc.

Group Possessive. The sign of the possessive, *-'s,* is appended to the last word of a short group of words forming a sense unit, as in "A man about *town's* apartment, the foreman of the *jury's* opinion, Beaumont and *Fletcher's* plays." When such a group of words is so long that the *group-possessive* construction would be awkward, use the *of* construction. "He is the son of the man who owns the farm," is better than "He is the man who owns the farm's son." The *of* construction should be used to avoid a bad sequence of *-s's.* "She is the daughter of my brother-in-law's second cousin," is better than "She is my brother-in-law's second cousin's daughter." Always write *someone else's, everybody else's,* etc., and not *someone's else, everybody's else.*

grub, *v.* Dig hard; *slang,* beg, acquire by importunate demand.

grub, *n.* Thick worm; *slang,* food.

guess, *v.* Can be used to mean *think, be of the opinion, imagine,* or *suppose* when it implies some uncertainty and is followed by an objective clause. "I *guess* the Browns haven't paid their rent yet."

Gullah, *n.* Dialect of certain Negroes of South Carolina and Georgia coastal district.

gum, *n.* Chewing gum, made of chicle ,or, less commonly, of spruce sap or paraffin; *dial.,* overshoe; *Br.,* mucilage.

gumbo, *n.* Okra soup.

gumption, *n. Colloq.* and *dial.* for *common sense, resourcefulness, shrewdness, enterprise.*

gusher, *n.* Fast-flowing oilwell; voluble sentimentalist.

guts, *n.* Modern slang for the old slang of the same meaning, pluck. *Intestinal fortitude* and *visceral stamina* are examples of polysyllabic humor.

guy, v. Ridicule, mock. [Guy Fawkes, don't you remember?]

guy, n. Steadying rope, guy-rope; fellow; slang, man, boy.

gym, n. Colloq. stump of gymnasium.

gyp, n. and v. Probably the stump of Gypsy. To swindle, a swindle, a swindler. "And then they gypped me out of what money I had." All slang.

gypsy, n. Romany wanderer, member of the Romany race; wanderer, migrant seasonal worker of unstable temperament. [L., Egyptian]

gyroscope, n. Spinning disc mounted on an axis; complex mechanism developed from such a disc. [Gr., ring watcher]

gyves (jīvs), pl. n. Shackles, leg-irons; slang, handcuffs.

H

haberdashery, n. Men's wear; shop in which men's clothes are for sale. "Harry had a haberdashery in old K.C."

hack, n. Hired vehicle; taxicab. [Stump of hackney carriage]

Hackneyed. Trite. A hackneyed expression is a cliché, a battered verbal ornament, a phrase that has "seen better days": rising tide of sentiment, last but not least, by leaps and bounds, clinging vine, cup that cheers, monarch of all he surveys.

had, p. and p. part. of have. Often used with adjectives, adverbs, or phrases of comparison, such as as well, as good, rather, better, best, followed by an infinitive or a that clause, and indicating preference or advisability. "We had as well go on to Boise, for there is no hotel here." "You had better watch out." Had ought is not a good substitute for ought, obliged, or should. "He should (not had ought to) get up earlier." Had have and had of are incorrectly used for had in sentences like "If the boys had have come this morning, they would have seen something," or "If they had of let us know, we could have met them." Had is low colloq. as a passive, as in "A good time was had by all," and stilted at the beginning of sentences like "Had I a dozen eggs, I could make an ome-lette." Write "If I had a dozen . . ." Had ought to is vulgar for ought to.

had it, Army slang borrowed from Br. colloq., lost. "You've had it, chum," means "Tough luck, Bud, you have failed."

hag, n. Witch; ugly old woman; colloq., plain woman, uncomely girl.

hair-do, n. Colloq., coiffure, manner of dressing the hair.

half, n. Although it is not strictly logical, one can say "I gave her the larger half of my apple." Both "half past ten" and "half after ten" are correct. Say "a half hour" or "half an hour," not "a half an hour." The phrases "didn't half try," and "isn't half bad" are colloq.

half-baked, adj. Underdone; colloq., incomplete, feeble-minded.

halitosis, n. Bad breath, stinking breath; what is called by Britons oral offense.

halt, v. Stop, cause to stop. H. is freely used in non-military contexts in the U.S. but not in Britain. Call a halt to means put a stop to.

halter, n. Head harness for a horse or other animal; triangular scarf worn in lieu of a blouse.

hamburger, n. Chopped beef, patty of chopped round steak, Hamburg steak. Cheeseburger, beefburger, and fishburger are patties shaped and cooked like hamburgers. [Ger. Hamburg with no suggestion of pork]

hammy, adj. Colloq., stilted, artificial, theatrical, like a sentimental actor playing Hamlet.

handbill, n. Advertising sheet intended for manual distribution.

handicap, handicapped, handicapping, v. Place at a disadvantage.

handicap, n. Artificial disadvantage for a contestant with superior record; disadvantage.

handle, v. Manipulate; deal with, deal in.

handsome, adj. colloq. Of pleasing appearance, inappropriately applied to scenery.

handy, adj. Useful.

hang out, v. Colloq., reside (with in or at).

hanged, hung. *Stand. lit.* prefers *hanged* to designate the execution of a criminal. "He was sentenced to be *hanged*." "Marjorie *hung* out the wash."

Hanging Participle. The same as **Dangling Participle,** q.v.

hangover, *n. Colloq.,* headache and illness after alcoholic indulgence.

happening, *n.* Occurrence.

harass (hăr'ăs), *v.* Tire by importunity; wear down by repetitious annoyance; wear down by a series of minor military attacks.

hard-boiled, *adj.* Boiled until hard inside. Purists in cookery insist that an egg dropped into boiling water or cooked in water brought to the boiling point until both yolk and white have become more solid than liquid should be called "hardcooked"; their point is that at no time in the cooking process does the liquid part of the egg boil. Figuratively, *h.b.* means tough, much-enduring.

hardly, *adv.* Correctly followed by *when*, not *than*, in sentences like "We had *hardly* pulled into the dock *when* (not *than*) the storm broke." *Hardly, scarcely, only, but,* do not need to be reinforced by a negative, as in "They had *not hardly* (right: They had *scarcely*) scratched the surface."

Harmony. Have you mixed literary types and different kinds of material, or the poetic with the literal, the serious word and the slang expression, indiscriminately? If so, you have not attained *harmony.* Make the transitions between the serious and the jocular, the imaginative and the matter-of-fact, easy and clear. Or exclude or subordinate whatever is discordant.

harp on, *v.* Talk monotonously about.

harum-scarum, *adj.* Reckless, wild.

hasenpfeffer, *n.* Pickled hare meat, stewed.

hassle, *n. Slang,* squabble; heated discussion.

haul, *v.* Drag; transport.

haul, *n.* Extent of transportation. "Rates are cheaper for long hauls."

hauteur (ō tŭr'), *n.* Proud bearing, haughty manner.

have got to, *v.* Must. See *get.*

have no use for, *v.* Dislike, scorn, disapprove.

hawker, *n.* Outdoor salesman, pitchman, pedlar.

hayseed, *n.* Grass seed; *colloq.,* farmer, rustic, rube.

haywire, *n.* Baling wire (which often becomes a tangled mass); *adj. colloq.,* deranged, crazy, unsystematic.

haze, *v.* Overwork; *collegiate tech.,* harass, torture, force to perform menial service or exhausting exercise.

head for, *v.* Start for, set out in the direction of.

healthy, healthful, *adj.* Strictly, *healthy* means *possessing health,* and *healthful* means conducive to health. A climate is not *healthy,* yet *colloq.* one may say "The climate of Maine is *healthiest* in the summer."

heap, *n. Stand. lit.* in *heap of toys, heap of old clothes,* but *colloq.* in the sense of *crowd of people, a great number or large quantity. Low colloq.* or *dial.* in the sense of *much,* as "I'd a *heap* rather stay home than go to that play." *Slang,* motor car.

heaps rather, *adv. phrase. Dialect,* much rather; *v.,* greatly prefer to.

hear to, *v. Am. colloq.* "She would not *hear to* (consent to, agree to) that."

heavy water, *n.* Liquid consisting of heavy hydrogen (Deuteron) and oxygen, formula D2 O.

heck, *n.* Euphemistic expletive. [Hell]

heckle, *v.* Badger, tease; harass with questions or other interruptions.

hectic, *adj.* Consumptive. *Colloq.* full of excitement, wild, feverish, restless.

heebiejeebies, *n. Slang,* the jitters.

hegemony (hē jĕm'ō nē), *n.* Leadership. [*Gr.*]

height (hīt). The pronunciation (hīth) is *colloq.*

heil, *interjection* Hail! Greeting! [Nazi German salutation]

helicopter, *n.* Airplane lifted and propelled by horizontally rotating blades.

heller, *n.* Hellion, imp, mischievous person, rascal.

help, *n. Stand. lit.* in the sense of hired helper or helpers. In rural America it means a man who works on the farm or a girl who works in the house.

help but. Not in good use. "I could *not help* hearing" is better than "I could *not help but* hear."

henchman, *n.* Feudal vassal; follower; worker in a political organization.

hep, *adj. Slang,* wise, sophisticated. *Hep to,* conversant with, aware of.

hepcat, *n.* Clever girl; skilful jazz dancer; appreciative listener to jazz.

here. *This here* and *that there* are vulgar. "*This (here)* hat is not as fine as *that (there)* coat."

her's, *pron.* Vulgar for *hers.*

heterodox, *adj.* Concerning, presenting, or characterized by false teaching. Contrary to orthodox right teaching.

hexameter, *n.* Metrical line of six feet.

hiatus, *n.* Gap, break; slight pause.

hick, *n.* and *adj. Slang* for a *hayseed, farmer, rustic.* "A *hick* town."

hickory, *n.* Shagbark tree; wood of any of a group of trees of the walnut family. [Indian name, liquor made from hickory nuts]

hie, *v.* Poetic for hasten, go in a hurry. It is often used reflexively and nearly always for comic effect. "Let's *hie* ourselves away to Coffee Pot Café."

hifi, *adj. Slang,* high fidelity.

highball, *n. Railroad tech.,* signal to go ahead; *colloq.,* tall glass, mixed drink in a tall glass, whiskey-and-soda.

highbrow, *n.* Impractical scholar, studious person, intellectual.

highfalutin, *adj.* High flown, bombastic. Spelled also hifalutin.

high-fidelity, *adj.* Very accurate in reproducing radio messages.

highlight, *v.* Cast strong light on, emphasize; stress like the brightly lighted portion of a picture.

hightail, *v. Sl.,* scram; depart rapidly and unceremoniously.

high-toned, *adj. Low colloq.* in the sense of *stylish.* "He's a *high-toned* man." In vulgar English it is always *high-tone.*

hijacking, *n.* Theft from motor trucks in transit; theft of smuggled or already once stolen property.

hike. *Colloq.* as a *n.* or *v.* meaning to walk or tramp, a tramp or tramping trip. *Hiker* is also *colloq.,* but *hitchhike* and *hitchhiker* are slang. In the meaning of *raise* (the amount of), as in "The next time you are brought to my court on the same charge, I'll see that the figures of the fine are *hiked* a bit," *hike* is slang.

himself, myself, yourself, *pron.* These are reflexives or intensives and should not ordinarily be used in place of the personal pronouns. "My brother and I (not *myself*) will attend to that." See **myself.**

hind, comp., **hinder,** superlative, **hind-most,** *adj.* Back, rear, following.

hire, *v.t.* Employ at a fixed wage; *New England colloq.,* borrow at a fixed rate of interest. "Well," said Calvin Coolidge, "they hired the money, didn't they?"

hire out, *v. Colloq.,* agree to serve for compensation.

hired, *adj.* Employed at a fixed wage; democratic euphemism for employed at domestic service, in service.

hisn, hern. *Hisn, hern, yourn, ourn, theirn, them* as demonstrative *pronouns,* are typical vulgarisms.

his or her. Correct but stilted or unnecessary as a substitute for the generic *his* in such sentences as "Each person who saw this disgraceful performance must have lost some of *his or her* (better *his*) respect for the Crescent Players."

hisself, theirselves, *pron. Dial.* or *vulgar.* "He got *himself* (not *hisself*) a farm."

Historical Present. Narrators occasionally use present verbs to describe past events vividly. It is humorously called the *hysterical present* when handled clumsily or employed sensationally or excessively.

histrionics, *n.* Theatrical oratory.

hit, *v.* As compared with *strike* (*p., struck, p. part., struck*), *hit* is the more familiar word. *Smite* is poetical, like the *p. part. stricken. Hit it off,* agree, and *hit one's stride* are *colloq.; hit for a loan,* ask for a loan; and *hit the ball,* work hard, travel swiftly, are slang. Hit, *n.,* besides its common meanings, denotes a stinging or telling remark that hits the mark, or a very successful book, play, etc., that *hits* the fancy.

hitch, *v.i.* Limp, hobble; *v.t.*, attach, harness (usually with *up*). "Hitch your wagon to a star."

hitched, *p. part. Sl.,* married.

hitchhike, *v.* Travel by alternate walking and riding; ride-and-tie; travel by begging transportation from motorists.

hither, *adv.* Like *thither,* rare except in poetry and in the phrase *hither and thither.*

hoarding, *n.* Saving illogically or illegally. Unrelated to *Br. hoarding* meaning billboard, board fence.

Hoax, *n.* and *v.,* having a similar meaning, is perhaps from *hocus,* as is also, perhaps, *hokum,* slang for stage talk or "business" intended to arouse laughter or sentimentality. Hence the slang meaning, stuff used by writers or speakers to move readers or audience to take a desired action.

hobo, *n.* Tramp, unemployed wanderer.

hock, *v. Slang,* pawn.

hocus-pocus, *n.* The juggler's trick, the magician's "spiel" or formula. Hence mock-magic, cheating nonsense, rigmarole, abracadabra, flimflam, humbug, charlatanism, quackery. The *v.,* meaning to cheat or trick, is *colloq.*

hokum, *n. Sl.,* peddler's patter; plausible nonsense; bunk.

hog, *n.* Mature or adult pig, swine. *Go the whole hog,* commit oneself utterly, go all the way, a phrase used by Abraham Lincoln.

hogtie, *v.* Fasten like a hog with a snubbing line attached to one foreleg and the diagonal hindleg; make helpless.

hoist, *v.* Principal parts, *hoist, hoisted, hoisted. Hist, histed, histed,* are vulgar forms.

hold, *v.* Principal parts are *hold, held, held.* The *p. part. holden* is *trade* or *tech.* (law), or archaic. *Hold a brief for,* usually in negative form, is used to mean defend or support. "I *hold no brief for* the doctors." *Hold a candle to,* compare with, and *hold the bag,* be left empty-handed, be left with the responsibility of facing consequences of an act, are *colloq. Hold out on,*

keep back secretly part of another's share, is slang.

Hold up is *stand. lit.* meaning display but *colloq.,* rob at gunpoint or with threat of physical injury. *Uphold,* support, is *stand. lit.*

hollow, *n. Dialect,* valley, valley neighborhood in mountainous country.

home, *n.* Domicile of a family; house in contradistinction to flat or apartment. In attributive use, *home, adj.,* means belonging to or associated with one's club, school, community, or city.

homely, *adj.* Plain, unbeautiful. The *Br.* equivalent is wholesome. [homelike]

Homeric, *adj.* Characteristic of Iliad or Odyssey, epic in quality or tone. An *H.* adjective is a compound of adjective and noun used as a verbal. An example is rosy-fingered. See *Epithet.*

homey, *adj. Colloq.* for *intimate* or *homelike,* "A *homey* atmosphere."

hominy, *n.* Hulled corn. [Am. Indian]

homogeneous, *adj.* Of the same kind, alike in composition. [The prefix *homo* is from Gr. meaning same.]

homogenize, *v.t.* Make of one consistency or substance throughout.

Homonyms. Words pronounced alike, but with different meanings, and usually with different spellings: *aisle, isle; be, bee; ceiling, sealing.*

honor. The *Br.* spelling *honour* is preferred for wedding invitations and other social forms.

honorable. Used as a title, it is not abbreviated, and is preceded by *The* and followed by the title *Mr.,* or by the name or initials. Not "Honorable Rumford" or "Hon. Rumford," but "The Honorable Rex Rumford."

hooch, *n.* Rum, hard liquor. [Alaskan Indian]

hood, *n.* Head covering attached to a monk's coat or cloak; folding cover; cover for automobile engine. The part of an academic costume called the hood is a conventionalized approximation of a monastic *hood,* the color of the lining indicating the university and that of the outer band symbolizing the field of scholarship.

hood, *n. Slang,* hoodlum, rough.

hoodlum, *n.* Destructive young ruffian. [*Ger.,* Bavarian dialect]

hoodoo, *n.* A variant of *voodoo. Colloq.* as *n.* or *v.,* a thing or person bringing bad luck; a Jonah. To bring or cause bad luck.

hook-up, *n.* Series of electrical connections by telephone or radio; affiliation; radio network of affiliated stations.

hooksey, *n. Sl.,* hook-and-ladder truck.

Hooper rating, *n.* Measure of popularity of a radio program.

hoopla, *n. Slang,* excitement; noisy demonstration.

hoosegow, *n.* Jail. [Spanish *juzgado,* court, whence also the slang, *jug*]

hootenanny, *n. Colloq.,* thing, tool, gadget; folk song concert. [avowedly adapted by W. W. Guthrie from the name of a Western singer, "Hootin' Annie"]

hop, *v. Colloq.* in the senses of *jump onto, dance.* Also as a *n,* meaning a dance, a trip by aircraft, and in the phrases *on the hop,* busy; and *on the last hop,* final part of distance to be covered. *Hop to it* is slang for *go to it.*

hop, *n. Sl.,* narcotic; *v. hopped up,* drugged with a narcotic.

hopes. The *pl.,* as in "She lived *in hopes* of seeing her son," is *stand. lit.* Some writers prefer the *sing.*

horrid, *adj.* Overworked feminine intensive. "He's just too *horrid.*"

horse, *n. Sl.,* heroin.

hot, *adj.* Since Chaucer, a favorite ingredient in many slang expressions. The *Am. hot air* has become naturalized in England and is replacing the *Br. mere vapouring.*

hot dog, *n.* Frankfurter; Coney Island red-hot; small sausage.

hot seat, *n. Sl.,* electric chair.

hound, *n.* Hunting dog; *sl.,* enthusiast.

hove, *v.* Archaic and *dial.* form of *heaved,* but *stand. lit.* in the phrase *hove in(to) sight.* "A big sailor *hove* into sight."

how. Now *dial.* as an interjection used to attract attention. Slang as an intensive. "Was he there?" "And *how!*" *How come?* is a *colloq.* clipped sentence and stands for "*How* did it happen that this is so?" For *what?, how?* is provincial. *Howdy* is *colloq.*

however, *adv.* and *conj.* Used in the place of *how,* as in "*However* (sometimes written *how ever*) did you know Nat was in town?" it is *colloq.* "*How* did you *ever* find those bills?" *Stand. lit.* in "They wondered *how* they *ever* got on without him." *But however* is *colloq.,* and the *however* after *but,* as in "*But* it must be remembered, *however,* that he made no definite offer," is redundant.

howler, *n. Am. sl.,* ludicrous error.

huarache (hwȧ rȧ′chĭ), *n.* Flatheeled shoe with upper of plaited leather thongs.

huckster, *n.* Unscrupulous pedlar; seller of cheap trash; agent for radio advertising.

human, humane, *adj.* The first means possessing qualities that characterize man as man. The practice of using it alone as a *n.* is of long standing; e.g., Chapman's *Homer* (1603), "Mars, plague of men, smeared with the blood of *humans.*" Many careful writers, however, always write *human beings.* See **canine** for adjectives that can stand alone as nouns. *Humane* means sympathetic, forgiving, benevolent.

humanity, *n.* Mankind; philanthropy. *Pl.* often capitalized, **the Humanities,** Greek and Latin classics; cultural studies as distinguished from applied science or vocational training.

humidify, *v.* Raise the percentage of water vapor in an enclosed space.

humor, *n.* Comic quality resulting from incongruity; mood. Originally, *h.* was a trait of personality attributed to the dominance of one of the four *humors* or bodily fluids, blood, phlegm, bile, and black bile. The *Br.* spelling is humour.

humorous, *adj.* Mirthful, mirth provoking; comical. Cf. *comic.*

hunch, *n. Colloq.* in the sense of intuition, a strong presentiment or feeling, an idea that comes suddenly and as if by itself.

hung. See **Hanged.**

hunk, *n. Colloq.,* a big piece or lump of something.

hunky, *n. Slang,* foreigner, especially one from Central Europe.

hunky-dory, *adj. Colloq.,* comfortable, perfectly satisfactory.

hunt, *v.* Seek, follow, pursue with a view to killing or capturing.

hurry, *adj. Stand. lit.* in "He sent a *hurry* call to the hospital," but *hurry-up, adj.,* is *colloq.* "It was a *hurry-up* operation."

husky, *adj. Am. colloq.* in the sense of *powerful, sturdy.* "The *husky* Purdue line." Also the *n.,* "He's a *husky.*"

hussy, *n.* Witty but discourteous girl; scolding slattern; also a mending kit containing needles and thread, a husswife. [housewife]

hustle (hŭs′el), *v.* To crowd, push along roughly. *Colloq.* in the sense of move or work rapidly or energetically; force onward. "He *hustled the work.*" Also *colloq.* as a *n.* meaning energetic activity, "push."

hybrid, *n.* A half-breed. A word made from two or more languages; e.g. *automobile, martyrdom.* See **Barbarism.**

hyperbola, *n.* Curve made by a plane cutting a cone through to its base. [*Gr.,* throwing beyond the mark.]

Hyperbole. The figure of speech having extravagant exaggeration as its distinctive trait.

hypercritical, *adj.* Excessively critical.

hypertensive, *n.* Excitable person, victim of high blood pressure.

hyphen, *v.* Print with a hyphen.

Hyphen. Punctuation mark (-) used to:
1. Separate the parts of a compound word that are not written separately nor yet written as one word: *self-taught, mother-in-law, twenty-one, man-eater.* The accent will sometimes help one determine whether to write words separately or as hyphenated compounds. In general, if each word has a major accent, the words are to be written separately. If one of the words (usually the second) loses its accent, use the *hyphen,* or write solid. Consult the dictionary.
2. Serve as the sign of a union made for the occasion only, as in the case of two adjectives, or an attributive *n.* and another *n.,* used as a unit to modify a *n.;* e.g., *The Smoot-Hawley Bill, a red-hot poker.*

3. Mark the division (between syllables) of a polysyllabic word which because of lack of space has to be broken at the end of a line of printing or writing. Words of one syllable are not split, and in ms. *-ed* is not turned over. See **Syllabication.**

hyphenate, *v.* Print with a hyphen. *Hyphenated* Americans are of presumably divided allegiance, such as German-Americans and Anglo-Americans, or even Irish-Americans.

hypocrisy, *n.* False pretense of virtue or religion; feigning to be what one is not. See **cant.**

hypocritical, *adj.* Falsely pretending to be moral or religious; dissembling.

hypodermic, *adj.* Beneath the skin; used for introducing medicine under the skin. Note that the *Gr. prep.* hypo means under. Do not confuse *hyper,* meaning over.

hypotaxis, *n.* Subordination in grammatical construction.

hypotenuse, hypothenuse, *n.* Long side of a right triangle, side opposite the right angle.

hypothecate, *v.* Promise as security for a loan; put up as collateral.

hypothesis, *pl.* **hypotheses,** *n.* Scientific guess; proposed explanation based on conjecture. An *hypothesis* that is found reliable upon thorough testing becomes a *theory.* If the explanation invariably fits a combination of phenomena, it is a *law.*

I

I, *pron.* Sometimes wrongly used for *me.* "Let you and *I* go" should be "Let you and *me* go." "Between you and *I*" should be "Between you and *me.*" "It is *I*" is *stand. lit.;* "It's *me*" is *colloq.*

IALA (Ē′á lá), *n.* International Auxiliary Language Association, a society for the purpose of constructing a practical international language.

iamb, iambus, *n.* Metrical foot consisting of an unaccented syllable followed by an accented, ŭ ⸗.

ibidem, *adv.* Latin for *in the same place.* Used in footnotes to save the trouble of rewriting a title that has just been referred to. *Abbr. ibid.*

-ic, -cal. Suffixes used to form adjectives. The shorter form should be preferred whenever a choice is possible and there is no difference in meaning; e.g., *heroic* and *aristocratic* are now preferred to *heroical* and *aristocratical.* Sometimes, however, there is a distinction of meaning. *Economic* means of or pertaining to the science of economics (and rarely *thrifty*); *economical* always means thrifty, saving, avoiding waste, as "an *economical* housewife." See *comic.*

ideational, *adj.* Having to do with ideas or mental processes; thoughtful.

idée fixe, *n. Psych.,* obsession. Usually *pron.* with an approximation of French, ĭ dā′fēks.

idem, *pron.* The same, Latin word often used in footnotes, *abbr. id.*

identical, *adj.* Exactly alike. Often followed by *with*, never by *to.* Two persons can never be identical, but two books may. "This copy is *identical* with the one you bought last week." *Identical same person* and *identically the same* are tautological.

identify, *v. Colloq.* in the sense of join, associate oneself with a business, party, or society, "I like to be *identified with* (better *associated with*) people interested in the welfare of the workers."

ideology, *n.* Besides its philosophical meaning, it denotes visionary theorizing, philosophy of life, way of thinking, or the ideas characteristic of an individual or class, as *proletarian ideology.*

Idiom. A form of expression or turn of phrase peculiar to a certain language. When one speaks of the *idiom of the language* he is referring to idiom in this sense. The word-for-word translation of the French *faire la barbe* would be *to make the whiskers,* which must be changed to *shave* to fit English idiom. The *idiom* requires certain prepositions after certain verbs or adjectives; e.g., *from* after *different.* Not to follow the custom of the language in regard to this is to be *unidiomatic,* to write a *solecism.*

In another sense, *idiom* (an *idiom)*

means an expression peculiar to itself either in grammatical makeup, or in being indecomposable, or in both. For instance, *beat all hollow* must stand as is, for if one says *bang all hollow* or *beat all empty* he is either not expressing the same idea or not speaking English. An idiom has developed a meaning that cannot be reproduced by synonyms of the separate words. Some idioms are not perfectly logical or exactly grammatical, but are correct since any expression that conforms to the custom of the language is correct. *Sit tight, pass muster, on all fours,* are idioms.

idle, *adj.* Not busy, not working; valueless; futile.

idol, *n.* Sculptured object of worship; image of a false god.

idolize, *v.* Worship, adore blindly or unreasonably.

idyl, idyll, *n.* Pastoral poem or story. [*Gr.*]

i.e. Latin *id est,* that is. Used chiefly in notes and technical reports.

if, *conj.* For introducing *n.* clauses dependent on verbs like *see, ask, know,* and *doubt, whether* is preferred to *if* in formal usage. "I will find out *whether (if)* I can raise the money or not." The second alternative, introduced by *or,* may be omitted. It is nearly always omitted in the *colloq.,* which prefers *if* to *whether,* especially after *see.* "Let's *see if* the door is open." "My husband asked me to see *if* you would change his sentence from a fine to forty lashes at the city jail."

Do not write *if's* for *and's, but's,* or *though's.* Write "He is a great poet, *although* a second-rate thinker," not "He is a great poet, *if* second-rate thinker." The *v.* after *if* may be omitted when the context makes the sense clear. "This is very important, *if* [this is] true."

if and when. Double-barreled, as are *unless and until, save and except, when, as, and if, etc.* One barrel is sufficient unless you are writing a legal document, and even here one is clearer.

iffy, *adj.* Full of doubts or conditions.

ilk. As *adj.* and *pron.* it is *Scot.* and *dial.* for of the same estate or name. But do not use as a *n.* to mean *breed, kind,* etc., as in "Athletes of Sullivan's *ilk,*" or "Peddlers and men *of that ilk.*"

ill, *adj.* and *adv.* Unhealthy, sick, unjust, harsh, bad, badly. The adv. *illy* should be avoided.

illinium, *n.* Metallic element No. 61 (Il.) Named from Illinois, the name of an Indian tribe, because discovered by Dr. B. Smith Hopkins, a retired professor of the University of Illinois. Other claimants of its discovery prefer to call it *promethium.*

illiterate, *adj.* Unable to read; unlettered; ignorant of books. [*L.,* not lettered]

illusion, *n.* Mistaken perception; a fallacy. See *Allusion.*

image, *n.* Composite of sensory impressions; mental combination of remembered sensations.

imagery, *n.* Figurative language conveying images.

imaginary, *adj.* Unreal; conceived in the mind.

imagination, *n.* Use of the powers of mental association to put sensory images together in new combinations; function of the mind whereby such ideas derived from sense perceptions come into existence; any complex of ideas consisting of memories of sensory perceptions.

In critical terminology, imagination suggests creation of consistent combinations, whereas *fancy* implies random sequences of associations.

immediate, *adj.* Next; without interruption or intervention.

immediately, *adv.* At once; without intervening action or time.

imminent, *adj.* Overhanging; threatening; impending; about to happen.

impact, *n.* Force of collision, power; *journalistic tech.,* influence.

impassable, impassible, *adj. Impassable* means that cannot be passed; *impassible* means that cannot suffer or be made to show signs of emotion. "The road is *impassable.*" "The Hindoo was *impassible,* although he must have been in extreme pain."

implement, *n.* Tool.

implement, *v.* Equip, fulfil, carry out; enforce.

Implication, Unintentional. Be careful not to word a title or statement so that ambiguity or an unintended implication or humorous effect will be produced. For instance, will the title *The Rise of American Oil* do for a scientific account of the part petroleum played in the economic life of the United States, or will *rise* be felt as a pun? The catchy title of a seriocomic book on seasickness, *Why Bring That Up?* is intentionally comical.

It is said that Lew Wallace dedicated the first edition of *Ben Hur* "to the wife of my youth," and that numerous inquiries about how many wives he had married caused him to add "who still abides with me" to the dedication. "Uncle Moses died at last" might imply that one was glad to see him die. The *double-entendre, the insinuation, innuendo,* and *hint* are intentional; the *faulty* implication is a mistake.

imply, infer, *v.* To *imply* means to contain by implication, include virtually, express indirectly; *to infer,* to derive through reasoning, conclude from acts or premises, indicate. "I *infer* that he is going to resign, but I did not mean to *imply* that by anything I said." *Infer* is used *colloq.* for *surmise* and *guess.*

imponderable, *adj.* Without weight, light. As a noun used by diplomats, **imponderables** mean important considerations that cannot be definitely measured.

impractical, impracticable, *adj. Impractical* means not practical, ideal, speculative, theoretical, unskillful from lack of practice; *impracticable,* not capable of being used, unmanageable, infeasible. "His ideas are *impractical,* his drawings *impracticable.*"

imprecise, *adj.* Vague, indefinite; inaccurate. Avoid this piece of jargon as you avoid *disadvise.*

impromptu, *adv.* and *adj.* Offhand, extempore.

Impropriety. In composition, using a fine pair of scissors to open a can. Using a good word as it was never intended to be used. *To proposition, to suicide, an invite,* using *like* as a *conj.* See **Barbarism.**

inadvertent, *adj.* Inattentive, unintentional.

in, into, *prep.* After verbs of motion, *in* denotes motion within a certain area: "The prisoner walked to and fro *in* his cell." *Into* denotes motion from one place to another: "The fly fell *into* the milk." The *colloq. in* often means *into,* as "Burt ran *in* the room and grabbed the first person he saw." Notice the difference between the incorrect "I took her *into* dinner" and the correct "I took her *in to* dinner." *Not in it* is slang for *outclassed.* "Their team was simply *not in it* at all."

in back of, *prep.* Behind. In *Br.* use, *in front of* is an acceptable equivalent for before, but *i.b.o.* is not common.

incidence, incidents, instance, *n. Incidence* means falling upon or affecting in some way; *incidents,* episodes or events; *instance,* illustration, request. "The angle of *incidence* was about 30 degrees." "Such harrowing *incidents* are a part of the day's work." "This is an *instance* of the man biting the dog."

incidentally, *adv.* Casually; by chance; as an aside. *Incidently* is vulgar.

Incoherence. Does every part of your sentence or paragraph have a natural and obvious connection with adjoining parts? If the connection is obscure or unnatural or lacking entirely, your sentence or paragraph is incoherent and must be revised. See **Coherence.**

incommunicado, *adj.* Without privilege or possibility of communication.

Incomplete Construction. Under certain conditions, words and even phrases may be omitted, especially in clipped sentences, but before leaving out a word or phrase make sure that the omission is in conformity with the requirements of the situation. Comparisons must be completed, at least implicitly; and often a connective must be repeated for the sake of clearness. Complete one construction before beginning another. Nothing must be left hanging in the air. "She was a young American who, coming to Paris, but she did not know

French or the French, yet was determined to know both," should be "She was a young American who, coming to Paris without a knowledge of French or the French, was nevertheless determined to know both." See **Omission** and **Clipped Sentences.**

incorrigible, *adj.* Not susceptible of correction; delinquent.

incunabulum, *pl.* **incunabula** (ĭn kū nă'-bū là), *n.* Book printed before 1500 A.D. Some scholars use an anglicized *pl., incunables.* [*L.,* cradle, birthplace]

Indent. Make an *indention* (which is the same as *indentation* but not as popular with students) or notch or recess in the marginal line of the text to indicate the beginning of a paragraph.

indestructible, *adj.* Permanent, not capable of being destroyed.

index, *n., pl.* **indexes** or **indices.**

individual, party, *n.* An *individual* is a single human being (as opposed to society, family, etc.); a *party* is a body of persons or one of the persons who make up one side of an action or affair; the plaintiff or defendant. Do not use either of these as a casual synonym for *person,* woman or man. "The *person* (not *party*) you mentioned did not appear." "That *man* (not *individual*) ought to be punished."

inductee, *n.* Person recently inducted into one of the armed services.

induction, *n.* Reasoning from particulars to generalizations, arguing from observation of individuals to a statement about the entire group of which they are members; installation, initiation.

indulge, *v.t.* Gratify, be complaisant toward a habit or desire; take one's pleasure in without check. As a *v.i.* it means to give oneself over to desires. See **engage in.** "He was prone to *indulge* in reverie."

ineluctably, *adv.* Inevitably; easier and fancier word than *irresistibly.*

Inexact Word. Use another word. Find one that more nearly expresses the thought.

infer. See **imply.**

Infinitive, Split. The infinitive is said to be split if an *adv.* is allowed to come between *to* and its infinitive: e.g., *to scarcely see.* It is nearly always a bad construction when stumbled into through carelessness, but when an author chooses it because it gives him the most effective and natural word order or the desired shade of meaning or emphasis, he is justified. In "If Mr. Hardy can find time to *thoroughly investigate* the Department of Parks, he will find waste that is shocking to him," the author has split the infinitive because he did not want the awkwardness of *time thoroughly to investigate* or to put *thoroughly* between *investigate* and its object. For similar reasons "Conservatives have been able *to greatly influence* public opinion" seems justified. But, in general, one should not split an infinitive if the *adv.* could just as well be placed outside the *to* and its infinitive. It is never advisable to allow an adverbial phrase to split the infinitive. Faulty: "They promised *to at once go to* Mr. Reed."

influence, *n.* Action invisibly exerted upon someone or something; whatever possesses the power of producing an effect without apparent force or direct or overt authority. Slang for political, financial, or social "pull," as in "He's got *influence.*" Better, "He is *influential.*"

influential, *adj.* Powerful.

informant, informer, *n.* Giver of information. *Tech.,* an *informant* is one who gives data about language, customs, behavior patterns to an anthropologist. An *informer* is a paid spy, often a traitor.

ingenious, ingenuous, *adj. Ingenious* means resourceful, talented, clever; ingenuous means artless, unreserved, naïve. "The boy was too *ingenuous* to equivocate." "How *ingenious* of him to think of that device!"

inhibition, *n.* Restraint, prohibition; *psychological tech.,* repression of a type of behavior.

in kind, *phrase.* By barter, in similar way, in the same type of property or goods.

innocent of. Chiefly jocular in the sense of *without* or *devoid of.* "The swimming pool was *without* (not *innocent of*) water."

in order that, *conj.* Commonly followed by *may* or *might.* "He tried to get all the voters out *in order that* his candidate

might be elected." In the poetic style the subjunctive without a modal *v.* may follow *in order that,* but not *shall* or *will,* as a rule.

inordinate, *adj.* Excessive; immoderate.

input, *n.* Electric or other power put into a productive system.

in regards to. Incorrect for *in regard to* or *with regard to. In regard of* is archaic or vulgar.

inside, *n.* The inner surface or part. *On the inside* is slang for *having special advantages, having inside information.* In the *pl.* it is *colloq.* for *entrails,* and as an *adj. colloq.* in the sense of *known to a select group,* e.g., *inside* information. *Inside of* is *colloq.* when applied to time. "She will be there *inside of (within)* an hour." *Of* is often superfluous with the *prep. inside.* "It is very cozy *inside (of)* his den."

insigne, *pl.* **insignia,** *n.* Badges, emblems, signs of authority or rank.

instant, *adj.* Present, in the current month. Avoid the triteness of "Yours of the 14th instant received and contents noted."

instrument, *n.* Tool for delicate and skillful work; mechanical contrivance for individual production of music.

intelligentsia, *n.* Like *illuminati* and *cognoscenti,* a fancy name for those having or claiming enlightenment; not like the others. It is synonymous with the slang *high-brows.*

intelligible, *adj.* Comprehensible, capable of being understood.

intensity, *n.* Strength, extent of power; *radio tech.,* degree of sound.

intensive, *adj.* Concentrated, exhaustive.

Intensives. Used here to mean words employed to add emphasis to what is said, as expletives and intensive adverbs. In formal writing do not make a practice of using *too, such, so,* as in "He is just *too* clever for words," "Life is *such* a bore," or "Margaret is *so* entertaining." *Awfully, dreadfully, horribly, terribly, simply* (as in *simply wild*), belong in *colloq.* speech, and even here are not always in the best taste. The more restrained expletives are chiefly *colloq.* and the unrestrained ones *low colloq.* or *vulgar.*

interdict, *v.* Prohibit, forbid; in ecclesiastical law, debar from certain rites, censure with penalty of such debarment.

interim, *adj.* For the time being; *ad interim;* in the meantime.

Interjection. Vocal expression or conventional symbol of an emotional reaction to a situation: *Oh! Ah! Aha!*

intern, interne (ĭn'tŭrn or in *Fr.* pron. ăn'tärn), *n.* Resident physician or surgeon or medical assistant in a hospital.

internship, *n.* Job or position of an intern.

interpret, *v.* Translate, explain, or clarify the meaning of foreign or technical phraseology, artistry, or emotion.

interpretive, *adj.* Clarifying, explaining the meaning.

interpretative, *adj.* Representing a performer's conception of another artist's composition.

interstice, *n.* Crack, narrow space.

interview, *n.* Meeting face to face, conference.

interview, *v.* Meet in conference, question for publication.

in the red, *phrase.* On the deficit side of the ledger, showing an unfavorable balance, losing or having lost money.

into, *prep.* From outside to inside.

intransigent (ĭn trăn'se jĕnt), *adj.* Irreconcilable; stubbornly committed to a course, esp. in politics.

intrigue, *n.* Scheme or plot depending for its success upon ignorance.

intrigue (ĭn trēg'), *v.* To form an underhand plot, carry on an illicit love affair, use secret influence with, complicate, perplex; hence, to arouse or hold the interest, beguile, fascinate. "That plot *intrigues* me." The *adj.* is *intriguing.*

introduction, *n.* Initial part of the text of a book; opening passage of an essay, article, speech, or theme. Do not make the introduction too long or elaborate. It may be used to explain the subject, title, terms, and plan, or to secure the reader's interest, but do not make it apologetic. The short theme rarely needs an introduction.

introvert, *n. Psychologists'* tech. or *jargon,* intuitive, self-centered person, dreamer.

Intruders. Intrusive elements, such as clauses, adverbial phrases, or appositives, that hurt the sentence by crowding in between subject and *v.,* or between *v.* and object; words allowed to split prepositional phrases, infinitives, or other groups that should usually be kept bound together.

1. Qualifying expressions may occasionally be allowed to come between subject and *v.,* but must not cause the sentence to lack unity or be swaybacked or confusing. In general, prefer "When father arrived he saw that everything had been nicely arranged for him" to "Father, when he arrived, saw . . ."

2. Only the modifiers of the object and occasionally a modifier of the *v.* should be permitted to separate *v.* and object. Prefer "As soon as father came he called for food" to "Father called, as soon as he came, for food."

3. A prepositional phrase should rarely be split. Prefer "He subscribed to the literary journals, although he showed no signs of being interested in them" to "He subscribed to, without showing a sign of interest in, the literary journals."

4. An *adv.,* but not an adverbial phrase, may, under the right conditions, split an infinitive. Correct: "I couldn't get him *to* really understand." See **Infinitive, Split.**

A word (or phrase) that comes between an auxiliary *v.* and its infinitive or *part.*— "have *never* played tennis"—or between a form of *to be* and its complement—"He is *also* Secretary of the Navy"—is not an intruder.

invalid (ĭn val'ĭd), **invalid** (ĭn'va lĭd), *adj.* The first means not valid, null, void; the second, not well, sickly.

invaluable, *adj.* Exceedingly valuable.

invariant, *n.* Constant; constant quantity.

invent, *v.* Devise something new. Cf. **discover.**

inventory, n. Taking stock.

Inversion. Placing the subject after the v. "What *did he* do?" "Never *will they* come again." Correctly used in questions, commands, exclamations, to link a sentence with the preceding one, and to help the metrics of a poem, but rarely to be used in a declarative sentence unless there is a definite need for it. The ornamental and elegant inversion is poetic or old-fashioned. "A cowboy could do twice the work that *could a city dude*" is awkward. "Tickets should I get at Rector's?" doesn't sound right. "Sang the birds and came the milkman," is bad.

invidious, adj. Tending to incite ill will; enviously and unfairly discriminating.

invite, n. Low colloq. for *invitation.*

invoke, v.t. Call for help from; materialize; conjure.

inwardness, n. Intrinsic quality; essence.

ion (ĭ'ŏn), n. Electrified particle, a *cation* if positively electrified and an *anion* if negatively.

ionosphere, n. Physics tech., ceiling of electrical particles, high in the Earth's atmosphere. At night the i. causes radio sky waves to rebound and thus makes distant reception better than it is by day.

Irony. A humorous or rhetorical effect in which the intended meaning is the opposite of what is seemingly said. "That's a sweet answer," if given the right intonation, means "That's a sour retort." *Irony* may be gentle, but *sarcasm* is always biting and reproachful.

irregardless, adj. and adv. An incorrect form of *regardless.* Often jocular.

Irrelevant. Not applicable or pertinent; material that is useless or foreign to the purpose of the theme. Omit what is possibly relevant but not clearly necessary. Material that is too good to omit but difficult to introduce into the text itself may sometimes be put into the footnotes.

Allusions are frequently partially or wholly irrelevant. Write "They were unmarried," not "They were *without benefit of clergy.*" Kipling's title *Without Benefit of Clergy* is a pun. The real meaning is *not having obtained the privilege of being*

tried by an ecclesiastical court. See **Allusion.**

irresistible, adj. Resistless; overwhelming; utterly charming.

ism, n. Doctrine; usually with connotation of disapproval.

isolationist, adj. Favoring separation of the U.S. from business and political entanglements with the rest of the world. n. Politician advocating a self-sufficient homeland cut off from the outside world.

isotope, n. Element in the same position in the periodic table as another and similar in chemical behavior but not in radioactivity. "A proton is the nucleus of the atom of the light isotope of Hydrogen."

issue, n. Used too often. It has a great many meanings, but all of them are related to *outlet;* e.g., the sending out of something, what is sent out, event, result, offspring, produce, profits. A less closely related meaning is point in debate or argument, the essential point in a legal conflict. Do not use to mean discussion, matter, details, question of principle, etc. Write "They will reopen the *discussion* (not *issue*) in the Senate."

is when, is where. *When* and *where* clauses should not be used as n. or adj. complements. Faulty: "A war *is when* nations attack each other on the field of battle." Faulty: "A market *is where* people buy vegetables and meats."

it, pron. The impersonal *it,* when it occurs in expressions like "*It says* in the paper that Lorillard has resigned," is *colloq.* Do not use an impersonal *it* construction where one expects an *it* with an antecedent; e.g., "The Supreme Court has given the New Deal a severe setback, but *it* is evident that readjustments will be made to clear away the uncertainties of our economic life." *It,* meaning what the French call the *je ne sais quoi,* is slang. *Colloq.* in expressions like "You can skip *it,*" "You can lump *it.*"

It, pron. Person of importance; central figure in a game.

Italian (ĭt ăl'yàn). Note the pronunciation.

Italics. A sloping style of type; indicated in manuscript by underlining. As a general rule the titles of separately published works (books and periodicals), letters and words considered as such, and foreign words, should be italicized. *Rome Haul;* the word *silk* is . . . ; *Gesundheit.* Old-fashioned writers sometimes italicize words they wish to emphasize.

it is me. Like *"Who* are you working for?" *it is me* is *colloq.* English.

it's, its. Often confused. The first is *it is;* the second, the possessive case of *it,* which, unlike most possessives, does not require the apostrophe. *You're* and *your* are similarly confused.

There are four kinds of *it's:*

1. *It* with a definite antecedent: "He ate the pie and liked *it."*
2. *It* with a vague antecedent: *"It* is my move now."
3. *It* used as an impersonal pronoun: *"It* is snowing. He is roughing *it."*
4. *It* used as an expletive (anticipatory subject): *"It* is easy to loaf."

J

jack, *n. Arch.,* manservant, unskilled worker; device which does the work of a man; portable mechanism for lifting weights by means of ratchet or screw.

jag, *n.* Tooth, notch; *colloq.,* condition of drunkenness, load of liquor; ragged projection.

jalopy, *n. Colloq.,* old Ford car, rebuilt automobile; rebuilt airplane.

jam, *n. Musical tech.,* free improvisation by members of a jazz band.

jamboree, *n.* Festival, grand festivity with connotations of jolly uproar and innocent gaiety. Capitalized, *J.* is the name for a general conference of Boy Scouts.

jar, *v.* Be discordant; cause to shake; shock; disconcert.

Jargon. Strictly, a form of speech, with almost no grammar or syntax, composed of a mixture of two or more existing languages. Pidgin English and Chinook are jargons. Sir Arthur Quiller-Couch used the term in a special sense meaning bombastic and badly written English, journalese.

This is A. P. Herbert's "Jungle English." Sometimes *jargon* is used to mean the special language of a group, but the term *trade* or *technical* is preferable. [*Fr.,* chattering of birds]

jaundiced, *adj.* Yellow; envious, jealous.

jay, *n.* Noisy bird, contemptuous of human interference; *slang,* self-satisfied rustic, country fellow visiting the city.

jay-walker, *n.* Pedestrian who disregards traffic lights and other regulations.

jazz, *n.* A kind of American music; a dance to such music; excitement such as is produced by jazz music; a literary style suggestive of the variety, exaggeration, distortion, and rapidity that characterize *jazz* music. In a score of other meanings it is slang, as is the *v.* meaning to transform into or make like *jazz.* [Creole, accelerate, speed up]

jeep, *n.* Small automobile; small car used by Army and Navy.

jeepers. *Interjection* expressive of enthusiasm or astonishment.

jell, *v.* Make jelly. Typical back-formation.

jeopardize, *v.* Place in jeopardy, risk.

jerk, *n. Sl.,* dolt, social misfit. [perhaps clipped from *soda-jerk*]

jerkwater, *adj.* Rustic, unimportant like a railroad station where trains stop only to take on water.

jerry-built, *adj.* Flimsy; cheaply and unsubstantially constructed.

jet, *n.* Shiny black mineral; blackness. [*Gr.* name of a town in Asia Minor]

jet, *n.* Gush of gas or liquid through a small opening under pressure. [*Fr.,* throw]

jet-propulsion, *n.* Means or fact of driving forward by power from a jet. The head of a rocket is a missile driven by such power.

jibe or **gibe,** *v.* Jeer or jeer at, mock, scoff. In this sense the preferred *sp.* is *gibe. Colloq.* in the sense of *fit, agree with.* "This doesn't *jibe* with what you said before." In this sense *sp.* with *j.*

jigger, *n.* Ingenious mechanical device, jig; measuring glass; volume of such a glass, about one and one-half fluid ounces.

Jimson-weed, *n.* Poisonous weed containing atropine and scopolamine. [Jamestown weed]

Jingle. Avoid accidental rhymes or the conspicuous repetition of the same or similar sounds, as in "The sole claim to fame of this name is the same." "His book is far from free from frivolity." A form of **Cacophony,** q.v.

jinx, n. Slang for a *hoodoo* or a *Jonah,* a person or thing causing bad luck.

jitney, n. *Sl.,* five-cent piece; motor vehicle (of Depression days) which carried a passenger for a nickel; jitney-bus.

jitter, v. To be nervous; be irritable or on edge. It is slang, as are also the n. *jitters* and the adj. *jittery.*

jitterbug, n. Enthusiastic dancer to swing music.

jive-talk, n. *Colloq.,* jazz lyrics; words sung to jazz accompaniment; slang of jitterbugs.

jocular, adj. Jocose, sportive.

johnny-cake, n. Hard corncake. [Mencken opines that *j.* is from Shawnee cake, not journeycake]

joint, n. Slang for gathering place, low resort, "dive," household, etc.

join up, v. Slang for *enlist.*

joker, n. Fifty-third card in a p..ck; deceptive clause inserted in a legislative bill to make its actual effect different from its apparent purpose; jester.

jolly, v. *Colloq.* in the sense of *rally, poke fun at, keep in good humor.* "We *jollied* them along." Also as an *adv.* "We'll *jolly* soon find out."

josh, v. *Sl.,* make fun of, banter, mock.

joshingly, adv. *Sl.,* in a spirit of fun; with a quality of deception, like a sophisticate ridiculing a rustic.

Journalese. Cheap and gaudy style as found in the more sensational newspapers, and sometimes elsewhere. The salient features are the use of pompous neologisms, flamboyant poetic words and expressions, genteelisms, and clichés. *Ban, pact, love child, slain, looms, probe, fistic encounter,* are used instead of *forbid, agreement, bastard, killed, impends, investigate,* or *fight.*

joy, n. Pleasure; ecstasy.

joy-ride, n. Hilarious trip by motor or plane with implications of recklessness.

judge, n. *Colloq.,* presiding officer of any court; any judicial official on the bench whether police court justice, justice of the peace, city magistrate, or Lord Chief Justice of England.

judgment, n. Judicial decisions; mental process of arriving at a decision; quality of mind which produces rational decisions, discretion. *Br.* authorities prefer the spelling judg*e*ment, but usage favors omission of the *e* even in Britain.

judicial, judicious, adj. *Judicial* means pertaining to a judge or a court, critical, involving judgment; *judicious,* wise, discerning, discreet. "This was a *judicial* decree." "Make a *judicious* choice."

judo, n. System for unarmed self-defense. To the Occidental it seems like a combination of wrestling and foul fighting. [Japanese]

jughead, n. Obstinate horse; mulish man or woman.

juke box, n. *Sl.,* automatic record-player, coin-operated. [Gullah, juke house, disorderly house]

jumping-rope, n. Skipping-rope.

junk, n. Discarded material, broken machinery; rubbish; old cordage; hard salted beef; lump, chunk; bottles, bones, and rags.

just, adj. Upright, due, correct; *adv.,* precisely, exactly, barely. *Colloq.* as an intensive meaning *quite, very, simply, decidedly,* as in "I am *just* dying to go," "You must be *just* starving," "It's *just* grand." *Just now* is correct, but *just merely, just recently* and *just exactly* are almost redundant. Prefer *just about to* to *just going to.* Avoid frequent repetition and mispronunciation.

K

kamikaze (kă′mĭ kă′zĭ), adj. Suicide. [Japanese]

kanaka, n. South Sea islander; strong man. [Hawaiian]

kangaroo court, n. *Colloq.,* unauthorized or not legally established court such as might be set up by a Vigilance Committee in a frontier town.

keef, *n. Slang,* dreamy tranquility, dopiness. [Arabic]

keen, *adj.* Sharp, eager, vehement, intense. Slang for *charming, delectable,* and in "to be *keen* about" in the sense of *be fond of.* "He is *keen* about her."

keep. *Keep* meaning *stay,* as in "He *keeps* in his room all the time," and *be in session,* as in "School *keeps* until four," is *colloq.* The following phrases are also *colloq.: keep on tap,* have on hand, *keep dark,* keep secret, *keep one's head above water,* keep going, and *keep in with,* stay on good terms with. *Keep company with,* go with, *keep tab* or *tabs on,* keep count of or check on, and *keep track,* watch, keep oneself informed, are *stand. lit.*

keynote, *n.* Key tone, basic note in a musical series; central idea, guiding principle.

keystone, *n.* Capstone of an arch. In *baseball tech.,* the *keystone* bag is second base.

kibitzer, *n.* Meddler; the onlooker who offers gratuitous advice but does not play. *Colloq.*

kick, *v. Colloq.* in the sense of *object forcefully or angrily.* The *n.* meaning *objection or protest, grounds of objection, thrill, excitement, powerful effect,* is slang. "The New Dealers expected a *kick* from the Newberg merchants." "He gets a *kick* out of the kiddies." *Kickback, n.,* is *colloq.* for *sharp or violent reaction,* and *trade or tech.* in the sense of returning part of one's wages to the employer to circumvent a wage scale.

kid, *n. Colloq.,* child; *v., sl.,* humbug, make fun of, mock, tease.

kidvid, *n. Sl.,* television program for children.

kimono, *n.* Loose coat or dressing gown. [Japanese]

kindly, *adj.* Humane, benevolent.

kindly, *adv.* Pleasantly, in a kind manner. "Thank you kindly," is an illogical expression. "Kindly let us have your opinion," is more sensible.

kind of, sort of. Usually preceded by a *sing.* demonstrative. "*This kind of* experience ages a person." There is little difference between *kind* and *sort,* although the latter sometimes may be slightly contemptuous or disparaging.

As adverbial substitutes for *somewhat, rather,* or *after a fashion, sort of* and *kind of* are *low colloq.* "You *kind of* startled me." "He *kind of* waved his hand." "She feels *sort of* tired."

The indefinite article *a(n)* is not needed in expressions like "What *kind (sort)* of *(a)* pen do you like?"

kin-mother, *n.* Mother-in-law without the comic or hostile connotations. This neologism has not become popular.

kit, *n.* Case for tools or other equipment; set of tools in such a case.

kitchenette, *n.* Little kitchen.

kiyote, *n.* Coyote, wolflike animal of western North America. [Nahuatl].

klux, *v.* Beat, maltreat; punish corporally without legal procedures. [Ku Klux Klan]

knobbly, *adj.* Bumpy.

knock, *v.* Slang for find fault with, speak evil of. **Knock,** *n.,* is slang in the sense of something said as carping criticism. **Knockdown** is slang (from the auctioneer) for social introductions. **Knock off,** *v.,* is slang in the meaning of stop working, deduct from a bill, do quickly. **Knockout,** *abbr.* K.O. and sometimes written *Kayo,* is *stand. lit.* in the senses of to knock out, and the blow that knocks out, but slang for an extremely attractive person or thing.

knocker, *n. Sl.,* officer, official. The *head-knocker* is an executive, a boss.

knockdown, *adj.* So-constructed that it can be taken apart and put together again.

knockdown, *n. Sl.,* introduction; social presentation.

know, knew, known, *v.* Be aware, be aware of; recognize.

know, *n. Colloq.,* information. *In the know* is post-war *colloq.,* well informed, and about as trite as "in touch with the situation."

know-how, *n.* Technical knowledge combined with knack.

koala (kō ä′la), *n.* Australian animal that lives in trees and looks like a teddy bear.

kow-tow (kou-tou'), *n.* Pay respect to, bow low. [Chinese]

K-ration, *n.* G.I. ration package for one day; principal contents of such a kit.

kudos, *n.* Praise, glory. Formerly *Br.* academic slang, *k.* is now in good *Am.* use. [*Gr.*]

L

laboratory, *pl.,* **laboratories,** *n.* Workroom for experimental study by scientists or students of science; to be distinguished from the *studio* of painters or sculptors and the *shop* of machinists or carpenters. In the U.S. the pronunciation in common use is lăb'rà tō rē and the approved pronunciation is lăb'ŏ rà tō rĭ. Some *Br.* scientists say lă bō'rà trĭ.

laconic, *adj.* Terse, brief and unemotional. [*Gr.*, Sparta]

lady, *n.* The feminine counterpart of *gentleman.* It is coming down in the world because it is made to stand for almost any woman and is used loosely and incorrectly in such compounds as: *chorus-lady, wash-lady, scrub-lady, sales-lady,* and *lady barber.*

lagniappe (lăn'yăp), *n.* Small gift to a customer. [*Fr.,* < Spanish, < So. Amer. Indian]

lambaste, *v. Sl.,* subject to a real or a verbal thrashing.

lambent, *adj.* Glimmering, lightly brilliant.

laminate, *v.* Press into sheets or layers.

lampoon, *n.* Abusive personal satire.

lapse, *v.* Die out, come to an end.

last, latest, *adj.* Strictly, *last* means the final item of a series and *latest* the most recent, the furthest advanced toward a certain time. "The *latest* (not *last*) number of *Time* is . . ." Yet one always says *last night, last Wednesday, last week, on the last occasion.*

late, the, *adj.* Former. Ambiguous because it does not indicate whether it is intended to mean that the person's life or his tenure of office is terminated, as *the late Governor of Utah.* It is better to use *ex-* with single words (*ex-President,* but **not**

ex-Chief of Police), *late* when the person described is dead, and *former* in other instances.

latter, *adj.* The more recent—opposed to *former.* "In these *latter* days." "If I have to choose between the hat and the shoes, I will take the *latter.*" A mere *pron.* as the antecedent of *the latter* is unsatisfactory. Faulty: "There they were—both he and she, *the latter* being the less perturbed of the two." *Latter* is not good as an elegant variation of *him* or *her,* but it is correct in *the latter part of the day (week, month,* or *year).*

latter-day, *adj.* Recent, modern. A Latter-day Saint is a Mormon. Note the hyphen.

laudable, laudatory, *adj. Laudable* means praiseworthy; *laudatory,* expressing praise. "She writes in the most *laudatory* (not *laudable*) *terms* of his work with the natives."

law-abiding, *adj.* Obedient to law, peaceable.

lay, *v.* A hen *lays,* betters *lay* a wager, sailors *lay* aloft or forward, and the worker *lays* to his oars. In its other meanings *lay* is transitive. *Lie,* with which *lay* is often confused, is always intransitive. The principal parts of *lay,* are *lay, laid, laid;* of *lie,* they are *lie, lay, lain.*

Lay for, clipped from *lay in wait for,* as in "You had better watch out, he is *laying for* you" is *low colloq. Lay off,* dismiss, is *stand. lit.,* but *lay off,* cease using, as in "I'm going to *lay off* cigarettes," and *lay off* meaning the opposite of *lay on,* attack, are slang. "You'd better *lay off* my brother." *Layoff,* shutdown, laying off workmen or work, is *stand. lit.,* and so is *layout,* plan, make-up of a newspaper, except when it means *dress, suit, dinner,* etc., *displayed.* In these meanings it is slang.

layout, *n.* Plan, diagram; preliminary outline for advertising; *slang,* show, spread, scheme of interior decoration.

l.c. Change capital letters to lower-case letters.

lead, led, led, *v.* Precede and direct.

lead, *n.* Heavy metal, symbol PB from Latin, *plumbum.*

leader, leading article, *n. Br.,* editorial, signed editorial.

learn, *v.* Vulgar when used to mean *teach.*

lease, *n.* Contract by which real property is held or occupied.

leatherneck, *n.* Member of the U.S. Marine Corps. The name is derived from the high protective collar on an early Marine uniform.

leave, let, *v.* To *leave* a person alone is to abandon him, *leave* him in solitude; to *let* him alone is to stop bothering him or having anything to do with him. For *permit* or *let, leave* is vulgar, and for *depart, set out* it is *colloq.* "I am *leaving* Chicago" is *stand. lit.,* but "I am *leaving* for Chicago" is *colloq. Leave off* is *stand. lit.* for *stop, desist from,* but *leave* in this sense is *colloq.,* e.g., "Now *leave* grumbling and get to work." The *n.* **leave** implies permission as well as departure. *Lief* is the correct form if the meaning is *gladly* or *freely,* as in "He would as *lief* walk as ride."

leer, *v.* Look sidewise, insultingly or maliciously.

leery or **leary,** *adj.* Slang for *knowing, wary, on one's guard.* "He's a bit *leery* about joining."

leeway, *n.* Side movement of a ship to the leeward (down wind). *Colloq.* in the sense of *delay, room to move freely in.* "He asked the landlord for a little *leeway* on the rent."

leftist, *n.* Radical, adherent of a "left wing" or revolutionary party.

legend, *n.* Extended title for graphic illustration in book or periodical; also popular tale ostensibly historical; saint's life.

legendary, mythical, *adj. Legendary* means fabulous as opposed to historical; *mythical* means fabulous or imaginary as opposed to actual. Strictly, a *legend* is the story of a saint's life but it has been extended to mean any traditional tale, and the *adj.* is often equivalent to *unauthentic, apocryphal.* The *mythical* person's existence cannot be verified; a *mythical* football team is one that is assembled on paper and has never played together as a team.

legible, *adj.* Plain; easy to read.

legionary, *adi.* and *n.* Belonging to a legion; **Legionnaire,** member of the American Legion.

legit, *n. Theatrical slang,* legitimate stage; drama as contrasted with vaudeville or motion pictures.

leisure (lē′zhr or lĕ′zhr), *n.* Ease; time free from vocational employment; time off.

length (pronounced *lengkth,* not *lenth*).

lengthy, *adj.* Remarkably long; too long.

less, *adj.* Refers to degree, value, or amount, as opposed to *more* and *greater,* and is the comparative of *little. Smaller* refers to size, dimensions, and amount; *fewer* to number, but *less* can be used in the sense of *fewer* with collectives; e.g., "To have *less clothes* than necessary." *Less* means inferior in rank or importance in one phrase, *no less a person than. Lesser* is more bookish than *less,* and often refers to size or importance. "He was one of the *lesser* poets of that period." *Lesser,* however, is not used adverbially or before *than.* "*Less* (*adv.*) steady men would have given up before now."

lesser, *adj.* Smaller, less. Prefer *fewer* of things and especially of people. Use *lesser* but rarely and only when cadence demands.

lest, *conj. Stand. lit.* but now considered somewhat formal. After *lest* the correct construction is *should,* or in elevated literary style, the subjunctive: "Lest he *be* angry."

let, *v.* Permit, allow, rent. See *leave. Let's,* let us, is often carelessly pronounced (*lĕs*). *Let's us* is redundant. *Let you and I* involves a false agreement. *Let's don't* is a bad substitute for *let's not.*

Let is frequently part of a *colloq.* verb-adverb combination; e.g., *let down,* fail; *let go,* act in a free and unconstrained manner; *let in,* get involved in, "You don't know what you have *let* yourself *in* for," *let on,* give sign of, "She never *let on* that she knew," *let up,* cease, stop, "He said that he would never *let up* until he got it." *Let off,* meaning to discharge a gun or spring a trap, is *stand. lit.,* but meaning to release from an obligation, is *colloq.*

Let in on, reveal a secret, make one a

party to, as in "I'm going to *let* you *in on* this," is slang. *Let* in *without let or hindrance* is a *n.* and means *hindrance*. *Letdown* in the sense of *drawback, disappointment, comedown,* is *colloq.*, but in the sense of a letting down, a slackening of speed, or effort, it is *stand. lit. Letup,* a stopping or slackening, is *colloq.*

Letters. It takes sense, tact, taste, and skill to write good letters. That is the reason there are so few of them. But all letters are interesting because they are so revealing. If the writer does not choose the standard sizes and styles of paper, it reflects on his taste. If his spelling, grammar, and diction cannot pass muster, it reflects on his education. If he brags, threatens, preaches, or is evasive and deceptive, it reflects on his character. And if the writer of a familiar letter tries to hide his shortcomings by completely submerging himself, he creates a dead and wooden thing.

The good letter writer observes the conventions of form, yet avoids stereotyped expressions. *Herewith enclosed, inst., noted the same, contents carefully noted, at your convenience,* and *your esteemed favor* never appear in his letters. Neither does he *beg to advise, advise* a person what he has done, or *beg to acknowledge.* And he finds a better way to begin or close a letter than with a participle in *-ing,* as in "Reply*ing* to your inquiry about," "Referr*ing* to yours of recent date," "Hop*ing* that this will find you the same," or "Trust*ing* that you will deign to grant me an interview."

The essential parts of a letter are: (1) the heading (or printed letterhead), (2) the inside address (omitted in personal letters), (3) the salutation, (4) the letter proper, and (5) the complimentary close with the signature. Personal letters are often written in longhand and sometimes both sides of the paper are used, but business letters are typed and only one side of the paper is ever used. Care should be taken in any kind of letter to keep a good margin and arrange the parts to present a nicely spaced, well-balanced, legible and attractive page.

Whether the writer chooses the diagonal (or indented) style or the newer and more popular block (or straight) style, he should be consistent and make sure that the whole letter, including the address on the envelope, conforms.

Mr. Charles M. Collyer
55 Prairie Avenue
Joliet, Illinois

inside address, block style

Freelands Stone Company,
830 Bowling Street,
Granite, Vermont.

inside address, diagonal style

75 Marshall Place
Charleston, Virginia
May 20, 1954

heading, block style

In the diagonal style usually the inside address and the entire letter, unless it is long, are double spaced. In the block style the punctuation of the display lines is open, and double spacing and not indenting (except in the semi-block style) separates the paragraphs; and the letter proper is single spaced.

The salutations in personal letters may be more or less informal, but business letters usually have *Dear Sir:* (or *Dear Sirs:*), *Gentlemen:, Dear Madam:,* or *Ladies:.* Most letters end with *Yours truly* or *Sincerely yours,* or some slight variation of either. *Faithfully yours* is only for close friends.

The personal letter should permit digressions freely, yet at the same time order its details in such a way as to make the wished-for impression and convey its message clearly. It should be colloquial in tone and diction. If it is direct, friendly, natural, and sincere and written with some skill and imagination, it may have some of the charm of the personal essay and capture the impressions of a day someone never wants to forget.

In the business letter attempts are made to keep the personal touch. Sales letters are friendly and cheerful and try to adapt their appeal to several different classes of readers. There is the bluff and business-like tone for men, the sprightly and poetic tone for women, and the jaunty, breezy, or juvenile tone for youth. Business letters must be clear and terse. Paragraphs are rather brief. One type of business letter requires exceptionally careful thought and great skill. This is the letter of application. In responding to an advertisement, the writer does not necessarily have to mention when or where he saw it, but he does have to make an effective beginning, and in the body of the letter give a clear and adequate account of his person, his education, and his experience. He should also give references (if possible, one with a telephone number); they are preferred to recommendations. And in doing these things, he must strike a happy balance between the ego which is too big and the ego that is too little. He must neither brag nor indulge in false humility. Let him have a reasonable confidence in himself and rest on his record rather than make wild promises or display overeagerness or anxiety, or make clumsy attempts to avoid the pronoun "I." A few "I's" are not objectionable, but let him stick to the facts and avoid statements of opinion about himself and his capabilities unless expressed in the most modest and tactful way.

The letter should not be so short that the addressee would get the idea the applicant is lazy or does not think the job important enough to justify any real effort. It should not be too long, yet long enough to give a satisfying account of the applicant's personality and training. The manner should be neither too familiar nor too stiff and formal; it should be frank, genial (not jocular), and well-bred. Florid and pompous verbiage is bad. In asking for a personal interview, the applicant should do it as simply as possible. And in the conclusion he should try no high-pressure salesmanship, give no veiled commands, nor indulge in an ornamental epilogue.

level, *adj.* Flat, flatly horizontal, having uniform altitude.

level, *n.* Plane; rank, grade of importance. Trite in favorite phrases of peda-gogical theorists and bureaucratic officials.

lewd (lōōd), *adj.* Obscene, indecent.

lexicon, *n.* Dictionary of a language; word list of a special subject.

liable, *adj.* Legally bound, under obligation to do, exposed or open to. It is used with *to* and (less often) *for. Colloq.* for *likely.* See **apt.**

liaison, *n.* Illicit cohabitation; bond.

libel, *n.* Written or printed slander.

liberal, *adj.* Neither conservative nor radical; generous, broadly inclusive. A liberal education is that which prepares for the privileges and duties of a free citizen.

liberal, *n.* Person of moderate political views, neither reactionary nor radical.

lid, *n.* Top, cover; *slang,* hat. *Put the lid on, sl.,* enforce blue laws.

lie, *v.i.* Rest, recline. "The book *lies* on the desk." "It *lay* there yesterday." "In fact, it had *lain* there since last Tuesday." See **lay.** *Lie low,* to lie prone, is *colloq.* in the sense of remain in hiding, as in "He's certainly *lying low* this time," but is slang meaning to conceal one's intentions.

lieu, *n.* Place; used chiefly in the phrase *in lieu of.*

lifelong, livelong, *adj. Lifelong* means enduring for one's life; *livelong,* very long.

lift, *v.* Raise, cause to move upward by power exerted from above; *colloq.,* steal, plagiarize, pilfer.

lift, *n.* Elevation of spirits, brief period of stimulation or inspiration; aid, help; *Br.,* passenger elevator.

lightning-bug, *n.* Firefly.

like, *adj.* Although originally adjectives, *like* and *unlike* are construed as prepositions and may govern nouns or pronouns in the objective case. However, they cannot govern an *adv.* or an adverbial phrase, as in the incorrect "We want it to be here *like in Buffalo." Like* is used correctly in the following. "He writes *like* (i.e., similarly to) an angel." "You treat me *like* (i.e., as if I were) a fool." "It's just *like* them to do that." "These are trees *like those* at home."

In the *colloq.* "He's lost *as like as not,"* *like* is an *adv. Like,* as in "She seemed so cheerful *like,"* is *dial.* and vulgar.

Like used for the *conj. as* is vulgar, e.g., "Few men have worked *like* you have." *Colloq. like* may be a *conj.* if the clause it introduces is a short clipped (elliptical) one, e.g., "The trousers fit him *like* a duck's foot [fits] in the mud," "These days cars come off the assembly lines *like* ants [swarm] across a lawn."

Like(d) to, adv., almost, is *dial.* "She *like(d) to* have died laughing." *The likes of* is *colloq.* "I never saw *the likes of* her."

When *-like* is added to another word to make a nonce word, the hyphen is used; e.g., *horse-like, cross-like.* Otherwise the compound is written solid.

For *something like, nothing like, anything like,* see **something like.**

likely, *adj.* and *adv.* Probable, suitable, promising, probably, in all probability. "I think that *likely* I'll be able to find it." See **apt.**

limit, *n.* Boundary (commonly in the plural, **limits**); *slang, the l.,* unbelievably bad, the worst possible.

limn, *v.* Portray, paint in miniature.

linchpin, *n.* Small metal bar inserted at the end of an axletree to hold the wheel in place.

line, *n. Colloq.* in the sense of business, *class of products, general idea of.* "We've got a *line* on his methods of marketing his *line.*" "He's in the oil-burner *line.*" Slang for *style of conversation.* "What a *line* he had!" *Along the line of* is crude for *about.* "He gave a talk *about* (not *along the line of*) camping and fishing." *Along these lines* is *colloq.* but stylistically poor. "We worked it out *along these lines.*" Better: ". . . *in this manner, according to these specifications.*" *In line with* is *colloq.* for *in harmony with.* "This procedure is *in line with* what we have always done." *Get a line on, v. Colloq.,* find out something about.

linen, *n.* Thread or textile made of flax; cloth or clothing of linen fabric or of cotton woven to imitate linen fabric.

line up, *v.* Wait in line, equivalent to *Br.,* "queue up."

line-up, *n. Police tech.,* presentation of recently arrested prisoners for scrutiny by assembled police officers.

lingerie (lăn′zhĕ rē), *n.* Linens; women's underwear.

lingo, *n.* Terminology peculiar to a certain profession or class; tongue.

linguistics, *n.* Science of language. This noun looks like a *pl.* but governs a *sing.* verb.

liquefy, *v.* Make liquid, reduce to fluid. Note the spelling.

liquidate, *v.* Pay off; eliminate, kill.

lira, *pl.* **lire** or **liras,** *n.* Unit of Italian money, formerly worth a nickel. Do not abbreviate.

literally, *adv.* According to the strict letter; not in a figurative or rhetorically exaggerated sense. "When he said that every man had his price, he did not mean to be taken *literally.*" Do not use for *very nearly, actually, practically,* or *virtually.* Faulty: "His teeth were *literally* (actually) yellow."

Literary Allusion. Indirect incidental reference to characters, actions, situations, or passages from books; a reference. "He's a perfect Babbitt." "When I saw all those fellows talking to my girl, I knew how Ulysses felt when he came home to Penelope." Do not use too many allusions, or those that are likely to be unfamiliar to your audience, or those that are trite or precious or irrelevant. See **Allusion, Irrelevant.**

Literary Language. The standard formal language. *Abbr.* stand. lit.

literate, *adj.* Able to read and write.

litre, liter, *n.* Liquid measure in the metric system, one cubic decimeter; 1.0567 U.S. quarts.

litter, *n.* Untidiness; rubbish; bed carried by poles; several young animals born at once.

little, comparative **less** or **lesser,** superlative **least.** *adj.* **Littler** and **littlest** are *colloq.*

livid, *adj.* Black and blue, ashy pale, discolored.

load down, *v.* Overload, burden unreasonably.

loaded, *adj. Sl.,* drunk; wealthy.

load up, *v.* Burden appropriately.

loaf, *v.* Idle, take things easy.

loafer, *n.* Idler, with implications of shirking responsibility; sport shoe.

loan, *v.* Principal parts, *loan, loaned, loaned.* Standard but not as firmly established as *lend,* which is identical in meaning.

loath, loathe. *Loath, adj.,* means disinclined; *loathe, v.,* means detest.

lobby, *n.* Anteroom; *polit. tech.,* group of people who dislike being called lobbyists but who make business of approaching legislators in anterooms of legislative halls and soliciting votes.

local, *n.* Chapter or branch of a trade union or lodge; railroad train that stops at all stations.

local, *adj.* In or of a place.

Local Color. The distinctive features of a particular locality at a particular time. Correct local color necessitates patient attention to details of the environment described, and close familiarity with them.

locate, *v. Am. colloq.* for *settle, establish oneself.* "They *located* in Nebraska." *Stand. lit.* in the sense of *find the place of* or *for.* "I was not able to *locate* the market."

lockout, *n.* Exclusion of workers by management.

Logic. Does your composition give evidence of sound judgment, accurate classification, valid reasoning, and systematic arrangement? If not, it is illogical in some respects. The most common faults are: (1) "blurred" or "loose" thinking, (2) undeveloped thought, (3) poor definition, (4) illogical comparison, (5) contradiction, (6) faulty or weak reasoning, (7) illogical arrangement of parts of sentence, paragraph, or composition. See **Arrangement and Fallacy.**

logistics, *n.* Science of transporting, quartering, and supplying military forces.

lollapalooza, *n. Sl.,* big one, heavy blow, excellent specimen.

loneliness, *n.* State of being without companionship; lonesomeness.

long-run, *adj.* Long-term, enduring, lasting.

look, *v. Colloq.* in the sense of *gawk, gaze in surprise.* "You should have seen them *look.*" Also in "Things are *looking up* (improving)," "It *looks like* rain," and "It's your *lookout* (concern)." In the sense of appear to be *look* is followed by an *adj.* "He *looked* kind." *Look to,* expect, take care of, count on, and *look up,* aspire, are *stand. lit.,* but *look in, n.,* chance of winning, is slang.

-looking. Usually superfluous in combinations like a *brown-looking dog,* a *bent-looking man,* a *sick-looking girl.* Write "A brownish dog, a bent man, a girl who looks to be sick."

loom, *v.* Journalese for *impends, is imminent.* In the papers everything from an investigation (journalese, *probe*) to a famine *looms;* sometimes it *looms large.*

loop, *n.* Curve of rope or line through which another rope may be passed; returning curve such as that of a noose; *baseball sl.,* league, affiliated group of ball clubs or teams, circuit.

lore, *n.* Wisdom, learning; traditional wisdom, folklore. [Old English, teaching]

lorgnette, *n.* Eyeglass with a long handle; pair of eyeglasses with a rigid handle.

lorry, *n. Br.,* motor truck.

lose (lōōz), **loose** (lōōs), *v. Lose* means to fail to keep; *loose,* to set free. The *adj. loose* means unconfined, not tight or fast or rigid. *Lose out* is *colloq.* for *lose.* "The party has *lost out* in its fight to reinstate Fredericks." *Lose out on,* like *miss out on,* is *low colloq.* or slang. Say *lose* or *miss,* "He *lost out on* (better *lost*) that bet."

lot, *n.* Unit of land; plot of any standardized size.

lot, *n. Stand. lit.* in "He bought this *lot* of shoes." But *colloq.* in the sense of *a great deal,* as in "I've had *lots* of trouble," "This is going to cause a *lot* of damage, and a *lot* of people will be sorry." The *adv. lots,* as in "I've wondered *lots* about that," is *colloq.,* but *lot* in "I think a *lot* of her" is *stand. lit. Lot,* sort of person, is *colloq.* "She's a bad *lot.*"

loth, *adj.* Acceptable variant of **loath.**

loud, *adj. Colloq.* when applied to sensations other than auditory in the figurative senses of *vivid, showy, blatant, offensively obtrusive, strong.* "His tie was as *loud* as his manners." *Loud* is an *adv.* as well as an *adj.* One may say "I wish you would speak *louder*" or "speak *more loudly.*"

lousy, *adj.* Pediculous; *sl.,* unpleasant, unhappy, bad, opposite of *swell.*

louver, *n.* Window, ventilating slit.

lovely, *adj. Colloq.* when used as a counterword and a feminine intensive. "What a *lovely* potato!"

low, *n. Stand. lit.* for *low level, low figure, low mark,* "The market has hit a new *low.*" *Low-down* is slang for *the facts, the truth.* "You must get the *low-down* on this deal." The *adj.* in the meaning of base, ignoble, mean, is *colloq. Low-brow* is the opposite of *high-brow.* Both are slang.

Low Colloquial or Popular English. English that pushes informality, the use of neologisms, contractions, slang, and expletives, to such an excess that it is not acceptable on the colloquial level. See **English, Levels of.**

lucid, *adj.* Clear; easy to understand; mentally alert and logical.

lug, *n. Scottish,* ear; earlike handle; projection; *colloq.,* with *the,* affectation; four-cornered sail set on a slanting spar; *sl.,* awkward swaggerer. "You great *lug,* stop putting on the *lug.*"

lumber, *n.* Wood sawn for use in construction as contrasted with *timber* or *firewood.*

luminosity, *n.* Quality of giving off light; degree or extent of shining.

luminous, *adj.* Brilliant; gleaming, shining.

lunch, *n.* Light meal, snack; midday meal, luncheon.

lurid, *adj.* Pale yellow, wan, ghastly. A *lurid* light is ghastly and sinister, as flames seen through smoke. Figuratively, it means shocking, sensational. "His eyes ran through the tabloid's *lurid* description of the murder."

lush, *adj.* Luxuriant.

lush, *n. Colloq.,* drunkard.

lustful, lusty, *adj. Lustful* means full of

sexual desires; *lusty,* hearty, vigorous.

luxuriant, luxurious, *adj. Luxuriant* means fruitful, teeming, abundant, as a *luxuriant* growth of hair; *luxurious* means giving delight, comfort; pertaining to extravagant indulgence, as *luxurious* food, life, climate, houses.

lycanthrope (lĭk'ăn thrōp), *n.* Werewolf; madman imagining himself to be a wolf.

lye, *n.* Caustic alkaline solution used in washing and cleaning.

lynch, *v.* Kill or execute without legal process. [name of Col. Charles Lynch, Virginian judge in the Eighteenth Century]

lynch law, *n.* Mob violence as a substitute for legal process in punishment of supposed criminals.

lyric, *n.* Song with musical accompaniment; poem like a song, expressing the poet's feelings.

lysozyme, *n.* Enzyme which lays the stomach wall open to erosion by acids and thus contributes to formation of ulcers.

M

macabre (mă kä'br), *adj.* Suggestive of the Dance of Death; morbidly grotesque.

machete, *n.* Heavy, single-bladed knife used in harvesting sugarcane.

mackinaw, *n.* Double-breasted plaid coat of blanket cloth.

mad, *adj.* Crazy, as in *"mad* as a March hare"; foolish, furious, enraged, frantic. "The poor fellow was *mad* with pain." *Colloq.,* angry.

magic, *n.* Action by or through supernatural forces; *colloq.,* personal magnetism, charm. Black magic is effected by evil supernatural power, that of Satan and his aides.

maintenance, *n.* Support; upkeep.

majority, *n.* Greater of two numbers, more than half; opposite of minority. See **Plurality.**

make, *v.* Make up, compose, invent, compensate for, and *make out,* get along, prove, discern, are *stand. lit. Make over,* reconstruct, is *stand. lit., Am.* but not *Br. Make good* is *colloq.* for the slang *make the* *grade.* To *make* a train, *make* a person (make the acquaintance of), be *on the make* (profiting at somebody else's expense), *make* (steal) something, and *make things hum* are slang. *Make* for *get a place on,* as in "He *made* the team," and *make no bones about* (make no scruple, not to hesitate) are *colloq.*

make like, *v. Low colloq.,* imitate.

make-up, *n.* Constitution; materials such as cosmetics, wigs, and pads used in preparing for a theatrical appearance.

make with, *v. Colloq.;* use, make use of.

maladjusted, *adj.* Ill adapted, deranged, mildly crazy.

Malapropism (măl'a prŏp'ĭsm). Wrong word chosen because of confusion between words of similar sound or appearance but of utterly different meanings. When Winifred Jenkins wrote, "Mistress was taken with the *asterisks,* but they went off," or "O Molly, the servants at Bath are devils *ingarnet,*" she meant *hysterics* and *incarnate.* The words she did write are malapropisms.

mandatory, *adj.* Compulsory, obligatory.

maneuver, *v.* Go through a tactical procedure; manage; manipulate. The spelling manoeuvre is stilted. [*L.,* handwork]

manifesto, *n.* Formal declaration of policy or program.

mannequin, *n.* Mannikin; dressmaker's dummy; anatomical model; model; woman employed to wear articles of apparel so that customers may observe them.

Mannerism. In writing, a stylistic trick, device, or peculiarity that recurs so frequently that it becomes conspicuous or offensive. The persistent use of inversion, or of the same number of adjectives before the nouns, or of poetic rather than common words, would be mannerism. The best style is free from mannerism and affectation.

manual, *adj.* By hand, hand.

manual, *n.* Handbook; keyboard played by hand; *military tech.,* prescribed way of handling a weapon.

Manuscript, *n.* The author's copy of his work, whether written by hand or typewritten as distinguished from the printed copy. *Abbr.* MS., Ms., or ms.; *pl.* MSS., Mss., or mss.

many, much. *Many,* a large number of; *much* a great quantity of. "*Many* snowflakes, *much* snow."

many a. Always requires a *sing. v.* "While there *has* (not *have*) been *many* a sly dig at his singing, he may surprise us all some day."

margarine (mär'gȧ rēn, mär'jȧ rēn), *n.* Edible fat as a substitute for butter.

marinate, *v.* Pickle, soak in brine, allow to lie in seawater; season (as meat for a salad) by soaking for hours in one type of dressing before adding another. [ultimately from Latin, sea]

markedly, *adv.* Conspicuously, notably. Cant word of newspaper critics.

marker, *n.* Memorial stone or plaque; grave stone; pledge, token of a debt.

Marks. See **Signs and Symbols,** and **Punctuation.**

markup, *n. Commercial tech.,* percentage added to cost of manufacture to determine retail price.

martyr, victim, *n. Martyr* means one who voluntarily sacrifices himself for principle or in support of a cause; *victim,* one sacrificed, hurt, or killed under circumstances not in his control or not completely so. *Colloq. victim* means dupe, one who has been cheated, and *martyr* a great or chronic sufferer.

mask-making, *n.* Manufacture of false faces.

masque, *n.* Type of Elizabethan or Jacobean dramatic entertainment with pageantry and music. *Comus* is a masque.

mass-meeting, *n.* Public assemblage, large political meeting.

master, *n. Music tech.,* primary phonographic recording from which commercial records are made.

masterful, masterly, *adj. Masterful* means domineering, powerful; *masterly,* indicating skill or knowledge of a master. "Fielding was a large, *masterful* man." "His treatment of the subject is *masterly.*"

mastermind, *v. Sl.,* solve, direct, coach.

mat, *n.* Small rug; cardboard backing for a picture; padded covering for a floor, especially the floor of a boxing ring.

maté, *n.* Beverage steeped from leaves of a Brazilian plant resembling holly; South American "tea."

material, *adj.* Physical, consisting of matter.

materialize, *v.* Appear as a material form, become realized fact. Should not be used for *appear, happen,* or *come* unless the idea of passing from the idea to the substantial is present. Write "He had the pleasure of seeing his dreams *materialize,*" but not "His breakfast didn't *materialize,*" unless for humorous effect.

materially, *adv.* Substantially. Trite in business letters as a synonym for *largely.*

mathematics, *n.* Science of relations between quantities or magnitudes and of ways in which quantities sought can be deduced. This pl. form is regularly construed as a *sing.*

matrix, *n.* Uterus; copper plate serving as a mold for metal type.

matter, *n.* Physical substance; earth; *colloq.,* pus; fault, defect. "What's the *matter* with Father?"

may. See **can.**

maybe, *adv. Colloq.,* perchance, perhaps.

mayflower, *n.* Trailing arbutus. This is not the *Br.* mayflower.

mayhem, *n.* Maiming; wilful disfigurement. "Modified mayhem" is slang for boxing.

McCoy, the real, *n.* Slang for reliable inside information; the genuine article.

mean, *adj.* Common, low, ignoble, ordinary, stingy, average, shabby. *Colloq.* in the senses of malicious, selfish in a small way, tough, ill. Slang in the sense of formidable: "He packs a *mean* punch." As an *adv.* it is *low colloq.:* "He acts *mean.*" **Meanie** is feminine slang: "You old *meanie.*"

means, *n.* Takes a *pl. v.* when the meaning is *resources, income, property.* "My *means are* slightly increased." Takes a *sing. v.* when the meaning is *way to an end.* "He found *a means* that *is* very effective."

meantime, *n.* Usually occurs in the phrase *in the meantime,* in the interval. **Meanwhile** is an equivalent. Both words

can be used as adverbs. **Mean time** is time measured by the mean sun.

measly, *adj.* Slang in the sense of *worthless, contemptible.*

measure, *n.* In substitute phrases for *much, a little, somewhat, many* and *greatly,* in danger of becoming overworked. "She had contributed *in no small measure* (better *much*) to the success of the penny sociable."

measure up to. Colloq. phrase meaning to qualify for, meet, be sufficiently excellent for or adequate to. "Will the boys *measure up to* these requirements?"

meat, *n. Arch.,* food; *stand. Am.,* flesh food.

meat market, *n.* Butcher shop.

Mecca, *n.* Used by journalists for any place which for some reason becomes the center of interest and is sought by many people. "Niagara Falls, *Mecca* of the newlyweds." Often not capitalized.

MECHANICS. See **Manuscript, Letters, Numbers, Syllabication, Abbreviation, Italics, Capitals, Spelling,** and **Plurals.**

mechanize, *v.* Strengthen by addition of mechanical equipment; substitute mechanical power for horses or men.

medieval (mē' dĭ ē'val, or *Br.* mĕd'i ē'-val), *adj.* In or of the Middle Ages.

meek, *adj.* Passively humble.

meet, *v. Colloq.* in the sense of make the acquaintance of by means of an introduction. "I *met* Mr. Zwilch in Shreveport."

megacycle, *n. Radio tech.,* one million cycles per second.

megaton, *n.* Explosive power equivalent to that of one million tons of TNT.

melancholy, *n.* Dejection; depression of spirits. [Latin, black bile]

meld, *v.* Merge; display honor cards in the game of pinochle.

melodrama, *n.* Sentimental drama with a happy ending.

memento, *pl.* **mementos** or **mementoes,** *n.* Token, reminder; souvenir. [*L.,* imperative "Remember!" first word of prayer for the dead]

memo, *n.* Stump of *memorandum.* Use only in business notes, catalogues, etc.

memorandum, *pl.* **memorandums or**

memoranda, *n.* Note of reminder; informal communication.

menu (mĕn'ū), *n.* Bill of fare; list of foods available in a restaurant.

merchandise, *v.* Sell. **Merchandising** and retail distribution are high-toned terms for selling.

merchant, *n.* Storekeeper, shopkeeper, trader; *Br.,* wholesale dealer.

meretricious, *adj.* Gaudy, alluring by false show, tawdry. [*L.,* prostitute, seller]

mess, *v. Colloq.* in the sense of spoil, meddle, putter, make a mess, and make a mess of.

Messrs., *abbr. Pl.* of Mr. when followed by proper names.

Metaphor. The most common of the figures of speech. An implied comparison; a simile without the *as* or *like.* "These rascals *fleece* the unsuspecting visitors." Here *fleece* is metaphorical for *cheat,* rob. The visitors are thought of as sheep shorn by shearers. But in "They *fleece* the *suckers*" and "Dodge *sifts leaks* in racket inquiry" the metaphors clash.

Meter or **Metre.** The rhythmical pattern in poetry. The four most important metrical feet in English verse are the iambic, ˘′; trochaic, ′˘; anapestic, ˘˘′; and dactylic ′˘˘.

methane (mĕth'ān), *n.* Marsh gas; colorless, odorless hydrocarbon used as fuel and for illumination.

meticulous, *adj.* Although this word has been severely criticized, it is thriving. In fact, it is used so often that it is in danger of becoming hackneyed. Those who use it take it as a term of high praise, and, overlooking its meaning of *too careful of unimportant details,* make it equivalent to *painstakingly exact, accurate, studiously careful.* It is true that *scrupulous* and *punctilious* mean what meticulous is commonly taken to mean, but their other meanings, conscientious, formal, very nice or careful in the observance of forms of conduct, handicap them as rivals of *meticulous.*

Metonymy. A figure of speech in which one thing is put for another, being so closely related that one can stand for the other. *America* for the American territory, people, reputation, history, etc.; *sail* for the boat and all its parts; *rum* for all alcoholic liquors; *board* for the food placed on the (board) table; and *skirts* for *girls.*

metre, meter, *n.* Basic measure of the metric system, about 39.36 inches.

mew, *n.* Breeding place of hawks, cage; *pl. mews,* stables.

microfilm, *n.* Minute photographic copy; film for such photography of manuscript, newsprint, or book page.

Middle Ages, *n.* Period between the Roman Empire and the Renaissance.

midriff, *n.* Diaphragm; part of body between chest and waist; garment which reveals this section; garment which covers this section.

midst, *n.* Occurs in literary phrases, as *in our midst, in your midst, in their midst,* but is rarely used in the spoken language except for humorous effect.

mighty, *adv.* Mightily. A *colloq.* or familiar intensive. "That was *mighty* nice of you to get those tickets."

migraine, *n.* Sick headache; pain on one side of the head. [*Gr.,* half-skull]

mill, *n.* Thousandth part of a dollar; *sl.,* harsh experiences, "through the *mill.*"

mimic, *adj.* Imitative, copying. [*Gr.,* mime, actor in a type of burlesque drama]

mind, *v. Stand. lit.* in the meaning of think of, heed, take charge or care of, dislike, be troubled about, remember, and intend. "Don't *mind* his teasing." "He's mad because he has to *mind* the baby." "I do *mind* his taunts." In the sense of *remind* it is chiefly *dial.* "*Mind* the maid to make the muffins." But "I shouldn't *mind* if I do" is *colloq.* for "Yes, I'll have some."

minimize, decrease, *v.* To *minimize* means to reduce to the least possible amount, or estimate at the lowest possible number or amount or proportion; to *decrease,* to diminish, lessen. "The value of the painting is *decreased* (not *minimized*) by the poor varnish."

minus, *adj. Colloq.* for *without, deprived of, deficient in.* "He was *minus* most of his clothes."

minuscule, *adj.* Very small. [*LL.,* name for a kind of handwriting]

minute (mĭ nŭt′, mī nūt′), *adj.* Very small, tiny, so small as to be hardly perceptible.

Minutes. In the terminology of parliamentary law, a minute is a record of some act or formal statement of an assembly. The minutes of a meeting constitute a record of the business transacted. It is one of the duties of the secretary (sometimes designated but never addressed as *recording secretary*) or clerk of the meeting to draw up the minutes from notes taken while the discussion is in progress.

In digesting his notes, he should endeavor to record what was done at the meeting rather than what was said. The minutes of inexperienced secretaries are often diffuse and misleading because of the inclusion of too many details. "All main motions (except such as are withdrawn) whether adopted or rejected should be entered, and usually the names of the makers of very important main motions but not the seconders; points of order and appeals, whether sustained or lost, and all other motions that were not lost or withdrawn." In short, the minutes should be a condensed and formal account of the business transacted, rather than a journalistic story of the debate.*

* General Henry W. Robert, *Parliamentary Law* . . . New York, 1923, p. 315. Cf. *Cushing's Manual of Parliamentary Practice*, new ed. revised by Albert S. Bolles (1925), pp. 32, 37.

minutia, *pl.* **minutiae** (mĭ nū′shĭ ē), *n.* Detail, minor point of information.

miscellaneous, *adj.* Various, heterogeneous.

mishmash, *n.* Jumbled mixture.

Misplaced Word. Words like *ever, almost, only, nevertheless,* and *however* are likely to settle down near words that they should not modify or affect in any way. A *conj.* like *nevertheless* should always be placed near or at the beginning of the clause to which it belongs; adverbs should as a rule stand near the words they modify. The italicized words in the following sentences are misplaced. "Jack *only* seems to become sentimental when he talks about

Margery." "I *only* need a few tubes of oil colors." "Kelly was ill but played a fine game which was lost *nevertheless.*" "She doesn't *ever* intend to speak to you again." See **Adverbs** and **Intruders.**

Misquotation. Try to quote accurately. If you quote from Bunyan or Shakespeare or Frost and make a mistake, that mistake will be discovered by some reader.

The man recovered from the bite;
It was the dog that died,

is a misquotation from Goldsmith's "Elegy on a Mad Dog." The lines are:

The man recovered of the bite;
The dog it was that died.

If you wish to verify a quotation, a concordance or a dictionary of quotations may be helpful.

miss, *n.* Miss is capitalized when it is a title of courtesy prefixed to the name of an unmarried woman or girl. It is rarely used to mean unmarried woman or girl except sportively, as in "What a pert *miss!*" or commercially, as in *Misses' and Ladies' Fashions.* Say "*Miss* West" if the person addressed is the elder daughter, "*Miss* Dorothea West" if a younger daughter, and "the *Misses* West" in referring to both.

misspell, *v.* Spell incorrectly.

mistreat, *v.* Maltreat, abuse.

mitigate, *v.* Make less severe.

Mixed Construction. A faulty construction caused by scrambling two ways of saying something. Some notorious examples follow. "The largest of any tree in Oregon" is a strange mixture of "larger than any other tree" and "largest of all the trees." "One of the, if not the, best car(s)" is a mixture of "one of the best cars" and "the best car." "Of one's own account" scrambles "of one's own accord" and "on one's own account." "Of all others" is a compromise between "of all ——s" and "beyond (or more than) all others." Write "You are the woman *of all women* I wanted to see," and not "You are the woman *of all others* I wanted to see."

When one mixes the construction of a whole sentence the result is quite disastrous. In "He felt that it was his duty *to supply* money as well as *giving his* time to see that contributions reached deserving people," *giving* should be *give* or the sentence changed to "He felt that *supplying* money as well as *giving* his time . . ."

Mixed Metaphor. The most common form of the mixed image or comparison. Do not superimpose two or more metaphors if they are alive and clash, or do not mix such figurative expressions indiscriminately with the literal. In the following sentence, the first comparison is with an object fixed in a firm stratum, the second metaphor is practically dead, the third changes the firm stratum into a stream, and the last comparison is with an abandoned boat. "But the problem remains *embedded* and *unsolved* in the *life stream* of our social system, a pathetic and abject *derelict.*" Better: "The problem remains in our social system and is still unsolved." In "The movement *ripened* into *bloom*" the first comparison is with a fruit and the second with the flower, but the second should come first since the flower comes before the fruit.

mixer, *n. Colloq.,* socially adaptable person; one who enjoys society, gets along well with people.

mob, *n.* Rabble, disorderly crowd; *sl.,* gang. [*L., Mobile vulgus,* slang that has become *stand. lit.*]

mobile (mō'bl, mō'bēl), *adj.* Susceptible of motion; able to move.

mobster, *n. Sl.,* gangster.

moccasin, *n.* Footgear of soft leather, often with sole and upper fashioned in the same piece. [Indian]

mock-heroic. See **Burlesque.**

mockup, *n.* Inexpensive or relatively simple full-size model of an expensive or complicated gown, piece of machinery, or ship.

Modifier Misplaced. Modifiers must be so placed that there can be no doubt about what they modify. They must not be intruders and split groups of words that belong together. Awkwardness, obscured meaning, or ambiguity results from dangling or squinting modifiers, intrusive words, and bad word order. "Nineteen killed by hailstones as big as coconuts *in*

Africa" and "What is good for the people *in the long run* is good for the government" contain *misplaced modifiers.*

An *adv.* or adverbial phrase preceding the subject of two verbs regularly modifies both verbs. The following sentence is faulty because the beginning phrase cannot logically modify *remained.* "*In the summer of 1934* the Burtons went to Italy and remained there *until the summer of 1936.*"

modulation, *n.* Smooth series of changes as of the speaking voice; *radio tech.,* variation of carrier wave to broadcast tones originated by audio wave.

monitor, *n.* One who, or that which warns; obsolete type of armored craft with one or more revolving gun turrets; listening post for checking of radio transmission.

monkey, *v. To monkey with* is *stand. lit.* meaning to tamper or meddle with. *Monkey* is slang in *monkey around* and as an *adj.* in *monkey business.*

monkeynut, *n. Br.* peanut.

monkeyshines, *n. pl.* Comic tricks, capers.

monkeysuit, *n.* Dress clothes; uniform.

monolith, *n.* Monument consisting of one rocky pillar or upright block of stone.

monologue, *n.* Speech uttered by one person.

monopoly, *n.* Exclusive control of a commodity or service; the company having a *monopoly;* the commodity or service thus controlled; exclusive possession of anything. With *of* (*Br.*) and *on* (*Am.*) "The government was given the *monopoly* on tobacco." *Entire monopoly* and *complete monopoly* are redundant.

monotone, *n.* Single tone; person who intones when he tries to sing.

Monotonous Sentences. To avoid monotonous repetition of the same kind of sentences, vary the length, diversify sentence beginnings, and change sentence types, as from loose to periodic or balanced, or from declarative to interrogative or exclamatory. If used with tact, the rhetorical question and quotation will give variety. Do not use inversion unless there is a purpose other than that of breaking the monotony. Artificiality and cheapness are worse than a decent but rather humdrum style. See **Variety for Effectiveness.**

montage (mŏn tägh′), *n.* Pictorial combination made by imposing parts of two or more pictures on a single background.

mooch, *v. Sl.,* beg, borrow with no intention of repaying; wheedle.

moocher, *n. Sl.,* person who borrows with no intention of repaying.

moose, *n.* Large mammal of deer family. A "Bull Mooser" or "Bull Moose" was a follower of T. Roosevelt in 1912. [Algonquian]

mop up, *v.* Clean thoroughly; glean the surviving enemies in territory beyond which a victorious battleline has passed; soak up.

moppet, *n.* Child, unpleasant child. An archaic term revived as a witty cant word of city sophisticates.

more than one. *Pl.* in sense but takes a *sing. v.* and agrees with a *sing. n.* "*More than one* fireman (not *firemen*) was (not *were*) overcome."

mores (mōr′ēz), *n. pl.* Customs; folkways. [*L., mos, sing., mores, pl.*]

moron, *n.* Feeble-minded person; adult of mental age 8, 9, 10, or 11; vicious fool; sexual pervert. [*Gr.,* dull, stupid]

morphology, *n.* Biological science of form and structure of living things; linguistic study of forms of words, especially of inflections.

mortician, *n.* Undertaker. Elegant variation for funeral director.

most, *adj.* Superlative degree of *many* and *much.* Used as an *adv.* to form the superlative of *adj.* or *adv.*; e.g., *most cheerful, most cheerfully. Colloq.* and *dial.* when used for *almost* in the sense of *nearly.*

mot (mō), *n.* A witticism. The expression is a Gallicism. *Mot juste,* the exact word, is still French.

motel, *n.* Hotel for motorists. See **Acronym.**

motif, *n.* Main theme of a work of art.

motivate, *v.* Impel, stimulate to action by showing or providing reasons of selfish advantage. (Overworked in the jargon of educationists)

motivation, *n.* Motive, driving force that causes decision or action.

motorcade, *n.* Procession or train of motorcars with a common goal or purpose.

motorize, *v.* Provide with motors or motor vehicles "motorized cavalry."

mountebank, *n.* Faker, cheap showman; quack doctor; charlatan. [Italian, climb up on the bench]

move, *v. Colloq.* in the senses of *show marked activity, get under way rapidly,* as in "Business is beginning to *move.*" With or without *on,* meaning to go away or depart, as in "Please *move on,*" it is also *colloq.,* but "Get a *move on*" is slang.

movie, *n.* Motion picture, usually in *pl.*

movie-struck, *adj. Sl.,* intent on becoming, or continuing to be, a motion picture performer.

Mrs. (mǐs′ǐz, mǐs′ǐs, Southern mǐz′ǐz), *Abbr.* of *mistress.* Mrs. has superseded *mistress* as a title of courtesy for a married woman except *dial.*

much, *adv.* As a rule, *much* modifies participles and comparative adjectives and adverbs, and *very,* positive and superlative adjectives and adverbs. *Much pleased, much older; very fast, very glad.* Never use *very* immediately before a *p. part.* in *-ed* unless it has become a true *adj.* in common use, as *tired* and *celebrated* have but *perturbed* has not. "He is *very tried,*" but "We shall be *very much perturbed* if she does not return."

much, *n.* A great or indefinite quantity. "This *much* he would say and no more." *As* is more formal than *that* in sentences like "I could have told you *that* (as) *much* myself." Sometimes *much* may be regarded as an *adj.* modifying a word that is expressed, and may therefore be modified by *as, so, too,* and *very.* "This is *too much* for the Martins."

Do not write *much less* for *much more. Much less* is used only in sentences that are negative in effect as well as in expression. "I did not even ask the price of it, *much less* (not *much more*) buy it." "It would be impossible for any American, *much more* (not *much less*) an American who was stupid and provincial to gain their confidence."

Muchly, like *thusly*, is a facetious formation.

muckraker, *n.* One who looks for crime or scandal. [Used by T. Roosevelt, alluding to *Pilgrim's Progress*]

mugger, *n.* Robber who chokes his victim and beats him in the face or "mug." This word is not connected with *Br.* Indian "mugger," crocodile.

mugwump, *n.* Independent in politics; politician who avoids taking sides on important issues. [Algonquian, chief]

mum, *n.* *Colloq.*, chrysanthemum, a clipped word.

muscle in, *v.* Intrude violently (with *on*), seize a share in, seize a share in the business of.

muse, *v.* Think deeply and quietly, ponder.

Muse, *n.* Goddess of lyric poetry. In systematic mythology there are nine Muses, one for each of nine types of creative art; Clio for history, Euterpe (ū tŭr′pē) for song with instrumental accompaniment of flute, Thalia (thá lī′ä) for comic poetry, Melpomene (měl pŏm′ē nē) for choral dance and song, Erato (ĕr′ä tō) for erotic poetry; Polyhymnia (pŏl ē hĭm′ nĭ á) for sacred song, Urania (ū rā′nē á) for astronomy, and Calliope (kál ī′ ō pē) for eloquence and epic poetry.

mushroom, *v.* Spread out.

muskellunge, *n.* Large game fish of the Great Lakes. [Chippewa Indian name]

muskrat, *n.* Big aquatic rodent with webbed feet, long scaly tail, and glossy brown pelt.

must not, must only. Often substituted for *may not, may only,* although strictly *must not* means is obliged not to and *may not* means is not allowed to. *May not* in the sense of is not allowed to is infrequent except in questions implying a positive answer. "*Mayn't* I have some?" implies "I suppose I am allowed to have some." Or in answers following a *may.* "*May* I enter the contest?" "I am sorry; you *may* not." *Must not* has therefore become the usual manner of expressing prohibition. "I am enter-

ing the contest." "Nó, you *must not.*" See **got.**

mutt, *n.* Mongrel; dull person; dolt.

mutual, common, *adj.* *Mutual* implies interchanged action. Strictly, whatever is *mutual* is reciprocally given and received, e.g., *mutual* esteem. *Mutual* things must at least bear the same relation to each other. One of the meanings of *common,* shared alike by two or more, is similar, but careful writers would say *common effort, common endeavor,* rather than *mutual effort, mutual endeavor.*

myriad, *adj., n.* Ten thousand; very numerous.

myself, *pron.* Do not use *myself* in the place of *I* or *me* unless you wish to emphasize *I,* as in "I have been there *myself*"; or unless you use it as a reflexive, as in "I shaved *myself.*" It is false modesty to say "The Smiths and *myself* were honored." "The Smiths and I" is better. But the *me* in the *dial.* or old-fashioned "I bought *me* a cigar" should be *myself.*

myth, *n.* A story of gods we no longer believe in; a story that explains how something was formed or made; why the water is salty and the opossum's tail bare; by extension, any fabulous tale. A person or thing existing only in the imagination. See **legendary.**

N

nacelle (ná sĕl′), *n.* Cabin or cockpit for passengers in a dirigible; inclosure for passengers in an airplane. [Fr., little boat]

Nahuatlan, *adj.* Belonging to a Mexican Indian linguistic stock or group of tribes.

naïve (nä ēv′), *adj.* Ingenuous, unaffectedly or amusingly simple. The feminine form of a French *adj.* that has become Anglicized. Do not bother with the masculine form *naïf.* The *n.* **naïveté** (nä ēv tä′) is also Anglicized and need not be italicized.

name, *v.* Appoint, designate.

narcosis, *n.* Stupor; treatment with narcotics. [*Gr.*, stun, benumb]

Narration. The account of an event or a series of events bearing upon the same issue. Some general directions: present the story graphically; arrange an ordered progression; know your reader and do not forget him; make the directing idea clear; and make the story self-explanatory and complete.

nary, *adj.* Never a, not one. Cf. *nairy,* not any, not the least, and *ary,* ever a, any. All *dial.*

nasty, *adj.* Foul, indecent, disgusting, dangerous.*Colloq.* in the senses of *disagreeable, offensive, objectionable, mean,* and *dishonorable.* "What a *nasty* day." "That was a *nasty* trick to play." Ironically used in a complimentary sense, as in "He slings a *nasty* pen," meaning he writes a trenchant style. Cf. *mean.*

naturalism, *v.* Realism based on a materialistic or determinist philosophy; the art of Zola.

naughty, *adj. Arch.,* worthless, bad; *stand. lit. Am.,* wayward, childishly mischievous.

near, *adj.* Immediate; close at hand.

near, *adv.* Not used as much as the *adv. nearly.* It is an *adj.* in *near relative, near silk, etc.* Meaning stingy it is *colloq.* like *close* in the same sense. *Near by,* or *near-by, adv.* is *colloq.* for *near, close by,* as "They are going to a camp *near by.*" *Near* is also a *prep.* meaning *close to.* Compounds made of *near* and an *adj.* are usually *stand. lit.,* e.g., *near-white, near-antique, near-related;* but *near-* and *n.* compounds are as a rule not established; e.g., *near-beer, near-shortage.*

nearby, *adj.* Neighboring; close at hand.

nebula, *pl.* **nebulae** (nĕb'ū lē), *n.* Cloud; gaseous structure of cloudlike appearance within our astronomical system; cloudlike concentration of billions of stars remote from our system.

necessary, *adj.* See **essential, necessary, requisite** for distinctions in meaning.

nee (nā), *adj.* Born. Used to introduce the maiden family name of a married woman: "Mrs. Bull, *nee* Wild."

need, *v.* Preferred to *needs* or *needed* in interrogative and negative sentences. Here it does not require a *to.* "She *need* not be called," but "He *needed to* be reminded." Do not use the *adv. needs,* needs must, as

if it were a *pl.* of *need, n.* Write "The coach gave him, when it was *necessary* (not *when needs were*), a day or two of rest."

needle, *v. Colloq.,* tease, heckle; *sl.,* strengthen by adding alcohol.

negative, *n.* Denial, exact opposition; the minus sign; picture, commonly transparent, on the front of which the relations of right and left and light and dark are the opposites of those in the object depicted.

Negatives. One must be very careful about the use of negatives such as *neither, not, no, nor,* especially when they occur in parallel clauses. One must remember that when the negative is attached to an auxiliary *v.* or similar word that is common to both clauses, the negative force is carried over into the second clause. "There is scarcely a clerk there who *has not* bought stocks and [has not] succeeded in drawing dividends from them." This sentence would be faulty if *is* were written for *succeeded in,* for then *has not* would not be supplied before the second *v.* Faulty: "There is scarcely a clerk there who *has not* bought stocks and *is* drawing dividends from them."

Do not let a negative carry over if the second clause is to be affirmative. "*No* writer who is given the award will want the decision to be set aside, or will (better *but any such writer will at least*) consider it an injustice if it is set aside."

The correlative *neither* is followed by *nor. Nor* commonly follows *not* in sentences like "They will *not* sign the contract, *nor* will they say positively that they will *not,*" where the second member expresses an alternative. But in sentences like "He is *not* interested in chemistry *or* any other science," where the second member expresses an extension, *not* is commonly followed by *or.*

negotiate, *v.* Sell, transfer, bring about by conferring. *Colloq.* in the sense of *tackle successfully, meet a test, surmount an obstacle.* "I suppose my car will *negotiate* that hill."

Negress, *n.* Female Negro, rare in the Northern U.S., where *Negro* is both *m.* and *fem.*

Negro (nē′grō), *n.* Person of the African dark race, Ethiopian; *Am. colloq.*, person of mixed ancestry, partly negroid. The *adj.* is also in good use.

Negroid, *adj.* Characteristic of the Negro race.

neighborhood, *n.* Proximity, vicinity; community; people living near one another. In the *neighborhood* of, awkward periphrasis for *about*.

neither (preferably nē ther), *pron.* Strictly, *not either of two*, but commonly *not either of two or more than two*. "I have *neither* time nor patience, nor the inclination, nor the right to do this thing." *Neither* is the correlative of *nor*. Cf. *either, or*. Correlatives are regularly followed by the same kind of grammatical construction; e.g., "They will *neither talk* nor *eat*." As a rule *neither* is followed by a *sing. v.*

As an *adv.* meaning *any more so,* and placed at the end of a clause to emphasize a preceding *nor, not,* or *no,* it is now chiefly *dial.* "He didn't like the cook, *nor* I *neither*."

nemesis (něm′ē sĭs), *n.* Capitalize when you mean the Greek goddess of retributive justice. It is given a *pl.* in *-es* and usually *sp.* with small letters when it means an act of retribution or one who inflicts condign punishment.

neoclassicism, *n.* European literary trend of the early Eighteenth Century, "analytic, objective, collective, and cosmopolitan," conforming to supposed critical standards of Aristotle and Horace and precedents derived from the classical writers of Greece and Rome.

Neologism. The general term for a word newly introduced into the language. A neologism may be good, as are most of the Greek and Latin loan words introduced in the Renaissance, or as most of the newly coined words that name the new inventions, the new ways of life and thought; e.g., *science, standpoint, skyscraper, outlook, airman, telephone, handbook, jaywalker*. Or it may be bad because unnecessary or badly made or unintelligible; e.g., *doughnutery, deinsectized, lovelify, oldfangled*. See **Coined Word.**

neo- suffix, *n.* Suffix newly introduced into the language or widely used in neologisms. American suffixes which have entered into the formation of many short-lived coinages are *-cade* (as in *cavalcade* whence *motorcade*), *-eria* (in analogues of *cafeteria*) and *-orium* (as in *lubritorium* meaning) an oil station). Here again we take a tip from Mencken (AL:S 1, p. 354).

neptunium, *n.* Element derived from uranium bombarded with neutrons.

nerve, *n.* Band of nervous tissue; mental stamina, courage, resolution. Slang in the sense of *impudence, effrontery, audacity*. Slang synonyms are *face, cheek, crust, gall, brass*. The *adj.* **nervy** is *colloq.* in the sense of *audacious*. The old meaning of *sinew*, *tendon*, is preserved in the phrase *strain every nerve*.

neutron, *n.* Uncharged particle nearly as large as a proton.

newscast, *n.* Broadcast news program.

next, *adj. The next man* means *anyone*. In this sense it is *stand. lit.* "He knows that as well as *the next man*." *Next* is slang in *get next to*, get power over, find out the truth about or secret of, bribe.

nice, *adj.* Accurately used to mean *requiring or having precision, critical taste, delicate sensitivity*, etc., but used too frequently as a mere counterword of approval. "The man was *nice* (considerate)." "The cake was *nice* (tasteful)." "The policeman was *nice* (friendly)." "We had a *nice* time (enjoyable time)." *Nicely, adv.,* in the sense of *satisfactorily,* is *colloq.* "The baby is getting along *nicely*."

nickel, *n.* Five-cent piece, whether of nickel alloy or other base metal. (There was once a five-cent silver piece.) Cf. *jitney*.

Nickname. An eke or added name. Nicknames include: (1) short and familiar forms of given names, *Al, Jack, Moll;* (2) names made up from habits, appearance, special abilities, peculiarities, etc., "Wild Bill" Hickok, "Fatty" Ross, "Dead-Eye" Dick, "Dizzy" Dean (quoted except in the sport pages); (3) sobriquets (sō′brĭ kā), names (usually laudatory) to take the place of given name and surname: *The Little Corporal, The Sage of Concord, The Lone*

Eagle, The Wizard of Menlo Park, Old Hickory (not quoted unless the surname is used with them).

nifty, *adj. Colloq.,* neat, charming, pretty, ingeniously adapted. It is radio slang as a noun meaning clever joke, smart quip.

nihilism, *n.* Nothingness; philosophy based on denial of objective reality; extreme political radicalism, advocating complete destruction of the present social system; practical anarchy.

nip-and-tuck, *adj.* Close, neck-and-neck, like a photo finish.

Nisei (nē'sā), *n.* American of Japanese ancestry; person born in the U.S. of Japanese ancestry.

nitwit, *n. Sl.,* fool, ignorant person, dullard.

nix, *adv. Colloq.,* no, never, not at all. *n.* Nothing. [*Ger., nichts,* nothing]

no-account, *adj. Dial.* as in "She wants father to sell that old *no-account* saddle horse."

nohow, *adv. Dial.* for *by no means, not at all.*

nom de plume (nŏm' de plōōm'), *n.* Pen name, pseudonym; e.g., Mark Twain. **Nom de guerre** is still French and pronounced as French. It means "war name," an assumed name under which one fights, plays, etc.; e.g., Joe Louis, Al Simmons.

nomenclature, *n.* System of names; naming used in classification.

nominal, *adj.* Existing practically in name only. A *nominal* price is so low that it is considered as having no quality of price left save the name. *Very nominal* is therefore redundant.

Nominative Absolute. The same as **Absolute Construction,** q.v.

no more, not more; no less, not less. *No more than five* means *five only. Not more than five* means *five at the most.* "She weighs *no less* than 200 pounds" expresses surprise that the person weighs as much as 200 pounds. "She weighs *not less* than 200 pounds" implies that the person weighs 200 pounds at least and perhaps more.

Nonce Word. Word coined for a special occasion but not taken into the language; e.g., Mark Twain's *cavalieress.*

none, *adv.* Not at all. "She will be none the wiser."

none, *pron.* Not one. Now used either as a *sing.* or *pl.* "*None* of these things *are* harmful." "There is *none* in this box."

non-objective, *adj.* Abstract, aesthetically expressive but not pictorial.

non sequitur (nŏn sĕk'wĭ ter). Latin for *it does not follow.* An inference or conclusion that is fallacious because it does not follow from the premises.

no ¶. Do not paragraph here.

no place, *adv. Am. dial.* for *nowhere.* "*No place* (better *nowhere*) could she find her keys."

norm, *n.* What is normal, general rule derived from the middle group of a large number of observed cases.

no sooner . . . than. Do not complete *no sooner* with *before* or *until.* "*No sooner* had they arrived *than* (not *before*) they decided to return."

no such a. Do not write *a* or *an* after *no such, kind of,* or *sort of.* "There is *no such* (a) person."

notable, noted, notorious, *adj. Notable* means worthy of fame; *noted,* well known for some particular thing; and *notorious,* known widely, usually for something bad. In reference to facts, *notorious* means well-known, talked of, but in reference to a person or thing it means unfavorably known, known to deserve an ill name. "Edmonds is a *noted* novelist." "That was a *notable* performance." "He was a public hero, although his private life was *notorious.*"

notarize, *v.* Attest or acknowledge (deed or contract); certify as a notary public.

notch, *n.* Nick, cut in a tally stick or rule, V-shaped indentation; mountain pass. *Topnotch* means first-rate, the best.

not hardly, not scarcely. Do not use *not* with *hardly* or *scarcely.* "The moose could (not) *hardly* swim the rapids." "There was (not) *scarcely* enough bacon for breakfast."

not only. See to it that *not only* comes at the right place in the sentence. "*Not only* had she now a chance to vindicate herself, *but* to do it in the most effective manner" should be "She had now a chance *not only* to vindicate herself *but* to do it in the most effective manner." The *also* in *not only . . . but also* is not always needed. "The number of ducks varied *not only* with the season *but* with the weather."

Noun. The name of anything presented as a thing; *weed, sign, patience, covey, word.*

no use. Established as an *adj.* meaning of no avail, of no advantage to, as in "It's *no use* to ask that fellow," "It's *no use.*" It is more formal if it follows *of.* "It's *of no use* to talk to him." Also as a *n.* "There's *no use* in that." To have *little* or *no use* for, means to account of little or no worth.

nova, *n.* New star; star newly discovered because of a sudden increase in its luminosity.

novice, *n.* See **amateur.**

novocaine, *n.* Alkaline used as a local anesthetic. [< *L.,* new + cocaine]

now, *n. Journalistic,* present time. "As of now" is awkward and trite; prefer *now* alone or *at present.*

nowhere near, *adv. Stand. lit.* for not nearly, not by a great deal. "Supper is *nowhere near* ready." **Nowheres,** *adv.* is *dial.* for *nowhere.*

nub, *n.* Kernel, seed; central idea, main point; knob.

nubbin, *n.* Stunted ear of corn.

Number. In grammar, difference in word form to indicate whether a word is *sing.* or *pl.* A mistake in *number* is usually a mistake in **Agreement,** q.v.

number, *n. Low colloq.* in the sense of *information serving to classify a person as being of a certain kind or type.* "I've got your *number.*"

number of. *A number of* takes a *pl. v.,* while *the number of* takes a *sing.* one. "A *number of* members *are* absent." "The *number of* members absent *is* alarming."

numbers, *n. pl.* Policy game, daily lottery. Also called *numbers pool.*

numerous, *adj.* Improperly used for *many* in its *n.* sense of *a large number.* "He has patented a score of inventions, *numerous* (better *many*) of which can be marketed." Do not use *numerous* when merely

several of, a few of, certain of which, many, or *a number* is meant. *Numerous* usually calls attention to the number of units in a collection; e.g., *a numerous library.* Write: "There were *a great number* of politicians on the platform"; not "There were *numerous* politicians . . ."

numismatics, *n.* Coin-collecting as a hobby. The *pl.* form is *sing.* in construction, by analogy from mathematics.

nut, *n. Sl.,* lunatic; insane person.

nut-factory, *n. Sl.,* hospital for nervous disorders; sanitarium; insane asylum.

nuts, *adj. Sl.,* demented, deranged, unstable. Sometimes spelled *nerts* in derisive representation of N.Y. provincial pronunciation.

nylon, *n.* Coal-tar derivative used in manufacture of hosiery, flat cloth, and brushes.

O

oaf, *n.* Awkward simpleton. [*OE,* elf]

oar, *v.* Row.

oasis, *pl.* **oases,** *n.* Island of fertility in a desert region.

objective, *adj.* Detached, impersonal; viewing events and phenomena apart from self-consciousness; *n.* goal, aim, end, purpose.

obligate, *v.* Indebt, place under moral or legal duty.

oblige, *v. Colloq.* in the meaning of perform, sing, etc., as in "Miss Perkins will now *oblige* with a recitation." Old-fashioned in the complimentary close of a letter; ". . . *and oblige* (better *I am*) Yours very truly."

oblivious, unconscious, *adj. Oblivious* means forgetful, no longer mindful; *unconscious* means not aware. "After this quarrel she was *oblivious* of all criticism, whether adverse or favorable." "He probably went away quite *unconscious* of the happiness he had given us." *Oblivious* is used with *to,* but is usually followed by *of.*

obscurantism (ob skyōōr' ant ism), *n.* Opposition to enlightenment and progress.

observance, observation, *n. Observance* is the keeping or carrying out of a duty, custom, or rule; *observation* is a taking notice, a noting of facts, that which is noted, a comment or statement. "The secretary was told that close *observation* (not *observance*) of foreign affairs was essential." "They wish us to enforce the *observance* (not *observation*) of this regulation."

Observation. In description the ability to observe closely and accurately is essential. A person with well-developed powers of observation will see a hundred interesting and significant things where another will see only the obvious. Most people see only what they are looking for. The attitude one takes toward the objects to be described affects his description of them. If one takes the *scientific point of view*, he will strive to be accurate and impersonal, seeking to free himself from bias due to *preconceived ideas, prejudices*, or anything that dictates what is to be seen or the manner of its being seen. If one takes the *artistic point of view*, he will give more freedom to the imagination and feelings. But no describer can afford to be led astray by illusions, to infringe upon *physical point of view*, or to be guilty of the *pathetic fallacy, false local color*, or the *anachronism*.

Obsolete. An obsolete word or expression is one too old to be used. Those like *yclept, eftsoons, lemman* (lover), have lost their meanings for the modern reader, who will, however, understand *hath, hast, thee, thou, doth, quoth*. These are archaic or obsolescent. See **Poeticism; Archaism.**

obstacle (ŏb′stĭkl, ŏb′stă kĕl), *n.* Hindrance, obstruction, that which stands in the way.

obtain, *v.* Especially useful in the sense of *be established in practice or use*, and *prevail* or *be in fashion*. "Widely different agricultural methods *obtain* in these districts." But in the sense of *acquire* it is often merely a formal word for *get*. "They *obtained* (*got*) that back number of *Fortune*."

occasionally, *adv.* Now and then, infrequently.

occur, occurred, occurring, *v.* Appear; happen.

occurrence, *n.* Happening; incident, event.

ocelot, *n.* American leopard. [Nahuatl]

octave, *n.* Any group of eight; first eight lines of a sonnet; interval between two musical tones one of which has twice the vibration frequency of the other.

octavo, *pl.* **octavos,** *n.* Book bound in units of eight leaves or sixteen pages.

odds, *n.* Correctly a *sing.* in "What's the *odds?*" and a *pl.* in "The *odds* are against us."

ode, *n.* Formal lyric; Greek choral song of the type perfected by Pindar.

of, *prep. Colloq.* in sense of before. "He left at a quarter of."

of, *prep.* Use the *of* phrase rather than the *'s* to indicate possession when the possessor is an inanimate object. Write *foot of the bed*, not *the bed's foot*. For exception see **Possessive of Inanimate Objects.** Sometimes *abbr.* as *o'*, as in *o'clock*, John o'Kent. *Of* is usually redundant in *feel of, taste of*, etc. Do not write *of* for *off*. *All of* . . . is good idiom even though the object of *of* has not been divided; e.g., "*All of the men* in the world."

Do not write (or pronounce) *of* (ŏv, ′v) after *might, would, should*, etc., for *have*, as in "She might *have* (not *of*) broken down the door." Do not pronounce *couple of* (kŭplŭ).

of course. Trite phrase. See **course.**

off, *adv., adj.,* and *prep.* One of the adjectival meanings of *off* is *away from the truth, divergent from a true line or exact figure*; hence *delirious, crazy, ill*, as in "He's a little *off* today." Another meaning is *below standard*. "The party is *off*" is *stand. lit.*, but "The game is *called off*" is *colloq. All off* is slang for *rejected, absolutely refused, ended*, but *well off* is *stand. lit.*

As a substitute for *of* or *from, off* is *dial.* or *low colloq.* "I got a dime *off* father." The *of* and *from* in *off of* and *off from* are usually redundant. "He helped get the cat *off* (*of*) the roof."

offhand, *adj.* Unpremeditated; casual; not based on studious preparation.

off the record, *adv.* and *adj. phrase.* Private, privately; not for publication or use as evidence.

officialdom, n. Group of persons in authority, administrative officers as a class.

often (awfn), adv. The t after an f in the middle of a word is often silent. **Oft** is poetic.

O.K. also written **OK, okay,** adv. All right. [Initials of Old Kinderhook, hometown of Martin Van Buren]

okie, n. Wanderer or refugee from the Oklahoma Dust Bowl; seasonal worker; hobo.

old, adj. Colloq. as a term of endearment or disapproval. "Where is that old fool?" Old fellow, old woman, old Nick. Old maid is the popular term for the obsolescent spinster. Colloq. old maid denotes a timorous, fussy, nervous person, especially nowadays a man. Old is colloq. also as an intensive with other adjectives: high old time, grand old man.

oligarchy, n. Government by a few; small ruling group. This is one of the 102 Great Ideas of Chicago U.

Omission. The omission of a necessary word or phrase is indicated by a caret (ʌ). Some omissions are obligatory, some are permissible, and some injurious. The omission of the relative pron. in the objective case is permissible but not obligatory. "He kicked every dog (that) he could corner." The omission of the anticipatory it is injurious. Write "What it was feared might happen, has happened."

Colloquial style admits of more clipped sentences and the leaving out of more dispensable elements than the formal, but no writer should emulate the recipe-telegram short-hand: "Beat eggs. Add flour, butter, sugar. Mix."

Do not omit anything that is not readily supplied by the context, or that is needed to make the sentence perfectly clear. "The duck I just missed won't stop before Florida (before it gets to Florida)." However, the omission of a necessary word is no worse than the repetition of words that should not be repeated. But connectives, pronouns, and auxiliary verbs must sometimes be repeated for the sake of clearness. "That is the singer who came from Dead Gulch, Idaho, and is called the Marvel of

the West (insert who after and)." Never omit transitions unless you are perfectly certain that the connection is obvious.

omnidirectional, adj. In all directions; receiving stimuli from various points and distances.

on, prep. Chiefly colloq. when, in combination with a v., the meaning is hindering, bothering, costing, as in "The pace told on him," "The furnace went out on him," "Have one on me." Slang in the sense of have special information about, advantage over; and with get in the sense of comprehend. "He has something on me." "They were quick to get on to that trick."

on, adv. In verb-adverb combination, often the v. alone is sufficient and the on superfluous, e.g., continue on. But often such a verb-adverb combination is stand. lit.: count on, push on, rely on. Bank on and plan on are colloq. On is superfluous in further on and later on.

Omit the from the phrases on (the) account of.

on hand, adj. phrase. Available, present, handy; in stock.

on purpose, adv. phrase. Colloq., intentionally.

on time, adj. or adv. phrase. Punctual, punctually; on credit.

once in a while, idiomatic phrase, adv. Occasionally.

once-over, n. Sl., for hurried examination, cursory survey. "He gave the mail the once-over."

one. One is the impersonal pron. It is usually followed by he or his in Am. usage, but sometimes a one seems preferable, as when it introduces a parallel clause. "One should always remember that he is not the only person to be considered." But "If one is sick, one ought to call a doctor." "You have to remember your friends on Christmas" is correct but less formal than the one construction.

The possessive is one's. Although normally sing. in meaning, with an adj., one can be pluralized: good ones, other ones.

oneself, pron. The reflexive and emphatic form of *one*. *Oneself* is preferred to one's *self*.

only, *adv.* Likely to be misplaced. The tendency is to write it too soon. Placed wrongly in "I *only* borrowed ten dollars," but right in "I *only* borrowed the ten dollars," or "I borrowed *only* ten dollars."

Onomatopoeia (ŏn'ō măt'o pē'yȧ). The formation of words imitating the sounds they stand for; the use of words whose sounds suggest the meaning; an echoic word. *Hiss, hoot, growl*, are *onomatopoetic* or *echoic* words.

onomatopoeic, *adj.* Suiting the sound to the sense; imitative in sound. Variant of *onomatopoetic*.

onto, *prep.* To and upon. May be written *onto* or *on to*, but *onto* is chiefly *colloq.* after verbs of motion where one would normally expect *on* or *upon.* "They ran out *onto* (*stand. lit. upon*) the stage." Cf. "They walked *on* to Smith's" where *on* is an *adv.* Old *slang*, conversant with, understanding, commonly as two words. See **hep.**

oodles, *n. pl. Sl.*, large quantities.

op. cit. *Abbr.* of the Latin for *title already cited*. Used in footnotes to refer to a book; e.g., Bryce, *op. cit.*, p. 26.

operate, *v.t.* and *v.i. Colloq.* for *deal in stocks speculatively*. An overworked *v.*, being used often when *work, run, conduct, carry on, deal in*, would be better. In careless English one *operates* a *pump, college, wagon, boat, canal*, or *park*. Write "Smithers was *operated* (*up*)*on*," not "Smithers was *operated*."

opinion, *n.* Belief; judgment; reasoned decision formally phrased.

Opinion or Fact? Is this statement opinion or fact? Let your reader know whether you are giving him what you believe or think about something (or what someone else believes or thinks) or *facts*. A *fact* is a thing done or existing, a real event, quality, or relation.

opossum, *n.* Omnivorous *Am.* marsupial with a prehensile, hairless tail. [Indian]

opposite, *adj.* Opposed; parallel.

opposite number, *n.* Man of corresponding position or rank or office in another organization.

optimistic, *adj.* Sanguine; inclined to put the most favorable construction on the world and all that happens in it.

optimum, *adj.* Best; most extensive. A cant word of bureaucrats.

-or. *Am. sp.* of words like ardor, armor, color. *Br.* ardour, armour, colour.

oral (ō'răl), *adj.* Concerned with the mouth.

oral, verbal, *adj. Oral* means spoken, uttered by way of the mouth; *verbal* refers principally to what is communicated rather than to the manner of communication. The opposite of oral is *written*. *Verbal niceties, verbal agreement, oral tradition.*

orate, *v.* Humorous barbarism based on *oration*.

orchestra, *n.* Arranged group of string, wind, and percussion instruments; main floor of a theatre in front of the stage; what is in *Br.* usage the pit. [*Gr.* dance]

order, *n.* Customary mode of procedure; propriety; brotherhood; class in society; regular procedure in forensic competition. *In order* means appropriate, admissible, or in working condition.

order, *v.* Direct; manage; instruct with authority; authorize.

order, *v.* In *Am.* usage *to be* is often omitted after *ordered*. "Filene *ordered* the shipment *held* in Boston."

Order of Climax. If the writer places the less important or interesting before the more important and interesting in a carefully planned crescendo, his material is arranged in the *order of climax*. If he does not use this order, he runs the risk of losing the reader's attention or of making an anticlimax. See **Arrangement.**

Organization. A composition should be organized so that the subject matter will be enhanced and the material presented in the most effective way. Some plan of attack should be adopted from the first. With the chief objective in mind it will be easier to keep a sense of proportion. The well-organized composition must meet the requirements of time, interest, facility, and expediency. The title must be exact, the subject properly limited, the beginning effective, irrelevant material rejected, false leads avoided, and the ending natural and concise.

Orient, *n.* Far East; the East, from North Africa to Hawaii, including the Near East.

originate, *v.t.* Produce, begin.

ornate, *adj.* Embellished; copiously or excessively adorned.

ornery (awn'ri), *adj. Dialect,* stubborn, ill tempered; bad; lazy.

ort, *pl.* **orts,** *n.* Bit of food left over after a meal; *pl.,* kitchen waste; peelings.

orthography. *n.* Fancy for *spelling.*

other, *pron.* Do not write ". . . *the one* of all the *others*" since you really wish to set off *the one* from the rest of the group. Write "From *all the others* he singled out *one.*" When *other* brings a series to a close by naming the genus to which the items of the series belong, make sure that the species belong to the genus named. "Clothiers, jewelers, and *other retail stores* (. . . and *other* retailers)." "Police detectives, G-men, and *ot*ᵏᵉʳ crime-hunting paraphernalia (. . . and *other* agents of the law)."

other, *adv.* With *than* it is *stand. lit.* but in certain constructions *otherwise* is preferable. "He could not do *other than* (otherwise than) admit her." After **other,** *adj.,* meaning *different in identity,* the idiom almost always demands *than;* but meaning *different in quality* or *kind,* the idiom demands *than,* or, less commonly, *from.* "Their speech, dress, and manners put them in a class of society *other than* ours." "Pets *other than* dogs." *But* is correct when *other* is omitted. "He had no offer *but* this."

ought, *v.* Commonly expresses the obligation of duty or moral demand. It is stronger than *should* in this sense. "You *ought* to tell him the truth right now." However, it is often used in the senses conveyed by *should,* i.e., fitness, propriety, expediency. "We have not done the things we *ought to have* (should have) done if we are to leave tomorrow." *Stand. lit.* in the sense of require, be in need of. "The fence *ought to have* a new coat of paint." Do not use *had* with *ought,* as in "*Hadn't* you

ought to (shouldn't you) ask the policeman?"

out, *adv.* Used in many verb-adverb combinations, as *try out, lose out, win out, watch out, sound out.* These are usually *colloq.* See the similar **up.** *Stand. lit.* as an *adj.* e.g., "The trial balance was *out* twenty-three dollars," "He was *out* ten cents," "We are *out* to win before the month is *out,*" and "She wears *out* sizes." Used as a *prep.* only in the phrase *from out. Out of the* in sentences like "She looked *out of the* window" is preferred to *out the,* "She looked *out the* window," although the latter is still commonly said in America.

outfit, *n.* Equipment for a journey or other undertaking; associated group; military unit.

outline, *n.* Line real or apparent marking the border of an object; contour; profile; sketch or tabular plan of the content of a piece of composition.

Outlines. Two types of tabular outlines are widely used in both analytical and constructive phases of rhetorical study. The topic-sentence outline consists essentially of the topic sentences of the paragraphs in a piece of composition. Conventionally, these sentences are introduced by Roman numerals and presented in the original order of paragraphs. In the analytical outline the topics of the main divisions of the composition analyzed or planned are introduced by Roman numerals, the principal subdivisions by capital letters, the secondary subdivisions by Arabic numerals, and yet inferior subdivisions by small letters. The outline of this type has the disadvantage of being difficult to prepare and the advantage of showing the relative importance of major and minor topics. It may consist of one continuous sentence (as in the argumentative brief), of phrases only, or of separate sentences for the main topics with appropriate indentation and subordination of modifying clauses or phrases. The conventional scheme of tabulation, often called the "Harvard" scheme, is indicated below:

Types of Outlines

I. There are two principal types of tabular outlines:
   A. topic-sentence,
   B. analytical.
II. The topic-sentence outline consists of the sentences summarizing the thoughts of paragraphs.
III. Analytical outlines may be of three kinds:
   A. continuous sentence outline,
   B. phrase outline,
   C. analytical sentence outline in which
      1. each sentence represents a main topic of the composition under analysis and
      2. tabulated subordinate ideas may be either
         a. phrases or
         b. clauses.
IV. This outline represents or exemplifies the analytical type composed of complete sentences.

out loud, *adv. Colloq.* for *aloud, loudly, audibly.* "He laughed *out loud.*" The *adj. out-loud* is also *colloq.*

outside of. Without or beyond the confines of. "*Outside of* his circle he is not very popular." *Colloq.* in the sense of *except for, besides,* "*Outside of (stand. lit. except for)* your approach shots, your golf is good." *Prep.* without *of.* "No one cares *outside* my nearest friends and relatives."

outstanding, *adj.* Conspicuous; important; obviously superior.

over. A *prep.* in "She nodded *over* her knitting," but usually *over* may be regarded as *prep.* or *adv.,* depending upon whether it is felt as governing a *n.* or as modifying an *adj.* or *v. Stand. lit.* in the sense of *more than.* "He ran *over* a mile." One of its meanings as an *adj.* is *ended, finished.* If *with* is added to *over* in this sense, as in "I'm glad that's *over* (*with*)," it is *colloq.*

over-all, *adj.* All inclusive, *preferable to* all-over but dangerously trite.

overcoat, *n.* Great coat; topcoat.

overly, *adv.* Excessively. Chiefly *Am.* "She was *overly* (*Br. over-*) excited by the situation."

override, *v.* Defeat decisively; cancel; overwhelm.

owing to. Safer to use than *due to. Owing to* can be used as either *adj.* or *prep.* "Boys, *owing to* (not *due to*) their love of action, hate to read stories in which nothing happens." *Due to,* of course, is correct in the predicate.

own, *n.* Own responsibility. "On your own" means independent, without support or backing.

oxymoron, *n.* Figurative use of contradictory terms, such as "cruel kindness." [*Gr.,* sharply foolish]

P

pack, *n.* Bundle; set, group; associated company (of animals).

pack, *v.* Make a pack of; crowd; cram, especially cram food into tin cans or other containers, prepare food for long-term preservation.

package, *n.* packet, parcel; radio and T.V. *tech.,* prearranged plan for a show or production to be sold as a unit for a flat sum.

package, *v. Tech.,* pack; put up in attractive containers.

pad, *v.* Stuff; falsify accounts or bills.

paddle, *v.* Spank, whack with a paddle; propel by means of a paddle.

page, *v.* Summon vocally; urge or induce a bellboy to summon thus.

pair, *pl.* pairs or slightly *arch.,* **pair,** *n.* Set of two, couple; *arch.,* series as in the phrase "up two pair of stairs."

pal, *n.* and *v.* Slang of Romany origin. *Buddy* is *colloq.,* and *pard* (for *partner*) is slang.

paladin, *n.* One of Charlemagne's twelve peers; champion; notable military follower. [Old Fr. < L. palace officer]

palimpsest (păl'ĭmp sĕst), *n.* Parchment from which one record has been erased to make room for another. [*Gr.,* scrape again]

palindrome, *n.* Word or group of words that is the same when read backward or forward. "Able was I ere I saw Elba." [*Gr.,* running back again]

palooka, *n. Sl.,* bumpkin; inept or unsuccessful prizefighter.

pan, *v.* Slang in the sense of *ridicule* or *criticize.* "They *panned* the life out of him." *Colloq.* with *out,* meaning to turn out, be realized. "This experiment didn't *pan out* very well." **Pan,** *n.,* is slang for *face.* The "*dead-pan*" comedian does not change the expression of his face. **Pan-handler** is slang for *street beggar* or *hobo who begs.* The *v.* is **panhandle.**

panel, *n.* Thin board fixed in a frame; lengthwise strip of ornamental cloth in a gown; associated group of workers, some on duty regularly, others available for consultation, consultative group.

panel discussion, *n.* Organized argument by a chosen group or panel of speakers,—in contrast with open-forum discussion.

panic, *v.* Rouse to panic, overwhelm with fright; *sl.,* delight, entertain to the point of hysteria. The past tense is *panicked.* [*L. < Gr.,* caused by the god Pan]

Pantheon, *n.* Temple of all the gods; with lower-case initial, list of all the gods of a people or a cult; place where national heroes are buried or memorialized.

pantomime, *n.* Dumbshow; dramatic entertainment without speech.

pants, *n. Colloq.* for *trousers, shorts,* or *drawers.* Femoral habiliments, unmentionables, and galligaskins are examples of polysyllabic humor.

pantywaist, *n. Sl.,* sissy, effeminate or sentimental person.

panurgic, *adj.* Like a character of Rabelais's, Pantagruel's licentious friend Panurge; picaresque.

papoose, *n.* Baby of American Indian parents. [Algonquian]

parable, *n.* See **allegory.**

paradigm (pă′rȧ dĭm), *n.* List of all the inflectional forms of a word; example of a declension or a conjugation.

paradox, *n.* A statement which at first blush may appear contradictory or opposed to common sense, but when examined further may prove to contain a truth. "The belly carries the legs." "The Child is Father of the Man." Also a statement that is really untrue or self-contradictory. The *adj.* is **paradoxical.**

¶. The symbol for *paragraph.* Paragraphing wrong.

Paragraph. Unit of composition commonly consisting of a series of sentences related by a common purpose. Its beginning is commonly marked by indentation.

Parallelism. Casting similar ideas into similar form, as a series of words, phrases, or clauses of the same kind. "To this preposterous court, whose *fearful prejudices, vile intrigues,* and *brilliant settings* the author so admirably describes . . ."; not "whose prejudices were fearful, and whose vile intrigues and the brilliance of whose settings the author so admirably describes." If the pattern is that of a series of subordinate clauses, do not make one member of the series an independent clause (false series). Incorrect: "That the most worthless of these lovers was chosen, and this choice was based on parental ambition as anyone could see." Better: "That the most worthless of these lovers was chosen, and that the choice was based on parental ambition, were obvious."

Theme-readers use the sign // to mean *not parallel.*

Parallel Structure. The same as **Parallelism.** *Parallel* means following like courses, similar. It is metaphorically applied to a series that is composed of similar units. When one starts a parallel pattern, one should complete it. The parallelism is misleading when the form but not the thought is similar. Incorrect: "He is treasurer, secretary, and neurasthenic."

paraphrase, *n.* A free (not word-for-word) rendering of the sense of a passage whether in the same language or another. If it is in the same language, it is usually an expanded restatement. A translation is a closer rendering from one language into another. **Paraphrase,** *v.,* means to interpret or render freely, as in a paraphrase.

Parenthesis, *pl.* **Parentheses.** Punctuation marks ( ) used for the following purposes:

1. To inclose a parenthetical inset. This inset may be explanation or general comment. "My next car (if I can ever get rid of this one) will be a Bliflex."

2. To inclose letters or numbers marking the divisions of a subject. However, parentheses are often omitted here, especially with Roman numerals.

3. To inclose bibliographical or other references inserted in the text. References are inserted in this way in textbook rather than in literary style. "The question of French influence, discussed in detail in another part of the book (p. 242), can only be touched upon here."

parimutuel, *n.* Procedure which regulates betting through mechanical calculation of odds and percentages.

park, *v.* Station, place in position in a row or series; *sl.,* in the sense of set or leave clothes, books, oneself, in a particular place. "Don't *park* on my desk."

parkway, *n.* Broad avenue, boulevard decorated with trees. This is an *Am.* word in good use throughout the U.S.

parlay, *v. Colloq.,* pyramid a series of wagers; arrange in advance to bet the money won on one horse on a second and so continue through three or four races or until one horse fails to finish first, second, or third. The corresponding *n.,* **parlay**, is a name for such a compound gamble.

parley, *n.* Conference; discussion of terms for settlement of a controversy.

Parliament (pär'lĭ mĕnt), *n.* Bicameral legislative assembly of the three estates of Great Britain and Northern Ireland; with *l.c.* instead of *cap.* initial, deliberative body, legislative assembly.

parliamentarian, *n.* One expert in rules of order or debate.

parlor, *n.* Drawing room; sitting room; reception room or hall. [Old Fr., talk]

parlous, *adj.* Dangerous. Use of this word in modern contexts is a literary affectation.

parody, *n.* Imitation of language, style, and pattern of a piece of composition; satirical imitation involving less exaggeration of defects than appears in burlesque. [Gr., song beside, parallel song]

parole, *n.* Word of honor; conditional release of a prisoner who has served only a part of his sentence.

parolee, *n.* Former inmate of a prison, at liberty on parole.

paroxysm, *n.* Fit.

partial, *adj.* Consisting of part only; affecting a part only; biased; illogically favoring (with *toward*).

partially, partly, *adv.* When these overlap, use *partly*. *Partly* is always to be used when the meaning is *as regards a part and not the whole,* and *partially* when the meaning is *to a limited degree.* "His hesitancy was *partly* due to fear."

Participle. A verbal *adj.* ending in -*ing*, -(*e*)*n*, -(*e*)*d*, or -*t: forlorn, burnt, fledged, running* (water). The participle in a phrase at the beginning of a sentence should as a rule modify the subject of the main clause. For participles that do not have to do this see **Dangling Participle.** A dangling *participle:* "Coming in on the Flyer the scenery was beautiful."

partisan, *n.* Loyal follower, adherent of party or cause; member of a guerilla band; scout.

Parts of Speech. The words of the language classified according to the manner in which they present the things they stand for, and to the part they play in the particular sentence in which they occur. Nouns, verbs, adjectives, adverbs, pronouns, prepositions, conjunctions, and interjections.

party, *n.* Slang for *person,* as in "Look at the *party* in the frock coat." See **individual.**

party-liner, *n.* Adherent to tenets and rules of a party; Communist.

pass, *v. Pass the buck,* to shift responsibility to someone else, is *stand. lit.,* but *pass the hat* for *take up a collection* is slang. *Pass the time of day* is *colloq. Pass up* is slang for *decline, refuse, disregard.* "I don't want you to *pass up* this opportunity." In the sense of faint, *pass out* is slang. But *pass on* meaning to die is *stand. lit.* in U.S.

passim, *adv.* Latin for *throughout, here and there.* Used in footnotes by writers who cannot or do not wish to give detailed page references to sources.

Passive, Double. See **Double Passive.**

Passive, The Weak. Do not use the passive voice unless you have a special need for it. "The fire at Cook Corners *was seen by me*" is not as good as "*I saw* the fire at Cook Corners." The passive is used if the agent is general or if there is no point in mentioning it; e.g., "Molasses *is made* from sugar cane."

past, *prep.* Beyond; close to and beyond in place or time.

past, *adj.* Pertaining to time gone; pertaining to a recent former time.

past, *n.* Former time; events in recent time gone. Do not confuse **past** with the preterit of the verb *to pass, passed.*

pasteboard, *n.* Paperboard, cardboard; *sl.,* playing card, ticket.

pastor, *n.* Religious leader of a congregation or parish. [*L.* <*Gr.,* pastor, a shepherd]

pastoral, *n.* Poem, drama, or narrative in prose dealing with shepherds and other rustics or with idealized Arcadian country life.

pastrami, *n.* Highly seasoned preparation of shoulderbeef.

Pathetic Fallacy. The attributing of one's emotions to objects or phenomena of external nature: "The sad trees groaned, all nature wept." It often seems affected and is always out of harmony with prosaic contexts.

pathogenic, *adj.* Causing disease.

pathos, *n.* Feeling combined of pity and sympathy; artistic quality productive of mob feeling.

patio, *n.* Garden courtyard of a house or other building of Spanish type.

patrol, *v.* Go the rounds, cover a beat. [*Fr.,* paddle through mud]

patrolman, *n.* Police officer.

patron, *n. Colloq.* in the sense of client or customer.

patroness, *n.* Woman patron; lady who gives public approval to a charitable or social enterprise of an artist, a club, or a society.

patronize, *v. Colloq.* in the sense of buy from, trade with.

patsy, *n. Sl.,* victim of bad luck; Jonah.

patty, *n.* Circular cake of meat, hash, or other foods mixed and molded by patting with the fingers; meat pie baked in a small round pan.

pavement, *n.* Paved roadway, hard road; *Br.,* sidewalk.

pay, *adj. attributive.* Concerned with or involving remuneration.

peal, *n.* Progressive tones from a series of seven bells; loud sound.

pecan (pē kǎn'), *n.* Species of hickory nut. [Amer. Indian]

pecuniary, *adj.* Related to money; cash.

pedal, *v.* Slang in *soft pedal* meaning not to stress, exercise restraint upon. "The committee had to *soft pedal* that issue."

pedal-pushers, *n. pl.* Short slacks for women (who may decide to ride bicycles).

pedantic, *adj.* Like a schoolmaster; exaggerating the importance of mere facts.

pediculous, *adj.* Lousy; elegant variation for unpleasant, objectionable.

pedigree, *n.* Genealogical tree; line of ancestors.

peek, *v.* and *n.* Glimpse; peer; peep.

peel, *n.* Small tower; skin or rind.

peel, *v.* Skin; *slang,* undress.

peeve, *n. Colloq.* grievance. [back formation from *peevish.*]

peeve, *v. Colloq.,* annoy, make querulous.

peevish, *adj.* Querulous; sensitive and stubborn; sulky. [Old English, whimpering, perverse]

peg, *v.* Fasten, hold; *baseball tech.,* throw.

pejorative, *adj.* Depreciatory.

pemmican, *n.* Preparation of dried meat and sometimes dried fruit, used in compressed cakes as food for travelers and explorers. [Cree Indian, grease]

pend, *v.* Hang; be about to occur; wait for settlement. **Pending** is used freely as a preposition, on condition of.

pendant, pendent. *Pendant* is a *n.* meaning a hanging ornament or appurtenance; *pendent* is an *adj.* meaning hanging. "The police recovered her stolen *pendants.*"

"The *pendent* strands of moss were white with frost."

penny, *n.* English coin formerly worth two cents; *colloq.,* one cent.

pentameter, *n.* Verse of five metrical feet. Iambic pentameter is English heroic verse, whether unrhymed (blank) or rhymed in "heroic" couplets.

people, persons, *n. People* are *persons* regarded indefinitely, as in "*People* say that he is honest," or as united by a common ancestry, culture, or similar characteristic. One would write "There were thirteen *persons* (rather than *people*) in the car" unless the car also was occupied by horses or other animals. *People* also means *the populace, the electorate, persons* as merely part of a human aggregate.

pep, *v.* and *n. Sl.* stump of either *pepper* or *pepsin,* meaning vigor, vim, and enthusiasm.

peplum, *n.* Uneven skirtlike flounce attached to the blouse of a dress at the waistline.

pepper-upper, *n. Sl.,* stimulant; cheerleader; encourager; deliverer of pep-talks.

pepsin, *n.* Digestive enzyme active in splitting proteins in the human stomach to form simpler, more soluble substances.

per, *prep.* By, by the. Latin phrases containing *per* are usually italicized: *per diem, per contra. Per capita* is used correctly only in reference to a certain method of sharing property, and is therefore incorrect in "The Americans spent two dollars *per capita* (better *each*) last year for paper." *Per* is not usually italicized in *per bearer,* twenty cents *per* pound, *per* enclosed bill, etc. *As per usual,* as in "Business as *per usual*" is jocular. *Per* belongs with legal and commercial phraseology, the expression *a dollar a yard* being more idiomatic than a *dollar per yard. Per* without the object is slang; e.g., "She earns fifty *per* (week)."

per cent, percentage. Always write *per cent* as two words, but omit the period after *cent.* The verb is *sing.* or *pl.* depending upon the context. "Three *per cent interest is* the usual rate." "Nine *per cent* is a large percentage (not *a large per cent*)." "Ten

per cent of the seeds *are* sterile." It means *so many per hundred,* and should not be used for *part,* or *proportion,* as in "What *per cent* (better *proportion*) of the customers return?" *Percentage* (with a defining term) is loosely used to mean *proportion* or *part of a whole.* "A large *percentage* of the pear crop was lost." Its stricter meaning is illustrated in "The *percentage* of games won is .624," and "His batting *percentage* is .301." Slang in the sense of *rake-off.* "Give me my *percentage* of the loot."

percentary, *n. Sl.,* agency which takes a percentage of the earnings of its clients.

percolate, *v.* Filter, filter through ground coffee for the purpose of deriving the flavor or essence; cause (liquid) to pass through a porous mass.

peremptory (pĕr ĕmpt'ō rĭ or pĕr'ĕmptō rĭ), *adj.* Arrogant; positive in expression of opinions; decisive without allowing opportunity for expression of opposition. [*L.,* take away entirely]

perfect, *adj.* Complete, utter, faultless. Yet *more* and *most* may be used with *perfect.* "In order to form a *more perfect* union."

Perfect Infinitive. Some writers prefer "I should have liked *to know* him" to "I should have liked *to have known* him," but both constructions are in good use, as is the equivalent "I *should like to have known* him." The perfect infinitive is regularly used to denote that it is no longer possible to hope or expect that something will be granted or done, or an intention carried into effect. "Natalie *was to have been queen* of the May."

perfectly, *adv. Colloq.,* utterly, entirely.

perhaps, *adv.* Usually set off by commas except when it begins a sentence.

Period. Punctuation mark used for the following purposes:

1. To mark the end of a declarative or imperative sentence: "We are late." "Come on." A period at the end of a quoted sentence is placed inside the closing quotation marks. "He said, 'Of course it didn't sell.' " The *period fault* is the mistaking of a part of a

sentence that cannot stand alone, for a complete sentence and closing this fragment with a period. See **Fragmentary Sentence.**

2. To mark an abbreviation: *Geo., ft.* (foot).

3. To indicate that words have been omitted from a quoted sentence (use three periods to indicate this), or that a sentence or more has been omitted from a quoted passage (use four periods to indicate this). "She stated that Wodehouse was '. . . the only Englishman who could make an American laugh at a joke about America.' " See **Ellipsis.**

Periodic Sentence. A sentence in which the leading member, generally the independent assertion, is placed last, or near the end, following a series of modifying clauses. Thus the grammatical structure is not complete until the period is reached. "Notwithstanding this difference in their opinions concerning the function of the central government, a difference that seemed to be insurmountable, both Fish and Fowl adopted, and worked with might and main to carry out, the policy of the Secretary of Agriculture."

Periphrasis (pĕ rĭf′rà sĭs). Circumlocution; the roundabout way of putting a thing; e.g., "The answer is in the negative" for "No." The *adj.* is *periphrastic* (pĕr′ĭ frăs′tĭk).

permissible, *adj.* Allowable.

persimmon, *n.* Plumlike fruit; tree bearing this fruit. [Virginian Indian name]

Person. *I am, you are, he is,* illustrate that relation between *v.* and subject called *person.* It is exemplified especially in the use of pronouns. *I* is first person, *you* is second, and *he, she,* or *it,* third person, all *sing.* See **Agreement.**

personage, *n.* Important man or woman; person. Avoid this overworked word.

Personal Attitude. After the writer has decided whether he is going to treat his subject impersonally (objectively) or subjectively, that is, make his own point of view or his own emotional attitude or imaginative interpretations prominent, he should stick to his decision. The sudden intrusion of the personal element is especially annoying. The kittenish autobiography is an example of the wrong method. For "The frantic author of these remarks found herself somewhere on the surface of mother earth near Flatbush Ave., July 21, 1915; and were her parents astonished!" write "I was born . . ."

personality, *n.* Individuality; a person, a being; the sum total of an individual's traits. Also personal remarks or observations that offend or disparage. Do not use as an *adj.* as in *"personality* traits, *personality* test," unless you are writing a technical paper on psychology.

Personification. A figure of speech in which animals, objects, phenomena of nature, or abstract ideas are made to act as persons: "Spring smiled; Winter frowned; Death threatens; the Rock cried out."

personnel, *n.* People; body of people employed in one organization, school, or military unit; *tech.,* professional activity of guidance, counseling; supervision of employees or students.

perspiration, *n.* Sweat. *Perspiration* is a formal word.

perspire, *v.* Sweat. "Horses sweat; gentlemen perspire; ladies simply glow."

persuade, *v.* Argue into believing or doing something.

Persuasion. Act of causing decision or action by force of argument or by emotional appeal, especially the latter.

persuasion, *n.* A jocular *colloq.* in the meaning of *kind, sort,* or *sex.* "Those of the female *persuasion* will not like this." Also *colloq.* for *persuasion by force.* Likewise the *n.* **persuader.** "My fists are my little *persuaders.*"

pet, *v.* Caress, fondle.

petrel, *n.* Species of seabird. [L., Peter, rock, because the bird seems to walk on the sea like St. Peter]

petrol, *n.* Gasoline; any light distillate of petroleum. This is the common *Br.* term for motor fuel. [stump of petroleum]

petroleum, *n.* Oil derived from the rocks, mineral oil, source of gasoline, kerosene, and many other fuels and lubricants. [*L.*, rock + oil]

phenobarbital, *n.* Sedative powder; phenyl-ethyl-barbituric acid; sleeping pill.

phenomenon, *n.* The *pl.* is *phenomena.* Fact or occurrence that appears, is perceived or observed. Popularly, *something strange or uncommon.* The *adj.* **phenomenal,** strictly, *apparent, perceptible,* is likewise extended to mean *remarkable, extraordinary,* or *prodigious.* "The sudden growth of enthusiasm for Ellery was *phenomenal* (extraordinary)."

philately (fĭl ăt′ĕ lē), *n.* Stamp-collecting, avocation of collecting and studying postage stamps. [coinage from *Gr.*, love + freedom from tax]

phone, *n.* and *v. Colloq.* stump of *telephone.*

Phonetics. The science of speech sounds. The phonetic symbols that follow stand for the English sounds most in need of this kind of representation. The sign (:) after a symbol indicates that the sound is long.

a: in	*father*
æ	*mat*
ai	*aisle, line*
au	*house*
ɛ	*met*
e	*mate*
ə	*about, china* (obscure e)
ei	*sleigh, way*
i	*sit*
i:	*machine, feet, meat*
ou	*note*
oi	*boy*
ɔ	*not*
ɔ:	*hall*
u:	*who*
u	*book*
ʌ	*but*
n	*sing*
b	*cloth*
đ	*clothes*
ʃ	*shoe, nation*
tʃ	*chin*
ʒ	*vision*
dʒ	*gin, judge*
j	*you, view*

phonological, *adj.* Concerned with the scientific study of sounds.

phony, *adj. Sl.*, not genuine; fake, or faked. The *n.*, meaning something that is not genuine, is also slang.

photo, *n. Colloq.* stump of *photograph.*

photogenic, *adj.* Likely to look good when photographed.

photograph, *v.* and *n.* Picture by means of effect of light on chemically prepared surface; a picture so produced. [coined word from Greek, light + write]

Phrase. Any group of words, as a *v. phrase, will have had; part. phrase, knowing what to do;* or *prep. phrase, of the night.* The *clause* is usually longer than the *phrase* and has a subject and a predicate.

Physical Point of View. When one disregards physical point of view, one describes something that he could not have possibly seen in the way he represents it as being seen. If one is standing on the ground, he cannot describe the color of the eye of a pigeon on the top of a three-hundred foot building.

physics, *n.* Science of energy and the phenomenal world.

pi, *n.* Greek letter; spilled or mixed type.

piazza, *n. Colloq.,* veranda, porch; *stand. lit.,* colonnade [public square in Italy].

pica (pī′ka), *n.* 12-point type, six lines per inch; type measure, 0.166 inches.

picaresque, *adj.* Full of rascality; characteristic of a type of novel in which the rogue or picaro is a central character. [*Sp.*]

picayune, *n.* Something of little value. The adjectives *picayune* and *picayunish* mean petty, cheap, small in conception and execution. "The waiters went on strike because of the *picayune* dining-room rules."

pick, *v.* Choose, select. See **out. Pick on,** choose as an object of attack or mockery.

picket, *n.* Pointed stake; sentinel; guard or watcher posted by a labor organization during a strike; body of soldiers on watch.

picnic, *part.,* **picnicking,** *past part.* **picnicked,** *v.* Go on a pleasure party involving eating a meal *al fresco.*

picture (pīk′cher), *n. Colloq.* in the sense of *picturesque person or thing,* or (with *the*) *the situation, the circumstances, the* *setup.* "He's out of *the picture* now." *Colloq.* as a *pl.* meaning *the art or business of motion pictures.*

picturesque, picaresque, *adj. Picturesque* means like a picture, striking, and when applied to language, graphic and vivid; *picaresque* means having to do with a rogue, or picaro; e.g., a *picaresque* novel.

pidgin, *adj.* Business, businesslike, chiefly in the expression Pidgin English, jargon of business in the Far East. [phonetic representation of Chinese pron. of business]

pie, *n.* Baked dish consisting of pastry crust and a filling of fruit, meat, or a mixture of meat and vegetables; also a concoction or confection of cake or ice cream bearing a resemblance to pastry in taste or appearance.

piece, *n. Stand. lit.* in the meaning of a single instance or specimen, and as short for a little piece of work, e.g., a short literary or musical composition, an article of furniture or a painting. "I bought a fine *piece* at the art auction." "That's a good *piece* of news." *Dial.* for a short distance, a short while, a portion of space or time, a person. "That *piece* of track between Dixon and The Forks is all upgrade." "We walked down the tracks a *piece.*"

pied, *adj.* or *participle.* Of two or more colors; *printing tech.,* mixed.

piedmont, *n.* Foothills, region at the foot of a mountain or range. [Fr., foot +hills]

piker, *n. Sl.,* person who does things meanly or poorly; a "tightwad," shirker, quitter, or coward. A small gambler who *pikes,* i.e., plays with extreme caution or makes small bets.

pile, *n.* Like *lot,* it is *colloq.* in the sense of *large amount or number.* When applied to money, as in "Jones has made his *pile,*" it is slang. Also slang in the *v.* phrases *pile out,* get out, *pile up,* get into a tangle, *pile in,* and *pile off.*

pilot, *n.* Steersman, helmsman; licensed expert who can steer vessels in certain difficult waters, such as the approaches to a harbor; man or woman who flies an airplane or has charge of the flying of a plane or dirigible; leader.

pin, *n.* Pointed piece of wire, usually with flat head or looped end; iron peg in such compounds as coupling *pin,* belaying *pin, tholepin, linchpin.*

pin-up, pin-up girl, *n.* Beauty; picture beneficial to *morale.*

pint, *n.* 16 fluid ounces. "A pint's a pound the World around," but in Britain it is 20 ounces!

pipe down, *v.* Navy *tech.,* be quiet or attentive in response to a bos'n's whistle; *sl.,* be still, shut up.

piquant (pē′kănt), *adj.* Sharply pleasant.

pit, *n.* Seed, shelled seed; deep hole.

pitcher, *n.* Wide-lipped jug with a handle for pouring; player who delivers the baseball to (or past) the batter.

pix, *n. Sl.,* or *theatrical tech.,* motion pictures, illustrations.

place, *n.* Location, locale, spot; *colloq.,* piece of real property; country home, whether large or small. *Any place* is now used by *Am.* speakers and even by many careful writers in lieu of *anywhere.*

-place. *Colloq.* when substituted for *-where* in *anywhere, somewhere,* or *everywhere. No place* is *Am.* dial. for *nowhere.*

placement, *n.* Location; putting in position; assigning to employment; finding jobs for people.

Place Names. The proper form of a place name is determined by local usage, the apostrophe being often suppressed: Pikes Peak, Kings County. The same is true of other proper names: Teachers College, Citizens Trust Company. The pronunciation must also follow local custom.

Plagiarism. Stealing and passing off as one's own the ideas or words of another. Also the ideas or words plagiarized. Of course, due notice of and credit for borrowings should be given in the text or footnotes.

plain, *adj.* Simple, direct; *colloq.,* without beauty of person. *Plain spoken,* outspoken, blunt.

plan, *v.* As an intransitive, *plan* means to devise or contrive. In the sense of intend or propose—often with *on,* but also with *to* or *for*—it is *colloq.* "The trip we **planned** *on* taking this summer must be given up."

planetarium, *n.* Mechanism for representing the motion of the heavenly bodies; room or building housing such mechanism.

plasma, *n.* Liquid portion of blood; liquid part of other organic tissues.

plastic, *n.* Organic substance, synthetic or natural, susceptible of being pressed or molded to make useful articles of various kinds; synthetic substance having qualities similar to those of hard rubber or celluloid.

plastic, *adj.* Worked or made by moulding or modeling; impressionable.

platform, *n. Archaic tech.,* pattern; plan; horizontal surface above the level of surrounding floor or earth; announced program of a political party or a candidate.

platitude, *n.* Flatness, triteness; trite truism.

platter, *n.* Large plate, flat dish for meat; *sl.,* phonograph record.

play-actor, *n.* Actor, player; stage performer; show-off.

plead, pleaded, pleaded. *Colloq. p. part.,* **pled.**

plenary, *adj.* Full, complete. A **plenary** session of a committee or a legislative body is attended by all who are entitled to be present.

plenty, *n.* An abundance. Chiefly *Am.* when preceded by *a,* as in "There was *a plenty* for one." See **aplenty.** *Plenty* can take the place of *plentiful* in the predicate. "Good houses to rent do not seem to be as *plenty* (plentiful) as last year." Chiefly *dial.* when used for *plenty of:* "She gave us *plenty* meat." *Colloq.* as an *adv.* "This one is *plenty* large enough."

Pleonasm or Redundancy. There is a *redundancy* of synonyms for *pleonasm.* They all mean a superfluity of words. Only one member of pairs like *if and when, refer back, both alike, pair of twins,* is needed. Do not repeat in a modifier a part of the idea contained in what is being modified. "He drew two parallel horizontal straight lines to join together two round circles" says no more than "He drew two parallel horizontal lines to join two circles." *The more preferable* is not as good **as** *preferable.* Be concise and come to the

point. Polysyllabic humor is the parody of pleonasm.

plexiglas, *n. Trade name,* acrylic resin sheets, etc., used in curved windows etc.

plot, *n.* Conflict of action leading to conclusion of a narrative. See **Action.**

plug, *n.* Stopple; spark plug; tired old horse; Radio *tech.,* commercial announcement.

plug, *v. Colloq.,* persevere.

plumb, *n.* Lump of lead; weight at the end of a line, used to determine the perpendicular. [*L.,* lead]

plummet, *v.* Drop straight down like the lead of a plumb line.

plump, *v.* Vote emphatically; argue forcefully; express vigorous approval.

plump, *adj.* Pleasantly fat.

plurality, *n.* Quality of consisting of more than one; *political tech.,* excess of number of votes cast for a winning candidate over those cast for another candidate. A *p.* is often less than a majority if there are several candidates. See **Majority.**

pluralize, *v.* Take a plural form; make plural.

Plurals. Words ending in the hissing sounds *s, z, x, sh, dg,* and *ch* form their plural by adding *-es,* or, if an *e* is written in the *sing.,* by adding *-s: hisses, noses, boxes, dishes, judges, churches.* Add *-s* to most other nouns except those ending in *y* and *o.* If the *y* follows a consonant, change *y* to *i* and add *-es: flies, ladies.* If the *y* follows a vowel, retain the *y* and add *-s: days, toys.*

Familiar words ending in *o* usually form their plural by adding *es: potatoes, echoes.* Those that have been shortened, that have a vowel before the *o,* or that are felt to be foreign, usually form the plural by adding *-s: photos, memos, folios, cameos, sombreros, kimonos.* See **Apostrophe.**

A few nouns form *pl.* without adding *-s* or *-es.* Examples are *sheep, oxen* or *ox, women, men, children.*

plywood, *n.* Building material made of veneer sheets so glued together that the grains of the layers of wood are at right angles.

pocket veto, *n.* Presidential failure to

sign a bill before adjournment of Congress.

podium, *n.* Platform or perch for the conductor of a musical performance; dais. **P.** is a neologism in this sense. [*Gr.,* little foot, foundation of the pavement for a row of columns in a temple]

poetaster, *n.* Bad versifier, weak imitator of good poets.

poetess, *n.* Female versifier. A woman who really writes poetry is a *poet.*

Poeticism. A word, usually an archaic one, suitable for poetry and not for matter-of-fact prose. Even in poetry, poetic diction often seems stilted and ineffective; in plain prose a poeticism sticks out like a sore thumb. Yet poeticisms still tempt the advertiser and the newspaper writer. *Beauteous, blithesome, direful, duteous, whilom, burden, canorous, clamant, lorn, plangent, full fain, ire* (for *anger*), *wed* (for *marry*), *full many a, perchance.*

poignant (poin′yănt, poin′ant), *adj.* Penetratingly keen like a poniard, painfully touching. Overworked word.

point, *n.* Tip like that of a needle; that which has position but neither parts nor extent; detail; dot on a map, place to be visited. *Pl.,* extremities of a horse.

pointer, *n.* Pointing rod used by teacher or demonstrator; beam of light projected for the same purpose; hint, suggestion.

point-free, *adj.* Not rationed, not requiring ration points for purchase.

Point of View. The author's attitude toward or relation to his subject. See **Physical Point of View.**

poke, *n. Colloq.,* bag, sack; purse.

poke fun at, *v. Colloq.* for deride.

Poke off, meaning to wander away, travel aimlessly, is also *colloq.*

pokey, *n. Sl.,* prison.

politics, *sing.* or *pl.* But don't change your mind in the same piece of writing.

polygraph, *n.* Manifold copying machine; lie-detector, device for measuring physical responses which accompany answers to questions.

Polysyllabic Humor. Deliberate use of pompous and ponderous words and roundabout speech for humorous effect. It is the parody of the pedantic weakness for elevated dignity. *Soft-palate calisthenics* (snoring), *matutinal ablutions* (morning bath), *vestigial remnant* (appendix), *domiciliary abode* (house), *sanguinary proboscis* (red nose), are examples.

pone, *n.* Hard johnnycake, cornpone. [Am. Indian]

pony, *n. Collegiate sl.,* translation, crib.

pool, *n.* Stagnant pond, small body of deep water; common stock, group of people from whom assistance may be drawn; artificial reservoir for swimming.

pooped, *adj. Colloq.,* exhausted, weary, languid.

poorly, *adj. Colloq.* for *unwell, in poor health.* "She is *poorly* (in poor health) today."

pop, *n.* Carbonated soft drink, soda-pop.

popular, *adj.* Make your reader understand whether you are using *popular* in its more favorable senses of *of or by all the people, in high favor,* or in the less favorable senses of *of* or *pertaining to the common people, cheap, generally believed but probably erroneous.* Thus, in the more favorable sense, *popular English* means plain, non-technical language, but in the less favorable sense, *low colloq.* careless language. A *popular definition* is one that sacrifices accuracy to interest.

porch, *n.* Front stoop, verandah, piazza (q.v.).

pore, *v.* Look with close attention.

pore, *n.* Little hole, hole in the skin for discharge of perspiration.

porgy, *n.* Species of food fish, red porgy. [Am. Indian]

porous, *adj.* Full of holes, provided with tiny holes like those of a sponge.

portfolio, *n.* Portable case for papers or prints; collection of securities held by a broker, an investor, or an institution.

portmanteau, *n. Br.,* traveling bag, suitcase. A **portmanteau** word is a telescoped combination of two or more words; e.g., travelogue combining travel and a part of monologue.

Possessive. See **Group Possessive** and **Apostrophe.**

Possessive of Inanimate Objects. In general, use the *of* phrase rather than the possessive *'s* with a *n.* standing for an inanimate object. "My horse*'s* shoes," but "the hood *of* my automobile." However, certain words denoting measure or extent such as *a hand's breadth, a week's wages, a month's notice, a boat's length,* and some old phrases like *at his wit's end, for pity's sake,* use the possessive *'s.* The use of it with *city* and *country* or the names of cities and countries, handy as it is for the newspapers, should not be encouraged unreservedly.

post, *v. Colloq.* in the sense of *to inform.* "He is well *posted.*"

post card, *n.* Mailing card without postage stamp imprinted.

postal card, *n.* Card with postage stamp imprinted.

posterior, *adj.* Later; behind; at the back; back.

posteriors, *n. pl.* Buttocks.

postfracas, *adj. Sl.,* after the war, postwar.

post-mortem, *adj.* After death.

post-mortem, *n.* Autopsy; *sports tech.,* analysis of records of a game.

potential, *adj.* Possible, latent.

potential, *n. Tech.,* voltage; latent power.

pother, *n.* Disturbance, fuss. *Obsolescent,* **pother** was revived by Robert Louis Stevenson.

powwow, *n.* Conference, long discussion. (Algonquian)

practicable, practical, *adj. Practicable* means usable, susceptible of being put into practice; *practical* means not theoretical, not speculative, skillful from practice. "His plan is *practicable.*" "He is no dreamer but a *practical* man." This distinction should be observed in *impracticable, unpractical,* and *impractical.* **Practically,** *adv.,* means to all practical purposes, virtually, not entirely or absolutely. Do not use as a synonym for *nearly, almost,* as in "They are *practically* (nearly) done with the job." Correct: "This material is *practically* worthless."

prairie, *n.* One of the vast tracts of open grassland in the Mississippi Valley. [L., meadow]

pram, *n. Br.,* perambulator, baby carriage, baby-buggy.

pre-. A prefix meaning *before, prior to.* When prefixed to a proper noun or a word beginning with *e,* the hyphen is commonly used. *Pre-engage, pre-exposure, prearrangement, preinstruct, pre-American, pre-Revolution, pre-war.*

precede, proceed, *v.* To *precede* means to come or go before in rank, place, or time; *to proceed,* to go on, continue. "Careful preparation should *precede* practice." "*Proceed* to the next step in the process." Notice the *sp.* of *proceeding, preceding, procedure.* The *n.* **precedence** (prē-sēd'ĕns) means priority, and the *n.* **precedent** (prĕs'ē dĕnt), a case taken as an example or rule. Prefer *go* or *pass* to *proceed* in all but dignified contexts.

precinct, *n.* Local subdivision, police district.

precious, *adj.* Costly, dear. Sometimes used ironically as an intensive; "You made a *precious* mess of that scheme." As applied to diction and pronunciation it means overrefined, fastidious, having the traits of preciosity. "This *precious* style is not likely to win more readers." *Colloq.* as an intensive *adv.* "You be *precious* (very) careful what you do."

précis (prā sē'), *n.* A summary preserving the gist, proportion, and atmosphere of the original, and about one-third of the original in size.

precisian, *n.* Formalist, scholar, or religious enthusiast rigidly exact in observance of rules.

precisionism, *n.* Philosophy and technique of painting with mechanical exactness.

Preconceived Idea. An idea born of legend, tradition, belief, or one's own desires, and tending to dictate what one sees or thinks and the way one sees it. Likely to hinder or make impossible true creative thinking or accurate observation.

preconception, *n.* Prejudice; idea accepted before observation of the facts of the matter; process of arriving at such an idea.

predicate, predict, *v. Predicate* means

to assert, affirm, or imply. Do not use for *to foretell, to found or base upon. Predict* means to foretell or prophesy.

predicative, *adj.* Making an assertion.

preempt, *v.* Seize or purchase a preemption; seize as if by right.

preemption, *n.* Right to purchase public land at a low price on condition of living on it and improving it.

prefab, *n. Sl.,* house or hut constructed of matched and finished pieces which are sold and delivered as a unit. Cf. **knock-down.** [pre-fabricated].

prefabricate, *v.* Make in sections which can be readily assembled and combined.

preface, *n.* Preliminary remarks by the author. See **foreword.**

prefer and **preferable,** *v.* and *adj.* Use both with *to.* "Silence is sometimes *preferable to* talk." *More preferable* is redundant. When the object of *prefer* is an infinitive and the construction is awkward, as in "I *prefer* to pay to losing her," change *prefer* to *choose rather* or *would rather*

Prejudice. Hasty or premature judgment; bias for or against; unreasoning objection to or favorable opinion of a person or thing.

preparedness, *n.* Readiness for war or other competitive activity. [popularized by T. Roosevelt]

Preposition. A word normally placed before a *n.* or *pron.* to show its relation to some other word; *at, against, through, by, over,* etc. A prepositional phrase, *on the river, of damask,* is either an *adj.* or an *adv.* in function. *Colloq.* the *prep.* is often omitted before the names of the days of the week; e.g., *Monday* for *on Monday.* "He writes it *Monday* and hands it in *Tuesday.*" This adverbial use is *stand. lit.* in expressions like *next Tuesday, last Wednesday.*

Do not be afraid to use a *prep.* "to end a sentence with."

prerequisite, *n. Collegiate tech.,* course which must be completed before another may be undertaken.

present, *v.* Formally introduce.

presently, *adv.* Before long; in the immediate future; not in good use in the sense of now, at the moment.

press, *n.* Printing press, machine for printing; the press, periodical publications in general, newspapers as a social force; treatment in newspaper stories.

press, *v.* Push; iron; *sports tech.,* be unduly tense like a batter who grips the bat too tightly.

press-agent, *n.* Public relations counselor; publicity director.

pressure, *n.* Squeezing.

pressure, *adj.* Influential, politically powerful.

Prestige. In reference to words, *prestige* means the esteem in which certain words are held owing to reputation or achievements of the people who use, or have used, them. An important factor in connotation.

presume, *v.* Venture, take on oneself without authorization; expect with confidence; assume; *colloq.* dare say.

pretence, pretense, *n.* Claim; false show.

preterit, preterite (prĕ'tĕr ĭt), *n.* Form of a verb in past tense.

pretty, *adv.* Moderately, slightly, to some degree, rather. "This play is pretty bad." *Pretty near* for *almost, well-nigh, a little short of,* is redundant. "The Tigers *pretty near* (better *nearly*) lost the game." Cf. the Southern *might' near.*

pretzel, *n.* Twisted brittle biscuit with salted surface. [Ger.]

prevail, *v.* Dominate, triumph; pompous synonym for be, exist.

preview, *n.* Advance showing of an art exhibit; advance showing of a motion picture; snatches of a motion picture displayed as advertising.

previous, *adj.* Preceding, antecedent, prior. One may write *previous to* instead of *previously to* in sentences like "He said that they had paid him a visit two days *previous to* Christmas." See **Quasi Adverbs.** *Previous* is *colloq.* for *premature* in "This statement is a little *previous.*"

prima donna, *n.* Female operatic star; leading woman singer; hence, selfishly temperamental person of either sex. "In my experience all very successful commanders are prima donnas and must be so treated."

primarily, *adv.* In the first place.

primary, *n.* Primary meeting, party election; meeting or designated time for selection of candidates by ballot.

principal, principle. As an *adj. principal* means chief, first, or highest. It is often misspelled *principle,* which means *a general rule.*

Principal Parts. Principal parts of a verb are the parts from which all the forms are developed; specifically, they are the first person singular form of the present tense, the first person singular of the past tense, and the past participle.

priority, *n.* Fact or privilege of going first.

prior to, *adv.* Prefer *before* or *previous to* except when there is more meant than the simple time relations, as in "The pledges must obtain the dean's authorization *prior to* the initiation." Write "*Before* (not *prior to*) going to El Paso, Ned stopped a week in Oklahoma."

prise, *v.* Pry, lift by leverage.

prissy, *adj. Colloq.,* sentimentally prim like a schoolma'am. [perhaps from Priscilla, Latin, somewhat old fashioned]

private eye, *n. Sl.,* private detective.

privilege, *n.* Grant of a special right or immunity; fundamental human right.

pro, *n.* One who votes or argues on the affirmative side. *Colloq.* stump of *professional.* "The *pro* taught him his stance."

probe, *n.* Journalese for inquiry, investigation, used chiefly in headlines; instrument for searching wounds.

problem, *n.* Question, task of discovering or guessing what will be the result of a given combination or complex of phenomena. *Fighting the problem* is objecting to the conditions instead of working out a solution.

procedure, *n.* Course of action; established way of doing things; progress.

proceed, *v.* Advance; go ahead.

process, *v. Military and political tech.,* put through a planned series of operations. Purists call this verb a barbarism.

process (prŏ'sĕs, prä'sĕs), *n.* Series of actions or operations, *esp.* in scientific experiment, cooking, or making industrial products. The *Br. pronun.* is prō'sĕs.

procure, *v.* See **acquire.**

producer, *n.* Manager or owner of a theatre or motion picture company; *Br.,* director of a production.

profession, *n.* Vocation involving extensive education and considerable social prestige; one of the learned professions, arms, law, medicine, divinity. Loosely the name is applied to skilled trades and types of business such as those of the "realtor" (*q.v.*), the mortician, the educator, the exterminator.

professional, *n.* Member of one of the three professions, medicine, law, divinity. This usage has connotations of Continental European influence.

professor, *n.* Dignified teacher. The title is used loosely in U.S. In colleges the title is conferred formally on experienced teachers of recognized scholarship and general ability.

profiteer, *v.* Take unfair proportion of gain from business transactions during a war or national emergency. As a *n., p.* means a man or woman who takes such profit.

progress, *v.* Advance; move toward perfection.

progressive, *adj.* Forward moving; *educational cant,* characterized by techniques involving development of activities connected with the interests of pupils or students. In grammar, the progressive aspects of a verb indicate that action is going on, beginning, or ending.

project, *n.* Undertaking; plan; *educational tech.,* product of a planned sequence of activities.

prom, *n.* Slang stump of prom*enade.* "She is a *prom* trotter."

prometheum, *n.* See **Illinium.**

prone, *adj.* Prostrate, face down.

Pronoun. The only kind of word in English that has three cases. Take care that the *pron.* that you put in the objective or nominative case should be in that case.

Remember that the *pron.* before the gerund is regularly in the possessive. "She couldn't account for all *her* comings and goings."

The *pron.* should have a definite antecedent. See **Reference.**

pronto, *adv. Colloq.,* at once, without delay. [Spanish]

Pronunciation. The chief arbiter in matters of pronunciation is the literate usage of the community in which you find yourself. The Utopian state of having just one correct and universal pronunciation of each word is not yet in sight. England cannot help much, for there is as much variation there as here. Boston cannot dictate to the rest of us, although its prestige has not entirely vanished; the "refined lady who will teach the purest Boston enunciation" still advertises in certain New York papers. Do not pronounce words that have become part of the language as if they were still foreign terms. Prairie du Chien, Wisconsin, is pronounced (prāry dōō shēn) and not as if it were French.

Proofreading. See **Signs.**

Propaganda, *n.* Takes a *sing. v.* Any organization or scheme for spreading a certain opinion or point of view; the opinion or point of view so spread. Often a synonym is preferable: doctrine, advertisement, belief, publicity, education, or teachings. The word has a rather low connotation. Consequently, one organization or party will call its efforts to make its creed or policy known an educational campaign or crusade, but the similar efforts of its rivals propaganda.

In the land of propaganda witch hunting takes precedence over fact finding, fool's gold is as valuable as real gold, and the trail of the herring is preferred to that of the fox. It is a land of half-truths, half-lights, and menacing shadows where danger and hateful things lurk; a place of glitter and tinsel and sham where all the pigs are sold in pokes and mercenary little simpletons choose a maniac to be their leader.

Propaganda is fool's logic. The following are some of its devices.

1. In *Name Calling* the propagandist appeals to prejudice and fear by giving bad names to persons, nations, groups, ideas, or whatever else he wishes condemned or rejected.

2. In *Glittering Generalities* he identifies his program with virtue and uses virtue words like truth, freedom, progress, democracy, the American way, as if they represented exclusively the ideals of his cause and those who support it.

3. In *Transfer* the propagandist places his article alongside a symbol or person or thing of great prestige, fame, or authority, and thus, having placed his buzzard next to an eagle, he confidently expects people to believe his bird much like the other, for do not birds of a feather flock together?

4. In the *Testimonial* device an important person is connected with whatever the propagandist is promoting.

5. In the *Plain Folks* device the person who uses it dresses and behaves and talks in such a way that the people he hopes to influence will believe him to be just like them—and therefore lovable and good.

6. In the *Card Stacking* device the public is given only part of the pertinent facts, so that it will draw the "proper" conclusion.

7. The *Bandwagon* device appeals to the all-too-human desire to join the winning side and a triumphant procession down Main Street.

propensity, *n.* Natural inclination or tendency. Use with *to* or *for,* not *of.* "That *propensity to* do what is easiest . . ."

proper, *adj.* Peculiar, right, fit, fine, correct, respectable, pertaining to or designating one individual only. *Proper* has a baffling collection of meanings. *Proper* for **properly,** *adv.,* as in "We did him up *proper*" is *dial.* and vulgar.

prophecy (prŏf′ē sĭ), **prophesy** (prŏf′ē sī). A *prophecy* is an inspired utterance, a foretelling or prediction. *Prophesy* is the *v.* and means to make a *prophecy.*

proponent, *n.* Advocate, proposer.

Proportion. Your composition is out of proportion, lopsided, or unbalanced if you have not assigned space to the several divisions of your subject in proportion to the relative importance of each. The main idea should be given first consideration, but your purpose as well as the value of your material, must be taken into account in organizing the composition.

proposal, *n.* Offer, tender.

propose, purpose, *v. Propose* means to make an offer, bring up for consideration. "He *proposes* terms that are too favorable to be rejected." It also means *to intend,* which is one of the meanings of *purpose.* One can say "I *purpose* to continue with the plan" or "I *propose* to continue with the plan" and mean the same thing. The other meanings of *purpose* are *resolve, consider as an aim for oneself.*

proposition, *n.* Assertion that is the subject of an argument, the question; terms suggested for an agreement; whatever is proposed or offered for acceptance or rejection. *Colloq.* for *affair, situation, plan, task* or *commercial enterprise.* "*Laissez-faire* is no longer the unquestioned *proposition (doctrine)* it was in father's day." Often used when *doctrine, problem, postulate, policy, prospect, process,* or *petition,* would be much better. As a *v.* it is vulgar.

Prosody, *n.* Versification; critical theory or science of metrics. See **Meter.**

prospect, *n.* View, beautiful view; *sl.,* prospective customer.

prospectus, *n.* Advance statement about a business undertaking.

protagonist, *n.* The actor or combatant who takes the chief part in a play or conflict; by extension, the most conspicuous figure in a movement; champion of a cause, advocate, principal spokesman or agent. Do not write "The *several protagonists in the novel . . .*" or "The *chief protagonist in the play . . .*" *Colloq.* a contender, a leader of the opposition (as if *protagonist* were the opposite of antagonist).

protest (prō tĕst'), *v.t.* and *i.* Remonstrate, make a formal statement of disapproval; voice formal objection to.

protest (prō'tĕst), *n.* Formal statement of disapproval.

proton, *n.* Positive charge of electricity within an atom. See **isotope.**

protrude, *v.* Thrust out, project.

protuberant, *adj.* Bulging, swelling.

prove, *v.* Principal parts, *prove, proved, proved.* A *p. part. proven* appears in freshman themes but rarely elsewhere. **Proven** as an *adj.,* as in "A man of *proven mettle*" is *stand. lit.*

provided, *conj.* Often followed by *that.* Use *provided* in formal statements to introduce a condition in which the provision is distinctly made, e.g., "We will accept your terms *provided* we are not forced to pay cash." In less formal statements *if* is preferable. **Providing** also may be used to introduce a condition, but it too is more formal than *if.*

provincial, *adj.* Countrified, narrow, limited. The *n.* means a person having these qualities. A *provincial* expression is one used in a certain district and differing from the *stand. lit.:* the New England *near* is a provincialism for *stingy.*

provocative, *adj.* Exciting; emotionally disturbing; rousing to love or hate; stirring up opposition.

prowl car, *n. Police tech.,* patrol car furnished with short-wave radio telephone.

prox, *adv. Abbrev.,* next month. Do not use such trite business English. [abbrev. of Latin proximo, in the next]

pseudo, *adj.* or *prefix.* Sham, spurious.

psychist, *n.* Spiritualist. A neologism.

psycho, *adj. Colloq.,* nervously or mentally disturbed or deranged. [stump of psychoneurotic Gr., soul + nerve]

psychodrama, *n.* Therapeutic acting out of a given situation, a psychiatric technique.

psychologist, *n.* Practitioner of the science which treats of the aspects of the mind.

pub, *n.* Saloon, tavern, barroom. [stump of *Br.* public house]

publicity, *n.* Quality of being open or known to the world at large; advertising, especially disguised or smuggled advertising not directly purchased.

publicize, *v.* Make conspicuous, bring to the attention of the public.

publisher, *n.* Producer of printed books; proprietor of a newspaper or other periodical.

pull, *n.* Slang for special favor, secret or illegitimate political influence, drawing power. "This ad has no *pull.*" As a *v.* it is slang in the sense of *arrest, hold, make, draw, hold back the full force of.* "He *pulls* down a big salary." "He *pulled* his punches." "The police *pulled* him." *Colloq.* in *pull off,* do something difficult, forbidden, or dangerous, *pull through,* survive, and *pull the wool over someone's eyes.*

pulp, *n.* Soft, sticky mass such as the edible part of a ripe apple; magazine printed on cheap paper and filled with stories that cater to the taste for sensationalism and fantasy.

Pun. Odd or comic play on words of the same sounds but different meanings, or play on the different applications of a word. Thought by some (especially by those incapable of making puns) to be a low form of humor. "Enjoyment of life depends upon the liver." "You earn your living and you urn your dead." "And the Kurds have their own whey."

punch, *n. Colloq.* in the sense of energy, effectiveness, vigor. "His editorials have more *punch* in them than ever."

Punctuation. The marks of punctuation are the period (.), exclamation point (!), question mark (?), colon (:), semicolon (;), comma (,), dash (—), hyphen (-), apostrophe ('), parentheses (()), brackets ([]), double quotation marks (" "), single quotation marks (' '), and the ellipsis (. . . .).

punk, *n.* Slang for young tramp, something not good. *Trade or tech.* (motion pictures), inexperienced helper of a cameraman; **punk,** *adj.* slang for no good, poor, inferior.

purely, *adv. Dial.,* utterly, thoroughly, completely. "Grandpa was a man who *purely* hated gadgets."

purge, *n.* Purification, thorough elimination.

purist, *n.* A linguistic die-hard. A person more positive in his opinions about language than learned in linguistics.

purpose (pĕr'pŭs), **purport** (pur'pōrt, purpōrt'), *v. To purpose* means to intend; *to purport,* to seem to mean or to mean. **Supposed** is preferable to the passive *purported.* "There were many allusions to the articles *supposed* (not *purported*) to have been written by Jenkins."

purposive, *adj.* Intentional; with avowed aim. .

pursuant to, *phrase.* In accordance with. Stiff old business style.

pursue, *v.* Chase, follow in order to overtake; be engaged in.

push, *n. Colloq.* for *vigor, driving force.* "The old boy seems to have lost his *push.*" Slang for *a set, crowd,* or *group.* "He's the whole *push* to hear him tell it." "She's in the social *push.*"

pushover, *n. Sl.,* easy task; enemy easy to defeat.

pussy-foot, *v.* Sneak, approach stealthily as if on catfeet; avoid open disagreement.

put, *v. Put it over* and *get it over* are *stand. lit.,* but *put over* and *put across* are slang for succeed in getting something done or accepted, present successfully, trick. "That rascal will *put* something *over* on you if you will let him." *Put on,* present, give, put on the stage; *put up to,* submit for a decision, are *colloq.* "The judge *put* it *up to* him whether he should work or pay the fine." But *put up to* is *stand. lit.* in the sense of *incite, suggest to,* as in "She *put* him *up to* it." *Put in,* spend, devote to, make, as in "He *put in* a good day's work," and *put off,* disconcert, as in "He spoke well until a heckler *put* him *off,*" are also *colloq.*

In the sense of *arrange a plot or scheme* **put up** is slang, but meaning to answer with, confront one with, as in "He *put up* a fight," it is *colloq.* The *adj.* **put-up,** dishonestly arranged, is slang. "It was a *put-up* job." The *adj.* **put,** fixed, is *colloq.* "These ties will stay *put.*"

As a *v.i.* **put** is *stand. lit.* meaning set one's course for, go hastily, betake oneself. Usually with *for, about, back, in, out, to,* and so on. "The pup will seize a bone and *put for* the cellar before you can even shout."

putt, *n.* Stroke made on a green to propel golf ball toward or, ideally, into the hole.

PX, *n.* Post Exchange; canteen.

pyrotechnics, *n. pl.* Fireworks; verbal fireworks, controversial eloquence.

Q

quad, *n. Printing tech.,* quadrat.

quadrat, *n.* Metal block used for spacing in setting type; an "em quadrat" is of the width of an *m* in the size of type being used.

quadruped, *n.* Four-footed beast.

quantity, *n.* Amount; in versification, length of time required to pronounce a syllable, length of the vowel in a syllable. Quantity is not in good use as a synonym for *number.*

quantum, *pl.* **quanta** *n.* Amount; unit of energy according to the notion of modern physicists that molecules are constantly taking in or giving out *quanta.*

quarter, *n.* Twenty-five cent piece.

quasi, *adj., adv.* Seeming; apparently.

Quasi Adverbs. Certain adjectives when but loosely attached to a construction that would seem to require an *adv.* may correctly stand for one. Such adjectives are *quasi adverbs.* In the sentence "He was smoothing down the topsoil *preparatory* to sowing the seeds," *preparatory* is a quasi adverb and does not have to be changed into the *adv. preparatorily.* Some of the quasi adverbs are: *according, pursuant, preliminary, preparatory, previous, prior, irrespective, regardless, contrary.*

quatrain, *n.* Four lines of poetry.

quay (kē), *n.* Wharf; landing place alongside a harbor or navigable stream.

queer, *adj.* Strange, odd, peculiar. *Colloq.* when used for suspicious, questionable, eccentric, unwell, or faint. "I feel *queer.*" Slang for *not genuine* or *honest.* "This is a *queer* deal." As a *v.* meaning to spoil, act so as to offend, make fun of, it is slang.

Question Mark. Interrogation point (?) used to mark the close of an interrogative sentence. "When shall we know?"

1. A question set within a sentence is not usually closed with a question mark. "This enmity sprang up, *didn't it,* almost overnight."
2. A sentence that is interrogative in form but only slightly so in meaning may end with a period instead of with a question mark. "Will you please send me the names now."
3. A sentence that is interrogative in form may be exclamatory in meaning. "What a day!"
4. The question mark within parentheses (?) is sometimes used to express doubt, as "My good friend (?) Nick is . . ." but is a rather crude device.
5. A question mark belonging to a quotation, or to an expression within parentheses, is placed before the second parenthesis or quotation mark. "He will ask, 'Do economists contend that depressions can be eliminated?' " (Will they?)

queue up, *v.* Line up, a vivid Briticism.

quicky, *n. Sl.,* motion picture made cheaply and quickly.

quiet, *adj.* Peaceful; gentle; still.

quisling, *n.* Political traitor. [Name of notorious Norwegian collaborator with Nazis]

quit, *v.t.* Leave, let go, give up, and *Am.* stop, discontinue, as "He did not like to *quit* work." As a *v.i.* meaning to leave one's job without intention of returning, it is *colloq.* "The cook *quit.*"

quite, *adv.* More often used in its *stand. lit.* meaning of *wholly, altogether, entirely,* in negative statements, as in "He is not *quite* ready yet; it is not *quite* three o'clock." It is also *stand. lit.* as an intensive meaning *positively, really, truly.* "This is now *quite* the fashion." *Quite* is *colloq.* when it means to a great extent or degree, as in "Aren't those prices *quite* high?" *Quite a(n),* meaning *of considerable size, excellence,* etc., with a *n.;* and meaning *very, rather, noticeably,* with an *adj.* is also *colloq.* "This is *quite a* house, *quite an* impressive speech." "He caught *quite a* few." *Quite some* for *considerable* is slang. "He waited in the anteroom for *quite some* (a considerable) time."

quiz, *pl.* **quizzes** *n. Br.,* practical joke; *Am. colloq.,* informal examination in school or college.

quiz, *v.* Examine, interrogate; *Br.,* mock, banter.

quondam, *adj.* Former.

Quotation. A *direct quotation* is the exact copy of spoken or written words; the *indirect quotation* is a restatement of the gist of what was said or written. Quotation marks enclose the direct, but no marks are needed for the indirect quotation. If there is any point (and there usually is) in indicating the source of a quotation, pass that information on to the reader, but do not do this in a pedantic or trite manner. Do not make parenthetical acknowledgment such as, "In the words of the immortal Swan of Avon" whenever you use a well-known Shakespearean phrase.

Single inverted commas mark *a quotation within a quotation.* "The impression he made on the House was expressed very well by Representative Sardine's 'Phooie!' "

Do not quote too much from books you have consulted in the preparation of a theme. Do not quote at all unless you need a writer's exact words for a special purpose.

Quotation Marks. Often *abbr. quotes* (" ") (' ').

1. Double *quotation marks* enclose direct quotations. When a quoted passage contains two or more paragraphs, the quotation marks are repeated only at the beginnings of the paragraphs, the closing quotation marks being omitted in all but the final quoted paragraph.

2. They also enclose the titles of shorter literary compositions (such as essays or poems) or parts of larger ones. When the larger ones are referred to as wholes, italics are customary. "The poem 'Trees' is found in *The American Anthology.*"

3. In quoting a question or exclamatory sentence, place the question mark or exclamation point inside the quotation marks. "She exclaimed, 'What a night!' "

4. Proverbs are not quoted.

5. *Quotation marks* are placed about words to be taken in a special way or those out of their natural context; e.g., slang in formal writing, a technical term not in a scientific treatise. "And this was the 'pillar' of the church!"

6. Single *quotation marks* enclose a quotation within a quotation. She said, "I do not like the way you keep repeating 'So's your old man.' "

quote, *n. Colloq. and radio tech.,* quotation; quotation mark.

quotes, *n. pl.* Quotation marks. [U.S. Govt. Ptng. Office Style Manual 1945, p. 5]

quoth, *v.* Archaic word meaning *spoke, said.* A poeticism.

R

racism, *n.* Conviction that pure races of human beings exist and that one race is inherently superior to others.

racket, *n.* Slang for questionable line of business, dodge, trick, fraudulent scheme. Better than slang in the sense of a criminal enterprise consisting in the systematic extortion of money by intimidation.

racketeer, *n.* Gangster.

racy, *adj.* Piquant, pungent; salacious, smutty.

radar, *n.* Method of discovering distant objects by reflection of ultra-high frequency point-to-point radio waves. [presumably coined from initials of *R*adio *Di*rection *A*nd *R*anging]

radical, *adj.* Revolutionary, extreme, root-and-branch. [*L.,* root]

radical, *n.* Advocate of sudden and complete change.

radio, *n.* Radiotelegraphy, wireless.

radio beam, *n.* Uniform radio signal from a landing field for guidance of approaching pilots. To be *on the beam* is to be on the right course and, therefore, smoothly effective.

radiorating, *n.* Declamatory broadcasting. Portmanteau neologism.

radon, *n.* Radioactive gas resembling argon.

raise, *v.* To cause to rise, cause to grow, rear, bring up. The principal parts are *raise, raised, raised.* Do not confuse with *rise, rose, risen.* To *raise Ned, the devil, the roof, the wind* (get money by any means possible) are slang. Parents may say that they *rear* children, but in many parts of the United States, especially in the South, they say that they *raise* them. **Raise,** *n.,* is *stand. lit.* in *get a raise,* i.e., an increase in wages or salary. Do not confuse with **rase,** q.v.

raison d'être, *n.* Elegant or scholarly variation for reason, justification, reason for the existence of.

raj, *n.* Rule; government in India; formerly, British rule in India.

rake-off, *n.* Slang for profit or commission, often an illegitimate one, received by a party to a transaction. "The contractors got a big *rake-off.*"

rally, *n.* Reassembling of forces after discomfiture or defeat; gathering of forces; mass meeting.

rank, *v.t.* Classify; outrank, take precedence over.

rap, *v.* Snatch away; strike a smart blow; reprove, condemn.

rap, *n. Sl.,* blame, penalty. *Take the rap* means accept the responsibility, pay the penalty.

rare, *adj.* Thin, not frequent, of uncommon nature or excellence. *Scarce* usually identifies something that is for the time being to be had in diminished quantities. "Herons are *rare* in this state." "A rainy summer has made the quails *scarce.*" *Am. rare* also means *underdone.* "I want my steak *rare.*" The *v.* **rare** is a *dial.* form of *rear. Raring to go* means eager, ready, anxious to go.

rarefy, *v.* Make thin, make less dense.

rarely, *adv.* In the sense of *seldom, rarely* usually precedes the *v.* "The Cannonball *rarely* makes a stop at Tinkersville." In the sense of *extremely, excellently, in an unusual degree,* it usually follows the *v.* "They are getting on *rarely.*" *Rarely ever* is *colloq.* for *rarely if ever.* See **hardly.**

rase, *v.* See **raze.**

rate, *v.* Mark, value.

rate, *n.* Mark; classification in the U.S. Navy, rating.

rather, quite, *adv.* The *colloq. quite* meaning noticeably, to a considerable extent, is similar to *rather.* See **quite.** *Rather* means somewhat, slightly, more precisely, more truly, to a greater extent, sooner, by choice. It can be used with *had* or *would.* "I *had* (or *would*) *rather* sit with you than dance with Miriam." It is *colloq.* for *certainly, assuredly.* "Do you know him?" "*Rather!*" (with the implication of knowing him too well).

rating, *n. Tech.,* enlisted man in the U.S. Navy.

rationalize, *v.* The general meaning is to make rational, explain or justify on logical grounds, interpret rationally, free from elements not in harmony with reason. The *trade or tech.* (psychological) meaning of *attribute one's actions to rational or plausible or presentable motives without analyzing or revealing the true motives* is widely used, and must not be confused with the more general meaning.

rattle, *v. Sl.,* fluster, frighten, confuse.

rave, *adj. Journalistic sl.,* enthusiastic, excessively favorable.

ravioli, *n.* Cereal food like spaghetti.

rayon, *n.* Textile fiber or yarn produced from cellulose; fabric made therefrom.

raze, *v.* Scrape, cut, shave off; destroy, level to earth; *rase.*

re. Usually in the phrase *in re,* used prepositionally to mean *in the matter of.* It is Latin, and when used in English, *trade or tech.* (law)

reach, *v. Colloq.,* get in touch with; arrive at; conclude.

reaction, *n.* A counter tendency, a return of a previous condition, return action or influence. *Trade or tech.* (chemistry), chemical process or change; (psychology) response to a stimulation of the nerves. Loosely, *impression, influence.* Much overworked and sometimes pompous in the sense of *response, impression, opinion, attitude.* "What was her *reaction* to that question?" is not as good as "What was her *reply* to that question?" if the writer means *response.*

readable, *adj.* Susceptible of being read; easy or pleasant to read. See **legible.**

Reading, The Art of. When one can translate sentences into one's own words, grasp all that the author wishes to convey, and pass judgment on the validity of the ideas presented, he can really read. The good reader attacks a new book with all the skill and knowledge acquired in previous readings and knows the value of a preliminary survey and any hint or fact that might throw light on the nature of the new book and what was back of it. So he reads the preface, examines the table of contents or the chapter heads, weighs the publisher's blurb, and looks up reviews or critical comments. As he knows that an author's life or his views usually affect his book, the expert reader may consult *Who's Who* or a biographical dictionary.

A tentative classification of the book or article may help him know what to expect and so get his mental bearings. If it is a short story, a special article on a popular subject, or a novel, it will most likely keep him interested to the end without much effort on his part. If it is study reading, it will doubtless be a strong challenge and he will have need for self-discipline and strong motivation. He will have to attack a small portion at a time, chewing and digesting thoroughly and never losing sight of the fact that he will have to remember what he is reading—at least until examination time.

If he is a truly good reader, he has overcome "dictionary paralysis" and so actually reaches for and consults his desk dictionary every time he encounters an unknown word. Besides he makes good use of the gazetteer, biographical dictionary, and lists of abbreviations and foreign phrases in the appendix. And he makes sure of topical and literary allusions. On occasions he may open the encyclopedia.

He does not have to read far before the style and method of presentation reveal what class of readers the author addresses and how he intended his book to be taken.

Is he pitching a straight ball or a curve? Is his book to be taken as a straightforward statement or as an allegory full of allusions to contemporary persons, vices, and foibles; or as a satire in which irony seems to turn everything topsy-turvy? The kind of material he selects and whether he looks at it from the point of view of comedy or tragedy or burlesque will provide the answer and also indicate whether he is inclined to be dreamy and romantic, realistic and satirical, or apathetic and coldly critical.

His quality is also revealed by the amount of figurative language he uses. The highly colored, flowery, Euphuistic style, ironically called "fine writing," is now laughed at unless it is in verse, yet even the scientist, who must be literal most of the time, still finds metaphors useful on occasion. The poet and the novelist without the concreteness, imaginative appeal, and beauty of figurative speech would be badly handicapped. In fact, the language itself would also suffer since much of it is made up of dead metaphors. One of the many reasons the reader must understand the figures of speech is to prevent him from mistaking the figurative for the literally real, as the girl did when she wanted to know where the electric *current* went when it was turned off.

The word *figure* in *figure of speech* means "that which contains hints or allusions," that is, contains an indication that something is meant other than the literal. In print it is the context and in speech it is the inflection of word or phrase that indicates that when the ironist says one thing he means the direct opposite. For instance, two girls who are having a tiff meet. One elevates her nose and remarks to the other, "Oh! what a *LOVELY* hat!" This under the circumstances will hardly be taken for a compliment. Compare this example of *irony* with the gangster's, "So you're a *WISE GUY?"* or an exasperated, "What a help *YOU* are!" When irony becomes bitter and cutting, it is *sarcasm.*

The imagination plays fast and loose with proportions in *exaggeration* and *understatement,* figures of speech used for emphasis. "The most colossal bargain in the world" illustrates how the first magnifies, and the very successful fisherman's modest "Oh! we caught a *FEW*," shows how the second gets emphasis by understating.

The *metaphor* is an implied comparison between two unlike things. In it the word which means one thing when taken literally is made to stand for another thing by virtue of a similarity of analogy discovered by the imagination. Thus, in "the *bottle-neck* in the automotive industry" bottle-neck literally means the narrow part of a bottle that slows the intake or outflow. Figuratively it stands for the untoward conditions slowing the output of automobiles, and the comparison is obvious. The underlined words in *community chest drive*, *spiral* of *inflation*, and "He's a '*ham*,'" are metaphors. In G.I. parlance a fine airplane pilot is a "rock" because he is "solid," and two slang metaphors are born.

Write out the comparison implied in a metaphor using *as* or *like* and you have a *simile*. "He behaves *like a 'ham.'*" In the similar *metonymy* the name of one thing stands for something closely associated with it, or if it is a part, it stands for the whole. In "The *kettle* is boiling" *kettle* stands for the contents of the receptacle. *Knife* stands for *surgery*, *board* for *table*, "*cop-(per button)*" for *policeman*, G.I. for *soldier*, and *leatherneck* for *marine*.

The figurative way of expression will not mislead the reader who understands it. Rather it will stimulate his imagination and add pleasure to his reading. But since authors may mislead him in another manner, he must constantly question the truth of any statement and the validity of any conclusion. The relation between a science textbook and reality will be close enough to satisfy anyone but a specialist, and although the names and the dates in a history text are undoubtedly correct, some historians might have a hard time justifying their theories, their strange perspectives, and their discreet suppressions. The word and the truth are still further separated in

biography, for the tendency of a biographer to make an idol of his subject is notorious. The campaign biography is worse still, for instead of faithfully rendering nature, it commonly embellishes it. The "debunking" biography is likely to fall just as short of the whole truth, but for the opposite reason. Imaginative truth to life is all that fiction claims; it does not pretend to tell what actually happened to real persons, although it often does just this.

By far the worst offender against truth is propaganda. It wears the uniform of a soldier enlisted in the cause of veracity, yet it has the heart of a mercenary and the soul of a traitor. It fights only to promote its own interest. The propagandist garbles quotations, distorts or suppresses facts, builds up emotional attitudes with bias words, and uses abstractionisms like liberty, democracy, and justice and makes them mean nothing or whatever he wants them to, for such terms are not "condensations" from experience and so do not have a definite content. The propagandist thrives because there are so many poor readers and so few thinkers in the world. The good reader will recognize propaganda for what it is and scorn it.

The skillful reader does not dawdle along but neither does he try to vie with the machine and press for speed and more speed. More important than speed are complete understanding and leisurely enjoyment. One of the joys of reading comes from accomplishment. Horizons constantly widen for the good reader because he discovers that the more he learns about any subject the more interesting it becomes.

read where. Too much has to be supplied by the reader in sentences like "I *read* in the *Times where* a taxi strike is imminent," and "I *saw* in the paper *where* Maginnis is paroled." Write "I read an article in the *Times* about the impending taxi strike." "I see in the papers that Maginnis is paroled."

ready, *v.* Prepare, make fit for use, make ready.

real (rē'ăl, not rēl), *adj.* In formal English *real* is nearly always an *adj.* since it scarcely ever stands for the *adv. really.* "He is *really* good" is not the exact equivalent of "He is *real* good." The *real* in the last sentence is an *adv.* meaning *very. Real* as an *adv.* meaning *very, much, extremely,* is chiefly *low colloq.* "She is *real* (better *extremely*) proud of her son." "He was *real* (better *much*) provoked by your remarks." "It's a *real* (better *very*) good thing."

real, actual, *adj.* In *real* the emphasis is upon objective existence. "Is this *real* or is it a dream?" In *actual* it is upon the act of coming into the sphere of action or fact. "Is he *actually* here?" The opposites of *real* are *imaginary, artificial,* and *counterfeit.* The opposites of *actual* are *possible, virtual,* and *theoretical.*

really, actually, *adv. Really* means in fact, existing objectively, and is often used for emphasis, as when it stands for *positively, I assure you, indeed. Actually* means in truth, in actual fact, and for the time being. *"Really,* is he *actually* here?"

realtor, *n.* Elegant patented name for a real estate dealer or agent who has had some specialized education and has joined a society of his fellows. Preferable to the vulgar *slang,* "landlord's Legree."

reason is because, the reason why. *Stand. lit.* usage is illustrated by "The reason he was dismissed is *that* he was impertinent." "The *reason* he was dismissed is *because* he was impertinent" is generally felt to be almost as redundant as "This is the *reason why that* he was dismissed," although examples of the first construction occur in the works of many good writers. It is best to complete *the reason is* with a *that* clause unless there is a special reason to do otherwise. However, there is no objection to *it is because,* as in "There is no mystery about why people make such mistakes; *it is because* they fail to think things through," although *it* refers to the idea of reason.

Why is not needed in "This is the reason *(why)* that he was dismissed," but *reason why* meaning *cause, motive,* as in "The reason why* is not hard to discover," is *stand. lit.*

receipt, *n.* "We are *in receipt of* your letter" is not as good as "We *have received* your letter."

receipt, recipe, *n.* Formula for combination of ingredients; pharmacist's prescription; formula for preparing a cooked dish. *Recipe* is preferable in the two special senses.

receive, *v.* Accept; permit to enter; get from the outside.

receptionist, *n.* Clerk who welcomes callers, gives information, and acts as a buffer between employer and clients or the inquisitive public.

recess, *v.* Adjourn.

recess (rē'sĕs, rē sĕs'), *n.* Adjournment; intermission; alcove.

recidivism (rē sĭd' ĭ vĭzm), *n.* Falling back, backsliding; return to criminal ways; relapse.

recitation, *n.* Oral delivery of memorized selection, prose or verse; repeating of prepared lesson; class meeting.

reckon, *v.* To ascertain number or amount by calculation; compute. In the sense of *think* or *suppose,* it is *colloq.;* and for *expect* or *intend* it is *dial.* "I *reckon (suppose)* he'll come back." "I *reckon (expect)* to get there Thursday."

recognize (rĕk' ŏg nīz), *n.* Admit the truth of, know the identity of, recall as having been known, give the floor to. Pronounce the *g.*

recollect, *v.* Recall to mind, remember by conscious effort.

recondite (rĕkŏn'dīt), *adj.* Subtle, deep, scholarly; abstruse, profound. [L., put away again]

reconditioned, *adj.* Repaired for second-hand sale.

recourse, resource, *n. Recourse* means resort for help or protection, the someone or something sought for that purpose. *Resource* means something that offers support, something resorted to in an exigency, a supply or stock that can be used. "We have missed every opportunity we had and must now have *recourse* to stratagem."

"He drew from *resources* no one knew he possessed."

recreate (rē′kre āt), *v.* Make again; bring to life; reanimate; take recreation.

red, *n.* Socialist, communist, radical, revolutionist. *In the red* means in debt.

red-baiter, *n.* Politician who derives pleasure and profit from accusing other politicians of communist leanings or affiliations.

redolent, *adj.* Heavily odorous.

Redundancy. A synonym for pleonasm, wordiness, tautology. The *redundant he,* or floating subject, is *low colloq.* "My father, *he* goes to town every day." Expressions like *join together, new innovation,* etc., are redundant. See **Pleonasm.**

refer, *v.* Point; direct attention; direct attention again; allude.

referee, *v.* Judge a contest, fight, or controversy.

Reference. The relation of a *pron.,* especially a relative *pron.,* to its antecedent. Ordinarily the reader expects a *pron.* to refer to the nearest eligible preceding *n.* If reference to this *n.* makes the meaning absurd or different from what the author intended, the reference is faulty. If the antecedent is in the possessive case or within parentheses, the reference is said to be *weak.* If the antecedent is vague and broad rather than a definite idea expressed clearly in clause or word, the reference is *broad.* If the *pron.* seems to refer to two ideas, the reference is *divided.* The types of *broad reference* illustrated in the following sentences are tolerated *colloq.*

"He has no political following, and *that* is the reason he was not nominated." "As soon as the fish stopped I checked him, *which* was, John told me, the worst thing I could have done." "There was a phone call *when* you were out." "Did *they* leave any message?"

In a broader sense, *reference* means an allusive statement or remark. A topical reference refers to such topics as a noteworthy happening, a notable trial, a witty retort made by a famous person, a notorious scandal. Reference also means a direction referring the reader to a certain passage or book.

refractory, *adj.* Stubborn, obstinate; hard to manage.

refuse, *v.* (rē fūz′), *adj.* and *n.* (rĕf′ ūs).

regard, *v.; n.* Used with *as* when the meaning is *consider* or *think.* "I *regard* her *as* my best friend." *In regard to* and *with regard to* are correct, but *with regards to* is a faulty mixed construction made from *with regard to* and *as regards.*

regardless, *adj.* Used with *of. Irregardless* is a faulty mixed construction made from *irrespective* and *regardless.*

regent, *n.* Governor, member of a governing body; capitalized Regent, *colloq.,* examination set by authority of the Board of Regents of the University of the State of New York.

register, *v.* Record formally, enroll, enter one's name in the register of a hotel.

register, *v.* Slang in the sense of feel, or convey the impression of feeling, or make an impression, as "The tiger *registered anger,*" or "Her smile didn't *register.*" In *trade or tech.* (motion pictures), it means to express emotion by attitude, gesture, expression, and action.

regular, *adj.* According to the accepted rules or manners; *sl.,* a *regular* fellow, i.e., one that thinks and does as other fellows.

rehabilitate, *v.* Restore to former capacity, efficiency, or social rank.

rehabilitation, *n.* Restoration of ability to be self-sufficient.

reimburse, *v.* Pay; repay.

relation, *n.* Recital, account; kinsman.

relative, *adj. Grammar,* referring to an antecedent.

relative, *n.* Kinsman, kinswoman.

release, *n.* News story or copy of speech or document made available for publication at or after a specified time.

religious, *adj.* Godly; concerned with a system or systems of faith and worship.

re-make, *n.* Journalistic *slang,* adaptation, revision, version.

remember, recollect, *v. Remember* means to bring to or keep in mind; *recollect,* to make a successful effort to remember. "Old Hickory *remembered* (not *recollected*) the remark he had made on that occasion." "I don't *remember* your name." "I can't *recollect* what I did with the screw driver." Do not *remember of*.

reminisce, *v.* Surrender oneself to reminiscences, indulge in reminiscent reverie.

remunerative, *adj.* Affording pay in return for service; profitable.

Renaissance (rĕn'e säns', rē nä'sans), *n.* New birth; revival. Capitalized when it means the period between the medieval and modern ages, or is used an an *adj.* meaning of or pertaining to this period. Generally preferred to *renascence.* "He prophesies an American *renaissance.*" "She is a student of *Renaissance* architecture."

renascent, *adj.* Revivified; sprung into new being.

renowned, *adj.* Famous. Illiterate persons mistakenly write *reknown.*

rent, *v.* Hire the use of real estate, machinery, or instruments.

rep, *n.* Slang stump of *reputation, repertory, repetition,* and *representative.*

repartee (rĕp'er tē'), *n.* Clever or witty retort, skill in making witty rejoinders. Also witty retorts collectively. "Hendricks is noted for his *repartee.*"

repeat again. With *repeat, again* is superfluous. Cf. *refer back.*

Repetition. The same word may be repeated in the same sentence or sentence sequence if it is used in the same sense each time. The following sentence does not meet this requirement: "He maintained that the rounds were *even, even* though the referee's decision did not bear him out."

In avoiding the natural or expedient repetition of a word, the writer may be guilty of the fancy variation; that is, variation for the sake of variety or for the sake of ostentation. But the writer must not let his mind or pen get into a verbal rut. Do not always say a thing in a way it has been said; avoid triteness and the stereotyped phrase. Do not let a favorite word run riot. Good wording is deft, fresh, and varied. Take special care to vary connec-

tives. Do not let *so* and *and* be the only conjunctions. See **Variations, Fancy.**

replete, *adj.* Full, very full; stuffed.

reportedly, *adv.* Bad journalese for *according to the report.* "Mrs. Doughby is in Reno *reportedly* seeking a divorce."

repossessed, *adj.* Taken back; reclaimed from purchaser who cannot keep up his instalments.

reprehensible, *adj.* Ethically or morally objectionable.

reputation, *n.* Estimation in which one is held. *Cf.* **character.**

repute, *n.* Reputation; favorable estimation as opposed to *disrepute.*

required, *adj.* Compulsory, prescribed.

research (rē sŭrch'), *n.* Scholarly investigation; careful, systematic study productive of new data. Too strong is this word to be applied to the studious exercises by which undergraduates acquire a little knowledge of scientific method. The pronunciation rē'sŭrch is *colloq.*

reservation, *n.* Limitation; personal accommodation set apart, booked in advance, or assigned.

residual, *adj.* Remaining, left over.

residuum, *n.* Remainder; part left over, residue. This *tech.* word is now often used *colloq.*

resilience, *n.* Elasticity; capability of withstanding shock without permanent change of shape.

respect, *n. With respect to,* with reference or regard to, is the usual expression, although *in respect of* is not incorrect. "There was nothing *with respect to* what was intimated this morning that would arouse our client's anger." *In respect to* means in relation to, as respects. *Without respect to* means without regard or consideration for.

respectively, respectfully, *adv. Respectively* means each to each, and relates members of one series to members of another series in the same order; *respectfully* means in a manner full of respect. "These are the items for which The Deaping Company and Rex, Inc. ask *respectively* $8000 and $8500." "Treat him *respectfully.*"

restaurant, *n.* Public eating place.

resuscitation, *n.* Restoring from unconsciousness or death.

retail distribution, *n.* Merchandising. Elegant variation for storekeeping.

retread, *n.* *Army sl.*, reserve officer recalled to active duty; *baseball sl.*, old player recalled to major league club.

rev, *v.* Change the number of revolutions per minute (*up* or *down*),–of airplane motors and propellers.

revamp, *v.* *Colloq.*, give new form to old materials; renovate.

reverent, reverend, Reverend, reverence. *Reverent* means showing respect; *reverend*, deserving respect. *Reverend* is a clergyman's title and is commonly used with the full name and preceded by *the.* Write "the Reverend William H. Wigging, D.D."; "the Reverend Mr. (or Dr.) W. H. Wigging," not "Reverend Wigging." In addressing a clergyman say "Dr. Wigging" if he has a doctorate, or "Mr. Wigging"; and not "Reverend Wigging" or "Reverend." *The Reverend,* as in *"The Reverend's* sermon was long," is in bad taste and is often somewhat derisive. *Reverence* is a strong feeling of respect and esteem.

Titles of respect preceding proper names should be capitalized. For officials of the Catholic and Anglican churches forms of address, salutation, and complimentary close are prescribed by ecclesiastical usage.

revers, *n. pl.* Lapels on a woman's coat.

revise, *v.* Look over with a view to correction or improvement.

rezone, *v.* Designate anew the limitations of an area or region.

rhetoric, *n.* Oratory; art of composition in words; speeches; technique of prose style.

Rhetorical Question. A question to awaken expectancy, to clinch conviction, and not to be answered unless by the speaker or writer. "The debater asked, 'Can these arguments that my opponents have brought forward be answered?' "

rhubarb, *n.* Pieplant; *sl.*, squabble, flurry of fisticuffs.

rhyme, rhythm, *n. Rhyme* means poetry; words or verses with corresponding terminal sounds. It is sometimes *sp. rime. Rhythm* means a particular metrical pattern or the regular flow or movement in verse, music, etc.

ride, *v. Colloq.* in *ride on a rail,* pu..ish, *ride the goat,* be initiated, *ride up,* work out of place, but *ride for a fall* is stand. *lit. Ride* in the sense of *pick on, bully, criticize,* as in "We are going to *ride* him ragged," is *colloq.* It is slang for *kill, play a joke on,* and *take for a ride.*

ridiculous, *adj.* Absurdly comic; not to be considered seriously.

right, *adv. Dial.* as an intensive meaning *rather, very.* "Mother is *right* (stand. *lit. quite*) well, thank you." "I'm *right* (very) glad to see you, Colonel." "There's *right smart* corn down there." *Colloq.* it means straightway, exactly, just. "You come *right* home." "Let's have it out *right* here and now." *Right away* and *right off* are *colloq.* for *at once.* "I want to go *right away* (immediately) after lunch." *Right along, adv.,* is *colloq.* for continuously. "It snowed *right along* through the morning." When **right**, *n.,* occurs in the phrase *have a right,* and the meaning is *should, ought,* it is chiefly *dial.* "You *have a right* to (should) obey mother." It is also *dial.* when the phrase means to have excuse, cause, reason, etc. "She *has no right* to cheat." It is vulgar in the sense of *deserve.* "Coming at that speed I *had a right* to break my arm."

rightist, *n.* Conservative in politics.

rise (rīz), *v.* and *n.* Ascend, ascent. The principal parts are *rise, rose, risen;* the *p. part.* is often used with *is* instead of *has.* The *n.* is slang in "We couldn't get a *rise* out of him."

roast, *v. Colloq.* in the sense of ridicule, criticize.

robot (rō'bot, rŏb'ot), *n.* A mechanical man, an automaton. Hence, an efficient but unfeeling person, a man capable of acting as a machine without human emotions or feelings. [First used by Capek in the play "R.U.R."; probably backformation from Czech *robotnik,* serf]

rock, *n.* Boulder, cliff; *colloq.,* stone; *sl.,* in *pl.,* diamonds, money. The *adj.*

rocky means fully of rocks; *sl.*, physically uncomfortable, mildly ill. *On the rocks*, without money, bankrupt, is *colloq.*

Rock-bottom, *adj.*, extremely low, *n.*, the very bottom; and *rock-ribbed*, with an abundance of rocky elevations, stern, unyielding, are *stand. lit.*

roger, *interj.* O.K., I understand, All right! [radiophone signal of receipt of message]

roil, *v.* Irritate, stir up. The *colloq. rile* means the same.

role, *n.* Actor's part; part or function assumed by anyone. The circumflex accent is usually omitted in *Am.* use.

romance, *n.* A novel or short story in which love and marriage are treated in idealistic fashion; a tale depicting chivalrous adventures, supernatural events, and fantastic experiences; heroic verse narrative in one of the Romance languages.

Romance Languages. All of the modern languages which have developed from Latin are classified as Romance. These include not only French, Spanish, and Portuguese but Roumanian, Sardinian, the Alpine Rhaeto-Romanic tongues, and the Dalmatian language (now obsolete like the horse-drawn fire engine). Colloquial American has been considerably influenced by Spanish, especially in the southwestern States, and by the French of Canada.

Roman Numerals. In the Latin system of notation, which is used in analytical outlines, tables of contents, and designation of the pages of an introduction, letters of the Latin alphabet are the numerals. The principal symbols are:

I =	1	C =	100
V =	5	D =	500
X =	10	M =	1000
L =	50	X̄ =	10,000

Placing a bar over a letter multiplies its value by 1000. The value of a letter preceding another is subtracted from that of the one following. Thus IX = 9. Lowercase letters may be used as numerals; they are often so used in pagination of prefaces or introductions.

rook, *v.* Cheat at cards; *colloq.*, cheat, defraud; *n.*, small, raucous blackbird; swindler.

rookie, *n.* Soldier in basic training, recruit, beginner, first-year man in major league baseball. This term is rather *colloq.* than *slang* because there is no precise synonym in good use.

room, *v.* Occupy a room as a tenant. *Roomer, n.*, is one who occupies a room as tenant or lodger, and *roommate* is a companion with whom one shares a room.

root, *n.* In linguistics, that part of a word which remains when inflectional endings, prefixes, infixes, and suffixes are taken away. The root of un tru th ful ness is tru.

rooter, *n. Sl.* But what other word can replace this term? The applauder? The encourager?

rope, *n.* Metonymy for the hangman's noose and also for the lasso. *Roped and tied* in the sense of at one's mercy, married to or under the domination of a woman, and *roped in,* inveigled into something, deceived, are *slang.*

rotatee, *n.* Soldier returned from active duty but subject to recall.

rote, *n.* Routine; by rote, by mechanical repetition of phrases without attention to the meaning.

rotten, *adj.* Decayed; *stand. lit.* in the figurative sense of unsound or corrupt. "He said that the local administration was *rotten* to the core." *Slang* in all the other pejorative senses, as bad, unskillful, uninteresting, disagreeable, inferior. "She is a *rotten* (poor) tennis player." "This is a *rotten* (uninteresting) book."

rough, *adj., adv. Rough-and-ready, rough-and-tumble, diamond in the rough, ride roughshod, rough rider, rough-spoken,* and *roughing it* are *stand. lit. Rough,* difficult, unpleasant, as in "It was a *rough* time"; "They had it *rough,*" is *colloq. Roughhouse* as a *n.*, meaning boisterousness, minor riot, fracas, and as a *v.*, meaning behave in a boisterous manner, is slang. *Roughneck, n.*, rowdy, crude fellow, is also slang.

round. See **around.**

route, *n.* Road or itinerary. It is pronounced (rōot) except in military (route step) and railroad use (The Shore Route), or the *colloq.* milk route, paper route, where it rhymes with out. The same practice is observable in the pronunciation of the *v.* "The mails were routed via Chicago."

rub, *n.* and *v.* As a *n.* meaning hindrance, difficulty, that which causes one to stop and reflect, rub is archaic and literary. To rub the wrong way, cause (one) annoyance or irritation, rub (it) in, repeatedly call one's attention to something disagreeable in an unpleasant manner, are *stand. lit.* Rub out, kill, is slang.

ruction, *n.* Uproar, fight, noisy outbreak. Chiefly *dial.*

rum, *n.* A generic name for spirituous liquors of all kinds, used chiefly by those who would like to forbid the sale of such drinks. As an *adj.* meaning queer, odd, poor, bad, eccentric; as in a *rum* customer, a *rum* thing, it is *Br. slang;* **rummy,** *n. sl.* for alcoholic.

run, *v.* The principal parts are run, ran, run. Because it is susceptible of being used with various significations, *run* has tended to become a word of all use. "Before the time of my stay *ran out.* I decided to *run* up to New York. While on the train I *ran* through the newspapers to get a brief *rundown* on the situation. In the city itself I had a brief *run* of luck. I *ran* into an old friend who *was running* a small cigar store in the station. I knew that he had *run* himself into debt a few years before, while *running* for public office. **Run in,** meaning arrest, is *sl.*

runway, *n.* Beaten path; elevated walk from stage of a theater into the orchestra; landing strip for airplanes.

rushee, *n.* Collegiate *sl.,* person who is being considered for membership in a fraternity or sorority.

ruthless, *adj.* Merciless. The antonym *ruthful* is archaic.

S

-s. Affix correctly used in certain adverbs, as *sometimes, afterwards, nowadays,*

but incorrectly added to compounds of where. Write *anywhere, nowhere, elsewhere, somewhere.*

sabbatical, *adj.* Pertaining to the Sabbath. The Sabbatical year was the seventh year, during which, according to the law of Moses, the land was allowed to lie fallow and all debtors and Israelite slaves were set free. Professors in some *Am.* colleges are allowed a sabbatical year of absence from professorial duties for study, travel, and a renewal of scholarly vitality.

sabotage (sab'ō täzh', sab'e tidge), *n.* Obstruction of production or waste and destruction of property by workers during war or during a labor dispute. It is loosely used to mean deliberate and malicious interference with any plan, program, or project. The *v.* is now acceptable in the literal and figurative senses. [*Fr.,* wooden shoes]

sack, *n. Sl.,* bed. Hit the *sack,* go to bed, and sad *sack,* an inept and bewildered person who by means well but is always unsuccessful in his efforts, are slang. *Sack* meaning dismiss from employment is *Br.* slang.

sacrilegious (sak'ri lē'jus), *adj.* Pertaining to profanation of holy things. Do not confuse it with *blasphemous.*

said, *v.* Low *colloq.* when followed immediately by an infinitive (except in passive constructions). See **say.** As *adj.* meaning previously mentioned, *said* should be reserved for technical legal documents.

sake, *n.* Welfare, benefit. The word that comes between *for* and *sake* is sometimes written without an apostrophe when it is a common *n.* whose possessive case is a syllable longer than its nominative. *For Margaret's sake* but *for conscience sake, for goodness sake.* The *pl.* of *sake* can be used with a possessive *pl.* "Do it for both our sakes."

salary, wages, *n.* Salaries are paid monthly (or at longer intervals) for clerical or professional work; wages are paid weekly or semi-monthly for labor. *Stipend* is more elegant than salary, and *honorarium* is more elegant than *tip.* [*L.,* money for salt]

sale, *n.* Disposal of goods for money;

selling of goods at reduced prices. *On sale* usually means offered to customers or purchasers at reduced prices; *for sale,* offered for selling, purchasable. *Salesclerk, salesgirl, salesman,* and *clerk* are in good use; *saleslady* is not.

same, selfsame, identical, *adj. Selfsame* is a stronger word than *same,* but they are synonymous. "This is the (same) selfsame dress you wore last night." *Identical* usually means alike in all perceptible details. "They are not *identical* twins."

It is in poor taste to use *same* as a substitute for a personal *pron.,* as in "We have seen your clients and will advise *same* (better *them*)," or "I have received your letter and read *same* (it)."

Do not use *the same as* as an adverbial conj., as in "Is your collector *the same as* mine?" This construction is *low colloq.* But the *adv.* (used with the) is correct in sentences like "He has to pay taxes *the same* as anyone else."

If it follows *same* closely, introduce a clause with *as* rather than *that.* "He referred to it in the same breathless manner that a hero worshiper mentions his current hero" should be "He referred to it in the same breathless manner as that of a hero worshiper mentioning his current hero."

Avoid *of* after *same.* "He had the same size of books." Prefer "He has books of the same size as those."

sanatorium, sanitarium, *n.* Used interchangeably in the sense of rest home for convalescents, health resort. *Sanitarium* is preferred when the meaning is institution for psychoneurotic patients; *sanatorium,* when the meaning is hospital where special (especially natural) curative treatments are available. Avoid the impulse to interchange the suffixes -arium and -orium.

sanguine, sanguinary, *adj. Sanguine* means optimistic, cheerful, confident; *sanguinary,* bloody, bloodthirsty.

sarcasm, irony, *n.* Sarcasm means bitter remarks made with the intention of giving pain. (By origin, it means to *tear flesh.*) *Irony,* saying the opposite of what is meant, is frequently found in a context which is sarcastic. Sarcasm, unlike irony, is direct.

"It was sarcasm when he called me a 'stuffed shirt,' but it was irony when he referred to me as a 'wise guy.' " See **Irony.**

sashay, *v. Stand. lit.,* perform a gliding dance step. In the senses of approach with affectedly graceful motion, whirl about, go, it is slang. [*Fr.,* chasser]

satellite, *n.* Heavenly body which revolves about a larger one, obsequious and servile follower of a wealthy or powerful man. As an *adj.* it is generally used in the phrase *the satellite nations* to describe nations which have come under the hegemony of a larger nation and lost autonomy in domestic and foreign affairs.

satin, *n.* Silk fabric woven closely to give a smoothfaced and glossy appearance.

satin, satiny, *adj.* Smooth, soft, and lustrous.

satire, satyr, *n.* Satire (săt′ĭr) is a literary piece marked by caustic wit or subtle humor which exposes and ridicules human foibles, vices, and absurdities. A **satyr** (sāt′er, săt′ er) is a lusty demigod, part human and part goat.

satirize, *v.* Subject to ridicule; use as the subject for a satire. *Satirization* is a bad coinage for *satire.* "This poem is a satire (not *satirization*) of pomposity."

saucy, *adj.* Pert, rude. (Dialectal pronunciation, să′sē.)

save. Archaic or literary for the preposition *except* and the conjunction *unless.*

saw, sawed, sawn or **sawed,** *v.* Cut with a saw.

say, *v.* A form of *say* followed directly by an infinitive is *low colloq.* (except in passive constructions). "She said to go away." Better: "She said 'Go away,' " or "She said that you should go away." Instead of "This article says to eat plenty of dark bread," write "This article advises one to eat . . ." But it is correct to write "He is said to be near here."

Say is impertinent or extremely informal as a form of address. "*Say,* who do you think you are?" Like *listen, well,* and *why,* it is a persistent but unnecessary sentence beginner. *Says* for said, as in "And then he up and *says* that he wouldn't," is *low colloq.* or vulgar.

The *n.* **say** is *stand. lit.* in "You have had
your *say*," i.e., chance to talk. **Say-so** is *colloq.* meaning a person's mere word. "We
have only your *say-so* for that." "I'll say
so!; I'll say!"; and "You said it!" as expressing emphatic agreement are *low colloq.* or
slang. **Said,** *adj.,* meaning aforesaid is
either *trade* or *tech.* (law, business) or trite
humor. See **said.**

scan, *v.* Examine closely and minutely;
analyze or describe the metrical structure
of verse; *tech.* (television), reproduce or
transmit an image by traversing a surface
with beams of light or electrons. In the
sense of *look over hurriedly, give a cursory glance to, scan* is *colloq.*

scarcely . . . than. Inelegant. Say
scarcely . . . before, or *scarcely . . . when.*
"Scarcely were the new pictures varnished
before (not than) several people came to
buy." Do not use *scarcely* after a negative.
Not "They don't scarcely ever speak," but
"They scarcely ever speak to one another
now."

scare, *v.i.* and *v.t.* Much less formal than
frighten. Stand. lit. in "He was scared by a
leak in the boat." *Low colloq.* in "She was
scared at (or *scared* of) mice." Write "She
was afraid of mice." Not "They were *scared*
to do that," but "They were *afraid* to do
that." *Scare up* is *colloq.* for find, get hold
of. "I can't *scare up* a nickel." *Scarehead* is
colloq. for very large headlines.

scare, *n.* Sudden fright or apprehension
without a real basis.

scarify, *v.* Make incisions or scratches;
criticize mercilessly.

scene, *n.* Subdivision of a play; locale of
action for a drama.

sceptic, sceptical. Also spelled *skeptic,
skeptical.*

schedule (skĕd'ūl), *n.* List, time table.
(*Br. pron.* shĕd'ūl.)

schism (sĭzm'), *n.* Division; in religious
history, division in the Christian church.

schizophrenia (skĭz ō frē'nē á), *n.* Mental illness or psychosis involving disinte-
gration of personality; split personality.
[*Gr.,* split mind]

schmaltz, *n. Sl.,* theatricality, overdone
sentiment; affected sentimentality, corn.

schmeer, *v. Sl.,* flatter. [Yiddish]

schnozzle, *n. Sl.,* nose, proboscis, trunk.
Schnozzola is a variant.

scholar, *n.* Commonly used to describe a
learned person, especially one who becomes a specialist in a particular field; one
who receives money, tuition, or other
emoluments to enable him to continue his
studies as a graduate student. Student is
generally used of those who attend classes
in secondary schools and colleges, pupil of
those who attend elementary schools. Student is also applied to those who like to
study.

schwa (schwä), *n.* Obscure vowel sound,
unaccented; commonly symbolized by an
inverted e (ə).

Scientific Point of View. The impersonal attitude toward what one is describing. It seeks to be rigorously accurate
through eliminating divergencies due to
faulty observation and the differing sensory equipment of the individual observers.
It tries to get rid of bias due to emotional
or intellectual set. Some of the evil consequences of disregarding scientific point of
view are misleading and inaccurate repre-
sentations, illusions, false proportion, the
pathetic fallacy, the anachronism, and in-
fringements upon **Physical Point of View,**
q.v.

scissors, *n. pl.* Pair of scissors, small
shears. Note that this is a plural noun, the
name for two blades.

scoop, *n.* Newspaper *tech.,* news story
published by one paper in advance of
other newspapers; Navy *slang,* the *scoop,*
the latest news, gossip, or rumor.

screen, *v.* Sift coarsely; pass through a
series of tests.

scrip, script, *n. Scrip* means stock certificate, unofficial currency; *script,* handwriting; anything written, manuscript;
written dialogue and directions for a motion picture or radio program.

scuff, *n.* Heelless, open slipper.

secular, *adj.* Literary in the sense of lasting for generations; happening once an
age or century. Commonly it means concerning this world rather than the next,
non-religious. Secular clergy are those who

do not belong to a monastic order, a society of men who are bound by vows of poverty, chastity, and obedience.

sedition, treason, *n.* Sedition means any act, speech, or writing stirring disorder and discontent with the government; **treason** is an overt act (and, according to law, witnessed by two persons) which aims at overthrowing the government, or, in time of war, aiding or comforting the enemy.

see, *v.* Principal parts, *see, saw, seen. Seen* for *saw* is vulgar. In formal style "See *whether* Fred is there" is preferred to "See *if* Fred is there." *See* is *colloq.* in the meanings of bribe, get support of, find to their liking or good enough to accept or agree upon. "The publishers couldn't *see* my novel." *See . . . through,* as in "I began it and I'm going to *see* it *through,*" and *see daylight* or *stars* or *red* are also *colloq. See to* is *stand. lit.* in the sense of tend, look after, provide for. *See where,* as in "I *see where* they had a drought out West," is *low colloq.*

seek, *v.* The principal parts are *seek, sought, sought.*

seem, *v. Stand. lit.* in negative constructions like "for some reason or other, I *can't seem* to get the sense of this statement," and "Good fruit *doesn't seem* (i.e., as far as I can find out) to grow in this section." It is also *stand. lit.* in the positive: "I *seem* to feel better."

seemly, *adj.* Fitting, in accordance with good manners, good taste, or common decency.

seize, *v.* Lay hold of forcibly; clutch; comprehend. Note the spelling.

seldom ever. *Colloq.* for *seldom if ever* or *hardly ever.* "Jenkins is *seldom ever* (*stand. lit. seldom if ever*) on time." Likewise *seldom or ever* is *colloq.* for *seldom or never.* Cf. the *colloq. rarely ever* for *rarely if ever.*
Seldom is not to be used as an *adj.* for *infrequent.*

selectee, *n.* Chosen person; man drafted for military service under the Selective Service Act. See **inductee.**

selection, *n. Colloq.* for poem or passage,

or piece of music selected to be read or played.

self, *pron.* Usually hyphenated when it is the first element in a compound: *self-assumed, self-approving, self-help.* Do not use such compounds when the word to which *self* is affixed suffices. Write "She is a *confessed* (not *self-confessed*) kleptomaniac"; "He admits that he violated his oath," not "He is a *self-admitted* perjurer." Do not use *myself, yourself,* etc., as substitutes for *I, you,* etc.

sell, *v.* Transfer or convey title to a purchase.

sell, *v. Slang* in the meanings of cheat, impose upon, take in, secure the acceptance of, convince of the desirability of. "He *sold* the public on Gold Pills, and kept them *sold.*" *Sell out* is slang in the sense of betray a cause or one's associates for money. The *n.,* meaning cheat, hoax, is *colloq.* "What a *sell* that show was."

semantics, *n.* Science of the meaning of words; science of the relationship between words as signs and the things signified and the effect of the use of words as signs on conscious and unconscious human behavior; semasiology.

semi-, *prefix.* Half.

Semicolon. The chief use of the semicolon is to separate the clauses of compound sentences of the following types:

1. When the comma and *conj.* are not used to connect the clauses. "The area of controversy in our politics is comparatively small; the really vital issues are relatively few."

2. When the clauses express a contrast or a marked change of thought. "Many persons think that *noisome* means noisy; only a few take *fatuous* to mean corpulent."

3. When a conjunctive *adv.* (*therefore, nevertheless, so, however, moreover, accordingly,* etc.) is the connective. "He is tiring rapidly; *nevertheless* I think he will finish first."

4. When the clauses have commas within themselves and the chief turn in the sentence must be clearly marked.

"If this doctrine is accepted, it must be granted also that financial losses and lack of the necessities of life are unavoidable for a large proportion of the population; but whether the unfortunate are doomed to dependency upon charity is another question, and one that will demand all our intelligence."

The *semicolon* is also used:

1. To punctuate a series of coordinate phrases when a stronger mark than a comma is desirable. "They discussed the problem of administration; the question of checks upon the chief executive; the attack upon the Constitution; the powers of the Supreme Court."

2. To precede connective phrases like *in fact, in short,* or *at that* coming between two independent clauses. It is also used before words like *namely, to wit, that is, for example,* introducing an explanation, example, or enumeration. "The two Corliss boys are coming; *in fact,* the whole class has been invited." "These men were employable; *that is,* the relief work kept them in training."

3. To separate the members of a series of clauses or phrases coming after a colon; and in addresses and references where a comma alone would not separate the items clearly. "His income for the last two years: 1935, $3210; 1936, $4286." "*Troilus and Criseyde,* 3:1–7; 4:3–10."

A semicolon is placed after closing quotation marks, not before. "He said that furs are worn by 'a large proportion of the population'; but whether this statement is correct or not I cannot say."

send, *v. Sl.,* rouse to ecstasy, delight, excite. **Send-off,** *n.,* is *colloq.* for a demonstration of good will to one beginning a journey or starting an enterprise.

sense, *v.t. Colloq.* for understand, grasp, realize, as in "He did not seem to sense the situation." *Stand. lit.* in the meaning of feel, become aware of without having to be told. "He sensed the danger before he knew what had happened." "She sensed his scorn."

sensible of, sensitive to, susceptible to. Generally, *sensible of* expresses emotional awareness, *sensitive to,* quick feeling, *susceptible to,* lack of resistance to. "I am profoundly sensible of his worth." "Are all writers sensitive to criticism?" "Many are very susceptible to flattery." *Susceptible of* means so constituted as to admit or permit. "Do you think that this new theory is susceptible of proof?"

sensory, sensual, sensuous, *adj. Sensory,* the scientific and technical term, means pertaining to sensation. *Sensual* means fleshly, inclined to indulge in gratification of the senses, voluptuous, carnal; *sensuous,* of or pertaining to the senses or the objects perceived by the senses. "*Sensual* men place their felicity in things that do not last, food, wine, and transient pleasures." "Since the young writer's world is mainly a world of sight and sound, he seeks to find words that will transfer to another the vividness of reality in *sensuous* experiences of his own." "His *sensory* perceptions were dulled."

Sentence. A statement, question, or request so worded and placed as to make sense. A compound *sentence* consists of two or more independent clauses. See **Complex Sentence** and **Forceful versus Languid Sentences.**

Sentimentality. The state of being sentimental, that is, dominated by, or having an excess of, tender and intense feelings. The quality of mawkish emotionalism. The sentimental person is apt to use expressions of ecstatic joyousness or of unrestrained gloominess: "How lovely!" "Isn't it just too adorable!" "Magnificent!" "Alas, O miserable me." Or poeticisms: *clamant, plangent, beauteous.* Or affected expressions of stock pathos: *a lump in one's throat, tug at one's heart strings, stricken, but it was not to be, the supreme sacrifice.*

separate (sep'a răt), *v.* (sĕp'a rĭt), *adj.* Followed by *from,* not by *between.*

sequence, *n. Tech.* (motion picture), a section of screen story represented as taking place at the same time and place without a break of any kind.

Sequence of Tenses. Relation in tense between verbs in main and dependent clauses. See **Conformity of Tenses.**

seraphim, *n. pl.* The singular is seraph.

serial, *n.* The serial room in a library contains magazines, journals, reports, and periodicals which are published at more or less regular intervals. Generally, *serial* refers to a narrative published in successive issues of a periodical.

serif, *n. Tech.* (printing), stroke finishing the top or bottom of a letter.

serigraph (sĕ'rē grăf), *n.* Picture or design produced by a series of printings through a silk screen which acts like a stencil.

service, *v.* Provide with maintenance, repair, installation, distribution, or the like.

session, cession, *n. Session* is a period of sitting, time of instruction in a school. *Cession* is the act of yielding rights or territories.

set, *v.* The principal parts are *set, set, set.* Cf. *sit, sat, sat.* As a *v.t. set* means to cause to sit, adjust, fix in a certain position or place, make fast, place a certain value on. As a *v.i.* it means to sit on a nest (said of hens), fit, as in "The coat *sets* well," fall below the horizon, and become rigid or fast.

Set one back is slang meaning to cost one so much money. "That dinner *set me back* (*stand. lit. cost me*) ten dollars." *Set up* meaning *treat to* is also slang. **Setup,** *n.,* is *stand. lit.* in the sense of manner in which something is arranged or ordered, make-up, manner of carrying one's body. "The senator has been studying the economic *setup* of Missouri." It is slang for unequal contest arranged so that one contestant may get experience or publicity, and for a treat. **Set-to** is *colloq.* for bout or contest.

Setting. In narration, the background—the time and place, the where and the when of the story.

settle, *v.* Close by payment. *Colloq.* when applied to the paying of an ordinary bill. "Who'll *settle* (*pay*) for the dinner?"

Also *colloq.* in the sense of *give a quietus to, stop, silence, make behave.* "That'll *settle* him."

severally, *adv.* Separately, one by one; opposed to jointly.

sew, *v.* The *p. part.* is sewed and (less frequently) sewn.

sexy, *adj. Slang,* characterized by great concern with the results of the anatomical differences which distinguish the human male from the human female; attractive. "The most important requisite for a historical novel is a sufficient number of sexy scenes."

sez, *v.* Phonetic spelling of says. See **say.**

shake, *v.* Cause to vibrate; *sl.,* get free from, evade.

Shake-down, extorted contribution, is slang. *Shakedown,* a pallet or straw bed, is *stand. lit.*

shall, will. One commonly regards *will* as the auxiliary *v.* that expresses pure futurity, especially in the second and third person. The *will* that expresses real volition (God *wills* it) is now most frequently met with in connection with *have* ("Who *will have* a sandwich?") or in negative sentences ("I *will* not allow that"). In the first person the auxiliary *will* often expresses a future colored by volition. "I *will* win that game." Consequently *shall* is generally used to express pure futurity in the first person. Yet there is a strong tendency, especially *colloq.* in America, to use *will* here. "We'll certainly have frost tonight." "What *will* I do when I get there?"

One reason for the prevalence of *will* over *shall* is that *'ll,* which is short for *will* and not *shall,* is easier to say than *shall.* Another is the inclination to use *shall* only when it is clearly necessary to indicate either that volition is not implied or that the idea of obligation, necessity, or restraint is present. Hence the preference for *shall* in the first person to express pure futurity, in conditional and relative clauses, and in promises or requests. Note that in questions *shall I (we)?* and *shall he?* ask about the will of the person addressed but that *shall you?* expresses pure futurity.

Is (am, are) going to sometimes takes the

place of the *will* of pure futurity, and *has to* or *is to* often takes the place of the *shall* expressing obligation.

Would is the *p.* of *will; should* is the *p.* of *shall*. In general, *would* and *should* follow the usage of *will* and *shall*, but see **would.**

shamateur, *n.* Amateur in name only; athlete who pretends that he is not paid for participation in games or contests. This portmanteau neologism combines sham and amateur.

shan't (shănt, shȧnt). Short for shall not. *Colloq.*

shanty, *n.* Dilapidated cabin, shack. [Irish or Canadian *Fr.*, old house, hut]

shape, *n.* *Colloq.*, condition. "The team is in *shape* to give the Bears a hard game." *v.* Show promise, begin to develop form, become efficient. "How is the new advertising campaign shaping up?"

shark, sharp or **sharper,** *n. Colloq.* A cardsharp (*sharper*) is one who cheats at cards, especially a professional gambler; a *cardshark* is an expert at playing.

shears, *n. pl.* Not to be used with *sing.* *v.* The *v., shear* has the *p. part. sheared* and *shorn;* the latter is used as an *adj.*

shew, *v. Br.* and *arch.* variant spelling of show. Now a literary affectation.

Shifts, Needless. In passing from clause to clause or from sentence to sentence, do not needlessly or unintentionally shift the subject of your sentences, the voice of the verbs, or number, person, or tense. A common fault is the shift from *sing.* to *pl.* in sentences which have an indefinite pronoun as subject. "If anyone has made an error, let them (better him) admit it." See **Stability** and **Directness.**

shimmy or **shimmey** (shĭm'ĭ), *n.* A jazz dance; excessive vibration, especially in the front wheels of an automobile. The *v.* means to vibrate or shake abnormally. [*Fr.*, chemise, an undergarment]

shine, shone or **shined, shone** or **shined,** *v.* Emit rays of light; be bright by reflection; polish; blacken or stain and polish. The preterite and *past part.* shone may be used when the *v.* is intransitive; in *Am.* usage *shined* may be used for the transitive

and intransitive *v.* "The sun has not *shone* (or *shined*) for three days." "I *shined* (not *shone*) my shoes yesterday." As a *n.* meaning mischievous trick or a liking, *shine* is *colloq.* **Shiner** is slang for black eye.

shivaree, *n.* Burlesque serenade of a newly wedded pair. [*Fr.*, charivari]

short, brief, *adj. Short* and *brief* mean not long; *short* refers to time and space, *brief* usually to time alone. *Short* sometimes implies a lack or incompleteness, as in "They are on *short* rations." It has the additional meaning of discourteously concise, as in "I gave him a *short* answer." *Short* is *stand. lit.* in such phrases as *short* of funds, *short* for (something), and make *short* work of. **Short-change** is *colloq. Brief* is *colloq. adj.* in the sense of extremely short when it is applied to spatial relations, as in "Bathing suits this year are briefer than ever before."

Shortly, *adv.,* is frequently ambiguous. It may mean soon, in a discourteous and concise manner, or briefly.

Short Story. This type of narration presents a situation or character involving a problem or a struggle. The solution or the outcome may or may not be conclusive or explicitly indicated. The short story is limited in length and in number of principal characters, and is usually built upon one main situation or scene. In many modern short stories mood is more important than the events. The author aims at evoking a single impression.

should, *v.* The *p.* form of shall as would is of will. *Shouldn't ought* is *dial.* and vulgar. See **would.**

shove off, *v. Sl.,* depart, leave, start off.

show, *n.* Demonstration, ostentatious display; spectacle, exhibition. *Show* business, theatrical production, administration, and participation in performances is a technical term. *Colloq.* for a play, chance, opportunity, as in "The poor fellow didn't have a *show*," and as a general term for theatrical performance. *Showdown* is *stand. lit.* for *decisive disclosure of facts, resources, motives.* **Show,** *v.,* is *colloq.* in the sense of *convince, prove.* "I'm from Missouri; you'll have to show me." *Trade or tech.* (racing), be third or better in a horse race. *Show off* is *colloq.* for *perform ostentatiously, display accomplishments in a spirit of vainglory.* **Show-off,** *n.,* is *colloq.* for the person who *shows off,* but *stand. lit.* for *the act of showing off.* **Show up,** *v.,* in the sense of *reveal the faults or weaknesses of, put in an appearance,* is *colloq.* "I *showed* him *up* all right; he won't *show up* today."

shut, close, *v.* Synonyms which differ in meaning in certain contexts. *Closed* is used to mean not allowing admission of the public, as in "The library is closed during the Christmas holiday." *Shut* is a stronger word in most contexts. *Shut up,* be silent, be less noisy, is *colloq.,* but *shutdown,* a closing of a factory, *shutin,* one who is confined to bed by a long illness, are *stand. lit.* A *shut-out,* a game in which one team makes no score, is sports *tech. Shut of,* rid of, free from, is *colloq.*

shy, *adj.* Timid, scant. Slang, often with *of* or *on,* for *lacking, short (of), deficient in.* "We are *shy* two clerks this morning." "We are *shy on* alligator pears." "I am *shy of* collars." *Short of* in this sense is *stand. lit.* **Shy,** *v.,* means to throw sidewise, swerve aside, shrink.

shyster, *n. Colloq.,* cheap pettifogging person, especially a lawyer without professional honor. Cf. *quack* and *charlatan.*

sibling, *n. Tech.* (psychology), brother or sister; children having one parent in common. [OE]

sic, Latin for *so.* Used after a quoted word or phrase to confirm, or more often, to question the accuracy of the statement. "The *Recorder* states that the County Fair will continue through Thursday and Saturday [*sic*]." The person who wrote in the [*sic*] wanted to call attention to the supposed mistake of substituting Saturday for Friday. "The *Freeport Booster* says in a recent editorial that it wishes to *enlighten* [*sic*] the citizens of our city as to their part in the recent paving scandal." The question mark within brackets can be used in a similar way.

sick, *adj.* The meaning in America is *suffering from any bodily disorder.* In British usage it means this when used as an attributive (*sick* people), but in the predicate (be *sick,* feel *sick*) it usually means *nauseated. Ill* and *unwell* are sometimes euphemisms. *Sick* is slang for *chagrined.* "They are *sick* about it all." *Sick* applied to specific parts in the sense of *diseased* is *low colloq.* "When this happens, the kidneys are *sick.*"

side, *n.* Space or region adjacent but neither before nor behind.

side, *adj.* Auxiliary, subordinate.

sideshow, *n.* Incidental diversion; small exhibition or entertainment associated with a circus.

sidestep, *v.* Evade, avoid.

sideswipe, *v. Colloq.* Strike a glancing blow. The *n.* is also *colloq.*

sidetrack, *v. Trade or tech.* (railroading), switch to a side track. *Colloq.* switch off from a purpose, prevent action upon, reduce to a subordinate position. "The delegates *sidetracked* poor Merton."

sight. As a *v.* it means to see, get sight of; as a *n.,* a thing seen. It is *low colloq.* in the sense of a great deal, a great many; much. "No, sir! Not by a long *sight* (a great deal)." "There was a *sight* of (were many) people at the fire." "The frost did a *sight* of (much) damage to the orchards." Do not confuse *sight* with **site,** *n.,* place of or for a building, or town, scene of something; or with **cite,** *v.,* bring forward, quote.

sight unseen, *adj. phrase.* Without inspection or test.

signature, *n.* Name of an individual written with his own hand; sound effects at beginning of a radio program regularly associated with that program; printing *tech.,* symbol placed at the bottom of the first page of each section of book or pamphlet; printed sheet containing 4 pages or a multiple of 4, folded as a unit and forming a section of a book or pamphlet. "I returned the dictionary when I discovered that the binder had omitted one signature and misplaced two others."

Signs and Symbols. For punctuation marks see **Punctuation.** Some of the signs commonly used in proofreading follow:

⌒ connect letters

\# leave space where caret is inserted.

∧ caret—used to indicate an omission, the insertion of letter, word, or symbol, or both.

⊙ insert period.

⸜ delete, strike out.

= insert hyphen.

Theme readers sometimes indicate faulty punctuation by / and faulty parallelism by //.

sign up, v. Colloq. for enroll, enlist. "He signed up thirty subscribers."

similar, adj. Like is both adj. and adv., but similar must be changed to similarly to form the adv. In substituting the more formal similarly for the adverbial like, writers sometimes forget to add the -ly. "They say that this species never raises its nestlings similar to (similarly to or like) the cowbird, which always lets other birds hatch and feed its young."

Do not confuse similar and same. If two things are identical in all respects or if there is no perceptible difference between them; similar means very much like (but with perceptible differences). "Exactly similar" is incorrect for same.

Simile. The simplest figure of speech. It is a comparison with something different in kind or quality and therefore not to be taken literally. "He eats like a bear," i.e., he eats ravenously. The like or as is usually expressed.

Because similes are simple they are dangerous. To use too many similes makes your style unnatural. The use of such trite similes, as blushing like a schoolgirl, as much privacy as a gold fish, fresh as a daisy, betrays your lack of imagination and makes your style flat. Similes which by their oddity call attention to themselves are more suited to verse or poetry than prose.

"The evening is spread out against the sky Like a patient etherized upon a table."

The epic or Homeric simile is an extended comparison which is applicable at one point only.

simply, adv. Plainly, in a simple or art-

less manner. Also a counterword and colloq. intensive to take the place of really, truly, absolutely, very. "Your dress is simply divine."

simulate, dissimulate, v. Simulate means to put on a false appearance or disguise; dissimulate, to conceal what a person or thing is, conceal one's true nature or motives. The same distinction should be made between the nouns simulation and dissimulation. Simulated, falsely appearing to be, is an elegant variation of artificial. Simulated leather means heavy paper disguised as leather.

since, conj. Since refers to the period intervening between a point in past time and another point in the past or present. "I had not seen her since I attended her wedding." It has also become a casual and less formal because. "Since she has evidently forgotten the appointment, I won't wait any longer." Use since when the meaning is since the time when, seeing that, or inasmuch as. Since in "Since I've been here I've been perfectly happy" should be while. Ago is not needed with since in sentences like "It is just two years ago since I saw her."

singlet, n. Br. and elegant, undershirt.

Sir, n. As a title it should be followed by the given name and not by the family name; as a form of address it is generally used by an inferior in addressing a male superior or a man with whom one wishes to maintain a relation of chill formality. It is used colloquially in addressing a friend on terms of social equality. Almost always accompanies a formal insult. "And you, sir, are a liar." "Don't sir me; you know my name."

sit, sat, sat, v. Be seated, lie, rest, be situated. Sit tight in the sense of refuse to move or be frightened into making concessions, and sit up, meaning show interest or surprise are colloq. But sit down (up)on, refuse, reject, repress, and sit pretty, be in excellent position, condition, are slang.

The confusion between sit and set is very old, and the attempt to settle the problem by saying that sit is intransitive and *set* is transitive is misguided. *Sit* is used as a transitive verb in such sentences as "She sits her horse well." "Sit yourself down." See **set.**

sitdown strike, cessation of labor by organized workers who remain in their place of employment, is a new formation already well established in the language.

sitter, *n.* Anyone who comes in to stay with children, dogs, canaries, or elderly invalids when those responsible are out.

Situation. The time, place, motive, or other circumstance essential to a complete view of an event or state of affairs, actual or imagined.

size, *n. Colloq.* in the sense of actual state of affairs or situation, as in "That's about the *size* of it—he's broke." **Size up,** *v.,* is *stand. lit.* for form an opinion of the situation, ascertain or estimate the character of a person, admit comparison. "This can't be sized up with that." "She had sized up the Baxters perfectly." It is *colloq.* in the sense of beginning to develop form, as in "How are things sizing up?"

Sized is the regular *adj.* in compounds, such as medium-sized, large-sized, etc. As a simple *adj. sized* or *size* may be used. "We had to use small sized (size) screws." Expressions which contain *size,* in its sense of magnitude, and **sized,** the *adj.,* are often tautological.

skilled, skillful, expert, *adj. Skilled* is used generally of workmen or craftsmen who have acquired proficiency through practice and training in a particular field; *skillful* is used of those who are not only proficient but also are unusually deft, adroit, and clever in the performance of any mental or physical operation. *Expert* is used to describe one who has special knowledge and a high degree of proficiency. "It is hard to find *skilled* labor." "Only a *skillful* mechanic could repair that motor." "He dominates the courtroom as only an *expert* trial lawyer can."

skulduggery, *n.* Wirepulling, fraud, trickery. Also *sp.* sculduggery.

slacks, *n.* Sports trousers, loosely-fitting for men, somewhat snug for women.

Slang. A word or expression, below the level of standard speech, substituted for the more orthodox or common term, out of laziness or sheer verbal exuberance, or with the aim of achieving the effect of vividness, force, novelty, directness, or humor. The chief creators of American slang are (according to H. L. Mencken) the wits of Broadway, gag-writers, newspaper columnists, and press-agents. Much of it comes from the burlesque house, the baseball field, and the county jails. Hence the low connotations which characterize most of it. The disease that often dispatches it in its youth is the triteness that springs from overuse. *Skirt, limey, lounge-lizard, hooch, hoofer, hook, scram.*

Not all slang is ephemeral. Some words, such as *debunk, highbrow, racketeer, boom,* become part of the standard language of educated speakers. Some words maintain themselves as slang for generations.

slant, *n. Colloq.,* particular or personal point of view, tendency, angle. "These articles have an optimistic *slant.*" "He has a new *slant* on the subject." **Slant,** *v.* Aim at a particular audience or purpose. "He slanted his articles to show that the law was also beneficial to labor." See **angle.**

slap, *n.* A blow administered with a flat surface. **Slapbang, slapdash,** hurried and careless, and **slapup,** excellent, are *colloq.* **Slap-happy,** *adj. Sl.,* punch-drunk, dazed from excessive beating about the head. **Slapstick,** characterized by crude comedy and boisterous antics, is acceptable in all but formal contexts.

slay, *v.* Kill, murder. Overworked in newspaper headlines.

slenderize, *v. Colloq.,* make thin and graceful; make appear less stout.

sleuth, *n. Journalese,* detective.

slick, *n.* Smooth place. An oil *slick* is a patch of oil on the surface of the sea where, presumably, an airplane or ship has sunk. As an *adj.* and *adv. slick* is slang in the sense of tricky, trickily, or very good. "He's a *slick* customer." **Slick up,** *v.,* is *stand. lit.* in the literal sense of polish, but *colloq.* in "Our town had better *slick* up."

Slicker, *n.* Cheat, gambler. City slicker is the yokel's term for the male city dweller. In trade or *tech.*, magazines are classified as *slicks* (printed on smooth paper) and *pulps, q.v.*

slip, *v. Colloq.* deteriorate, become worse, drop, and put on or take off hurriedly. "Your work is *slipping.*" "Wait here while I *slip* into something more comfortable." *Slipshod, adj.*, is *stand. lit.* as is the *v. slip up,* make a mistake; move up stealthily. The *n., slip-up,* error, small mistake, is *colloq. Slippy* is *dial.* or *colloq.* for *slippery.*

slow, *adj.* and *adv.* Quite as good an *adv.* as *slowly.* "When you pass a school you had better drive *slow.*"

slurp, *v. Sl.,* drink or suck in noisily.

slurry, *n.* Watery mud; thin mortar.

slush, *n.* Wet and dirty snow; overly sentimental piece of writing. A *slush fund* is money collected for use in political bribery, propaganda, or lavish entertaining to influence votes, usually with the implication that the money was either collected or used illicitly.

smack, *v.* Slap smartly; kiss noisily.

smart, *adj.* As applied to a person *smart* means witty (sometimes pertly facetious), shrewd, dashing, fashionable. *Dial.* in the sense of rather large amount of, as in "He has right *smart* of brass." *Smart aleck,* often shortened to *smarty,* is *colloq.* for one who shows off.

smear, *v.* Deface; defame, undermine the reputation by unproved accusations, lies, and innuendo; *sl.,* defeat thoroughly.

smell, *v.i.* and *v.t. Smell out* as in "They will *smell out* the secret" and *smell at* in the sense of inhale or smell odor are *stand. lit.* But **smell up,** make odoriferous, is *colloq.*

smog, *n.* Mixture of smoke and fog. Portmanteau word used freely in Los Angeles.

smoke, *v.* and *n.,* Smoke out, force the revelation of something hitherto undisclosed, smoker, smoking car, one who smokes, are *stand. lit. Smoke,* any alcoholic drink of inferior quality, and *smokes,* cigars, cigarettes, pipes and tobacco, are slang. *Smoker,* party at which only men are present, is *colloq.*

snafu, *adj. Sl.,* confused, utterly confused.

snap, *v.* Slang in *snap out* of it, *snap into* it, and as a *n.* meaning an easy job or remunerative position. The *adj.* is *stand. lit.* "A *snap* decision is one that is made in a hurry." In the technique of story-telling a *snapper* is a surprise ending, an unexpected but not utterly unreasonable or implausible turn at the close of a story.

so, *adv.* and *pron.* As a *pron., so* is usually the object of *say, think,* etc. "The decision was unfair but I was the only one there who said *so,*" i.e., that it was unfair. Make sure that this *so* does not cause vague reference, as in "When he realized that he did not know enough algebra, he set out to do *so.*" Prefer "When he realized that he would have to learn more algebra, he set out to do *so.*"

As an *adv., so* corresponds to *thus* as *that* to *this.* In the meanings of *accordingly, as it seems, also, in actual fact, positively,* do not try to yoke *so* with a *that.* As a conjunctive *adv., so* is overworked and does not properly belong in formal style. Introduce a result clause with *so that.* Avoid, if you can, the following:

1. The exclamatory or intensive *so,* except when the sentence is very short and simple, and the experience appealed to is general. "Maxwell, like *so* many (better *like very many*) wealthy men, started his business career selling papers."

2. The *so* deliberately inserted before a descriptive *adj.* "Here is a scholar who has chosen the task of investigating the English satirists of this complex but always *so* (omit this *so*) attractive period."

3. The *so* that follows close on the heels of other *so's* and *such's.* "It is too bad that *so* many men who can *so* barely meet their daily expenses have to be *so* careful with the *so* little that they get." (Omit *so's.*)

4. The explanatory *so* after *for,* as in "He could not run, *for* he was *so* frightened."

(Omit *so,* or write "He was *so* frightened he couldn't run.")

5. The *so* with superlatives and words that do not admit of degrees (absolutes). "And now, as *so* oft-times (better *often*) happens, the investor finds that he has thrown his money away."

So-so is *colloq.* for *fair.* "She's getting along *so-so.*" Also written *soso* and *so so. So that's that* is a *colloq.* conclusion.

For *so* with a *p. part.,* see **Very with Passive Participles.**

sociable, social, *adj. Sociable* means affable in the company of others, inclined to seek the company of others, friendly. **Social** is more often used in the sense of characteristic of high society, and in the modern compound words of social reformers and politicians, concerned about the good of mankind in general, interested in betterment of society. As a *n.,* **sociable,** gathering of friends, members of an organization, church, etc., is a *colloq.* variant of *social.* **Socialite,** member of high society, one of the Four Hundred, is *colloq.*

sock, *n.* Short stocking. A *pl.,* **sox** is in common *Am.* use in advertising but is not *stand. lit.*

soft, *adj. Colloq.,* sentimentally lenient, not hardboiled, luxurious; non-alcoholic. **Softly,** *n.,* is also *colloq.*

So Habit. The proper place of the *so* joining independent clauses is in colloquial, not in formal style. The writer with the *so* habit uses this *so* in formal writings, and uses it on all occasions, whether they call for *and then, therefore,* or *so that.* For purpose clauses *so that* should be used. A *semicolon* before a *so* joining main clauses is better than a comma. Not bad: "He held out his arm; *so* she took it." Better: "She took his arm because he held it out." See **so.**

solecism, *n.* See *barbarism.*

solid, *adj.* Not liquid; *colloq.,* reliable, dependable; *slang,* consistently stimulating.

solidarity, solidity, *n.* **Solidarity** means union between members of a group or between groups rising from common pur-poses or interests; **solidity,** the quality of being solid.

soliloquy, *n.* Monologue; talking to oneself. Cf. colloquy and dialogue, speech between two or more.

soluble, *adj.* Susceptible of being solved; susceptible of being dissolved.

solvent, dissolvent, *n.* Both mean that which liquefies a substance or causes it to mix with another. Except in scientific treatises **solvent** is the more usual word.

some, *adj.* and *pron. Colloq.* as an *adv.* meaning *somewhat, rather, to some extent.* "She feels *some* (somewhat) better today." *Some* is a *slang* intensive (understatement) in "*Some* style to Chloe," i.e., there is a great deal of style to Chloe. "That's going *some*" means going very rapidly, and "*Some* fight!" means "This is a fight if there ever was one!" *Some of these days* in "*Some* of these days you're going to decide to buy Funkos" is clipped from "*On* some *one* of these days . . . ," i.e., *sometime.*

some more, *adv. phrase. Colloq.,* to a somewhat greater degree.

someone else's. Established idiom.

someplace, *adv. Colloq.* for somewhere.

something, *n. Low colloq.* as an *adv.* meaning very, to some extent, in some degree. "The car was skidding something fierce."

something like, *adj. Colloq.* in the sense of almost as it should be, wholly as it should be. "Now that's *something like* it." *Something like, anything like,* and *nothing like,* adverbs meaning to some, any, or no degree approximating to, are *stand. lit.* "This sketch is *nothing like* so well drawn as that one."

sometime, *adj.* Former, who or which was in the past; *adv.,* in the indefinite future.

someway, *adv.* Also written some way, someways. It is *colloq.* for somehow, in some way. "We have to get home *someway.*"

somewheres, *adv. Vulgar* for somewhere.

sonar, *n.* Method and apparatus for detecting location of submarines. [*sound navigation ranging*]

sonic, *adj.* Of sound; at the speed of sound.

Sonnet. Lyric of fourteen iambic pentameter lines. The Petrarchan sonnet consists of an octave and a sestet. The Shakespearean or English sonnet consists of three quatrains and a couplet.

sooner, *n.* One who moves ahead of others; one who settled in former Indian territory before it was legally open to immigration; Oklahoman. The *adv. sooner* for rather is an acceptable locution in all but the most formal types of discourse and writing.

sophisticated, *adj.* Also *sophisticate.* Most of the unfavorable meanings, artificial, deprived of naturalness and simplicity, etc., seem to have given way to the favorable meanings of worldly-wise (not credulous), urbane (not provincial), and subtle (not ingenuous). In danger of being used too often and indiscriminately.

sophomore (sŏf'ō môr), *n.* Second-year student in an *Am.* college. [Gr., wise fool, doubtful etymology.]

sorry, *adj.* Rueful, regretful; *Br.* type of apology, merely formal.

sort of. See **kind of, sort of.** The usual construction is *this sort of,* and not *these (those) sort of.* But the latter may be used *colloq.* before nouns in the *pl. Low colloq.* when used to reduce the strength of a statement. "Guess they'd be fightin' still if they all hadn't got *sort o'* tuckered out." *Of any sort or kind* is redundant.

Of a sort and *of sorts* are *stand. lit.* and mean *so-called, rather poor specimen or kind* of and *of different kinds.* "This was a horse *of sorts.*" "I found a doctor, at least a doctor *of a sort.*" *Out of sorts* is *colloq.* for cross, disturbed, ill.

sound, *v.* Seek to find out about a person or thing, test, is *stand. lit.* The out, frequently heard in *colloq.* language, is unnecessary. "I shall sound his motives before appointing him."

Sound off, *v. Military tech.,* identify oneself by announcing name, rank, and errand; *sl.,* talk noisily. The *adj.,* **sound** means solid, safe; healthy all the way through, financially solvent.

source material, *n.* Original documents, such as personal letters, diaries, public records, manuscripts, early editions, writings of contemporaries, used in literary or historical research.

Space Pattern. The device of comparing the main pattern or shape of a scene or object to a simple familiar form; e.g., cloverleaf crossing. Sometimes called *fundamental image.*

spanner, *n. Br.,* monkey wrench.

special, especial, *adj. Special* and the *adv. specially* may be used to mean practically everything covered by *especial* and *especially,* and are by far the more common. *Especial* is still possible or preferable in the senses of *exceptional in degree,* as in "He acts this part with *especial* cleverness," and *of or for someone or something* (specified by a possessive *adj.* or the possessive case), as "Did you do that for *my especial* benefit?" or "This play is given for the *especial* benefit *of* the crippled children." But *special* should be used in sentences like the following: "The Steel Corporation is paying a *special* dividend." "This is a *special* edition." "Congress passed this *special* act."

Special pleading is popularly taken to mean dishonest evasion of the real issues by presenting or arguing upon one point or phase of a controversy as if this point or phase covered all of the question at issue.

specialty, speciality, *n. Specialty* is the commoner word. "What's his *specialty?*"

specie, species, *n. Specie* means hard money, coined money; it has no plural. *Species* means sort, kind within the large group or genus. In a scientific name the designation of phylum, class, family, or genus is capitalized but that of the *species* is not capitalized. Note that *species* is both *sing.* and *pl.* "One *species* is the . . . ; there are four other species."

Specific. The definite, particular, or precise is nearly always more forceful than the general.

specimen, *n.* One of a number, a sample; *sl.,* individual.

spectator, n. Spectators watch; an audience listens, or watches and listens.

speech, pl. **speeches,** n. Expression of thought in spoken words; formal public address. Address is more formal, lecture more academic, and talk much less formal.

speed, speeded or sped, speeded or sped, v. Move rapidly. For speed up, accelerate, the preterite and p. part. is speeded up.

speed-up, n. Acceleration; increase in speed of operation; means used to increase output of workmen.

spell, v. Relieve by undertaking to work for a fixed time; place in order the proper letters of a word. The n., spell, means fixed length of time; duration. **Spellbind** means to charm, fascinate. In Am. stand. lit. **spellbinder** is used of an orator who holds his audience captivated.

spelunker, n. Explorer and student of caves.

Spenserian, adj. Pertaining to Edmund Spenser, author of the Faerie Queene. The S. stanza consists of eight iambic pentameter lines followed by an alexandrine, with the rhyme scheme, a b a b b c b c c.

spill, spilled or **spilt, spilled** or **spilt,** v. Sl., give information. As a n. spill is arch. in the sense of strip of paper or wood used for lighting a fire; colloq., a fall.

Spill-over Sentence. A sentence so full that it spills over into the following one where the overflow does not belong. False division. "The howling northeaster rocked the porch and rattled the windows of the little stucco house, which was none too sturdy. The walls were thin, and it was the home of the Scotts who had lived in it for a score of winters." The walls were thin belongs with the first sentence.

spiritual, n. Religious song; Negro folksong religious in tone and theme.

spit, v. Expectorate, eject from the mouth. The preterite is **spat.** The preterite of **spit,** impale, put on a spit, is spitted.

spiv, n. Br. sl., loafer, drone in the social hive; grafter.

Split Construction. Do not needlessly break up the natural order of sentence parts or let words or punctuation marks separate constructions whose parts normally belong together, as the parts of a phrase. Avoid the awkwardness of "The attitude the people take toward, without ever actually taking a part in, a political conflict of this kind, is astounding." A misplaced comma can break up a natural order; e.g., "The fox, turned back again, from the brook." See **Intruders.**

Split Infinitive. To + adv. + infinitive; e.g., to thoroughly analyze. Not always a fault. See **Infinitive, Split.**

splurge, v. Colloq., make an ostentatious display, show off, spend money lavishly. There is a corresponding n.

sponsor, n. Guarantor, patron; backer; radio tech., advertiser who pays for a show. The sponsor in baptism is the godparent who promises to inculcate religious principles in a child.

spoof, n. and v. Slang word coined by Arthur Roberts. Swindle, hoax.

Spoonerism. An unintentional ludicrous distortion of words through transposing initial letters. The happy Sam becomes the Sappy ham, a well-oiled bicycle, a well-boiled icicle, and smelling salts, selling smalts.

sport, n. Colloq. in the sense of one who follows racing, football, etc., chiefly for the purpose of gambling; or one who is a devotee of sports and pastimes; a good loser. v. Colloq., display clothes, personal belongings, expression, or manner, in public. "They lounged about as if they had nothing to do but sport their sunburned faces and fancy clothes."

spot, v. Colloq. in the sense of recognize, tell, as in "He can spot a winner every time." **Spot,** n., in on or upon the spot, meaning in danger—often in put on the spot, to kill—is slang.

spotlight, n. Theatrical limelight; publicity.

sprain, strain, n. A sprain is an injury to a joint and to its ligaments; a strain, injury to a muscle or muscles from excessive exercise or stretching.

square, v. Sl., secure silence or acquiescence of the police or those in authority by persuasion or bribery; *n.*, odd person, social misfit, square peg. **On the square** is *colloq.* for honestly, fairly. *Squarehead* is derogatory slang for a German, Swede, or Holsteiner. *Square deal, square dealer,* and *square shooter* are *colloq.*

squeal, *v. Colloq.*, protest, complain, give away secrets, or inform the authorities.

squeeze, *v. Sl.*, take graft, extort cash or other gifts in return for the use of political influence.

squib, *n.* Brief, clever, malicious piece of writing which is much like a lampoon. Originally a kind of firecracker which made a hissing noise before it exploded.

Squinting Modifier. A word or phrase that modifies in an uncertain manner because it is so placed that it looks two ways and is therefore ambiguous. "I could begin work tomorrow *if necessary* for twenty dollars a week."

Stability and Directness. Stability as applied to the sentence means evenness and steadiness. To get stability the writer must avoid needless shifts and must not waver between two possible constructions, as beginning the sentence with a subject that fits the first *v.* but that will have to be tacitly modified before it will fit the second one.

Directness is the straightforwardness obtained by the correct placing of modifiers and antecedents, and by keeping together sentence elements that naturally belong together.

staccato, *adj.* Abrupt, disconnected; *adv.*, brokenly, abruptly. [musical term Italian, disconnected]

Staccato Style. Disconnected sentences cut short or apart by gaps of silence which are indicated by periods, exclamation points, dashes, or omissions. Usually keyed to sensational pitch. Headline style. A style to whip up jaded nerves, and therefore bad. See **Style.**

stadium, *pl.*, **stadia** or **stadiums,** *n.* Ancient Greek straightaway racetrack, about 630 feet long, partly surrounded by tiers of seats; modern outdoor enclosure for spectacular athletic contests and shows.

stag, *n.* Male deer; man, man alone, bachelor, predatory bachelor; party for men, in contrast to a "hen party."

stag, *adj.* For men only.

stall, *v.* To stop, refuse to go, as an automobile; deceive by not doing one's best in an athletic contest. *Colloq.* in the sense of *keep at a distance by force or wile.* "Can you *stall off* the collector?" Slang in the sense of fight for time by prolonging a situation. In this sense the *n.* also is slang.

staid, stayed. *Staid* means serious, sedate, sober. *Stayed* is the preterite of the verb *stay.*

stand, *v. Colloq.* in the sense of bear, endure, as in "I can't *stand* that fellow." *To stand to,* have to, be in position to, as in "What will he *stand to* lose if he votes this ticket?" is also *colloq.* like *stand for,* permit, suffer, treat, pay for, as in "She won't *stand for* that," and "He'll *stand* cigars *for* the crowd." *Stand off, v.,* postpone payment, etc., and *n.*, tie, draw, are *stand. lit.,* but *stand in with,* join, be partners with, be in favor with, is slang.

Standard English. The English used by the majority of intelligent and self-respecting speakers and writers of the language. It includes the formal or literary English and the colloquial, popular, but not the low colloquial, popular, or vulgar English. See **English, Levels of.**

standpoint, *n.* Can be used instead of *point of view,* especially when another *of* would follow the *of* of point *of view;* e.g., "from the point *of* view *of* medicine." Better: "From the *standpoint of* medicine." Elsewhere *point of view* is in slightly better standing than *standpoint,* and either is generally preferred to *viewpoint* or *angle.*

stanza, *n.* Group of lines of verse or poetry arranged according to a pattern, a smaller unit in a long verse composition. See **Spenserian.**

starlet, *n.* Little star; *colloq.*, young actress who has had a small role in a motion picture and is being held under contract to a studio.

start in, start out, start up, *v. Colloq.* where the adverbs are merely intensifying and not directional. But *stand. lit.* in "That was how he *started* me *in* business."

stash, *v.* Put away, conceal safely.

state, *n.* *Colloq.* Condition of anxiety or confusion. "You see what a *state* she's in." "Now don't get yourself in a *state.*"

State, *v.*, more formal than say, means to assert formally.

stateside, *adj.* In, to, or characteristic of the United States.

stationary, stationery, *adj.* and *n.* *Stationary* means not moving, immovable; *stationery,* writing material.

statue, stature, statute, *n.* *Statue* means a sculptured image; *stature,* height, influence; and *statute,* a written law.

status quo. Latin term meaning the state in which things are at present, have been till the present, and were formerly, or had been before some definite time in the past. With the prep. *in,* write *in statu quo,* not *in the status quo.*

stay, *v.* *Legal tech.,* delay for the time being; *stay put,* remain fixed, be immovable, is *colloq.*

steer, *n.* *Sl.,* direction, suggestion of action.

step up, *v.t.* Speed up, key up efficiency, production, machinery, or electric current. When used loosely to mean raise in price or standard, it is slang.

-ster. Suffix of agency, originally feminine but now of common gender as in huckster, rhymester; *cf.* spinster.

stere, *n.* Cubic metre.

stereophonic, *adj.* Projecting sounds from a number of outlets to accompany three-dimensional motion pictures.

stet. Latin. Let the word or letter inadvertently cancelled stand; *trade* or *tech.* of proofreaders.

stick, *v.* Chiefly *colloq.* in the sense of *place, put,* as "*Stick* any old hat on your head," and *puzzle,* as "That problem *sticks* me." Also *colloq., smear with sticky substance,* and *apply oneself steadily to.* "I'm all *stuck* up with paste but I'll *stick* to my job." Slang in the sense of *trick, cause to pay,* as in "He's *stuck* with the bill." Also slang in *stick around,* linger, *stick it there,* shake hands, *stick up for,* take a stand in an argument or fight, *stick them* (the hands) *up,* and the *n. stick-up,* a robbery.

The *adj. stuck-up,* conceited, self-important, is *colloq.*

sticker, *n.* Gummed label; *Am.* for *Br.,* poster; philatelic *tech.,* gummed hinge.

stick up, *v. Sl.,* hold up; rob.

Stiff Style. To avoid stiffness do not make excessive use of technical devices or allow the skeleton of your composition to become too prominent. Try not to be too formal or dignified in diction. The stiff style lacks ease and fluency.

stigma, *n.* Mark of disgrace (with *pl. stigmas*); sacred mark (with *pl. stigmata*). It is safer to use *stain, brand, mark, reproach, defect, taint, blemish, blot,* or some such word. The *v. stigmatize* is usually followed by *as.* "He *stigmatized* this act *as* monstrous."

still more, yet more. Intensive of more. Do not write "There is yet still more . . ." or "There is still more yet . . ." for "There is yet (or still) more to be done."

stimulant, stimulation, stimulus, *n.* A *stimulant* is that which increases or quickens activity, a spur; a *stimulus* (*pl. stimuli*) is an incitement to activity; impulse; whatever rouses or stirs to action. *Stimulation* is the state of increased activity which results from the application of *stimulants* or *stimuli,* or the act of applying them.

sting, stung, stung, *v.* Prick, stab with a sharp point; *colloq.,* cheat. Past tense *stang* is archaic.

stink, *n.* and *v. Sl.,* in the sense of disturbance, trouble, as in "She raised a big *stink* about my absence," and as a *v.,* meaning be unsatisfactory, lack aesthetic value or charm. "This book *stinks.*" The excessive use of the word as slang causes some to avoid it even in its *stand. lit.* senses, stench; smell bad, be malodorous.

stinkeroo, *n. Sl.,* extremely inept performance, very bad play.

stock, *n.* Shares in a company; cattle; group of players presenting a series of old plays.

stooge, *n.* Theatrical *sl.* for foil, the comedian's foil; the zany or subordinate fool or clown.

stool-pigeon, *n. Police tech.,* informer.

stop, *v. Low colloq.* in the sense of stay,

spend a short time (with). "We are *stopping* (*stand. lit. staying*) at the Morraine Hotel." *Stop in,* call on; *stop by,* call on; *stop off,* get off; *stop out,* stay overnight; and *stop over,* are *colloq.*

story, *n.* Narrative, tale; journalistic *tech.,* unit of news, written account of an event.

straddle, *v.* Ride astride of, walk with feet on opposite sides of (a line); *colloq.,* hedge, appear to favor both sides.

straight, strait, *adj. Straight* means direct, not curved; not mixed; *fig.,* neat; upright, not crooked, direct in thought and speech; undiluted. *Strait, arch.,* means narrow, strict, difficult. As a *n. pl.* meaning difficulty, emergency, it is *stand. lit.;* and the phrase, in straitened circumstances, impecunious, in financial difficulty is hackneyed. *Strait,* in its *archaic* sense, survives in the compounds strait jacket and strait laced (not straight laced), excessively prudish, puritanical.

stratosphere, *n.* Outer layer of atmosphere about seven miles from the surface of the earth. **Stratospheric,** *adj.,* means rare, high, intense; journalistic *sl.,* highbrow, offensively intellectual, not easily understood.

stratum (strā'tum, străt'um), *n.* Layer, level, geological level. *Pl.* is either *stratums* or *strata.*

straw vote, *n.* Unofficial ballot; test or sampling of voting strength.

streamline, *v.* Construct or reconstruct (a vehicle or missile) to minimize retardation due to air pressure; simplify, make more efficient.

strike, *v.* Chiefly *colloq.* when meaning to hit upon, come upon suddenly, arrive in. "His eye *struck* an odd letter." "Morgan *struck* town yesterday." *Strike up,* as in "We *struck up* a friendship," is *colloq. Strike* meaning *make urgent request of,* as in "George *struck* my boss for a job," and to *strike oil,* make a lucky investment, are *slang.* The *p. part. stricken* is obsolete, except in a few phrases such as *stricken with palsy, stricken out.*

string, *n.* and *v.* Twine, cord; sequence, series; *colloq.,* condition attached (to an

agreement). *Strung* is preferred to *stringed* in almost all contexts (except when referring to musical instruments).

Stringy Sentences. Sentences strung out to inordinate length should be broken up, especially if they have been allowed to grow up like Topsy. If a stringy sentence is made of a long series of co-ordinate clauses, some of these should be made subordinate. "And she said that it would be all right and sat down and the woman next to her said that she was glad and that the children would be just as happy without their father and that anyway things were never as bad as they seemed but were sometimes worse and one should never lose hope."

strive, strove, striven, *v.* Contend vigorously, try hard.

strong-arm, *adj.* Involving the use of force and violence.

stub, *n.* Stump of a sapling in a clearing; short remnant of a pencil or a cigarette; *v.,* bump as against a stump.

studied, *adj.* Intentional. "That was a studied slight."

study, studio, *n. Study* is a room in a private home (usually furnished with books) where a student or scholar studies or writes; a *studio* is the work-room of a photographer, artist, musician, or a room equipped for television or radio broadcasts, recording of phonograph records, or filming of motion pictures.

Stump Words. A *stump word* is a long word trimmed down for convenience and ease. Words that are overused often are made into stump words: *ad* for *advertisement, gym* for *gymnasium, cab* for *cabriolet, auto* for *automobile.* Some stump words are *stand. lit.,* a very few are even poetical, e.g., *fount* for *fountain, morn* for *morning,* but most of them are either *colloq.* or slang.

stunt, *n. Colloq.* A feat, a gymnastic trick, a notable performance. The *v.,* "He is *stunting* in his plane," is also *colloq.*

Style. Manner of writing or speaking developed by cultivation and made evident by characteristic adaptations and shadings in the use of language. Some of the most common faults of style are: (1) awkwardness, (2) stiffness, (3) staccato sentences, (4) journalese, (5) fine writing, (6) exaggeration, (7) monotony, (8) lack of harmony, (9) intrusion of the personal element, (10) telegraphic sentences.

stylize, *v.* Create with conscious artifice in conformity to a pattern, mark with identifying peculiarities.

subatomic, *adj.* Existent within the nuclei of atoms.

Subject Too Broad. If your subject is too broad you will not be able to develop it with any thoroughness or originality in a short theme. Your paragraphs will read like summaries or you will leave phases of the subject undeveloped. Space for the concrete and specific will be lacking. Limit your subject by attacking only a small part, phase, or aspect of it, and word your title accordingly.

subjective, *adj.* Determined by personal traits; *crit.,* affected by emotional or temperamental bias of the observer; *gram.,* nominative.

Subjunctive. Verbal mood of the unreal and imaginary. "If he be sick . . ." "Were I the boss."

Subordination. To connect a series of sentences with *and, or,* or *but* is the easiest, but not always the best thing to do, especially in formal writing. Think through what you are going to write and you will use more adverbial and adjectival clauses. Many an *and* should give way to an *if, although, when, because, that,* or *so that.*

suborn, *v.* Induce to illegal behavior; accomplish unfairly or by underhanded methods.

subsequent to. See **Quasi Adverbs.** *Subsequent to* can introduce an *adv.* phrase as well as *subsequently to* can. "The baths will not be open *subsequent to* October 15." *After* is simpler than either.

subsist, exist, *v. Subsist* means to support life; *exist,* to live, to have life. A subsistence diet is a diet sufficient to maintain life; as a *n.,* subsistence means enough to live on; not quite enough to live on.

Substantive. A noun; any word or word

group that performs the work of a *n.* in a sentence.

substitute, replace, *v.* The central meaning of *substitute* is put one person in place of another, or put something in the place of something else. "I can *substitute* for you." "Boys are being *substituted* for men." *Replace* means put something or someone back in the same place as before, restore to former state. It has the secondary meanings of supply an equivalent of, return, repay, and put in a new place. "His strict views were *replaced* by (not *substituted by*) more tolerant ones." "Boys are being *replaced* by (*not substituted by*) men." A similar distinction should be drawn between the nouns **substitution** and **replacement.** The former is followed by *for* not *by.*

subversive, *adj.* Undermining, tending to destroy or overturn the government. A **subversive** movement need not be secret.

such, *adj., adv.,* and *pron.* Do not use as a substitute for a demonstrative, as in "But I could not do *such.*" *Colloq.* as an intensive. "She has *such* a sweet disposition." But *stand. lit.* in "I never saw *such* big eyes," or "Did you ever hear *such* convincing evidence?" and when followed up by a *that* clause. "She had *such* an attractive voice *that* even her enemies liked to hear it." When *such* is followed by a relative clause, this must be introduced by *as.* "He demanded only *such* laws *as* were absolutely necessary." If followed by a result clause, this should be introduced by *that,* not by *so that.* "It was *such* a foggy day *that* we left the plane and took a train." *Such as* requires a *n.* for its completion. "Some were improving their skill in one art, *such as,* for instance, *painting* (not *in painting*), some in another." Archaic in the sense of *all who, those who* or *which,* etc. "*Those who* (not *such as*) are unable to pay their own way cannot go."

sucker, *n. Colloq.,* gull; person easily deceived.

sulfa drugs, *n.* The sulfonamides, a class of synthetic drugs used in treating infectious diseases.

sump, *n.* Pit, reservoir; *colloq.,* dumping place for waste and oil; *Br.*, oil-pan.

super. Too popular as a prefix with which to make windy or hyperbolic words; e.g., the movie producer's *superproduction* and *superfilms*, the *supercriminal*, *super-love*, *supersalesman*, *supersanity*, *super-satisfaction*, *superscandal*, and the use as an *adj.* strengthener in words like *super-perfect* and *super-American*. The excessive use of *super* is a superabomination.

superior to. The correct idiom. Do not use *than* for *to*. "He found a scabiosa that, for this kind of garden, would certainly be *superior to* (not *than*) either irises or zinnias."

superlative, *adj.* Highest in degree. See **comparison** (of adjectives and adverbs).

supernova, *n.* Vastly bright new or newly discovered star.

supersede, *v.* Replace, displace, take the place of; supplant.

supersonic, *adj.* Pertaining to a speed greater than that of sound; beyond the sound barrier.

supine, *adj.* Prostrate; flat on the back.

suppose, *v.t.* Accept as true for the time being, assume as a hypothesis, presume, presuppose; and, in the passive, expect, "I am *supposed* to buy it before tomorrow." As a *v.i.* it means to opine, think, conjecture. *Suppose* is slightly preferable to *supposing* for introducing clauses like "*Suppose* they will not accept your terms (what will you do then?)."

supra-, *pfx.* Above, over and above, beyond.

sure, *adv.* Stands for *surely* in sentences like "And *sure* enough the thing capsized," and "That day will come as *sure* as fate." *Sure* is vulgar as a directly modifying *adv.* (intensive) as in "She *sure* can dance." Prefer *surely* or *certainly*. It is slang when used for *certainly, indeed,* or a similar intensive affirmative answer. "Do you think you can do it?" "*Sure.*" *Sure thing* in the same construction is slang. *Would sure* is low colloq. for *would be sure to*. "He had a sister who *would sure* (would be sure to) tell his mother." *Sure-enough,* meaning real, actual, genuine, as in "Will you give me a *sure-enough* pony?" is *dial.* The *adj.*

sure-fire is slang. "This will give *sure-fire* results."

surrealism, *n.* Type of art which represents ideal reality rather than conventionally consistent visual impressions.

surrogate, *n.* Judicial officer having jurisdiction over probate of wills and settlement of estates.

suspense, *n.* Hanging; emotional tension caused by desire to know the outcome of a conflict.

suspicion, *v. Dial.* for *suspect*. The *n.* is a Gallicism in the sense of *a mere trace, a touch*. "There is just a *suspicion* of paprika in this soup."

sustain, *v.* Rather formal as a synonym for *suffer, receive,* or *get*. "He has *sustained* (suffered) a sprained ankle." Most useful in the senses of bear up against, endure. "The city was capable of *sustaining* a two-month siege."

svelte, *adj.* Elegantly slim. [Fr.]

swank, swanky, *n.* and *adj.*, *Sl.*, pretentiousness, elegance; stylish, pretentious, high-toned.

swap, *n.* and *v. Colloq.*, trade or exchange.

swat, *v.* Hit hard. Hence the nouns *swat* and *swatter*. Chiefly *Am.*, but from English *dial.*

sweat, *v.* Principal parts, *sweat, sweat* or *sweated, sweat* or *sweated.* Perspire, force witness or accused person by means of insistent questioning to give information; exploit, drive hard. *Colloq.* in the sense of *work hard* or *suffer for*. "I'll make you *sweat* for this insult."

sweat out in the sense of *await, wait for,* under unpleasant conditions, is war slang.

swell, *adj. Colloq.* counterword for *smart, fashionable, stylish*. "We live in a *swell neighborhood.*" Slang for *great, magnificent, tiptop.*

swing, swung, swung, *v. Swang* is *arch.* and *dial.* As a *n., swing* means a type of modern music. The *swing shift* is the working time from four in the afternoon to midnight.

switch, *v.* Change abruptly; turn aside; *n.,* theatrical *tech.,* clever new turn for an old joke or piece of stage business.

switchblade, *n.* Pocket knife with long blade which can be extruded instantly.

switcheroo, *n. Sl.,* clever and theatrically effective variation of a reliable formula or established routine.

Syllabication. Dividing words into syllables. If your syllabication is faulty, you have put the hyphen in the wrong place. Try not to carry over a word from one line to another, and never divide a monosyllable or a personal name, or split off an *-ed,* a single letter, or a part that cannot be pronounced separately.

If you have to split a word at the end of a line, divide it according to syllables. A consonant usually goes with the second syllable: *sa hib, in ti mate.* Words containing double consonants are nearly always divided between these: *ses sion.* Separate prefix or suffix from the root and divide compounds at the hyphen, or if written solid, into their elements: re verse, ware house.

syllabus, *pl.* **syllabuses, syllabi** (sĭl'à bī), *n.* Outline or abstract of a course of study; main heads of a treatise. [Gr., piece of parchment, label]

symbols, *n. pl.* Signs, objects, things that stand for other things: the hooked cross, the crescent, the red star. Proofreaders' signs: ꝺ dele, ʌ caret. See **Punctuation, Signs and Symbols,** and **Phonetics.**

sympathy with, sympathy for. One has *sympathy with* what he is in harmony or agreement with, *sympathy for* one who, or that which, suffers. There may be *sympathy between* persons.

syncopate, *v.* Music *tech.,* shift the regular metrical accent. "Syncopation occurs when a tone begins after the beginning of one beat and progresses into the middle of the second beat."

synecdoche, *n.* Rhetorical figure by which a part is taken for designation of the whole. "I'll ride my wheel down the hill."

Synonyms. When two or more words in the same language have the same or similar meanings in most of their applications, they are called synonyms: enough, sufficient; obese, fat, stout. Only a few pairs are exactly alike in both denotation and connotation. Words which have roughly similar meanings are called analogous terms: feat, adventure; loot, steal. A word is a synonym *to* or *for* another word, or synonymous *with* it.

Syntax. That division of grammar which deals with the relation between parts of a sentence.

synthesis, *n.* Composition, putting together in harmonious combination, putting together; artificial creation. Cf. analysis.

systematic, systemic, *adj. Systematic* means arranged according to a plan; in line with planned procedure; *systemic,* going through the whole body, permeating the physical structure as a whole.

T

tab, *n.* Check, paper or pasteboard slip or ticket; end torn off such a ticket and used in accounting; *colloq.,* bill; *v.,* keep tabs on, to keep account of, watch carefully.

table, *v.* Place on a table, defer action on, postpone.

tabloid, *n.* Small tablet, pellet; newspaper of small size; paper known for sensational journalism.

taboo or tabu, *n.* A setting aside as sacred or accursed; a prohibition by general consent. The *adj.* means prohibited, and the *v.,* to put under *taboo.* For examples of linguistic *taboo* see **Genteelism.**

tackle, *v.* Grapple with, come to grips with; *colloq.* in the sense of attack food, approach a person with a request. "He tackled me for a dollar." *n.* Equipment, gear.

tag, *n.* Label, pasteboard label with a string; hackneyed or trite word or phrase.

take, *v.* Principal parts, *take, took, taken. Have took* is vulgar. The following phrases are *stand. lit. Take in,* cheat, deceive, visit, attend. "I was completely *taken in.*" "Let's *take in* the art gallery." *Take on,* assume, undertake, accept a challenge. "If elected he will *take on* many a responsibility."

The following are *colloq.*: *Take,* win favor, gain a favorable reception. "His play *took.*" *Take it,* bear, suffer. "He can't *take it.*" *Take stock in,* rely on, have faith in. *Take on,* assume airs, act as if under stress of emotion, make a fuss. *Take off, n.* and *v.,* caricature, parody. *Take it out of* (*on*), make pay for. *Take one about,* escort publicly. *Take care of,* dispose of, deal with. *Take down* (*with*), as in "He was *taken down with* the measles." *Take up with* is *colloq.* in the sense of associate with, but *dial.* meaning to become interested in.

Take it or leave it is slang. *Take sick* is chiefly *dial. Take and,* as in "Father *took and* wrote the mayor," is also chiefly *dial.* The construction in "It did not *take* him much time" is unidiomatic. Write instead, "He didn't *take* much time in doing this." *Take to,* become fond of, as in "She may *take to* him," is *dial.,* but meaning begin to settle into a habit or apply oneself to a regular practice or occupation, as in "Those who *take to* begging rarely ever work," it is *stand. lit.*

taking, *adj. Stand. lit.* in the sense of charming, pleasing, attractive. "Taking ways," however, should be avoided as an overused pun. "He remarked upon her taking looks." Equivalent **fetching** is *colloq.*

Talent, Genius. *Talent* implies an unusual aptitude or ability which one may or may not exercise; *genius* is used to describe an innate ability so overwhelming that the exercising of it cannot be controlled. *Genius* is appropriately applied only to creative pursuits; *talent* to pursuits which are not necessarily creative. A *talent* may be acquired, and it is frequently used in pejorative sense in contrast to genius. A talented person is one who possesses aptitude for important achievement; a genius, one who possesses innate ability for overwhelming achievements.

talk, *n.* Informal for address or lecture; *colloq.* style of speech. *Talk back v.* Be saucy, answer discourteously, retort. **Talkie,** *n., colloq.* Motion picture with synchronized sounds and dialogue.

tall, *adj.* High; *colloq.,* grandiloquent, exaggerated. A *tall* story is a brief narrative characterized by exaggeration, a typically American form of fiction.

Tandem Construction. A series of dependent units coming one after another like riders on a tandem may give a weak and straggling effect or result in ambiguity, a hopelessly involved sentence, or a cacophonous jingle. A bad tandem of participial phrases: "The home team's line gave way, leaving large gaps, lowering the morale of our backfield, encouraging the opponents, laughing at our consternation." One with too many *of's*: "On the third morning of the third week of the month of September of 1936, of such tremendous import, we arose early." Two *of* (*in, for to,* etc.) phrases in a row are enough; three are too many. A series of *but* clauses should be avoided at all costs. See **But, The "But" Habit.**

tangible, perceptible, *adj. Tangible* means capable of being perceived by the sense of touch; having objective reality, substantial. *Perceptible* means noticeable in any degree.

tap, *n. Br.* spigot, faucet.

taste of. When taste is transitive, *of* is usually redundant. "*Taste* (not *taste of*) *this sauce.*" When *taste* is intransitive, *taste of* sometimes means *have a certain flavor.* "The cake *tasted of* rancid butter."

tasty, *adj. Colloq.* for savory, tasteful. "*Tasty* bread and *tasty* furniture."

Tautology. Another synonym for *wordiness.* Strictly, a form of wordiness consisting in the useless repetition of an idea in different words: *combining together, visible to the eye, static stability, mongrel cur.* On rare occasions some such expressions may be proper, e.g., "It is now *plain* and *evident* why the appeal was rejected."

tawdry, *adj.* Showy, cheap and gaudy, not elegant. [English, St. Audrey or Ethelreda, because cheap laces were sold at a fair named for the Saint. St. Audrey lace became *tawdry* lace]

taxi, *n.* Stump of taxicab. Both *n.* and *v.* are *stand. lit.* "We taxied to the game."

T.C., *abbr. adj. Tech.,* Teachers-College; *colloq.* characteristic of Doctors of Education.

Technical Terms. The special terminology of an art or science or game is inappropriate in any but technical writing or on the sport page unless used in moderation and carefully (though unobtrusively) defined for the general reader.

There is always a grave danger that the popularized technicality will lose all or some of its original meaning. The popular meanings of *acid test,* the *devil's advocate,* and *protagonist* misrepresent the original senses of these terms. The *abbr. trade or tech.* includes technical terms and others that belong to a special class.'

technics, technique, *n. Technics* means the science or doctrine of an art; *technique,* skillful routine in any kind of work.

techy or **tetchy, testy,** *adj. Techy* (or *tetchy*) is a synonym of the more modern touchy, overly sensitive, quick to take offense. *Testy* means easily roused to anger by minor irritations.

tedious, *adj.* Tiresome, wearying; causing ennui. (The pronunciation tē jus is *colloq.*)

teen, *n. Colloq.,* age between twelve years and twenty; adolescent.

teenager, *n.* Person in his *teens*; journalese and *colloq.*

teetotaler, *n.* Abstainer from all alcoholic drinks. **Teetotal, teetotally,** *adj., adv.* Absolute, complete; completely, used in *colloq.* and humorous contexts.

telegenic, *adj.* Aesthetically suited to television.

television, *n.* Transmission of visual images by means of radio waves. *Televise* and *telecast* are used to describe the act of transmitting a television show; *teleview* is sometimes used for the more usual "watch television."

tell, *v. Tell on,* inform, as in "She *told on* us," is *colloq.* Also *tell the world. Tell good-by* is *colloq.* for *bid good-by* or *say good-by.* "They wished to get up early to *tell* (*bid*) them good-by."

temperamental, *adj.* Sensitive, easily excitable. Note the spelling.

temperance, abstinence, *n. Temperance* means habitual and voluntary moderation; *abstinence,* habitual and voluntary giving up.

temporal, temporary, *adj. Temporal* means connected with the present life only, worldly as opposed to spiritual; *temporary,* lasting for a short time only. **Temporal** is opposed to everlasting; **temporary,** to permanent.

temporize, *v.* Delay or evade action to gain time; bow gracefully to the force of the present circumstances.

tend, attend, *v.* One may *tend* the children, the sick, the store, the fire, or the pump; or one may *attend* to the children, but one *attends* church, school, or a meeting.

tendentious, *adj.* Having a definite purpose. Not a synonym of quarrelsome, contentious, or dissentious.

tender, *v.* Offer, present.

Tense. The form a *v.* takes to indicate the time of an action or state; e.g., *goes* is present tense, *went* is past (preterite) tense.

The past tense does not as a rule indicate connection with the present moment. It simply refers to some time in the past. It is the tense to use whenever the sentence contains a time indication, such as *yesterday, the other day, last week, in 1930,* or when the sentence is a question about the time. "When *did* he leave?" The absence of a time indication with the past sometimes causes obscurity. "When describing his early experiences in the West, Captain Cody said that reticence *was* considered a prime virtue." This would be clearer if *in those days* were inserted between *was* and *considered.* The fault of leaving out such a time indication is called *the undated past.*

The perfect tense connects a past occurrence with the present. The perfect therefore is the tense to use whenever the time indicated in the sentence is not yet completed (*this week, today, not yet*). "I have been very busy this week."

For tense sequence see **Conformity of Tenses.**

termed as. The *as* is redundant. "Boston

is *termed* (not *termed as*) The Hub."

terminate, *adj.* Grammatical *tech.,* associated with completed action. See aspect. The *v.* is pompous or officialese for end, finish.

terrible, terribly, *adj.* and *adv. Colloq.* counterwords when mere intensives. "Isn't this pie *terrible?*" Do not use the *adj.* for the *adv.* "The cat yowled something *terrible.*" Write *terribly* and omit the *something.*

testament, testimony, *n. Testament* means a legal document by which a person disposes of his property, a will; Bibl., solemn pact or covenant. *Testimony* means the statements of witnesses under oath in court, or, more loosely, all the evidence.

tetrameter, *n.* Line of verse having four metrical feet.

than, *conj.* There is a tendency to use *than colloq.* as a *prep.*; e.g., "She is smaller *than me.*" The *stand. lit.* is "She is smaller *than I*" (*am* is understood after the *I*). But the *stand. lit.* requires the objective case in "They will take you rather *than me*" because *take* is implied before *me.* The *than whom* in such sentences as "They elected Fredrichs, *than whom* no politician is more wily," is old-fashioned and awkward.

After *different* prefer *from* to *than.* "Her present style is different *from* her style of ten years ago." After *hardly* and *scarcely* do not use *than* for *when* or *before.* "He had *scarcely* finished the second year *before* (not *than*) they called him home." Do not use *than* after *prefer.* "I *prefer* a brush *to* (not *than*) a pen." "I *prefer* staying home *to* (not *than*) riding in that car."

After a comparative pronounce the *than* clearly and do not let it become a mere *'n,* as in "I can do this *better'n* that."

that, *pron. Low colloq.* or *dial.* when used as an *adv.* to take the place of *so, so very, to such a degree,* with words denoting quality or action. "I'm *that* tired I could sleep standing up." However, before *much* and *far* the adverbial *that* is no worse than *colloq.* "We went about *that far.*" "He could not have erred *that much.*" The similar adjectival use, as in "She has *that* assurance that she would speak to the

president himself," is *colloq.* In *stand. lit. such* or *so great* would be used instead.

Do not use *that* as a relative *adv.* made to stand for *with which, in which, for which,* or *as that in which.* "Politicians dream of it in the same fond manner *that* (better *as that in which*) a boy of ten dreams of a gun and a pony." "I then read his letters in the spirit *that* (better *in which*) he had written them."

Do not omit the *in* in the phrase *in that way.* "He did it *in that way* (not *that way*)." *That there* like *this here* is vulgar. "*That there* sign is going to fall." "*That* sign *there* is going to fall." So *that's that,* i.e., that's finished, is *colloq.* Likewise the *at that* for *even so, anyway, nevertheless.*

It is usually advisable to write *the* for the *that* or *those* in sentences like "*That* (the) part of the book describing the French watering places is especially well done."

The *that* or *this* in sentences like "*That* (*this*) silly grin of his gave him away" implies familiarity with, or general notoriety of, the object so qualified, and is often disparaging.

that, which. In actual practice these pronouns are interchanged freely except in a few constructions, yet ideally *that* is the restrictive and *which* the nonrestrictive. "The bill-of-fare contained many items *that* stimulated his imagination." "His Spanish omelette, *which* was cooked perfectly, took the prize." *That* is not less formal than *which,* but there are more *that's* than *which's* in speech.

If a *prep.* goes with the relative, use *which*; or, if feasible, use *that* and put the *prep.* at the end of the clause or sentence. Write "the situation *in which* he found himself . . ." or "The situation (*that*) he found himself in . . ." *Whose* may be used as the possessive of *that,* but it is often avoided and *of which* used instead. *That* is often omitted if it is not the subject. "The *Handbook* you bought is neat and useful."

Notice that the second of two coordinated relative clauses nearly always begins with *which* or a form of *who.* "He had a style *that* was not more impressive than theirs, but *which* was much simpler and therefore more telling." *Which* is no longer used to refer to persons, as in "The gentlemen *which* are now preparing . . ."

The, *definite article*. As a general rule *the* used as part of a proper name or title is capitalized. But in common practice this rule does not apply to the names of periodicals, ships, or companies. Books and periodicals are never catalogued in a library under *the* or *a*.

theft, larceny, *n.* Both mean the illegal taking of what belongs to another. *Larceny* is the more specific and applies to the taking and carrying away of what belongs to another. Larceny can be proved only when it can be clearly shown that the thief had the stolen property in his personal possession. *Larceny, colloq.,* means the desire to make profits by questionable means.

their, *pron.* Do not confuse with there or they're. Do not use *theirselves* for *themselves*.

them, *pron.* Vulgar when used for those, as in "*Them* women make me tired," and "*Them* are the tickets I want."

theme, *n.* Topic, subject; composition, essay.

then, *adv.* At that time, next in order of time. The use of *then* as an *adj.* is archaic but not unjustifiable. "The then archbishop . . ." is a stiff phrase, but it appeared in the *New Yorker*.

theorem, theory, *n. Theorem* means proposition susceptible of rational proof; rule or law (generally expressed by an equation or mathematical formula). A *theory* is a combination of propositions (drawn from observable evidence or based on inferences) which explains or accounts for known facts; the principles of an art as opposed to its practice; *colloq.*, best guess, conjecture.

therapy, *n.* Treatment; healing quality; used of remedies for diseases. Compounded with other classic roots it forms such words as hydrotherapy, physiotherapy, electrotherapy, names for specialized and highly lucrative systems of treatment for chronic ailments. **Therapeutic**, *adj.*,

means curative, remedial, concerned with the art of healing. [Greek, attendant, minister]

there, *adj. Sl.* in the sense of ready, dependable, able. "He's certainly *there* when it comes to spelling."

there, *adv.* and expletive (anticipatory subject). The *v.* following **there** in "there is" and "there are" constructions must agree with the subject (which follows). "There is a lesson to be learned from that," but "There are many lessons to be learned." Error is likely to result if *there is* or *there are* is separated from the subject by phrases.

therefor, *adv.* For this, for that. Somewhat stilted. "The reason *therefor* is my lack of interest."

therefore, *conjunctive adv.* For that reason; consequently.

thesaurus (thē saw′rŭs, thĭ saw′rŭs), *n.* This word is derived from the Greek word meaning treasure or treasury. It means a very helpful kind of dictionary; a repository of analogous terms and synonyms.

thesis, *n.* A proposition; academic essay; key sentence or central assertion of a controversial essay.

they, *pron.* The indefinite *they,* as in "*They* had war and pestilence in Spain that year," and "*They* don't have central heating plants in their houses," is *colloq. They say* (French *on dit*), as in "*They say* that the floods are receding," that is, "it is said that the floods . . ." is *stand. lit.*

think, *v.* "*I don't think* that (so, etc.)" is correct since *think* means not only *carry on the process of thought* but also *entertain a particular opinion. I think not* is not the equivalent of *I don't think* because *I think not* means "I have a contrary opinion." "*I don't think* so" means "I do not accept the particular opinion advanced." *Think* is *stand. lit.* in "I didn't *think* of leaving the back door open." *That* is usually omitted after *think*. "I *think* (that) he is witty." *Think up* is *stand. lit.* for *devise, invent*. "Let me *think up* an excuse." *Think for*, suppose, suspect, is also *stand. lit.* "Her plans are more selfish than you *think for*."

this, *pron. This* as an *adv.* to take the place of *so is, colloq.* "Yesterday we went about *this* far." But notice that *this* is an *adj.* and *much* a *n.* in "*This much* is certain, I am hungry." *This, adj.,* means *at hand, just mentioned.* In sentences like "Then he pitched *this* curve of his," *this* implies that the curve is well known or that it is not to be regarded very highly.

this here, that there, these here, those there. Vulgar.

thou, thee. *Pron. sing.* Archaic, you. *Thou* is in the nominative and *thee* is in the objective case.

thrash, thresh, *v.* Both mean to separate grain from chaff; to go over and over as an argument, usually with out. *Thrash* means beat (usually with a stick, cane, etc.), toss about or move one's arms and legs violently.

thrill, *n.* Moment of ecstasy; *colloq.,* pleasant experience.

through, *adj. Colloq.,* arrived at completion, finished.

through, *prep.* From one end to another (of time, space, or degree), by means or reason of. As an *adj.* meaning having given up, as "I am *through* with smoking," having come to the completion of, as "Are you *through* with the job?"; finished with, as "She is *through* with the scissors," and at the end of the period of usefulness or efficiency, as "That tenor is *through,*" it is *colloq.*

Through is sometimes used where *throughout,* meaning in every part or respect, from end to end, would be better. "One reads his advertisements *through* (better *throughout*) the land."

It is an *adv.* in "They shipped the goods *through* to Denver," and "I have read the chapter *through.*" Also after a *part.* or *adj.* in the sense of thoroughly, entirely, "The travelers were wet *through.*"

throughout (the whole, the entire). Tautological since *throughout* means in every part.

throw, threw, thrown, not **throwed,** *v.* Sports *tech.,* lose dishonestly, throw away the victory; **throwaway,** *n.* ʰʳinted notice distributed by hand.

thug, *n.* Brutal criminal; in India, cheat, swindler, one who murders by strangling.

thumb, *v.* Secure or direct by signal with *thumb;* touch or push with the thumb. *Thumb* a ride (his nose, the doorbell).

thus, *adv.* To this degree or extent, in the manner that has been or is about to be shown, in accordance with what has been said, and (by extension) therefore, accordingly. The *thus* introducing a *part.* is often admission that the writer is not quite sure of the syntax of the *part.* "The uncertainty about the cattle prices has caused the cattlemen to cut down their herds, *thus* running less chance of losing." Avoid this use of *thus.* **Thusly** is a jocular variation of *thus. Thus* is a formal word.

ticket, *n.* Associated group of candidates; *v.t.,* put a ticket on. **Ticket-of-leave,** *Br.,* parole (of a prison inmate).

tickle, *v.* Amuse, please, gratify; titillate.

tidewater, *n.* and *adj.* Coastal region; pertaining to the coastline.

tie, *v. Tie up to* and *tie up with* are *stand. lit.* in the sense to join forces with, go in with. **Tie-up,** *n.* means traffic stoppage, and breakdown or suspension of business. **Tie-in,** *n.* and *adj.,* means combination. A *tie-in* sale is one by which an article on which the price is fixed is sold at that price on condition that accessory articles be purchased at a higher price.

tight, *adj. Colloq.,* nearly even, with a low score; stingy; *sl.,* drunk; *stand. lit.,* difficult. *Tight*-lipped and *tight*-fisted are *stand. lit.,* but tightwad is slang.

tilde, *n.* Mark placed over *n* (ñ) in a Spanish word to indicate that the *n* is to be pronounced *ny,* as señorita (sän yōr-ēt'ä).

till, until, *prep., conj.* In meaning practically equivalent. *Till* is the commoner form. *Until* is slightly more formal and is usually preferred as the opening word of a sentence. Both are sometimes misused for *when* or *before* after *hardly* or *scarcely.* "We had scarcely entered the woods *till* (better *before*) he wanted to go home."

timeless, *adj.* Unending, not restricted by time; not representative of an era.

titan, *n.* Fabulous giant; powerful financier.

title, *n.* Name of a piece of composition; official or honorary designation used as part of the personal name. Such a title is regularly capitalized: Chairman Smith, Sir John More, Ambassador Jusserand.

Title, Inexact. Walter Scott did not like a title that revealed what was in one of his novels. Do not imitate him when giving a title to your theme. Word your title so that the subject and nature of your composition will be clear from the start.

TNT, *n.* Trinitrotoluol, a high explosive.

to, *prep.* It can mean *till;* e.g., "We shall be at home from three *to* eight," "She believed this *to* the end." *Cf.* "We went in *to* dinner," and "We went into the water." *To* is vulgar when used for *in* or *at.* "He works over *to* (at) Maxwell's." *Colloq.* when used with the name of a place visited. "Have you ever been *to* (in) Denver?" See **and, to.**

to-do, *n. Colloq.*, bustle, stir, ado.

toggle, *n.* Crosspiece or loop in a chain to bar or prevent twisting.

token, *n.* Piece of base metal used as currency; metal ticket, especially one used in automatic coin machines.

tolerant, *adj.* Lenient, able to endure or put up with. Usually followed by of.

tong, *n.* Chinese businessmen's club or lodge.

tongue in cheek. To write with tongue in cheek is to write waggishly. It implies that the real attitude of the author differs from what he says or what he seems to say. In danger of overuse and of being misinterpreted by the literal-minded.

tony, *adj.* Old *colloq.*, fashionable, of the bon ton.

too, *adv.* Excessively, more than sufficiently; in addition. *Colloq.* as a mere intensive meaning very. "I am just *too* happy." As a rule, well, much, or some similar word should stand between *too* and a *past part.* "He is *too* (actively) engaged to pay attention to you." "The house is *too* (well) heated for that."

top-brass, *n.* Generals (who wear gilded helmets), bosses, men in high office.

topflight, *adj.* Superior.

Topic Sentence. A condensed or leading statement that contains implicitly what is made explicit in its paragraph. The chief types are: the forecasting statement, the envelope sentence, the question, the summarizing sentence, the implied topic sentence, and the transition topic sentence.

tortuous, torturous, *adj. Tortuous* means winding, twisting; not straightforward or morally straight; *torturous,* causing severe pain.

totalitarian, *adj.* Characteristic of a political system which allows no opposition parties.

tough, *adj.* Stubborn, strong, violent; *colloq.* unfortunate. The *n.,* meaning a ruffian, and *adj.,* meaning disorderly, having criminal proclivities, are *Am. stand. lit.*

toward (tō'ard, tōrd), **towards** (tō'ardz, tōrdz), *prep.* Both mean *in the direction of, in relation to.* The English prefer the *towards* but the Americans prefer *toward* except where *towards* would be more euphonious. The *adj. toward* is archaic and rarely occurs except in the negative compound *untoward,* perverse, unpropitious, inconvenient, as in "That was an *untoward* event."

traditional. See **legendary.**

tragedy, *n.* Drama which excites pity and fear in readers or listeners; a play with an unhappy ending; a disastrous or fatal event.

tragic, tragical, *adj. Tragic* is generally used to mean pertaining to a tragedy as a literary form; disastrous; **tragical** means gloomy, resembling tragedy.

tragicomedy, *n.* Play or other literary piece in which comic and tragic elements are mingled; a serious play with comic elements and a happy ending.

trailer, *n.* Object drawn or dragged; small house constructed on wheels so that it can be drawn by an automobile; *tech.*, scenes from a motion picture to arouse the interest of the audience and induce them to return to see it.

tranquility, tranquillity, *n.* Calmness, composure.

Transcendentalism, *n.* Philosophy dealing with the reality of ideas not derived from human experience.

transcript, *n.* Copy; copy from a copy; college record; bureaucratic record.

transcription, *n. Radio tech.,* a broadcasting of phonograph records.

transient, transitory, *adj.* Both mean short-lived, temporary, fleeting. *Transient* emphasizes the idea of brevity of existence; *transitory,* of the inevitability of the end. "He grasped eagerly at the few *transient* joys of this *transitory* life."

transistor, *n.* Electronic *tech.,* device using a small crystal, commonly of germanium, instead of an electron tube in amplification of signals and in other electronic applications.

Transitions. In passing from one idea to another build bridges, put up sign posts, show by word, phrase, or sentence that a new but logically related thought or phase of the subject is being broached. Do not be niggardly with connectives like *for this reason, therefore, afterward, consequently, while on the contrary,* etc. Use the exact connective; do not write *although* when you mean *yet.* The common types of transition are transition in space, transition in time, transition in thought, and imaginative and emotional linkings.

transmittal, *n.* Sending. *Transmittal* differs from *transmission* in having stronger connotations of legal formality and no connotation of machines.

transpire, *v.* Strictly, exhale, be exhaled, become known, leak out; loosely, happen, take place, turn out, go on. "Much of what happened never *transpired.*" "They had no way of finding out what was *transpiring* (most authorities would demand going on) in their absence."

Transpose. Change the order of words, clauses, or sentences as indicated. Printer's direction. Abbr. *tr.*

trans-sonic, *adj.* At or near the speed of sound.

trauma, *n.* Injury or wound caused by violence; shock; resulting emotional condition.

traumatic, *adj. Psych. tech.,* resulting from or causing, trauma; *colloq.,* shocking.

travesty, *n.* See *burlesque.*

treat of. Discuss, deal with, handle a subject. "The third volume treats of (not with) modern literature." *Treat with* means to have dealings with, carry on a discussion with.

trek, *v.* and *n.* Draw or drag a load; migrate; migration, slow journey overland. Journalese for any journey.

tribute, *n.* A payment, a sum of money, an acknowledgment of service or of worth. *A tribute to* does not mean *a proof* or *illustration of,* as in "The manner in which they dealt with the problem is *a tribute to* (better *a proof of*) the honesty of the aldermen."

trifling, *adj.* Good-for-nothing, worthless, petty. Southern provincial when applied to people.

trimeter, *n.* Line of verse with three metrical feet.

triphthong, *n.* Three vowel sounds combined in one syllable.

Trite. From Latin *tritus,* rubbed. As applied to words or phrases, *trite* means hackneyed, worn to a frazzle. "Bosom of the family"; "those with whom we come in contact"; "bright and shining faces"; "cradle of the deep"; "to be or not to be." H. W. Fowler calls expressions like these *battered ornaments.* Some persons cannot resist the temptation to adorn their sentences with such ornaments, whether decrepit and irrelevant allusions, musty quotations, worn-out proverbs, ancient sobriquets, or old poetic words that hardly belong in prose. The writer must, of course, avoid these, and also old puns, pedantic humor (*thusly, muchly*), playful archaisms (hight, yclept), and legal (*the said*) or other technical terms brought in for the sake of "wit."

trochaic, *adj.* Consisting of trochees. "Four and twenty blackbirds."

troche, *n.* Medicinal tablet, lozenge. [*Gr.,* wheel]

trochee, *n.* Metrical foot of two syllables, the first accented.

troubled, troublous, troublesome, *adj. Troubled* means disturbed, agitated; *troublesome,* causing annoyance. *Troublous* is literary for troubled.

try, *n. Colloq* for *trial, test, chance.* "He had a *try* at (*stand. lit.* attempted to solve) the problem." **Try out,** *v.,* is *colloq.* in the sense of make a test of vocal ability, athletic efficiency, etc. The *n.* **tryout** in this sense is also *colloq.,* but it is *stand. lit.* meaning a trial to determine whether an athlete may remain in a certain class.

try and. *Colloq.* for *try to* in constructions like *try and forget it, try and do it,* but *try and* may soon be *stand. lit.* here.

trylon, *n.* Pyramidal triangular spire.

tu quoque. Latin for *you also.* Turning a charge or argument upon its user instead of attempting a reasoned refutation. The so's-your-old-man argument. Saying "Why don't you invest in it yourself?" in reply to the person urging you to buy.

turn, *n. Colloq.* in the sense of nervous start or shock. "What a *turn* Fred's appearance gave me." **Turn in,** *v.,* is *colloq.* in the sense of go to bed. *Turn out,* to get up, is also *colloq.* But *turn down,* meaning to refuse, reject, is *stand. lit.* "Madge *turned down* the offer." *Turn on the heat,* put under pressure, subject to a grilling, is slang.

tutelary, *adj.* Guardian, having natural or supernatural supervision. **Tutelar** is a variant. See *daemon.*

tutu, *n.* Projecting sylphlike skirt for a ballet dancer.

TV, *n.* Television.

type, *n.* Particular class or kind; model or exemplar, rectangular block of metal having its face so carved as to print a letter or other character.

typhoon, *n.* Tropical cyclone. Malapropism for *tycoon, n. colloq.,* powerful industrialist.

U

ugly, *adj.* Repulsive, unpleasing to sight; *colloq.,* quarrelsome, ill-natured, unpleasant, disturbing. **Uglify,** to make ugly, is *stand. lit.*

un-, *pfx. Un-* when attached to a word frequently negatives the simple form and implies neither praise nor blame, *e.g., un*advised, without advice, ill-advised, rash; *un*believer, one who does not believe or who suspends belief, disbeliever, one who denies; *un*moral, without moral sense, immoral, wicked; *un*religious, having no religious belief, irreligious, impious, wicked; *un*interested, having no interest in, disinterested, impartial.

unaware, *adj. Unawares* is the *adv.*

unbeknownst, *adj. Dial.* for unknown, unbeknown. "He did all this unbeknown (not *unbeknownst*) to me." Often jocular.

uncomparable, *adj.* See **incomparable.**

Uncompleted Idea. Do not abandon an idea you have brought up until all its implications that are pertinent have been brought out. Supply everything that you have led the reader to expect, or that he cannot readily supply himself. "That day wasn't as good, and the audience applauded Bert Smith heartily at the closing curtain." Here the comparison is incomplete, and, although the context might have supplied what was needed to complete it, the sentence would still be unsatisfactory, for the reader expects *but* instead of *and.* Something necessary to the completion of the first idea has dropped out and must be supplied. See **Omission.**

undergraduate, *n.* College student who has not taken a degree.

underground, *n.* Secret organization for opposing a victorious enemy or the government in power.

underhand, *adj.* Secret, sly; fraudulent. Preferable to underhanded, but the *adv.* is underhandedly, and the *n.* underhandedness.

underline, *v.* Draw a line beneath. Underline in MS. all words which are to be printed in italics.

underprivileged, *adj.* Deprived of rights, social or economic; *colloq.,* handicapped. "The child is mentally *underprivileged.*"

underscore, *v.* Underline.

Understatement. Securing emphasis by

understating. "Who are all these people?" "Oh, a few of my friends." "He's all right"; i.e., he is so excellent that we give him our hearty approval. "She isn't half bad": i.e., she is very good indeed.

underworld, n. Kingdom of the dead, in classical mythology; the criminal group.

Undeveloped Thought. Do not let a thought get only halfway into a sentence or paragraph. If the thought is pertinent, bring it all the way in. If it is not important or relevant, shut the door in its face. "As Kelly, the Yale end, ran toward the side lines, a Princeton tackler was within an arm's length of him, and Kelly proceeded up the field to make a touchdown and win the game." Why mention the Princeton man if we are not told how the Yale man eluded him?

undoubtably. Wrongly written for undoubtedly.

undulatory, adj. Wavy, wavelike; moving smoothly in a rising and falling series like waves.

unequal, adj. Followed by to (with a gerund if with a verbal phrase), not for. "The completion of these negotiations, to (not for) which the Premier at his age was quite unequal, will be left to his younger successor."

unicellular, adj. One-celled.

unilateral, adj. One-sided; done by one party to a contract.

uninterested, adj. See un-.

union shop, n. A business establishment which, though free to hire nonmembers of a union, has agreed with the union to retain only those who subsequently join the union. It differs from a closed shop in that in a closed shop the management is not free to hire nonmembers of a union.

unipod, n. One-legged support.

unique, adj. The only one of its kind. Do not use for odd, unusual, marvelous, or rare. More unique, most unique, very unique, are grammatically illogical, but are sometimes found. It is better, however, to use quite unique for emphasis. It is also permissible to use almost unique, nearly unique, and unique in some respects.

Unity. A sentence has unity if it contains one independent thought and no more. If there are several ideas in the sentence, they must be closely related to one another and to the main thought. The most common violations of sentence unity are: (1) two sentence ideas in one sentence, (2) the spill-over sentence, (3) excessive detail in one sentence, (4) choppy sentences, (5) stringy sentences, (6) lack of subordination. The paragraph and the whole composition have unity if they stick to the subjects announced in the topic sentence and the title.

universally by all, phrase. The by all is redundant.

unmeasurable, adj. Not to be measured. It is used literally. Immeasurable is used in figurative contexts; it means not limited.

unquote, n. Journalistic and radio tech., "end of quotation." An unpleasant locution.

unreadable, adj. See illegible.

unsanitary, insanitary, adj. Synonymous; there is a tendency to restrict unsanitary to contexts which imply lack of sanitation.

unselfdetermined, adj. Passive, enslaved, subject to coercion.

until, prep., conj. See till.

up, v. Colloq., raise.

up, adv. Against gravity; colloq., completely. In verb-adverb combinations up often adds something to the meaning of the v. but is superfluous in many phrases such as ascend up, beat up, close up, connect up, divide up, end up, finish up, open up, rest up, and wash up. Combinations like the stand. lit. clean up and check up on are useful and fit colloq. contexts better than the more dignified and formal verbs.

The adj. up is colloq. in "He wondered what was up," and "He is up for petty larceny." Up against, confronting or confronted with, is colloq. but slang when the object is it, as in "He's up against it." All up with meaning utterly hopeless for, as in "It's all up with him," is slang. Up to, engaged in, capable of doing is stand. lit., but in the meaning of incumbent on is slang. Up and about, moderately well, up and *coming,* alert, promising, *up in the air,* unsettled, excited, *hard up,* without money, *up the stream,* in difficulties, are *colloq.* **Getup** is *colloq.* for costume. *Up until* is incorrect for *up* to or until. Write "She will be busy up to July."

upon, on, *prep.* In general, prefer *on* if there would be no strong accent on *upon.* Contrast "Upon my word!" with "On hearing the command, we marched." But usage varies with different adjectives and verbs. For instance, depend takes *on* when the meaning is to be con..ngent. "Whether he can go or not depends *on* his parents' wishes." But it takes either *on* or *upon* when the meaning is to be dependent on for support. "They depended *on* (or *upon*) the income from their savings account."

up to date, *adv. Stand. lit.,* abreast of the times, up to the present. "This brings my account up to date." Hyphenated, an attributive *adj.* "His was an *up-to-date* factory."

uptown, *adj.* In the upper part of the town; *colloq.,* snobbish; as an *adv.* toward the upper part of the town.

upwards of. More than. *Upwards of a hundred* means slightly more than a hundred, not about a hundred or nearly a hundred. Also **upward of.**

urban, urbane, *adj. Urban* means pertaining to a city, citified; *urbane,* gracious, polite, polished.

U.S. *abbr.* United States. In formal context always preceded by the. Prefer the *U.S.A.*

Usage (ūs'ĭj, ūz'ĭj). In language, the customary or habitual practice of speakers and writers. Good usage is the use of the best speakers and writers of the day, and the criterion (rather than logic or etymology) in matters of diction, grammar, and pronunciation.

use (ūs) *n.* Custom or practice, as in "This festival was an ancient use of the Celts," "What's the *use?*", "It's no *use* to try," and the *use* in "She had little (or no) *use* for dogs," are *stand. lit.*

use (ūz), *v.* The intransitive *use* is now employed only with to, and as an auxiliary to denote habitual or repeated action, as in "He used to play tennis every Saturday," or a permanent state in the past, as "I used to live in Utah." The used in "He was used to driving at night" is the *p. part.* of the transitive *v.,* which means inure, accustom, treat, or employ.

It is generally advisable to avoid the use of the past tense of *use* with a negative. It is either stilted, as in "I *used* not to visit the library," or awkward, as in "I didn't *use* to visit the library." I *used to could* for I *used to* be able to is vulgar.

utter, *v.* Issue, put in circulation; give public expression to; speak.

utter, uttermost, utmost, *adj. Utter* is the comparative of the O.E. adj. *ut,* out, and *uttermost* is the superlative. *Utter* now means complete, extreme, unmitigated, as in "He is an *utter* fool." *Uttermost* is chiefly a literary word, which is obsolescent in the senses of farthest and last, and now serves as a rough synonym of *utter. Utmost* as an *adj.* means greatest, highest, furthest; as a *n.,* one's best.

utterance, *n.* Speech, vocalization.

V

vacuum, *n. Colloq.,* vacuum bottle, container protected by vacuum jacket to retard the escape of heat or cold from the contents; and for vacuum cleaner, device for cleaning by suction. As a *v.* meaning to clean with a vacuum cleaner, it is also *colloq.*

vagrant, vagabond, *n.* Both agree in meaning a person with no fixed place of abode. Vagrant is always used in a derogatory sense for one who has no visible means of support. Vagabond can be used in the derogatory sense, but it now frequently means a carefree wanderer.

Vag, an ugly specimen of the headline-writer's coinage of stumpwords to fit limited space, is short for vagrant.

valuable, valued, invaluable, *adj. Valuable* means worth much money, precious, or highly serviceable; *valued* means highly regarded, appreciated, or appraised as worth so much. *Invaluable* means priceless, with a value that cannot be estimated.

value, *n.* Write "Of what value will it

be?" not "What value will it be?" *Value* is a favorite word with persons who write pompously or pretentiously and are fond of scientific or semiscientific terms. Instead of writing fun, they write entertainment *value,* instead of beauty, aesthetic *values,* for euphony, euphonic *value,* and for attention, attention *value.*

vamp, *n.* Upper part of a shoe; patch or trimming to make an old thing look new. In the sense of an unscrupulous and heartless flirt, one who uses her feminine wiles to charm and prey upon men, *vamp* is slang; the verb meaning to charm and harm like a vampire is also slang.

van, *prep. Du.,* of. See *de.*

Variations, Fancy. It is not wrong to use the same word more than once in a sentence or sentence sequence, provided that the repetition is natural and that the word is not used in different senses. If feasible use a *pron.* the second or third time a word comes up. If you use a fancy variation, it may give your reader the idea you are showing off, or it may distract his attention from the thought of the sentence. This is especially true of names. In a paper about William Wordsworth the reader will naturally expect Wordsworth's name to appear a few times. He need not become "the author of Michael," "the leader of the Romantic Movement," "the friend of Coleridge," "the poet of lakes and mountains," "the creator of a new theory of poetry," with each successive appearance.

Avoid using fancy variations for plain words to give a "literary" effect to your writing. Hirsute adornment for beard, habiliments for clothing, fraught with peril for dangerous, etc. are neither ornamental nor effective.

Variety for Effectiveness. Normally there should be many more loose sentences than balanced or periodic ones.

Most of your sentences will be declarative. Occasionally vary by using interrogative or exclamatory sentences. To get variety of sentence structure, (1) place an *adv.* or *adv.* modifiers at the beginning of the sentence, (2) begin the sentence with a participial construction, (3) make some of

the "and" and "but" sentences into subordinate clauses.

variorum, *n.* and *adj.* An edition of the works of an author containing all the notes and comments of various editors.

various, *n. Am.,* several different ones. "This problem has arisen in *various* of our colleges and universities." The British prefer to write several, many, a few, or certain of.

venal, venial, *adj. Venal* means purchasable by bribe, corrupt; *venial,* excusable or pardonable. "It was hardly a *venial* fault for the *venal* judge to render such a biassed charge."

venomous, *adj.* Poisonous, bitter. Note the spelling.

Verb. The name of something presented as an action, state, or process. The function of the verb is to assert in most sentences.

Verb-Adverb Combinations. In "They bring the fruit round to the houses" the verb and the adverb are used in their ordinary senses. But in "They couldn't bring the drowned man round," bring round has the new meaning of resuscitate and is a verb-adverb combination. "They looked up the wall" is not a verb-adverb combination, but "They looked up his friends" is. The verbs that enter into these combinations are usually short and of native origin. They combine with at, in, down, up, over, and the like to form new verbs, and from these are developed nouns and adjectives (layout, make-up, send-off, letdown, write-up, long-drawn-out, broken-down) and derivatives and even inflectional forms (dressing-down, leftovers, goings-on, hangers-on).

Whether a writer chooses to use a verb-adverb combination or its more dignified classical equivalent—catch on or comprehend, break up or disintegrate, size up or estimate, put out or extinguish—should depend entirely on the requirements of the situation. If the demand is for the novel, the emphatic, the racy popular, the colloquial, he should choose the verb-adverb combination. If for the more formal, accurate, and unambiguous, he should select the more highly specialized, longer-established verb. Some verb-adverb combinations and derivatives are recognized as standard. Most of them, however, are colloquial, and not a few are slang. For example, *setup* is standard when it means arrangement, organization, or make-up, but slang when it means a contest arranged to the advantage of one contestant or side. *Push-over*, put across or over, and *put-up* as in put-up job, are slang. To *put on*, meaning to feign, and *getup*, meaning costume, composition, or structure, are colloquial. A writer should strike out a superfluous adverb such as the out in "They tested (out) the engine."

verbal, *adj.* Of words, concerned with words. A *verbal* slip is a misuse of a word in speech or writing. Do not use in the sense proper to oral. "This applies to all promises whether *oral* (not *verbal*) or in writing."

Verbal. In grammar, a verbal is a verb form used as a noun or adjective. Though employed as nouns or adjectives, verbals are regularly modified by adverbs not adjectives, and retain the function of governing an object. "Studying mathematics is a difficult task." "To do this well is my desire."

verbalism, verbosity, *n. Verbalism* is the excessive attention to words which commonly results in a stilted style or in empty wordiness. *Verbosity* is the use of more words than necessary for clearness or emphasis, a superfluity of words.

verbatim (vėr bā'tĭm), *adv.* and *adj.* Word for word; exactly.

verdict, *n.* Judgment, decision. Do not use for mere opinion, as in "He said that it was his *verdict* (better, opinion) that the melons were ripe." But it can be used to mean opinion pronounced, as in "They stand condemned by the *verdict* of the people."

verisimilitude, *n.* Appearance of conforming to reality; consistency of descriptive background. "It is not enough for a narrative to be true; it must also have *verisimilitude*."

vernacular, *adj.* Pertaining to the native language; peculiar to the language of a certain country, region, or district. As a *n.*

in the sense of native language, *vernacular* is *stand. lit.*; in the sense of vulgar language or low colloquial language it is *colloq.*

Verse. Verse is used as a general term for anything composed in a set rhythmic pattern. It is also used to designate a composition which, though following a metrical pattern, cannot be dignified with the name of poetry. In this sense limericks, parodies, and popular songs are verse, but Milton's *Paradise Lost* is poetry. *Verse* is inaccurately used for stanza. The second *verse* means the second line of poetry not the second stanza of the poem.

verso, recto, *n.* The *verso* is the left-hand page of any book or manuscript; the *recto* is the right-hand page. *Verso* of a coin is the reverse, "tails," as opposed to obverse or "heads."

vertical union, *n.* A labor organization which admits all those who work in a certain plant or industry to membership regardless of the work which they perform. Opposed to horizontal union which is organized by crafts. In general, the C.I.O. favors vertical unions; the A.F.L., horizontal unions.

Very with Passive Participles. As a rule much, well, or some similar modifying word should be inserted between very or too and a *p. part.* in -ed. Participles like tired and celebrated have become true adjectives in common use and do not fall under this rule. "He is very celebrated, . . . very tired," but "They are very much interested," and "Who could say that he was not very well entertained?"

So does not come under this rule, yet the insertion of a much, well, etc., between it and a *p. part.* is frequently desirable. "Pam writes that her pies have been so much admired that she is tempted to become a professional cook."

Very is regarded as an emphatic word, but it loses its power to emphasize when it is overworked. See if you cannot substitute a more appropriate word for very.

For the rule concerning whether much or very should be the *adv.* used with the *p. part.*, see *much*.

vet, *n. Colloq.* stump-word for veteran, old soldier, any ex-service man, and veterinarian, physician for animals, person skilled in treating injuries and ailments of beasts.

veterinary, *adj.* Pertaining to the science and art of prevention or cure of diseases of animals other than man.

via (vī a), *prep.* By way of; *sl.*, by.

vicar, *n. Arch.*, substitute in office, deputy; *stand. lit.*, ecclesiastic representing the Pope; Anglican or Protestant Episcopal clergyman in charge of a parish of which he is not rector, or in charge of a chapel, church, or mission which is in some way dependent on another church. The *adj. vicarious* means substitutive, done by a substitute. "The growing practice of vicarious pilgrimage is merely another indication of the lessening of religious fervor."

vicious, *adj.* Defective, imperfect, faulty; corrupt, criminal; general condemnatory term to describe weather, animals, statements, and men. Do not confuse with *viscous,* sticky.

vide, *v. Abbr.* Usually the second member in *q.v., quod vide,* which see.

video (vĭd'ē ō), *n.* Television. Television is the commoner term.

view. The idiomatic phrase *in view of* means considering, taking into account. "*In view of* his expressed sentiments, we cannot do this and still keep his respect." *With a view to* means with the intention of. "*With a view to* conciliating his enemies, he sent gifts." *On view* means displayed for public inspection. "The new paintings are *on view* all week." *In view* means in sight, in prospect. "There is no hope *in view.*"

viewpoint, *n.* Place from which one looks; way of looking. Conservative writers prefer point of view.

vigilante (vĭj ĭ lăn'tē), *n.* Member of an unauthorized body of citizens who band together to quell violence by dealing out prompt punishment.

vignette, *n.* Running ornament of vines and leaves; small decoration or illustration at beginning or end of a chapter; dainty or small picture or written description; sketch. [*Fr.*, little vine]

villain, *n.* Scoundrel, base fellow; theatrical character capable of crime, bad man. [L., *villa,* country house, whence *villanus,* belonging to the country house or villa, whence the English word *villain,* a serf attached to a country house or manor, a baseborn fellow capable of ungentlemanly behavior. The word *villein* is used by historians in the sense of serf attached to a manor.]

vintage, *n. Stand. lit.,* wine; production of wine; all the produce of certain vineyards in one season. *Colloq.*, production or crop of anything but wine. "A dress of prewar *vintage.*"

virtually, *adv.* Not exactly synonymous with almost or nearly. It means effectually, to all practical purposes, not actually, not entirely or absolutely. "She is *virtually* the head of the firm."

visa (vē'zȧ), *n.* Mark or stamp placed on a passport to indicate that it has been examined and approved. Note spelling and pronunciation.

visit, visitation, *n. Visit* means a short stay with a friend; *visitation,* a routine inspection, a formal or official visit, or an affliction (compared seriously or humorously to divine dispensation). "This pestilence is a visitation." The *v. visit* is *colloq.* in the sense of chat with, as when paying a call. "We were visiting over the phone." It is *stand. lit.* in the sense of call upon, be a guest of; carry on social converse with.

vitamins, *n.* Pronounce vĭt'ȧ mĭns.

vocalize, *v.* Make into a vowel; utter; practice singing vowel sounds.

vocation, *n.* See **avocation.**

volplane, *v.* Glide through the air, float to earth without engine power.

voluptuous (vŏl up'tū us), *adj.* Characterized by or inclined to give sensuous pleasure; gratifying the senses in a subtle or sumptuous manner.

voodoo, *n. and adj.* Magic. [Haitian *Fr.*, African, *vodu*]

vortex, *n.* Whirlpool; middle of a whirlpool; place of concentration. "He was drawn into the *vortex* of this brilliant society." *Vertex* means the highest point, summit.

vs. *abbr.* Versus; opposed to, as opposed to.

Vulgar or Illiterate English. Incorrect ungrammatical or provincial English, such as is usually employed by the uneducated. "She ain't got nary a bit of hern left." A *vulgarism* is a word, phrase, or construction belonging to this type of English, or one for which euphemisms are universally substituted in polite society. See **English, Levels of.**

vulgar, *adj.* Of the common folk rather than refined or educated. "Spit is a *vulgar* word." Professor Fries defines vulgar language as "as nearly illiterate as writing may become and still fulfil the function of communication."

Vulgate. The Latin version of the Bible translated by Jerome at the end of the fourth century and commonly accepted as standard for the services of the Roman Catholic Church. As an *adj. vulgate* means pertaining to that Bible. In the sense of every day American language it is *tech.*

W

wack, *n. Sl.,* eccentric person, simpleton.

wacky, *adj. Sl.,* insane.

wade into, *v. Colloq.,* denounce vocally; attack with blows; begin energetically; *stand. lit.* in the sense of walk into a pool or body of water.

wages, wage, *n.* The use of a singular verb with *wages* is archaic. "The *wages* of sin *is* death." Currently: "His *wages were* collected by his wife." *Wages* is the more usual word for money paid to laborers, as *a day's wages, a week's wages; wage* is commonly used for an element in compound words, as *wage* earner, *wage* slave, *wage* scale, *wageworker,* the hourly *wage.*

wait, *v. Colloq.,* postpone. "Shall we wait dinner, father?" *Stand. lit. v.i.,* "Shall I wait?"; and *v.t.* be prepared for and be quiet and expect. *Await* and *wait for* are more common in these senses. "He waited (or awaited) his turn quietly." "Punishment waits (or awaits) those who fail."

waive, *v.* Put away, give up; disregard;

reject. Do not write: "He *waved* his right to speak," for "He *waived* his right to speak."

walkie-talkie, *n.* Portable radio set including transmitter, used principally for communication between military units in the field.

walkout, *v.* Go out on strike; desist from work without formal strike; *n.,* concerted departure of working people from office or factory without actual vote to strike.

walkover, *n.* A "race" in which a horse traverses the track in a walk because he is the sole starter; hence *colloq.,* one-sided contest, easy victory. *Cf.* the *sl. setup, pushover,* and *in the bag.*

want, *v.i.* and *v.t.* The primary meaning is to be without, lack, need, feel the need of. Hence developed the meaning roughly synonymous with wish and desire. But *want* is the more informal, *wish* the broader, and *desire* the more emotional term. *Wish* can take an objective clause, e.g., "I wish that it would clear up." *Want* cannot, and such sentences as "I *want* that she should go," "I *want* for her to go," are chiefly *dial.*

Want is often used *colloq.* in clipped constructions, as "She *wants* [to get] off," "The cat *wants* [to get] in." Perhaps these are patterned after "She *wants* (lacks) air," "He *wants* (lacks) food." The *colloq. want,* as in "You *want* to keep your eyes open or you will miss it," expresses mild obligation or command. It is less common in the third person. "She *wants* to watch her p's and q's when she visits those people." "You are *wanted* in the outer office" is *colloq.* for "Your presence in the outer office is desired."

warmongering, *n.* Propaganda designed to cause war.

warn of, warn against, *v. Warn of* means inform of an approaching danger; *warn against,* caution to be on one's guard against someone or something or performing a certain action. "He was warned of the approach of the enemy." "He was warned against trying to get through here."

was, *v.* Past tense first and third person

of *to be.* Vulgar as pl. or second person. "Where *was* you when the lights went out?" "There *was* six men in the elevator." For the condition contrary-to-fact subjunctive, *was* has almost displaced were, especially *colloq.* "If I *was* a man I'd show them." The usual practice in more formal writing is to use *was* after if in cases where doubt is not strongly implied, and *were* if doubt is strongly implied. "I wonder if that *was* the book he meant." "If this *were* the book he meant, it would not be here."

watch, *v.* Look at attentively, be a spectator. *Watch out,* be on guard.

way, *n.* Road, track, route, traveling distance, course or manner of action. *Colloq.* for condition, neighborhood, section. "Poor Smith is still in a bad *way.*" "Out my *way* they are oiling the road." *Ways* in the meaning of distance, as in "Walk a *ways* with me," and "That is a long *ways* off," is *dial.*

As an adverb, *way* is *colloq. abbr.* of away, far. "She lives *way* (away) up in the Bronx." "That is *way* (away) below what I paid for it." *Colloq.* in "She doesn't dance the way I do." But it is *stand. lit.* in "She doesn't dance in the way I do (or my way)." *By way of being,* as in "I am *by way of being* a writer," is *colloq.*

Write "The ship is underway," not underweigh. *Anyways* and *cornerways* are *dial. This a way* and *that a way* are vulgar. See *away.*

we, *pron.* If you are writing an editorial, or are the spokesman of a board or committee, and feel that you should use *we* (our, us, ourselves) instead of I, the paper, the committee, etc., you are using the editorial *we.* It is correct but a little pompous, and is likely to result in confusion if you allow the *we* to refer to yourself, to your paper or group, and then to your political party or country, all without informing the reader. The use of *we* merely in order to avoid I is inexcusable.

Weak Ending. The end of a sentence, paragraph, section, or whole composition is emphatic by position. Do not therefore allow hanging or vague expressions such as and so forth, and whatnot, and the like,

or "so what?" to fill this position. Try to place important words or sentences here. The endings of the larger units should be real climaxes. The writer who knows his business builds up to his final statements. If he fails, the result is an anticlimax. See **Order of Climax.**

Weak Passive. The passive voice has legitimate uses and is therefore needed, but do not get the bad habit of using the passive indiscriminately. The active voice is stronger. "A long and dismal day was spent by me" is weak. Write "I spent a long and dismal day."

Weak Reasoning. Make sure that your conclusions have been arrived at logically, and that you have not suppressed evidence which has a direct bearing on the question, and which the reader has a right to see produced. See **Fallacy.**

wedding, marriage, *n. Wedding* is used for the ceremony and also for the social festivities connected with the ceremony; *marriage* is used for the ceremony, the state of being married, and, figuratively, for any close union. "We were invited to the *wedding.*" "It was a civil *marriage,* since there was no minister in the town." "I have no active dislike of *marriage* (or married life) as such." "Let me not to the *marriage* of true minds / Admit impediments." **Wed,** *v.,* is *stand. lit.*

weird (wērd), *adj.* Fateful; magical; uncanny. *Weird* as a noun meaning fate, destiny is *archaic* or Scot. *dial.*

well, *adv.* The opposite of ill; satisfactorily, favorably, fully, rightly. As an interrogative or interjection it expresses vague surmise, annoyance, pleasure. "Well?" "Well, why not?" "Well, let's get to work." Do not let it become a persistent sentence beginner. In America it is used as an attributive *adj.* "Stevenson at that time was far from being a well man." It is often the first element in a compound: well-able, well-disposed, well-mannered. These are hyphenated when used attributively (a well-established concern) but are usually treated as separate words in the predicate (it is well timed).

went, *v. Went* is the past tense of go;

gone is the *p.* participle. Always say have gone, never have *went*. *Went and . . .* as a mere intensive, is *low colloq.* "He *went and* did it again."

were, *v.* Literary and archaic for would be, as in "It *were* (would be) idle to try to describe that tremendous scene," or in introducing a subordinate clause, as in "*Were* I (If I *were*) to send for him now, you would be angry."

wetback, *n.* Migratory Mexican illegally working in the United States. Presumably he swam the Rio Grande.

whale, *v. Colloq.,* whip, hit hard, thrash. "I'll *whale* the daylights out of him." *Whale of a, adj.* phrase, means large, very large; ironically, very bad.

wharf, *n.* Quay. Both wharfs and wharves are correct for the *pl.;* **wharve,** *n.* Whorl of a spindle.

what, *pron.* "*What?*" is a very abrupt and impolite substitute for "What did you say?" *What* often occurs in clipped sentences, as in "What (shall we do) about supper?" and the *sl.* "And what a man (he is)!" *What . . .* for, as in "*What* did you do that for?" is *colloq.* for "Why did you do that?" Often clipped to "*What* for?" This occurs as a *colloq. n.* in "His father gave him *what for,*" i.e., a scolding or beating. But notice that "*What* did he sing for?" is not exactly equivalent to "Why did he sing?" **What not** as a kind of et cetera at the end of an enumeration, as ". . . the question of the day: law enforcement, taxes, and what not," is rather bookish, but less trite than what have you. **Whatnot,** written solid, means a thing of no particular class or kind, and a bric-a-brac shelf.

What is an *adv.* in "*What* with the grasshoppers and *what* with the drought, the crops are ruined," and in "*What* good does it do him?" i.e., "In what respect or how much does it do him good?" Also in the *colloq.* "*What* do we care!" (Cf. "What care we?" and "A clever girl, what?")

In the sense of as much as, as far as, as in "She helped him *what* she could," *what* is *dial.* But *what* is equivalent to but that in sentences like "Never fear but *what* they will come."

Make up your mind whether a singular verb or a plural verb should follow *what* and do not let the introduction of a plural complement make you change your mind in the middle of a sentence. "*What* is of absorbing interest is (not are) the remarkable effects of this treatment." But "He demanded a halt in what are called 'soak-the-rich' taxes" is correct. When *what* stands for that which, it is always followed by a singular verb. "*What* the country needs is better politicians."

As a substitute for what?, whatever? is *colloq.* "*Whatever* (stand. lit. what) did he say?" *Whatever* is *stand. lit.* in "He said *whatever* he wished to say."

wheel, *n. Sl.,* important person; more often *big wheel.*

when, *conj.* What time, time at which. *When* can be used for in which or on which after expressions of time like hour, day, month, year, etc. "On the day *when* it happened I was not here." Avoid the illiterate formula *is when* in defining a word and after what is . . . "What is important *is when* a man decides on his career." Better: "The moment *when* a man decides on his career is important." *When* should never introduce a clause of prime importance.

whence, thence, hence, *adv.* Archaic and formal, being largely replaced by from where, where . . . from, or from which (for *whence*), from there, from that (for *thence*), and from here (for *hence*). But *hence,* used as a *conj.* meaning consequently, therefore, still is in active use. See *from whence.*

where, *adv. Where* can, of course, be used relatively to mean at or in which (place, situation, respect, etc.). "That is the place *where* Victor was born." "Can you remember *where* we were reading?" "*Where* do I come in?" "I could not find out where he got his information." "Let's look where I lost it." The use of where for that in referring to something that has been read or heard is *low colloq.* "I see *where* they had a tornado near Little Rock." "I saw in the *Booster where* the new Mayor is having a hard time."

Where is a *pron.* in "That is where you are wrong," and the *colloq.* "Where do you hail from?" The construction in *"Where* will you be *at* tomorrow?" and in *"Where* are you going *to?"* is *low colloq.* Omit the *at* and the *to.* Clauses which begin with where should not be used in defining nouns, as in "A decathlon is *where* there is a competition in ten different events."

whereabouts, *n. sing.* Also written whereabout. The place where someone or something is. The *adv.* is nearly always *whereabouts.* It means about where, near what place, and is not synonymous with where. "They do not know where (not *whereabouts*) he left the cache."

whereof, wherein, whereby. These compound relative adverbs are now generally considered stiff and pedantic. The preference is given to which and a *prep.* "There lay the field on the south side *whereof* (of which) Custer made his last stand."

Wherever, sometimes written where ever, as an interrogative *adv.,* as in *"Wherever* did you get that hat?" is *colloq.* As an *adv.* in "He will go *wherever* he is sent," it is *stand. lit.*

whether, *conj.* The original meaning was which of two, and it was formerly used only in disjunctive questions, being followed by or no or or not. "I do not know *whether* to go or not." It can now be used also without the or no, or not. "Let's see *whether* you can swim." For introducing object clauses *whether* is preferred to if, except *colloq.,* for the general feeling is that *if* should be reserved for the introduction of conditional clauses. "They do not know *whether* (*colloq.* if) Frances can go." Neither of nor as to should precede *whether,* as in "The question (of, as to) *whether* it is or is not correct for men to wear hats in elevators is now settled."

which, *rel. pron.* Conservative writers use that or no relative pronoun in a restrictive adjective clause and *which* in a nonrestrictive clause when the antecedent is neuter singular. The use of *which* to refer to a statement, fact, or idea is *colloq.* as in "He was absent from class, besides *which* he did not turn in his theme." "He served as chairman of the committee, *which* shows that he has school spirit." See **and which, but which** for those constructions.

whichever, *pron.* and *adj.* It refers to a choice between a number of persons or things, and is used as an interrogative, relative, or *adj.* It is an *adj.* in *"Whichever* (no matter which) plan you adopt, you will encounter difficulties." It is a *pron.* in "We agreed that *whichever* arrived first in Camden should dine at the expense of the Walking Club." The *rel. pron. which* cannot be used in this construction.

while, *adv.* and *conj.* As a *conj. while* can be properly and safely used in the sense of during the time that, for as long as. It can be used for although or whereas, but such use frequently causes ambiguity, as it does in *"While* the Turners are friendly, they might be more useful to their neighbors." It is not to be used for and or but in introducing coordinate clauses. Wrongly used in "The rector preached the sermon *while* Miss Perkins sang the offertory."

while, *v.* Spend time pleasantly; sometimes misspelled *wile* by those who confuse it with the verb which means to entice or lure as by a magic spell.

whingding, *n. Sl.,* party; social meeting; convivial gathering.

white, *adj. Colloq.,* term of approbation, as in "That was *white* of you." The terms white collar worker, and white-haired or white-headed, favored, favorite, are also *colloq.* as is the *v.* whitewash, to cover up crimes, to use an official inquiry to exonerate. But white elephant, white flag, and white feather are *stand. lit.*

who, which, *interrogative* and relative pronouns. Some differences in the use of these should be noted. Use *which* to indicate choice between an undetermined number of things or persons. *"Which* of the players do you prefer?" As a relative *who* corresponds to he, she, they, I, we, and you, *which* to it. "Her child, *who* is able to read, chose this book, *which* is the best I ever read." But *which* formerly referred to persons. Either *who* or *which* may be used in reference to animals and countries. "Britain *who* . . ." "Norway *which* . . ." Use *which* when the antecedent is a verbal or predicative idea, though it must be remembered that such a construction may be ambiguous and is almost always clumsy. The *which* can almost always be replaced by *and* or *and that*. "The farmers are permitted to hunt, *which* (and) the mayor is not." "I go sketching whenever I have time, *which* (and that) is not often."

The interrogative possessive *whose* is never used of things, but the relative *whose* may be so used. "A river *whose* mouth was shaped like a triangle . . ." Note here that the possessive of the relative is *whose*, the contraction for who is, who's.

Both *which* and *whom* may be omitted when in the objective case. "The man (whom) I admire is . . ." "That is a thing (which) I am always forgetting."

See **that, which**, and **Reference**.

who, whom. In *stand. lit.* the case of any pron. is determined by its function within its own clause, but in colloq. English the position in the sentence is often decisive. *Colloq.* the tendency is to reserve the position immediately before the *v.* usually taken by the subject, for nominative pronouns; and the other positions for objective pronouns.

Moreover since *whom* is often omitted in both *stand. lit.* and *colloq.* English (the man [whom] I admire), there is often a lack of assurance in writing it, and it seldom occurs in informal speech. Indeed, the only places in which *whom* is naturally used is immediately before the subject of the following *v.*, as in the archaic *than whom* construction, "They elected Johns, *than whom* no one is more corrupt"; or in the same position after prepositions, as in "This reveals the spirit of the people by whom and for whom these laws were made." In "This is the person whom I am told is responsible," the *whom* should be *who* since it is the subject. But in "This is the man *whom* I met yesterday," the

whom, though unnecessary, is correct.

Colloq. the interrogative *who* is used instead of the *stand. lit. whom* in sentences like "*Who* are you working for?" **Whomever** is established in the following construction: "You may follow *whomever* you please."

whodunit (whoo dŭn'-ĭt), *n. Sl.*, story of crime detection.

whoever, *pron.* The case of *whoever*, just as that of any relative pron., is decided by the part it plays within its own clause, not by the main sentence. "He invited whomever he met," but "He invited *whoever* came to his office," and "For *whoever* was responsible for that false report there can be no forgiveness." *Who ever,* or whoever, as in "*Who ever* can it be?" is *colloq.*, but separated as in "But who could ever have supposed that he was really mad?" is *stand. lit.*

The possessive is *whosever*, not *whosever's*. "We couldn't find out whose pen this was, but *whosever* it was, it is mine now."

whole, *adj.* In the sense of uninjured, sound, restored to health, *whole* is archaic and literary. It is used in a number of phrases, as *as a whole*, taken as a complete unit; *in whole* or in part, completely or partially; *on the whole*, all things considered, made out of the *whole* cloth, completely false, with no basis in reality.

With the exception of *wholesale, wholesome*, salutary, promoting mental or physical health, and *wholewheat*, all the common compounds with *whole* are hyphenated, as *whole-souled*, noble, magnanimous, completely sincere. Note that the *adv.* form of *whole-hearted* is *whole-heartedly* not *whole-heartily*.

whoopee, *n. Sl.*, wild pleasure. To *make whoopee* is to make a strenuous and determined effort to have a gay time.

whopper, *n. Colloq.*, exceedingly big one, especially a big lie.

whose, *pron.* Possessive case of the relative *pron.* who often used for the possessive of which or that, especially to avoid the postponed *of which.* "He scaled the mountain *whose* summits (the summits of which) were visible from our camp."

who's, contraction, who is. *"Who's* that fellow?"

wicked, *Sl.,* brilliant, excellent, superlatively efficient.

wide-open, *n. Colloq.,* used of places where the enforcement of the laws is extremely lax.

wiener, *n.* Type of small sausage, wienerwurst. *Wienie* is a slang variant. Not to be confused with *wiener schnitzel,* which is a breaded veal cutlet.

wildcat, *adj.* Irresponsible; contrary to regulations or agreements; not in accord with established standards or custom, as *"a wildcat* banking venture, a *wildcat* strike." A *wildcatter* is one who prospects for oil in places where no oil has been discovered or who engages in rash or unreliable business projects. A vivid Americanism.

will, *v.* See *shall.*

win, *v.* Principal parts, *win, won, won. Wan* and *win* for past tenses are vulgar forms.

window dressing, *n.* Hollow display, specious favorable reports of financial condition, political situation, etc., intended to mislead voters, prospective customers, and any others who do not see behind the false façade.

wind up, *v. Colloq.,* come to a finish, bring to an end, end, conclude as in "I *wound up* in Toledo."

windy, *adj.* Given to empty chattering; boastful; having no substance, empty. *Windy* in these senses is *stand. lit.* "He has formulated some *windy* plan for taking the pain out of paying taxes." "We heard the usual *windy* speeches at the rally." *Windbag,* a wordy and stupid talker, is also *stand. lit.*

win out, *v.* Achieve victory. Although the *out* is logically tautological the expression is *stand. lit.* "After protracted negotiations the State Department won out."

wire, *v. Colloq.,* send word to by telegraph. As a *n.* wire means message sent by telegraph. *Live wire,* a busy energetic extrovert, is also *colloq.*

wirepulling, *n. Colloq.,* use of secret

means to influence or control a person or an organization, especially in politics. The *v. wirepull,* and the *n. wirepuller,* are also colloq.

wise, *n. Archaic,* way, manner, habit, custom. *Wise,* in this sense, survives as the second element in such words as cross*wise,* like*wise,* no*wise,* other*wise,* clock*wise.* Its use with other adjectives is literary or poetic, as in "Let us tie them posie *wise* . . ." "Geraldine in maiden *wise* . . ."

wise, *adj. Sl.* in such phrases as *get wise* to, become informed about, *"wise* up," be wise to, know about, put one *wise,* inform. *Wise guy, n.,* and *wisecrack, n.* and *v.,* are *sl.* Wiseacre (wīz′ăk ĕr), *n.,* stupid person who pretends to wisdom, is *stand. lit.*

wish, *v.* Care for, desire, invoke, bid. It is usually used with for or an infinitive. The sentence "Good morning, Mr. Smedley, do you *wish* coffee?" is clipped, the full sentence being "Good morning, Mr. Smedley, do you *wish* to have coffee?" "Do you *wish* for . . . ?" is low *colloq.* See **want.**

wishful, wistful, *adj. Wishful* means based on desire rather than sound logic, expressing a wish; *wistful,* pensive, wishful without hope of having one's wish fulfilled. *Wishful* is trite in combination with thinking.

wit, *n.* Cleverness in pointing up concealed relationships between ideas; person with power to express ideas in a clever and amusing manner. The original meaning of *wit,* mental power, survives in the phrases at one's *wit's* end, completely puzzled, have one's *wits* about one, be in full possession of one's mental power, live by one's *wits,* make money by mental agility, especially outside the law, out of one's *wits,* insane.

with, *prep.* Do not use to introduce an agent, as "Stung *with* a wasp." It may express instrumentality, as in "Stung *with* a whip," or cause, as "Shake *with* fright," or accompaniment, as "He came *with* his son." A singular verb is usual in such constructions as "Bill, with his father, is going to the fair."

within, *prep.* The use of *in* for *within* in

expressions of time is *colloq.* "I can get to Chicago in (better *within*) five hours."

without, *prep.* Dial. as a *conj.* meaning unless, except, if . . . not, as in "She won't go *without* she gets permission." *Without hardly* and *without scarcely* are low *colloq.* for *almost without.* Write "The circus moved into town silently and almost *without* the citizens' being aware of what was happening," not ". . . *without* the citizens' hardly being aware . . ." The phrase *without* benefit of the clergy is frequently taken to mean cohabiting without having had a religious or civil marriage ceremony; actually, the benefit of the clergy was the ancient right of the clergy to be tried in an ecclesiastical court which was usually much more lenient than the civil court. This benefit was later extended to all who were literate.

witness, *v.* Often used for a fancy see. "I want you to *witness* this performance."

wolf, *n. Sl.,* amorous young man more charming than scrupulous; male flirt.

woman (woom'ăn), **women** (wĭm'ĕn). *Woman's* is used as general descriptive possessive; e.g., *woman's* rights movement, but *women's* is used when the meaning is specific, e.g., *women's* club, i.e., a club for women. *Female* for woman, *n.,* once frequently employed by the best writers, is now in consequence of an unattractive connotation, commonly avoided, and a new *adj. woman* (*women* with a *pl. n.*) used for female, *adj.* "Not all *women* students are cooks."

The *adj. womanly* is commonly used for desirable traits, as *womanly* sympathy; *womanish* is generally used in a derogatory manner, as in *womanish* spite, a *womanish* man.

Woman is unnecessary in the phrase *widow woman.*

wonder, *v.* To be greatly surprised. Usually with at, but sometimes with an infinitive. "I wonder to see such an assemblage." It also means to be curious to know. "I *wonder* what she is doing now."

wonder, *adj.,* used in newspapers in the sense of amazing, marvellous. Probably coined to take the place of *wonderful,* which had become a mere counterword, *wonder* has now suffered the same fate.

wont (wŏnt, wŭnt), *n.* Custom, habit. *Wont,* accustomed, is a predicate adjective with forms of the verb to be.

won't, *v. Colloq.* contraction of the obsolete *woll not,* will not. Sometimes used to form *adj.* compounds, as a won't-learn, a won't-wait, a won't-work. "He's a won't-work student."

woo, wooing, wooed, *v.* Court, seek the love of. The *n.* woo in the senses of affection, sentimental lovemaking, sexual play, is slang.

wood, *n.* A forest. In this form it takes a *sing. v.,* but as *woods* it takes a *pl. v.,* "The wood is dark and dismal." "The woods are green." The last form is more common, and *colloq.* may take a *sing. v.* "The *woods* is not far from the shack." *Out of the woods* is *colloq.* for past the difficulty.

woodcut, *n.* Design cut with a chisel or knife on a block cut with the grain of the wood; picture printed from such a block. Unlike a woodcut, a wood engraving is made with a burin or graver on a block cut across the grain.

Wordiness. Redundancy, pleonasm; verbosity; using two or more words where one would be better. Strike out ponderous periphrases, useless separate predications, floating subjects, and deflate generally unless you wish your style to be windy and pompous. See **Pleonasm.**

Word Order. The normal order of sentence parts in a declarative sentence is subject-verb-object. When the main *v.* precedes the subject, the order is said to be inverted. See **Inversion.** In a sentence with proper word order adjectives and adverbs are placed near the words or expressions they modify and not pushed from their proper place by intruders. See **Intruders.** Also, the antecedents of pronouns must be nearest the eligible preceding nouns. See **Reference.** Virtually, still, soon, and almost are misplaced in the following sentences. "Her head virtually was severed from her body." "The United States still is neutral." "He soon is expected." "Almost it is impossible."

work, *v.* In the sense of obtain something by trickery, flattery, deceit, *work* is *stand. lit.* "She *worked* the manager for a free pass." But *work it,* as in "I'll *work it* so he won't ask you," is *colloq.* In the sense of make use of, use, as in "For her plots she systematically *worked* her own past," *work* is *colloq.*

workaday, *adj.* Everyday; commonplace.

workday, *n.* Day on which people work; weekday rather than rest day or Sabbath.

Workout, *n. Sl.,* test or trial, as in "Give him a workout to test his voice"; *stand. lit.,* athletic exercise. The *v. workout,* exercise briskly until healthily weary, train in preparation for an athletic contest, is *colloq.*

Compound words formed with *work* as their first element are usually not hyphenated, as workbench, workbook, workday, workman, workshop, etc.

The plural of *work* in the phrase *the works,* is slang for perfection, completeness, the best ever, thorough defeat.

worriment, *n. Colloq.,* worry, a harassing annoyance.

worsen, *v.* Deteriorate, become worse; make worse.

worsen, worser, *adj. Low colloq.* for worse.

worst, *adj. Worst* follows numbers, as in "The five *worst* (not the *worst* five) players were dropped from the team."

worst way, worst kind, *adv. Colloq.,* very much, badly, very difficult. "He needs it the *worst* way." "They want to go home the *worst* kind (of way)."

worth, worth while. *While* after worth is sometimes superfluous and often gets one into grammatical trouble. "This scheme is *worth* studying" is correct, but "This scheme is *worth while* studying" is not. **Worth-while,** *adj.,* is of questionable value. "This is an excellent (entertaining, valuable, meritorious, profitable, rewarding) book" is better than "This is a worth-while book."

would, should. Although these verbs are the past forms of *will* and *shall,* they seldom express a real past. However, *would* may express past volition in negative sentences like "He called but she *would* not

hear him," or power or capacity in the past in sentences like "He tried glue but it *would* not hold," or it may imply habit in the past, as in "She *would* sing for hours at a time." But *would* is chiefly used in reference to an imaginary state or condition.

The same is even more true of *should,* which rarely refers to a real past except in expressing surprise at some past occurrence, as in "And when I got off the boat whom *should* I see but Ruggles!"

In the conclusion of sentences of rejected condition *would* and *should* in strictly formal English are used as follows:

If he did that,
I *should* be surprised.
you *would* be surprised.
shouldn't you be surprised?
she *would* be surprised.

If he had done that,
we *should* have been surprised.
you *would* have been surprised.
shouldn't you have been surprised?
she *would* have been surprised.

But there is a steadily growing tendency, especially *colloq.,* to use *would* for *should* in this as well as in other similar constructions.

Use *would* also for the following purposes:

1. To express volition under hypothetical conditions, or to express a wish or request. "I *wouldn't* go if you gave me a thousand dollars." "I wish he *would* stop." "*Would* you please tell me the time?"

2. To express probability or expectation. "That is what most women *would* do."

Use *should* for the following purposes:

1. To express obligation or duty under hypothetical conditions. "If I did what is right, every shirker *should* be dismissed immediately."

2. To express present obligation, duty, or simple propriety or advice. Ought (to) expresses present duty more strongly than *should.* "A citizen *should* vote." "You *should* see their exhibit."

3. To express an emotional attitude (suspicion, joy, surprise) toward something which may, or may not, be a fact. "Why *should* the products of this company be called inferior?"

Do not use *would have* in place of *had* in conditional clauses. "If he had (not *would have*) invited us, we would have come." Do not use *would have* for did in negative statements. "She wonders that you did not write (not *wouldn't have* written) as soon as you arrived."

I'd is a *colloq.* contraction of *I would. Would better* and *would best* are *dial.* or *low colloq.* for had better and had best; but *would rather* is preferable to *had rather* in most cases.

wow, *v. Sl.,* overwhelm; cause to applaud deliriously. *n.,* Emphatic conclusion; exclamation of delight. "Go out and *wow* them!" "A good story starts from a situation and ends in a *wow!*"

wrack, *n.* Wreckage; preferred to *rack* in the expression "go to *wrack* and ruin."

wrecker, *n.* Destroyer; one who salvages material from partly destroyed buildings.

wrench, *v.* Twist violently. Do not write or pronounce *wrench* when you mean rinse.

wrestle, *v.* Răss'ul is an illiterate pronunciation.

write, wrote, written, *v.* "I shall write her today" is as correct as "I have not written to him for a year," or "I shall write insurance." *Write up* in the sense of praise someone or something in a newspaper article, is *colloq.*; in the sense of complete the writing of, describe, write an account of, *write up* is *stand. lit.*

Write-up, *n. Sl.,* laudatory article in the press; *colloq.,* description, account, report.

Y

yammering, *n.* Talk, loud talk.

yank, *n.* and *v. Colloq.,* quick pull; to jerk. "They *yanked* me out of bed."

Yank, *n.* and *adj.* Slang stump of Yankee, originally a nickname for a New Englander, now by extension a Northerner, or by further extension, and in contrast with foreigner, any inhabitant of the U.S. [presumably *Du.* Jan Kaas for John Cheese]

yarn, *n. Colloq.,* tall tale, imaginative story.

yaup, yawp, *n.* Howl, loud cry. "Whitman's barbaric yawp!"

ye, *pron.* Old form of you, and the *pl.* of thou. Poeticism. *Ye* as in *Ye* Olde Tea Shoppe is the result of an error. Printers used the *y* to represent the thorn (þ) which was pronounced *th-.*

yeah, *adv. Low colloq.,* yes.

yell, *n.* Cheer, whoop; systematic memorized rigmarole used in encouraging teams in competitive sports.

yellow, *adj.* Jealous; unscrupulous; cowardly; sensational. "That newspaper is a *yellow* sheet." "What a *yellow* quitter he is!"

yen, *n. Sl.,* desire.

yes man, *n. Sl.,* man who always agrees with his superior.

yesteryear, *n.* Time a few years ago. Analogue from yesterday. "Where are the snows of yesteryear?"

yon, *adv.* Yonder, moderately far away; **hither and yon,** hither and thither.

you, *pron.* Frequently used as an indefinite *pron.*; less formal and more direct than one. "When you reach the top and look out over the city, the first thing you see . . ." More formally this would be "When a person reaches the top . . ." or "When one reaches the top, the first thing one (or he) sees . . ." Do not aimlessly shift from you to one or from one to you, especially in the same passage. But the shift from *one* to *he* is usual and established. *You all* is Southern and is almost always used as a *pl. Youse* is an illiterate *pl.* Note that *you* always takes the *pl.* verb, "You are, you were," never "You was."

youngster (yŭng'stẽr), *n.* Chiefly *colloq.* A young person or animal; the opposite of the *colloq.* oldster. *Younker* and *young'un* are *dial.*

yourself, *pron.* See **himself.**

youth, *n.* While a *youth* now generally means a young man, a young person generally means a young woman. Yet collectively, *youth* means both young men and women. "The *youth* of the land."

yrs. Do not sign a letter *Yrs.* truly. Write Yours truly, and sign your name.

Z

zany, *adj.* Silly, clownish. *n.* A clown or comedian who performs humorous antics.

zed. *Br.* pronunciation of the letter *z.* *Izzard* is *Am. dial.*

zenith, *n.* Highest point, summit.

zip, *v.* Move rapidly, whizz past; *n., colloq.,* vigor, energy.

zircon, *n.* Semiprecious gem, transparent silicate of the element *zirconium.* [Arabic < Persian, gold]

zombie, *n.* Magically stimulated corpse operated as a robot; *tech.,* extremely potent drink or cocktail with a rum base. [African, serpent]

zone, *n.* *Arch.,* belt, girdle; one of the latitudinal divisions of the surface of the earth; region; area, commonly circular, measured from a central point, as a shipping zone or parking zone.

zoom, *v.* Aviation *tech.,* climb steeply.

zwieback, *n.* Sweetened bread toasted lightly, rusk. [*Ger.,* twice baked]